Contributors

Ana Almeida
Department of Educational Psychology
University of Minho
Campus de Gualtar
4710–057 Braga
Portugal
aalmeida@ie.uminho.pt

Amy Barnes
School of Exercise and Health Sciences
Faculty of Computing, Health and
Science
Edith Cowan University
2 Bradford Street, Mt Lawley,
WA 6050
Australia
a.barnes@ecu.edu.au

Sheri Bauman
Department of Disability and
Psychoeducational Studies
University of Arizona
P. O. Box 210069
Tucson, AZ 85721–0069
USA
sherib@u.arizona.edu

Sofia Berne
Department of Psychology
University of Gothenburg
Box 500
405 30 Gothenburg
Sweden
Sofia.Berne@psy.gu.se

Catherine Blaya
IUFM
Université Nice – Sophia Antipolis
Grand Château
28 avenue Valrose BP 2135
06103 Nice Cedex 2
France
cblaya@aol.com

Luigi Bonetti
Department of Psychology
University of Bologna
Piazza Aldo Moro, 90
47521 Cesena (FC)
Italy
luigi.bonetti2@unibo.it

Vera Boronenko
Institute of Social Investigations
University of Daugavpils
Parades str., 1–421
LV-5401 Daugavpils
Latvia
veraboronenko@inbox.lv

Antonella Brighi
Department of Education Studies
University of Bologna
Via Filippo Re, 6
40127 Bologna
Italy
Antonella.brighi@unibo.it

Cyberbullying through the new media

Cyberbullying is one of the darker and more troubling aspects to the growing accessibility of new media technologies. Children in developed countries engage with cyberspace at younger and younger ages, and the use of the internet as a means to bully and harass has been greeted with alarm by educationalists, parents, the media, and governments.

This important new book is the result of a four-year international collaboration, funded by the EU, to better understand how we can cope and confront cyberbullying, and how new media technologies can be used to actually support the victims of such abuse. The chapters in this book initially define the historical and theoretical context to cyberbullying, before examining key issues involved in managing this pervasive phenomenon. Coverage includes:

- The definition and measurement of cyberbullying.
- The legal challenges in tackling cyberbullying across a number of international contexts.
- The role of mobile phone companies and internet service providers in monitoring and prevention.
- How the media frame and present the issue, and how that influences our understanding.
- How victims can cope with the effects of cyberbullying, and the guidelines and advice provided in different countries.
- How cyberbullying can continue from school into further education, and the strategies that can be used to prevent it.
- The ways in which accessing 'youth voice', or maximizing the contribution of young people themselves to the research process, can enhance our understanding.

This book will be an invaluable resource for researchers, students, policy makers and administrators with an interest in how children and young people are rendered vulnerable to bullying and harassment through a variety of online channels.

Peter K. Smith is Emeritus Professor of Psychology at the Unit for School and Family Studies at Goldsmiths College, University of London. He chaired COST Action IS0801 on Cyberbullying (2008–2012), and is currently PI of a European–Indian Network project on bullying, cyberbullying, and school safety and wellbeing (2012–2015). His research interests are in social development, school bullying, play and grandparenting.

Georges Steffgen is a professor at the University of Luxembourg. He directs a research group on aggression – especially violence – in school and cyberbullying, as well as approaches to health promotion. He has been project manager of national and international scientific projects on violence in school and anger. He has authored and co-authored more than 40 papers in international journals and books, and he is editor or co-editor of 14 books. He co-chaired COST Action IS0801 on Cyberbullying.

Cyberbullying through the new media

Findings from an
international network

**Edited by Peter K. Smith and
Georges Steffgen**

Psychology Press
Taylor & Francis Group
LONDON AND NEW YORK

First published 2013
by Psychology Press
27 Church Road, Hove, East Sussex BN3 2FA

and by Psychology Press
711 Third Avenue, New York, NY 10017

Psychology Press is an imprint of the Taylor & Francis Group, an informa business

© 2013 Peter K. Smith and Georges Steffgen

The right of Peter K. Smith and Georges Steffgen to be identified as editors of this work has been asserted by them in accordance with sections 77 and 78 of the Copyright, Designs and Patents Act 1988.

British Library Cataloguing in Publication Data
A catalogue record for this book is available from the British Library

Library of Congress Cataloging in Publication Data
A catalog record for this book has been requested

ISBN: 978-1-84872-253-8 (hbk)
ISBN: 978-1-84872-254-5 (pbk)
ISBN: 978-0-203-79907-9 (ebk)

Typeset in Bembo
by Saxon Graphics Ltd, Derby

Printed and bound in the United States of America by Publishers Graphics, LLC on sustainably sourced paper.

Contents

Juan Calmaestra
Facultad de Formación del
Profesorado y Educación
Universidad Autónoma de Madrid
Ciudad Universitaria de Cantoblanco
C/ Francisco Tomás y Valiente, 3
28049 Madrid
Spain
juan.calmaestra@uam.es

Marilyn Campbell
School of Learning and Professional
Studies
Queensland University of
Technology
Kelvin Grove QLD 4059
Australia
ma.campbell@qut.edu.au

Lucie Corcoran
School of Education
Trinity College Dublin
Arts Building
Dublin 2
Ireland
corcorl@tcd.ie

Angela Costabile
Department of Languages and
Educational Sciences
University of Calabria
Via Ponte Pietro Bucci, cubo18B,
4°piano
87036 Arcavacata di Rende (CS)
Italy
a.costabile@unical.it

Helen Cowie
Faculty of Health and Medical
Sciences
Duke of Kent Building
University of Surrey
Stag Hill, Guildford
Surrey GU2 7TE
United Kingdom
H.Cowie@surrey.ac.uk

Iain Coyne
University of Nottingham
YANG Fujia Building
Jubilee Campus
Wollaton Road
Nottingham
NG8 1BB
United Kingdom
Iain.Coyne@nottingham.ac.uk

Donna Cross
School of Exercise and Health
Sciences
Edith Cowan University
2 Bradford Street
Mt Lawley, WA 6050
Australia
d.cross@ecu.edu.au

Gie Deboutte
Department of Communication
Studies
University of Antwerp
Sint-Jacobstraat 2
2000 Antwerp
Belgium
Gie.Deboutte@ua.ac.be

Francine Dehue
Faculty of Psychology
Open University
Valkenburgerweg 177
6401 DL Heerlen
Netherlands
Francien.dehue@ou.nl

Rosario Del Rey
University of Seville
C/ Pirotecnia, s/n
41013 Seville
Spain
delrey@us.es

Anders Eklund
Lärarförbundet
Box 12 229
Segelbatsvägen 15
102 26 Stockholm
Sweden
anders.eklund@lararforbundet.se

Rasa Erentaite
Psychology Department
Mykolas Romeris University
Ateities g.20
LT-08303 Vilnius
Lithuania
Rasa.erentaite@gmail.com

Hildegunn Fandrem
Centre for Behavioral Research
University of Stavanger
4036 Stavanger
Norway
Hildegunn.fandrem@uis.no

Susan Flocken
European Trade Union Committee
for Education – ETUCE
Bd. Du Roi Albert II, 5
B-1210 Brussels
Belgium
Susan.flocken@csee-etuce.org

Ann Frisén
Department of Psychology
Gothenburg University
Box 500
405 30 Gothenburg
Sweden
Ann.frisen@psy.gu.se

Marta Fulop
Institute of Psychology
Hungarian Academy of Sciences
Victor Hugo utca 18–22
Budapest 1132
Hungary
Martafulop@yahoo.com

Vasiliki Gountsidou
Solid State Section, Physics
Department
Aristotle University of Thessaloniki
54124 Thessaloniki
Greece
iakovou@auth.gr

Tali Heiman
Department of Education and
Psychology
The Open University of Israel
108 Ravutski Street
43107 Ra'anana
Israel
talihe@openu.ac.il

Sameer Hinduja
School of Criminology and
Criminal Justice
Florida Atlantic University
5353 Parkside Drive
Jupiter, FL 33458–2906
USA
hinduja@fau.edu

Catarina Katzer
Cyberpsychologie, Medienethik and
Jugendforschung
Bismarckstr. 27–29
50672 Köln
Germany
Nc-katzerca@netcologne.de

Jette Kofoed
Department of Learning
University of Aarhus, DPU
Tuborgvej 164
DK 2400 Copenhagen NV
Denmark
jeko@dpu.dk

Marjo Kurki
Department of Nursing Science
University of Turku
20014 Turku
Finland
Marjo.kurki@utu.fi

Piret Luik
Institute of Education
University of Tartu
Salme la Tartu 50103
Estonia
Piret.luik@ut.ee

Magdalena Marczak
Institute of Work Health and
Organisations
Nottingham University
Wollaton Road
Nottingham
NG8 1BB
United Kingdom
lwxmim@nottingham.ac.uk

Conor McGuckin
School of Education
Trinity College Dublin
Dublin 2
Ireland
conormcguckin@gmail.com

Ersilia Menesini
Department of Psychology
University of Florence
Via di San Salvi, 12
Complesso di San Salvi Padiglione 26
50135 Firenze
Italy
ersilia.menesini@unfi.it

Carrie-Anne Myers
Social Sciences Building
City University London
Whiskin Street
London EC1R 0JD
United Kingdom
Carrie.myers.1@city.ac.uk

Karin Naruskov
Institute of Education
University of Tartu
Salme la Tartu 50103
Estonia
Karin.naruskov@ut.ee

Annalaura Nocentini
Department of Educational Science
and Psychology
University of Florence
Via di San Salvi, 12
Complesso di San Salvi Padiglione 26
50135 Firenze
Italy
Annalaura.nocentini@virgilio.it

Dorit Olenik-Shemesh
The Open University of Israel
108 Ravutzky St.
43107 Ra'anana
Israel
doritol@openu.ac.il

Mona O'Moore
School of Education
Trinity College Dublin
Dublin 2
Ireland
momoore@tcd.ie

Rosario Ortega
Psychology Department
University of Cordoba
San Alberto Magno S/N
14004 Cordoba
Spain
ortegaruiz@uco.es

Benedetta Emanuela Palladino
Department of Educational Science
and Psychology
University of Florence
Via di San Salvi, 12
Complesso di San Salvi Padiglione 26
50135 Firenze
Italy
benedetta_palladino@yahoo.it

Justin W. Patchin
Department of Political Science
University of Wisconsin – Eau Claire
105 Garfield Avenue
Eau Claire, WI 54702–4004
USA
patchinj@uwec.edu

Sonja Perren
Jacobs Center for Productive Youth
Development
University of Zurich
Culmannstr. 1
8006 Zurich
Switzerland
perren@jacobscenter.uzh.ch

Maili Pörhölä
Department of Communication
University of Jyväskylä
PO Box 35 (Pitkäkatu 1A)
FI-40014 University of Jyväskylä
Finland
Maili.Porhola@jyu.fi

Virginia Sánchez
Department of Developmental and
Educational Psychology
University of Seville
C/ Pirotecnia
s/n. 41013, Seville
Spain
virsan@us.es

Herbert Scheithauer
Department of Psychology
Freie Universität Berlin
Habelschwerdter Allee 45
14195 Berlin
Germany
hscheit@zedat.fu-berlin.de

Anja Schultze-Krumbholz
Department of Psychology
Freie Universität Berlin
Habelschwerdter Allee 45
14195 Berlin
Germany
Anja.schultze-krumbholz@
fu-berlin.de

Anna Ševčíková
Faculty of Social Studies
Masaryk University
Jostova 10
60200 Brno
Czech Republic
asevciko@fss.muni.cz

Roma Simulioniene
Psychology Department
Klaipeda University
S. Neries g. 5
92297 Klaipeda
Lithuania
r.simulioniene@gmail.lt

Ruthaychonnee (Ruth) Sittichai
Faculty of Humanities and Social
Sciences
Prince of Songkla University
Muang, Pattani 94000
Thailand
Ruthsittichai@gmail.com

Phillip Slee
School of Education
Flinders University
GPO Box 2100
Adelaide 5001
South Australia
Australia
Phillip.slee@flinders.edu.au

Peter K. Smith
Unit for School and Family Studies,
Department of Psychology
Goldsmiths, University of London
London SE14 6NW
United Kingdom
p.smith@gold.ac.uk

Barbara Spears
School of Education
University of South Australia
Magill Campus
Magill 5072
South Australia
Australia
Barbara.spears@unisa.edu.au

Christiane Spiel
Faculty of Psychology
University of Vienna
Universitätsstr. 7
A-1010 Vienna
Austria
Christiane.spiel@univie.ac.at

Gitte Stald
Digital Cultures and Mobile
Communication Research Group
IT University of Copenhagen
Rued Langgaards Vej 7
DK-2300 Copenhagen S
Denmark
Stald@itu.dk

Georges Steffgen
Integrative Research Unit on Social
and Individual Development
University of Luxembourg
Route de Diekirch
L-7201 Walferdange
Luxembourg
georges.steffgen@uni.lu

Keith Sullivan
School of Education
National University of Ireland,
Galway
University Road
Galway
Ireland
keith.sullivan@nuigalway.ie

Efthymia (Efi) Sygkollitou
Department of Psychology
Aristotle University of Thessaloniki
54124 Thessaloniki
Greece
Syngo@psy.auth.gr

Fran Thompson
Unit for School and Family Studies
Department of Psychology
Goldsmiths, University of London
London SE14 6NW
United Kingdom
f.thompson@gold.ac.uk

Panayiota Tsatsou
Department of Political and
Cultural Studies
Swansea University
Singleton Park
Swansea
SA2 8PP
Wales, United Kingdom
p.tsatsou@swansea.ac.uk

Zehra Ucanok
Psychology Department
Hacettepe University
06800 Ankara
Turkey
Ucanok@hacettepe.edu.tr

Maritta Valimaki
Department of Nursing Science
University of Turku
20014 Turku
Finland
mava@utu.fi

Heidi Vandebosch
Department of Communication
Studies
University of Antwerp
Sint-Jacobstraat 2
B-2000 Antwerp
Belgium
Heidi.Vandebosch@ua.ac.be

Anne Vermeulen
Department of Communication
Studies
University of Antwerp
Sint-Jacobstraat 2
B-2000 Antwerp
Belgium
Anne.Vermeulen@ua.ac.be

Trijntje Völlink
Open University Netherlands
Valkenburgerweg 177
NL-2960 Heerlen
Netherlands
Trijntje.vollink@ou.nl

Ales Završnik
Institute of Criminology
Poljanski nasip 2
SI-1000 Ljubljana
Slovenia
Ales.zavrsnik@pf.uni-lj.si

Rita Zukauskiene
Department of Psychology
Mykolas Romeris University
Ateities str. 20
LT-08303 Vilnius
Lithuania
rzukausk@mruni.eu

Preface

Amongst a number of recent books on cyberbullying, this book presents an unusual perspective. It is based on a four-year networking collaboration involving 28 European countries, plus Australia, in a sustained program of research, and training activities. This was financed by a COST Action, and altogether six Working Groups of researchers collaborated across a range of activities within the action theme 'Cyberbullying: Coping with negative and enhancing positive uses of new technologies, in relationships in educational settings'.

The action produced a considerable range of academic and practical outcomes, and this book brings them together in a way which we hope will be interesting for all those researching in, or actively concerned about cyberbullying, and how Information and Communications Technology (ICT) can be abused, but also used positively, in schools.

In the introductory section, Peter K. Smith and colleagues give a brief overview of the topic, and then describe what a COST Action is and how this program of networking was organized.

The second section deals with definitions and measurement issues. In Chapter 2, Ersilia Menesini and colleagues discuss how cyberbullying has been defined. Surveying two empirical studies and recent literature on the topic, the chapter presents a thorough comparison of different approaches and criteria, and proposes an integrated definition. In Chapter 3, Ann Frisén and colleagues describe the results of a systematic review of 44 instruments used to assess cyberbullying, emphasising structural and psychometric properties, such as validity and reliability, as well as the conceptual and definitional basis. An important aim is to provide criteria for readers to evaluate and choose instruments according to their own aims.

The third section is on regulation, and the media. In Chapter 4, Marilyn Campbell and Ales Zavrsnik explore whether cyberbullying should be criminalized, by examining the purposes of the law and its application to cyberbullying. The role of the law in reflecting social norms and legal influences on anti-bullying policies in educational settings is also reviewed. Current legal applications in different countries are considered and challenges to updating the law provided. In Chapter 5, Iain Coyne and Vasiliki

Gountsidou consider the role of Internet Service Providers (ISPs) and Mobile Phone Companies (MPCs) in the cyberbullying process. It debates the notion of industry self-regulation and outlines the EU Safer Social Networking Principles as a guide to evaluating the effectiveness of industry action. In Chapter 6, Heidi Vandebosch and colleagues point out that the amount of attention that media pay to cyberbullying, and the way they frame the issue, influence the general public and policymakers. They report the findings of a content analysis of national, daily newspapers in eight countries; these indicate that cyberbullying has become an important news issue, with the tone of the majority of articles often being alarmist.

The fourth section looks at coping with cyberbullying and guidelines. In Chapter 7, Conor McGuckin and colleagues explore current knowledge on coping with cyberbullying, providing a systematic review of the literature in the area. The issues regarding the research agenda in this area are explored, and attention is directed towards what is known and what those interested in the area should focus on for current and future research. In Chapter 8, Mona O'Moore and colleagues review nationally published guidelines already in place in various countries. Criteria for assessing best practice were determined to assess the two most prominent national guidelines in each of 27 countries, according to school ethos, policies and programs, skills and collaborative partnerships, and as they targeted parents, young people, schools, and teachers. For each target group, they review the research evidence, present key findings from their content analysis, and make recommendations of practical importance.

The fifth section is on research challenges. In Chapter 9, Helen Cowie and colleagues examine research on cyberbullying among university students. Although prevalence rates are lower for university students than for school pupils, the effects of being bullied at school can persist into young adulthood. They present both qualitative and quantitative data from four countries, explore the nature and incidence of cyberbullying, discuss continuities and discontinuities and identify some possible interventions to alleviate the problem. In Chapter 10, Barbara Spears and colleagues point out that electronic and virtual environments have become increasingly important in the social lives of adolescents. They describe the impact of ICT use on cognitive skill, academic development, social development and relationships; and discuss the range of positive uses that these new technologies can have. In Chapter 11, Barbara Spears and Jette Kofoed point out that traditionally, bullying research has focused on survey methodologies and what has been largely missing is the voice of young people and methodologies to allow for carefully listening to youth voices. The insights into youth life and social media that can be gained through qualitative methods can add valuable and important knowledge to what we already know from surveys and quantitative studies, including the subtleties of youth life mediated by technologies and the variability of it. In Chapter 12, Donna Cross and colleagues, who formed the Australian representation in COST IS0801, describe four major cyberbullying research initiatives conducted and the outputs generated from each in Australia during the COST Action. They consider the implications for policy and practice for Australian education systems and for schools, their staff, students and their parents. In Chapter 13, Vera Boronenko and colleagues review the opportunities for networking, and training of early career researchers, provided by COST IS0801. The first part of the chapter reviews the use of Short Term Scientific Missions, with six case study examples. The second part provides an overview of the organization, and the outcomes of two Training Schools; one in Australia, and one in Finland.

Finally, we invited three sets of commentators to reflect on the work of COST IS0801, and on the field of cyberbullying. All had attended at least one of our events, but none were on the Management Committee of the Action. Justin Patchin and Sameer Hinduja provide a commentary from the perspective of leading researchers in the USA, looking at the work primarily done in Europe, and Australia. Anders Eklund and Susan Flocken, from ETUCE, provide a practitioner commentary, from the perspective of potential users of the knowledge gained through the research such as described in the book. Keith Sullivan provides some thoughts on bridging research and practice. This seems particularly appropriate in an area where much of the research is inspired by the aim of improving the well-being, and happiness of young people in schools.

We would like to thank our many academic colleagues who have contributed to this book; but we also wish to thank the Science and Administrative Officers in the COST Office in Brussels, who worked with us over the four years. For much of this period Dr Julia Stamm was our Science Officer, and a special thanks must go to her for her advice and help for our First Training School in Melbourne. We also wish to thank Ms Felicitas Ambrosius, Ms Geny Piotti, Ms Solène Droy, Ms Anja van der Snickt, and Dr Andreas Obermaier; their support has always been helpful. A special thanks also to Ms Marie Abel for her systematic and helpful format checking of the manuscript of this book.

Peter K. Smith, London
Georges Steffgen, Luxembourg
April 2013

Part 1

Introduction

1   The nature of cyberbullying, and an international network

Peter K. Smith, Georges Steffgen and Ruthaychonnee (Ruth) Sittichai

"Cyberbullying" refers to bullying and harassment of others by means of new electronic technologies, primarily mobile phones and the internet. There has been much research and action on traditional forms of bullying in schools, with some success, but cyberbullying has arisen and increased in the last decade. This chapter starts with a review of cyberbullying, and how research on the topic has developed this century. It continues with explaining what a COST Action is, and how an international network of 28 countries took forward aspects of research into cyberbullying. The progress and outputs of the network were organized on a website, which is described.

Review of cyberbullying research

A few journal reviews of cyberbullying already exist (e.g. Mora–Merchán & Jäger, 2010; Smith, 2012; Smith & Slonje, 2010; Tokunaga, 2010), but the area is developing very rapidly, in part as new technologies develop and new fashions (such as particular social networking sites) appear. In this review we briefly highlight some important aspects, including definitional criteria; types of cyberbullying; age and gender differences; overlap with traditional bullying and sequence of events; differences between cyberbullying and traditional bullying; motives for perpetration and impact on victims; student coping strategies, and school-based prevention/intervention.

Definitional issues

Over the last decade, awareness of cyberbullying, followed by research activity and publications, has increased dynamically. Much of the literature (though not all) is on cyberbullying in young people. Also, much of the literature (though not all) stems from a psychological perspective, and has built on a thirty-year tradition of research on what is often called "traditional" bullying, or "offline" bullying. This carry-on includes both early definitions of cyberbullying, as well as the kinds of topics pursued (such as characteristics of cyber-bullies and cyber-victims). Nevertheless, other disciplinary perspectives are also present, and the area presents some new challenges as well as opportunities for researchers (Bauman, Walker, & Cross, 2013; Smith, 2010).

Bullying is generally seen as intentional behaviour to harm another, repeatedly, where it is difficult for the victim to defend himself or herself (Olweus, 1999). It is based on an imbalance of power and can be defined as a systematic abuse of power (Rigby, 2002; Smith & Sharp, 1994). By extending the definition from traditional bullying, cyberbullying has been defined as "an aggressive act or behaviour that is carried out using electronic means by a group or an individual repeatedly and over time against a victim who cannot easily defend him or herself" (Smith, Mahdavi, Carvalho, Fisher, Russell, & Tippett, 2008). From this perspective, cyberbullying is a systematic abuse of power which occurs through the use of information and communication technologies (ICTs).

Although the definition mentioned above (or similar ones) is quite common within the cyberbullying context, some of these definitional aspects are under debate. Two criteria in particular separate bullying from more general aggression (i.e. intent to cause harm). These are the aspects of repetition, and power imbalance. Both can be seen as relatively clear for traditional bullying, but have more difficulties in application to cyberbullying.

First, the idea of repetition within cyberbullying is not straightforward; one cyberbullying act may readily "snowball" out of the initial control of the bully, due to the technology used. An example is a picture that is sent (or uploaded onto the Internet), that at a later stage is distributed by other people (not the initial perpetrator). Thus a single act by one perpetrator may be repeated many times by others, and experienced many times by the victim. If the repetition is not carried out by the perpetrator, is this still cyberbullying?

The second definitional issue is that of power imbalance. In traditional bullying this might refer to physical strength, psychological confidence, numbers, or popularity/rejection in a peer group context. But physical strength is not necessary for perpetration of cyberbullying, nor is strength of numbers. However, two rather new possibilities of power imbalance in cyberbullying are technical ability with ICTs, and anonymity (Vandebosch & Van Cleemput, 2008). For example, it is more difficult to respond effectively if you do not know the identity of the perpetrator; conversely, if a victim does know the perpetrator, then the more conventional criteria of physical/ psychological strength and peer group popularity may come back into play (i.e. a victim may be fearful of retaliating against a popular and stronger pupil who may take further revenge offline).

Although it is possible to mount a defense of the criteria of repetition and imbalance of power in the cyberbullying domain, there are clearly difficulties (Smith, del Barrio, & Tokunaga, 2013). In practice, some studies actually measure cyber-aggression or cyber-abuse since they do not clearly include these two aspects (Bauman, Underwood, & Card, 2013). These issues are also discussed in Chapter 2.

Types of cyberbullying

Some studies just look at cyberbullying as a single construct. While suitable for some purposes, many aspects of cyberbullying (such as gender differences, or impact) seem to vary by the specific type of cyberbullying experienced. Some studies have divided cyberbullying into the two main media of Internet and mobile phone bullying (e.g. Ortega, Elipe, Mora-Merchán, Calmaestra, & Vega, 2009). However, in recent years the advent of smartphones makes it possible to send and receive emails via a mobile phone as well as use these phones to access the Internet more broadly; this makes the earlier distinction between mobile phone and Internet bullying problematic.

Some studies have investigated cyberbullying via a range of more specific media. Smith *et al.* (2008) used seven main media described by secondary school pupils: mobile phone calls, text messages, picture/video clip bullying, emails, chatroom, instant messaging, and websites. Hinduja and Patchin (2010) used a nine-item cyber victimization scale, covering similar media. Wachs and Wolf (2011) used a five-item scale, again covering similar media but grouping some of those together (e.g. text message/mobile phone call). In South Korea, cyberbullying in Internet game contexts has been found to be a very common form (Tippett & Kwak, 2012). These lists of types of cyberbullying and aggression are not exhaustive, and as technology develops, new forms of cyberbullying emerge.

An alternative to looking at the medium used in cyberbullying is to look at the type of action, or its content. There are a range of types of action, including flaming (online verbal fights); online harassment; cyberstalking (online intimidation/harassment); denigration (put-downs); masquerade (pretending to be someone else to send/post material to damage someone); outing (sharing embarrassing information or images of someone); exclusion (from an online group); putting up false profiles; distributing personal material against someone's wishes. Pyzalski (2012) listed 20 such categories of "electronic aggression". These are, to some extent, independent of the media used. Rivers and Noret (2010) described the content of abusive text messages and emails, in an English sample. Their ten main categories were: threat of physical violence, abusive or hate-related, name calling (including homophobia), death threats, ending of platonic relationship(s), sexual acts, demands/instructions, threats to damage existing relationships, threats to home/family, and menacing chain messages.

The ways young people communicate through ICT are rapidly changing. Over the last few years the spread of smartphones has enabled someone to use his/her mobile phone both for Internet as well as text messaging and calling. There has been a rapid increase in popularity of social networking sites such as Myspace or Facebook. Twitter has been another social networking development that has seen very rapid growth in recent years. New descriptive words are coming in: for example "sexting" describes the circulation of sexualized images on mobile phones or the Internet; "trolling" describes persistent abusive comments on a particular website; "griefing" describes harassment of someone in a cyber game or virtual world. Researchers in the field need to keep up to date with such changes and expansions regarding new modes of cyberbullying and cyber aggression.

Age and gender differences

Tokunaga (2010) argued that the trend with age across studies is for a curvilinear relationship for victimization, with the greatest incidence at seventh and eighth grades (around 13–15 years). Involvement in cyberbullying continues through adult life, but does appear to decrease after older adolescence (Ševciková & Šmahel, 2009).

Tokunaga (2010) described the area of gender differences as more complex and "fraught with inconsistent findings" (p. 280). Examples can be found of boys being more involved than girls (e.g. Calvete, Orue, Estévez, Villardón, & Padilla, 2010; Fanti, Demetriou & Hawa, 2012; Salmivalli & Pöyhönen, 2012), few or no significant differences (e.g. Livingstone, Haddon, Görzing, & Ólafsson, 2011; Smith et al., 2008), and girls being more involved than boys (e.g. Rivers & Noret, 2010). Nonetheless, there may be *relatively* greater involvement of girls in cyberbullying, just as there is in relational bullying, when compared to traditional physical (mainly boys) or verbal bullying (Smith, 2012). The inconsistency across studies may be due to different samples, methodologies (definitions, and types of cyberbullying assessed), and historical changes (such as increased use of social networking in girls especially; Patchin & Hinduja, 2010).

Overlap with traditional bullying and sequence of events

A well-replicated finding is a large overlap between involvement in traditional bullying and cyberbullying, whether as bully or victim (e.g. Livingstone et al., 2011; Raskauskas & Stoltz, 2007; Salmivalli & Pöyhönen, 2012; Smith et al., 2008).

Little is known about the sequence of events that may lead up to cyberbullying. Ybarra and Mitchell (2004) suggested that some cyberbullies may be traditional victims who, being unable to retaliate face-to-face, may do so by electronic means as a form of compensation. This was not confirmed by Vandebosch and van Cleemput (2008), but partially supported by Smith et al. (2008) as well as Steffgen and König (2009) who found a trend for traditional bully-victims to also be cyberbullies.

Differences between cyberbullying and traditional bullying

Cyberbullying has been found to differ from traditional bullying in a variety of ways. Smith (2012) described seven features: (1) it depends on some degree of technological expertise; (2) it is primarily indirect rather than face-to-face, and thus may be anonymous; (3) relatedly, the perpetrator does not usually see the victim's reaction, at least in the short term; (4) the variety of bystander roles in cyberbullying is more complex than in most traditional bullying (the bystander may be with the perpetrator when an act is sent or posted; with the victim when it is received; or with neither, when receiving the message or visiting the relevant Internet site); (5) one motive for traditional bullying is thought to be the status gained by showing (abusive) power over others, in front of witnesses, but the perpetrator will often lack this in cyberbullying; (6) the breadth of the potential audience is increased, as cyberbullying can reach particularly large audiences in a peer group compared with the small groups that are the usual audience in traditional bullying; (7) it is difficult to escape from cyberbullying (there is "no safe haven"), as the victim may be sent messages to their mobile or computer, or access nasty website comments, wherever they are.

Motives for perpetration and impact on victims

The motives for cyberbullying were investigated by Varjas *et al.* (2010) in a qualitative study using semi-structured individual interviews with 20 students aged 15 to 19 years. Motives could be categorized as either internal (based on emotional state), such as revenge, boredom, jealousy, trying out a new persona or redirecting feelings; or external (based on victim characteristics or the situation) such as no consequences, non-confrontational (not face-to-face), or that the target was different in some way, such as appearance.

All forms of bullying have negative impacts on the victims, and indeed on all those involved. However, the relative impact of traditional and cyber bullying may be affected by the differences between them, summarized above. Some factors, such as the breadth of audience or anonymity, may particularly contribute to the negative impact (e.g. Slonje & Smith, 2008; Wang, Nansel, & Iannotti, 2011). Ortega *et al.* (2009) compared what different emotions victims might feel if they experienced traditional bullying (direct, indirect) or cyberbullying (mobile, Internet). The emotions reported were not bothered, embarrassed, angry, upset, stressed, worried, afraid, alone, defenseless, and depressed. More of the negative emotions were reported when being traditionally bullied, in particular being the victim of direct bullying, than in cyberbullying. Nevertheless, although many victims do feel distressed after cyberbullying incidents, many studies (e.g. Ortega *et al.*, 2009; Patchin & Hinduja, 2006; Smith *et al.*, 2008) also report that some victims do "not feel bothered". In Ortega *et al.* (2009), between 36–44 per cent reported being not bothered, with the highest frequencies found in Internet bullying and the lowest in mobile phone bullying.

The research on the relative impact of being a victim of traditional bullying and cyberbullying is rather mixed. Hay, Meldrum and Mann (2010) found a greater impact of cyber victimization compared to traditional victimization on internalizing measures such as self-harm and suicidal ideation. But Hinduja and Patchin (2010) found that being a victim of cyberbullying was significantly associated with suicidal thoughts, but only at a comparable level to the association with traditional bullying. In a study of Austrian adolescents, Gradinger, Strohmeier, and Spiel (2009) found that being a cyber victim was significantly associated with both depressive and somatic symptoms, but the association was about the same strength as for traditional victims.

Olweus (2012, p. 534) went further and tentatively concluded that "if the student is exposed to both traditional and cyber bullying, the additional impact of cyberbullying seems to be negligible". But some research contradicts this. For example, Gradinger, Strohmeier and Spiel (2009, Table 5) found that depressive symptoms in victims of both traditional and cyber bullying was significantly greater than victims of either form alone. Similarly, Brighi *et al.* (2012) found significantly poorer self-esteem and higher loneliness scores in such poly-victims when compared to victims of traditional or cyberbullying alone.

Student coping strategies

When children and adolescents are asked what they think they would do if cyberbullied, the most often suggested ways of coping has been through different ways of technically protecting oneself from harassment online (Aricak *et al.*, 2008; Smith *et al.*, 2008). These technical solutions can consist of blocking certain people from contacting you online, changing passwords, user names or email addresses and deleting anonymous text messages without reading them. Smith *et al.* (2008) asked respondents to choose the best ways to stop cyberbullying from a list of suggestions produced by focus groups; "blocking messages/identities" was the option chosen by most respondents. Aricak *et al.* (2008) also found this to be the most selected way to stop cyberbullying.

Other coping strategies are often mentioned by cyber victims. These include switching one's name on online accounts or changing phone numbers (Aricak *et al.*, 2008; Juvoven & Gross, 2008; Smith *et al.*, 2008). Some respondents select more confrontational ways of online coping such as responding online, telling the bully to stop (Aricak *et al.*, 2008) or even bullying back (Dehue *et al.*, 2008).

Adults generally encourage student victims to tell a teacher or parent if they are being bullied. This has had some success in traditional bullying; although many victims are unwilling to tell adults about their victimization, especially older pupils and boys (Smith & Shu, 2000). Slonje and Smith (2008) found this reluctance to tell to be even more marked in cyberbullying, and in their Swedish sample not a single cyber victim had told an adult at school about being targeted.

In a study with Dutch adolescents, Dehue *et al.* (2008) found that 13 per cent had told a friend when cyberbullied, 9 per cent had told their parent(s),

7 per cent did not tell anyone and only 2 per cent had told a teacher. Smith *et al.* (2008) found that 16 per cent of cyberbullied respondents had sought help from parents and 9 per cent from teachers. However, the EU Kids Online study, involving children aged 9–16 years old in 25 European countries, found that 77 per cent of the cyber victims had talked to someone about their experience; 52 per cent told a friend, 13 per cent told a sibling, 42 per cent talked to a parent, 8 per cent to another adult they trust and 7 per cent told a teacher (Livingstone *et al.*, 2011). Coping strategies are reviewed further in Chapter 7.

School-based intervention/prevention

There are many programs devised for traditional bullying which, as Ttofi and Farrington (2011) have shown, often have reasonable success rates. Some aspects of these can be extended to include cyberbullying without major changes; clearly cyberbullying needs to be incorporated in components of these programs, such as a whole-school anti-bullying policy, and awareness-raising and curriculum-based activities. An example of a successful general anti-bullying program is the KiVa program in Finland, which includes computer-based classroom activities and support for victims from high-status peers. Although primarily designed with traditional bullying in mind, evaluations so far show that KiVa is as effective in reducing cyberbullying as it is for a range of traditional forms (Salmivalli, Kärna, & Poskiparta, 2011).

Other programs dealing with bullying advocate that it is important for the bully to understand what s/he has done (e.g. Pikas, 1989). This idea may be of particular importance within the cyberbullying context compared to that of traditional bullying. Slonje *et al.* (2012) investigated the difference of remorse felt by students after bullying others; 70 per cent of those who had only traditionally bullied others reported feeling remorse after their actions whilst only 42 per cent of those who had only cyberbullied others reported the same. If pupils do not feel remorse for what they do, there could also be less opportunity for any empathy to occur. Some research findings show that cyberbullies have less empathy for others being victimized than do non-cyberbullies (Steffgen, König, Pfetsch, & Melzer, 2011).

Another intervention used occasionally in traditional bullying is quality circles; here, students in small groups find out information about a problem, use structured discussion techniques, and come up with solutions which are presented and considered by teachers and the school. This has been used successfully in cyberbullying, and is particularly helpful for teachers aiming to keep abreast of fast-moving changes in the kinds of cyberbullying students are experiencing (Paul, Smith, & Blumberg, 2012).

In addition, new technical developments may help. A UK charity, Beatbullying, launched a new form of virtual peer support called CyberMentors in 2009. Students are trained as cybermentors, log on and mentor on demand. Cybermentors can refer mentees on to senior cybermentors and counselors for further support if necessary. This scheme has been evaluated quite positively by Banerjee, Robinson, and Smalley (2010) and Thompson and Smith (2011).

Not many intervention or prevention programs exist that deal specifically with cyberbullying; a Campbell review by Mishna, Cook, Saini, Wu, and MacFadden (2009) documented four short-term programs, that had had little effect. However, resources are being developed. For example, in England, Thompson, Robinson, and Smith (2013) evaluated two e-safety films used by secondary schools, Childnet International's *Let's Fight It Together*, which deals with cyberbullying, and Child Exploitation and Online Protection's (CEOP) *Exposed*, which is about sexting. Both films and resources were rated as "good" by pupils and staff.

Summary

Although cyberbullying research is vigorous and has already achieved a good deal, it faces some notable challenges. In particular, definitional and measurement issues need to be more fully resolved. Issues that need to be addressed more clearly include when the incidents should be regarded as cyberbullying (with repetition) or cyber aggression (a one off act); and the notion of power imbalance (see Chapter 2). A more standardized approach to measurement in this area is needed (see Chapter 3). A complication here is that the rapid historical changes in ICTs means that researchers need to continually modify instruments and be aware of new developments. These developments may have an influence on a variety of aspects such as gender and age differences or distribution processes of the bullying material. The field has also lacked an overall theoretical approach, although this can be said to be true of the field of bullying research generally (Monks *et al.*, 2009).

However, there are also many opportunities in cyberbullying research (Smith, 2012). One is a broader disciplinary basis of research than is found in traditional bullying, including besides psychology and education, strong input from sociology, media studies, public health, law, and other social sciences; and a greater combination of qualitative and quantitative approaches perhaps following from this disciplinary breadth. There is the potential to make more use of young people, not only as participants in focus groups, but also by involving them as researchers themselves, in the design of the study, and gathering data (Spears *et al.*, 2009; and Chapter 11).

The nature of cyberbullying phenomena also inevitably directs us to broader contextual and developmental aspects. Contextually, we know that (even for school-aged children), most cyberbullying is not experienced in school; the perpetration, the witnessing, and the reception of cyberbullying acts will often be in homes, clubs, outside areas. Developmentally, cyberbullying may show more age permeability than traditional bullying; traditional bullying appears to vary substantially between the school setting and the workplace setting; but cyberbullying occurs in cyberspace, whatever age group is taking part. We need to explore and contrast in more detail the motives for cyberbullying, compared to traditional bullying. There also appear to be important national or cultural differences in cyberbullying which call for explanation (Genta *et al.*, 2012).

If we face the challenges and build on the opportunities that the field offers us, this will be an important and exciting program of research that may help us minimize the abuse of new technologies and ensure that cyberspace is primarily a happy and satisfying arena for human relationships.

The COST Action on cyberbullying: an international network

COST stands for Co-operation in the field of Scientific and Technical Research, and a COST Action provides funding for meetings, workshops and seminars, scientific visits, training schools, and dissemination in its particular disciplinary area. COST Actions primarily cover European countries, but a number of other countries have affiliation arrangements and possibilities. Many COST Actions are in operation at one time, over a wide range of disciplinary areas (see http://www.cost.eu/about_cost).

COST Action IS0801 started in October 2008 and like most COST Actions, lasted four years. Its full title was 'Cyberbullying: Coping with negative and enhancing positive uses of new technologies, in relationships in educational settings'. The aim of this Action was to share expertise on cyberbullying in educational settings, and cope with negative and enhancing positive uses of new technologies. The more detailed objectives were:

- sharing of developing expertise in knowledge base and measurement techniques across researchers;
- sharing of input from outside the research community, specifically from legal experts, and from mobile phone companies and internet service providers;
- sharing of already nationally published guidelines, and recommended coping strategies, in different countries, including positive uses of new technologies in the relationships area; moving towards a common set of guidelines applicable for the European Community;
- increased awareness of the issue, and of the outcomes of the Action, to likely beneficiaries of the Action.

The Action started with 17 countries at its inaugural meeting in Brussels but by the fourth year of the Action it had grown to include 28 European countries. The European COST countries participating are shown in Table 1.1. In addition, four institutions in Australia affiliated with COST IS0801, and played a very significant role in the activities (see Chapters 4, 8, 10, 11, 12 and 13). One institution in Ukraine was also affiliated, but unfortunately due to visa and other problems, the Ukrainian representative was never able to attend the meetings.

Table 1.1 List of COST countries (with acronyms), and date of joining COST IS0801

AT: Austria 03/10/2008	GR: Greece 22/09/2008	PL: Poland 01/10/2008
BE: Belgium 21/08/2008	HU: Hungary 22/09/2009	PT: Portugal 13/10/2008
BG: Bulgaria 21/08/2008	IS: Iceland 23/03/2009	Romania –
Croatia –	IE: Ireland 27/01/2009	Serbia –
Cyprus –	IL: Israel 13/01/2009	Slovakia –
CZ: Czech Rep. 10/04/2010	IT: Italy 08/10/2008	SL: Slovenia 10/04/2010
DK: Denmark 16/01/2009	LV: Latvia 10/09/2008	ES: Spain 21/08/2008
EE: Estonia 04/10/2010	LT: Lithuania 21/10/2008	SE: Sweden 27/01/2009
FI: Finland 05/09/2008	LU: Luxembourg 21/10/2008	CH: Switzerland 21/08/2008
FYR of Macedonia –	Malta –	TR: Turkey 13/01/2009
FR: France 12/02/2010	NL: Netherlands 20/02/2009	UK: United Kingdom 21/08/2008
DE: Germany 21/08/2008	NO: Norway 22/09/2008	

– means country did not join

Countries which joined could, through their national COST Office, nominate up to two full members and two substitute members to the Management Committee (MC) of the Action. At the inaugural meeting, MC members elected Professor Peter Smith as Chair of the Action, and Professor Georges Steffgen as Vice-Chair. To take forward the aims of the Action, six Working Groups were set up, with a Chair and Deputy for each; these, together with their active membership, are shown in Table 1.2.

The MC met at approximately six-month intervals, to discuss the progress of the Action's aims and objectives. The meetings are shown in Table 1.3. Each meeting was in a different country, and opportunities were always taken to hold a (usually one–day) conference, with speakers from the COST Action but also local speakers, and a small number of invited speakers from overseas. In addition, two Training Schools were held, as discussed in Chapter 13. Chapter 13 also describes the use of Short Term Scientific Missions (STSMs), which enabled researchers to visit an institution in another country for periods varying from one week up to three months.

The website of the Action was developed by Dr Ruth Sittichai, who also helped with much of the administrative work over the four years. The website can be found at http://sites.google.com/site/costis0801/. On the homepage

Table 1.2 Working Groups of COST IS0801 and their composition

Working Group 1   Sharing of developing expertise in knowledge base and measurement techniques across researchers; organization of Workshop 1.

Co-ordinator: Ersilia Menesini (IT). Deputy: Rosario Ortega (ES). MC Members: Sofia Berne (SE), Catherine Blaya (FR), Rasa Erentaite (LT), Ann Frisén (SE), Catarina Katzer (DE), Piret Luik (EE), Katya Mihailova (BG), Joaquin Mora-Merchán (ES), Karin Naruskov (EE), Piotr Plichta (PL), Jacek Pyzalski (PL), Herbert Scheithauer (DE), Anja Schultze-Krumbholz (DE), Tolya Stoitsova (BG), Rita Zukauskiene (LT). Overseas MC: Phillip Slee (AU). Affiliated: Juan Calmaestra (ES), Dorothy Grigg (UK).

Working Group 2   Sharing of input from outside the research community; specifically from legal experts and from mobile phone companies and internet service providers; organizers of Workshop 2.

Co-ordinator: Iain Coyne (UK). Deputy: Heidi Vandebosch (BE). MC Members: Vasiliki Gountsidou (GR), Mitja Muršič (SL), Roma Simulioniene (LT), Nika Skvarca (SL), Nelli Tolmaca (LV), Janis Vandans (LV), Aleš Završnik (SL). Overseas MC: Marilyn Campbell (AU).

Working Group 3   Sharing of already nationally published guidelines in different countries, including positive uses of new technologies in the relationships area; organization of Workshop 3.

Co-ordinator: Maritta Valimaki (FI). Deputy: Ana Almeida (PT). MC Members: Sofia Berne (SE), Gie Deboutte (BE), Hildegunn Fandrem (NO), Marta Fulop (HU), Tali Heiman (IL), Anastasia Kapatzia (GR), Marjo Kurki (FI), Dorit Olenik-Shemesh (IL), Mona O'Moore (IE), Gitte Bang Stald (DK), Efi Sygkollitou (GR). Overseas MC: Donna Cross (AU).

Working Group 4   STSMs, and on maximizing opportunities for early-career researchers (e.g. through co-supervisions, visits, conferences, and possibly training events).

Co-ordinator: Vera Boronenko (LV). Deputy: Zehra Ucanok (TR). MC Members: Yair Amichair-Hamburger (IL).

Working Group 5   Sharing of research on coping strategies, in different countries, and of research that will inform the work on guidelines carried out by Working Group 3.

Co-ordinator: Sonja Perren (CH). Deputy: Conor McGuckin (IE). MC members: Francoise Alsaker (CH), Stephanie Pieschl (DE), Gaute Auestad (NO), Lucie Corcoran (IE), Helen Cowie (UK), Francien Dehue (NL), Aysun Dogan (TR), Monika Finsterwald (AT), D'Jamila Garcia (PT), Erling Roland (NO), Ana Sevcikova (CZ), David Smahel (CZ), George Spiel (AT), Trijntje Vollink (NL). Affiliated: Panayiota Tsatsou (GR).

Working Group 6   Positive uses of new technologies, in relationships in educational settings.

Co-ordinator: Angela Costabile (IT). Deputy: Bassam Aouil (PL). MC members: Haukur Arnthórsson (IS), Antonella Brighi (IT), Pernille Due (DK), Jette Kofoed (DK), Luca Pisano (IT), Maili Pörhölä (FI), Rosario del Rey (ES), Virginia Sanchez (ES), Christina Salmivalli (FI), Christiane Spiel (AT), Dagmar Strohmeier (AT). Overseas MC: Barbara Spears (AU).

[AU = Australia; for other country acronyms see Table 1.1. Composition of Working Groups did vary over the four-year period.]

Table 1.3 Schedule of main meetings of COST IS0801

Date	Venue	Organizer	Main events
October 2008	Brussels, Belgium	COST Office	Initial MC meeting; organization of the Action.
April 2009	Lodz, Poland	Dr Jacek Pyzalski	Second MC meeting; one-day conference, *Electronic aggression among youth – the new manifestation of old phenomenon?*
August 2009	Vilnius, Lithuania	Professor Rita Zukauskiene	First Workshop, *Cyberbullying: definition and measurement.* Invited speaker from USA (Professor Michele Ybarra). Abutted the European Conference in Developmental Psychology.
October 2009	Sofia, Bulgaria	Dr Katya Mihailova	Third MC meeting; one-day conference, *Social Media for Children: Cyberbullying and Media Literacy.* Invited speaker from Germany (Mr Thomas Jäger).
April 2010	Melbourne, Australia	Professors Phillip Slee, Donna Cross	Training School: *From research to policy and practice: Innovation and sustainability in cyberbullying prevention*; a collaborative venture between COST and DIISR, Australia (see Chapter 10).
May 2010	Antwerp, Belgium	Dr Heidi Vandebosch	Fourth MC meeting; Second Workshop, *Legal issues regarding cyberbullying.* Invited speakers from Belgium (Mr Luc Beirens), Ireland (Mr Paul Durrant) and Australia (Professor Sally Kift). Abutted e-Youth conference.
October 2010	Florence, Italy	Professor Ersilia Menesini	Fifth MC meeting; one-day conference, *The always-on-generation: risk and benefits of new technologies.*
May 2011	Turku, Finland	Professor Maritta Valimaki	Sixth MC meeting; Third Workshop, *Adolescents and social media: Guidelines and coping strategies for cyberbullying,* combined with two-day Training School: *Adolescents and social media interventions: methodological issues, and guidance and coping strategies for cyberbullying* (see Chapter 10). Invited speakers from USA (Professor Sheri Bauman) and ETUCE (Dr Susan Flocken).
November 2011	Dublin, Ireland	Professor Mona O'Moore	Seventh MC meeting; one day International conference, *Bullying at school: Sharing best practice in prevention and intervention.* Invited speaker from Norway (Dr Gaute Bjornsen).

Date	Venue	Organizer	Main events
June 2012	Paris, France	Professor Catherine Blaya	Eight MC meeting; International conference *Cyberbullying*. Invited speakers from USA (Professor Sheri Bauman, Professor Justin Patchin), Canada (Professor Shaheen Shariff), UK (Professor Sonia Livingstone). Many non-academic organizations attended.
October 2012	Vienna, Austria	Professor Christiane Spiel	Ninth MC meeting; International conference *Bullying and Cyberbullying: The Interface between Science and Practice*, held jointly with Austrian Ministry for Education, Arts and Cultural Affairs. Invited speaker from Council of Europe (Mr Childerik Schaapveld). Besides COST presentations, a session was devoted to the Austrian national strategies on violence prevention in the public school system.

there is information about the Chair, Vice-Chair, 28 participant countries, the Action's main objectives, aims, and a brief introduction about cyberbullying, as well as information about timetable and management. The Management Committee page provides the information about MC members (address, contact details and publications) sorted by country. The Management Committee Meetings page has the minutes of meetings. The Working Group page has information about Working Groups 1 to 6. A workshop and conference page has information on workshops and conferences. The Training School page has information on the two Training Schools; and the STSM (Short-Term Scientific Missions) page provides the reports of STSM that have been concluded (see also Chapter 13). There are also links to the Action Poster, books and publications. Finally, on this site is a link to the *Guidelines for preventing cyber-bullying in the school environment* booklet (see Chapter 8), including translations into Czech, German and Turkish, and there is also a direct link to this booklet on the homepage.

At the end of the four years, the Action was evaluated by COST officials and by Professor Kaj Björkqvist from Åbo Akademi, Finland. The evaluation was very positive; besides the conferences organized, many useful STSMs, and the Training School developed with Australian colleagues followed up by the second Training School in Turku, the Action had fostered or facilitated a considerable number of grant applications and successes, and many publications and other outreach activities. At least four books and five journal special issues were closely associated with the Action. This book aims to present the major activities, findings and outcomes of COST IS0801.

References

Aricak, T., Siyahhan, S., Uzunhasanoglu, A., Saribeyoglu, S., Ciplak, S., and Yilmaz, N. (2008). 'Cyberbullying among Turkish adolescents'. *CyberPsychology and Behavior, 11*, 253–261.

Banerjee, R., Robinson, C., and Smalley, D. (2010). *Evaluation of the Beatbullying Peer Mentoring Programme.* Report for Beatbullying. University of Sussex.

Bauman, S., Underwood, M.K., and Card, N. (2013). 'Definitions: Another perspective and a proposal for a beginning with cyberaggression'. In S. Bauman, J. Walker, and D. Cross (eds.), *Principles of cyberbullying research: Definition, methods, and measures* (pp. 87–93). New York and London: Routledge.

Bauman, S., Walker, J., and Cross, D. (eds.). (2013). *Principles of cyberbullying research: Definition, methods, and measures.* New York and London: Routledge.

Brighi, A., Melotti, G., Guarini, A., Genta, M.L., Ortega, R., Mora-Merchán, J.A., Smith, P.K., and Thompson, F. (2012). 'Self-esteem and loneliness in relation to cyberbullying in three European countries'. In Q. Li, D. Cross, and P.K. Smith (eds.), *Cyberbullying in the global playground: Research from international perspectives* (pp. 32–56). Chichester: Wiley-Blackwell.

Calvete, E., Orue, I., Estévez, A., Villardón, L., and Padilla, P. (2010). 'Cyberbullying in adolescents: Modalities and aggressors' profile'. *Computers in Human Behavior, 26*, 1128–1135.

Dehue, F., Bollman, C., and Völlink, T. (2008). 'Cyberbullying: Youngsters' experience and parental perception'. *CyberPsychology and Behavior, 11*, 217–223.

Fanti, K.A., Demetriou, A.G., and Hawa, V.V. (2012). 'A longitudinal study of cyberbullying: Examining risk and protective factors'. *European Journal of Developmental Psychology, 9*, 168–181.

Genta, M.L., Smith, P.K., Ortega, R., Brighi, A., Giasrini, A., Thompson, F., Tippett, N., Mora-Merchán, J., and Calmaestra, J. (2012). 'Comparative aspects of cyberbullying in Italy, England and Spain: Findings from a DAPHNE project'. In Q. Li, D. Cross, and P.K. Smith (eds.), *Bullying goes to the global village: Research on cyberbullying from an international perspective* (pp. 15–31). Chichester: Wiley-Blackwell.

Gradinger, P., Strohmeier, D., and Spiel, C. (2009). 'Traditional bullying and cyberbullying: Identification of risk groups for adjustment problems'. *Zeitschrift für Psychologie/Journal of Psychology, 217*(4), 205–213.

Hay, C., Meldrum, R., and Mann, K. (2010). 'Traditional bullying, cyber bullying, and deviance: A general strain theory approach'. *Journal of Contemporary Criminal Justice, 26*, 130–147.

Hinduja, S., and Patchin, J.W. (2010). 'Bullying, cyberbullying, and suicide'. *Archives of Suicide Research, 14*, 206–221.

Juvoven, J., and Gross, E.F. (2008). 'Bullying experiences in cyberspace'. *Journal of School Health, 78*, 496–505.

Livingstone, S., Haddon, L., Görzig, A., and Ólafsson, K. (2011). *Risks and safety on the internet: The perspective of European children. Full findings.* LSE, London: EU Kids Online.

Mishna, F., Cook, C., Saini, M., Wu, M-J., and MacFadden, R. (2009). *Interventions for children, youth and parents to prevent and reduce cyber abuse.* Oslo, Norway: Campbell Systematic Reviews.

Monks, C.P., Smith, P.K., Naylor, P., Barter, C., Ireland, J.L., and Coyne, I. (2009). 'Bullying in different contexts: commonalities, differences and the role of theory'. *Aggression and Violent Behavior, 14*, 146–156.

Mora-Merchán, J.A., and Jäger, T. (eds.). (2010). *Cyberbullying. A cross-national comparison*. Landau: Verlag Empirische Pädagogik.

Olweus, D. (1999). 'Sweden'. In P.K. Smith, Y. Morita, J. Junger-Tas, D. Olweus, R. Catalano, and P. Slee (eds.), *The Nature of School Bullying: A Cross-National Perspective* (pp. 7–27). London and New York: Routledge.

——(2012). 'Cyberbullying: An overrated phenomenon?' *European Journal of Developmental Psychology*, *9*, 520–538.

Ortega, R., Elipe, P., Mora-Merchán, J.A., Calmaestra, J., and Vega, E. (2009). 'The emotional impact on victims of traditional bullying and cyberbullying: a study of Spanish adolescents'. *Zeitschrift für Psychologie/Journal of Psychology*, *217*(4), 197–204.

Patchin, J.W., and Hinduja, S. (2006). 'Bullies move beyond the schoolyard: a preliminary look at cyberbullying'. *Youth Violence and Juvenile Justice*, *4*, 148–169.

——(2010). 'Trends in online social networking: adolescent use of MySpace over time'. *New Media and Society*, *12*, 197–216.

Paul, S., Smith, P.K., and Blumberg, H.H. (2012). 'Revisiting cyberbullying in schools using the quality circle approach'. *School Psychology International*, *33*, 492–504.

Pikas, A. (1989). 'A pure concept of mobbing gives the best results for treatment'. *School Psychology International*, *10*, 95–104.

Pyzalski, J. (2012). 'From cyberbullying to electronic aggression: typology of the phenomenon'. *Emotional and Behavioural Difficulties*, 17, 305–317.

Raskauskas, J., and Stoltz, A.D. (2007). 'Involvement in traditional and electronic bullying among adolescents'. *Developmental Psychology*, *43*, 564–575.

Rigby, K. (2002). *New Perspectives on Bullying*. London: Jessica Kingsley.

Rivers, I., and Noret, N. (2010). '"I h8 u": findings from a five-year study of text and email bullying'. *British Educational Research Journal*, *36*, 643–671.

Salmivalli, C., and Pöyhönen, V. (2012). 'Cyberbullying in Finland'. In Q. Li, D. Cross, and P.K. Smith (eds.), *Cyberbullying in the Global Playground: Research from International Perspectives* (pp. 57–72). Chichester: Wiley-Blackwell.

Salmivalli, C., Kärna, A., and Poskiparta, E. (2011). 'Counteracting bullying in Finland: The KiVa Program and its effects on different forms of being bullied'. *International Journal of Behavioural Development*, *35*, 405–411.

Ševciková, A., and Šmahel, D. (2009). 'Online harassment and cyberbullying in the Czech Republic'. *Zeitschrift für Psychologie/Journal of Psychology*, *217*(4), 227–229.

Slonje, R., and Smith, P.K. (2008). 'Cyberbullying: Another main type of bullying?' *Scandinavian Journal of Psychology*, *49*, 147–154.

Slonje, R., Smith, P.K., and Frisén, A. (2012). 'Processes of cyberbullying, and feelings of remorse by bullies: A pilot study'. *European Journal of Developmental Psychology*, *9*, 244–259.

Smith, P.K. (2010). 'Cyberbullying: the European perspective'. In J. Mora-Merchán, and T. Jäger (eds.), *Cyberbullying: A cross-national comparison* (pp. 7–19). Landau: Verlag Empirische Pädagogik.

——(2012). 'Cyberbullying and cyber aggression'. In S.R. Jimerson, A.B. Nickerson, M.J. Mayer, and M.J. Furlong (eds.), *Handbook of School Violence and School Safety: International Research and Practice* (pp. 93–103). New York: Routledge.

Smith, P.K., and Sharp, S. (eds.). (1994). *School bullying: Insights and perspectives.* London: Routledge.

Smith, P.K., and Shu, S. (2000). 'What good schools can do about bullying'. *Childhood, 7,* 193–212.

Smith, P.K., and Slonje, R. (2010). 'Cyberbullying: The nature and extent of a new kind of bullying in and out of school'. In S.R. Jimerson, S.M. Swearer, and D.L. Espelage (eds.), *Handbook of Bullying in Schools: An International Perspective* (pp. 249–262). New York: Routledge.

Smith, P.K., del Barrio, C., and Tokunaga, R. (2013). 'Definitions of bullying and cyberbullying: How useful are the terms?' In S. Bauman, J. Walker, and D. Cross (eds.), *Principles of cyberbullying research: Definition, methods, and measures* (pp. 64–86). New York and London: Routledge.

Smith, P.K., Mahdavi, J., Carvalho, M., Fisher, S., Russell, S., and Tippett, N. (2008). 'Cyberbullying: its nature and impact in secondary school pupils'. *Journal of Child Psychology and Psychiatry, 49,* 376–385.

Spears, B., Slee, P., Owens, L., and Johnson, B. (2009). 'Behind the scenes and screens. Insight into the human dimension of covert and cyberbullying'. *Zeitschrift für Psychologie/Journal of Psychology, 217*(4), 189–196.

Steffgen, G., and König, A. (2009). 'Cyber bullying: The role of traditional bullying and empathy'. In B. Sapeo, L. Haddon, E. Mante-Meijer, L. Fortunati, T. Turk, and E. Loos (eds.), *The good, the bad and the challenging. Conference Proceedings* (Vol. II; pp. 1041–1047). Brussels: COST Office.

Steffgen, G., Pfetsch, J., König, A., and Melzer, A. (2011). 'Are cyber bullies less empathic? Adolescents' cyber bullying behavior and empathic responsiveness'. *Cyberpsychology, Behavior, and Social Networking, 14,* 643–648.

Thompson, F., and Smith, P.K. (2011). *The use and effectiveness of anti-bullying strategies in schools.* DFE-RR098. London: DfE.

Thompson, F., Robinson, S., and Smith, P.K. (2013). 'An evaluation of some cyberbullying interventions in England'. In M.L. Genta, A. Brighi, and A.Guarini (eds.), *Cyberbullismo: Ricerche e Strategie di Intervento* [Cyberbullying: research and intervention strategies] (pp. 136–153). Milan: Franco Angeli.

Tippett, N., and Kwak, K. (2012). 'Cyberbullying in South Korea'. In Q. Li, D. Cross, and P.K. Smith (eds.), *Cyberbullying in the Global Playground: Research from International Perspectives* (pp. 202–219). Chichester: Wiley-Blackwell.

Tokunaga, R.S. (2010). 'Following you home from school: A critical review and synthesis of research on cyberbullying victimization'. *Computers in Human Behavior, 26,* 277–287.

Ttofi, M.M., and Farrington, D.P. (2011). 'Effectiveness of school-based programs to reduce bullying: a systematic and meta-analytic review'. *Journal of Experimental Criminology, 7,* 27–56.

Vandebosch, H., and Van Cleemput, K. (2008). 'Defining cyberbullying: A qualitative research into the perceptions of youngsters'. *CyberPsychology and Behavior, 11,* 499–503.

Varjas, K., Talley, J., Meyers, J., Parris, L., and Cutts, H. (2010). 'High school students' perceptions of motivations for cyberbullying: An exploratory study'. *Western Journal of Emergency Medicine, 3,* 269–273.

Wachs, S., and Wolf, K.D. (2011). 'Correlates between bullying and cyberbullying. First results of a self-report study'. *Praxis der Kinderpsychologie und Kinderpsychiatrie, 60,* 735–744.

Wang, J., Nansel, T.R., and Iannotti, R.J. (2011). 'Cyber and traditional bullying: Differential association with depression'. *Journal of Adolescent Health, 48*, 415–417.

Ybarra, M.L., and Mitchell, K.J. (2004). 'Online aggressor/targets, aggressors, and targets: a comparison of associated youth characteristics'. *Journal of Child Psychology and Psychiatry, 45*, 1308–1316.

Part 2

Definition and measurement

2   Definitions of cyberbullying

Ersilia Menesini, Annalaura Nocentini,
Benedetta Emanuela Palladino, Herbert
Scheithauer, Anja Schultze-Krumbholz,
Ann Frisén, Sofia Berne, Piret Luik,
Karin Naruskov, Rosario Ortega,
Juan Calmaestra and Catherine Blaya

This chapter will discuss how cyberbullying has been defined, starting from early studies conducted using the definition of traditional bullying proposed by Olweus (1993), up to recent contributions specifically focused on cyberbullying. The first group of studies, from the background of traditional bullying definitions, highlighted some fundamental aspects of bullying and cyberbullying, such as intentional harm, repetition over time and power imbalance between perpetrator(s) and victim(s). From the more recent literature, it is still unclear whether these criteria are completely applicable to the phenomenon of cyberbullying. On the other hand, media research has proposed new criteria specific to the ICT environment, such as anonymity and publicity. Summarizing two empirical studies conducted within COST Action IS0801, the chapter will present a discussion on definitional criteria of cyberbullying taking into account recent literature on the topic.

Introduction

Several types of aggressive behaviours can be observed in information and communication technology (ICT) environments: flaming (a written form of verbal aggression); sexual aggression (ranging from repeated enquiries in relation to the age and gender of a user, to more forceful and upsetting explicit proposals, repeated harassment and even "virtual rape"); cyberstalking (online harassment that includes threats of harm or is excessively intimidating); visual aggression (disseminating harmful visual material such as videos, photos); disruption of online activities (different kinds of acts capable of disrupting online activity of a user, such as breaking into internet accounts and servers, impersonating other users, abusing authority, restricting access to areas of the internet); flooding (IRC flooding consists of sending many lines of text repeatedly in such a way that the user's screen is visually flooded with text); spamming; ignoring or excluding others.

All of these acts can be defined as aggressive acts because they are characterized by intentionality, meaning that the perpetrator has the intention to harm others. Internet harassment (Ybarra & Mitchell, 2004), online harassment (Finkelhor, Mitchell, & Wolak, 2000), and electronic aggression (Pyzalski, 2012) are all terms used to define aggressive acts conducted on the internet or through ICT characterized by the intention to harm others. However, these acts do not necessarily constitute cyberbullying, because we do not know if there is a power imbalance between those involved, or if the negative acts were carried out repeatedly over time.

In fact, there is still a debate among researchers on whether a negative act in the ICT environment has to fulfill the three criteria (intentionality, power imbalance and repetition) relevant to school bullying to label this particular negative act as cyberbullying (Cassidy, Brown, & Jackson, 2011; Langos, 2012; Law, Shapka, Domene, & Gagnè, 2012; Monks *et al.* 2009; Pyzalski, 2012; Slonje, Smith & Frisén, 2013; Smith, 2012a; Ybarra, Boyd, Korchmaros, & Oppenheim, 2012). Although these three features are generally accepted, they are still discussed critically in the literature in terms of the specific meaning assumed in the cyber context (Dooley, Pyzalski, & Cross 2009; Langos, 2012; Menesini & Nocentini, 2009; Menesini *et al.*, 2012; Nocentini *et al.*, 2010; Slonje *et al.*, 2013). However, some authors assume that components of the Olweus-based definition of bullying translate well to the online context (Ybarra *et al.*, 2012). Despite this ongoing discussion, a majority of studies define cyberbullying as: "an aggressive, intentional act carried out by a group or individual, using electronic forms of contact, repeatedly and over time against a victim who cannot easily defend him or herself" (Smith *et al.*, 2008, p. 376).

Besides the traditional bullying approach, there is also another approach to the definition of cyberbullying coming from the media literature: this approach stresses new criteria specific to the ICT environment which can be considered to define cyberbullying, i.e. anonymity, that occurs when the victim does not know the identity of the bully, and publicity (as opposed to private exchanges between two parties) that characterizes the acts where a large audience is involved (i.e. emails, SMSs, MMSs sent to a large audience, or offences occurring in a public forum, or videos and pictures distributed via social networking) (Langos, 2012; Nocentini *et al.*, 2010; Slonje & Smith, 2008).

The aim of the present chapter is to present an updated definition of cyberbullying starting from the discussion of the three "traditional bullying" criteria (intentionality, repetition and power imbalance) and the two "specific cyberbullying" criteria (anonymity and publicity). There are other relevant issues related to the cyberbullying definition: the specific ICT used (i.e. internet and mobile phone), the specific medium used (i.e. email, chatroom, instant messaging, social networking sites), the specific type of behaviours used (i.e. written, exclusion, impersonation, visual, stalking, denigration), and the specific communication mode (i.e. voice, text messaging, online) (Hinduja & Patchin, 2010; Menesini, Nocentini, & Calussi, 2011; Ortega, Elipe, Mora-Merchán, Calmaestra, & Vega, 2009; Smith *et al.*, 2008; Willard,

2006; Ybarra *et al.*, 2012). However, these issues will be omitted from the present chapter, since our aim is to investigate the relationship between traditional and cyber bullying definition. We will discuss the results from two empirical studies carried out in Working Group 1 (WG1) as part of COST Action IS0801: these studies aimed to investigate the applicability of the criteria discussed above to the cyberbullying definition, and to compare findings across different European countries. In the next section we will present a synthesis of the two studies, while readers can find more details in the published articles, as referred to below.

Studies carried out in the COST Working Group

The Focus Group Study

The Focus Group Study was a qualitative study conducted in five European countries: Italy, Spain, Germany, Sweden and Estonia. The results of the study conducted in Italy, Spain and Germany are presented in *Cyberbullying: Labels, Behaviours and Definition in Three European Countries* by Nocentini, Calmaestra, Schultze-Krumbholz, Scheithauer, Ortega and Menesini (2010). Results of the Estonian study are presented in: *Estonian students' perception and definition of cyberbullying* by Naruskov, Luik, Nocentini and Menesini (2012). Finally, results of the Swedish study are presented in *Adolescents' view on how different criteria define cyberbullying* by Berne and Frisén (2011).

The aim of the study was to examine students' perception of the term used to label cyberbullying, the perception of different forms (written–verbal, visual, exclusion and impersonation), and the perception of the criteria used for the definition (imbalance of power, intention, repetition, anonymity and publicity). The first aim of the study was to identify the most suitable term to describe cyberbullying behaviour, which can then be used by researchers and practitioners who are in contact with adolescents to assess cyberbullying (e.g. professors, educators, counsellors). Second, we wanted to examine if the four forms of behaviours proposed all represent the cyberbullying construct. Finally, the adequacy of the different criteria of the cyberbullying definition was examined, including the three conventional criteria of traditional bullying and the new ones (anonymity and publicity) related to the specific cyber context.

Focus groups with mixed gender were held, using the same interview guide across countries. Three key questions were considered: (1) Which is the best term to label four scenarios presented in the posters describing different situations or behaviours that could be considered cyberbullying or not?; (2) Do all the four typologies of behaviours represent the cyberbullying construct?; (3) Are the three criteria for defining bullying (intentionality, imbalance of power and repetition) relevant in order to define a cyberbullying act? Are the two additional specific criteria for cyberbullying (publicity and anonymity) relevant in order to define a cyberbullying act?

The participants in Italy, Spain and Germany were 70 adolescents aged 12–18 years: 27 adolescents in Italy (20 boys, 7 girls), 23 in Spain (9 boys, 14 girls), and 20 in Germany (11 boys, 9 girls). In Sweden, 48 boys and girls, aged 12 and 15 years, participated. The focus groups were not conducted with mixed gender groups but instead the groups were divided by gender. In Estonia, two focus group interviews were conducted with 20 secondary school students: each focus group had five boys and five girls, in one group from Grade 6 and aged 12, and in the other group from Grade 9 and aged 15.

Results from this Focus Group Study are briefly reported below, integrating findings from the five countries. The first aim tried to find the best term to label cyberbullying in each country: overall, although the term *bullying* emerged spontaneously through all the focus groups in each country, the term *cyberbullying* was spontaneously proposed only by German (*cyber-mobbing*) and Swedish adolescents. Swedish young people often used the term *mobbning* or *nätmobbning*. The best label for cyberbullying in Spain was *acoso* (harassment). In Italy, it was *bullismo virtuale* (virtual bullying) and other terms involving electronic bullying, internet or online bullying (*bullismo elettronico*). In Estonia, the more specific term *cyberbullying* did not emerge so clearly from the focus group interviews although there were terms that referred to the cyber context (*internetis kiusamine; mobiiltelefonidega kiusamine; tekstisõnumitega kiusamine*); these three terms are respectively the Estonian translation of: internet bullying, bullying via cell-phone, and text-bullying.

In relation to the three bullying criteria, for the majority of the students the intention to harm was not the only important characteristic that defined cyberbullying, because the effect on the victims and his/her perception of the acts can also be more relevant than the intention of the aggressor (Naruskov *et al.*, 2012; Nocentini *et al.*, 2010). Repetition was a very strong criterion to be used for the definition because it can differentiate between a joke and an intentional attack and it can characterize the severity of the action. However, participants in Italy and Germany paid attention to the relation between repetition and publicity: if the act is public and thus it is sent (or showed) to several people, although it is done only once, this can be considered as done several times.

The other two additional criteria, anonymity and publicity, did not constitute a requisite for labelling an action as cyberbullying, but they were relevant because they connote the severity and the nature of the attack and the victim reaction. Overall, the results underlined that in order to define a cyberbullying act, adolescents need to know if the action is done intentionally to harm the victim (criterion of intentionality), the effect on the victim ("the victim was upset" is part of the power imbalance criterion), and the repetition of the action (criterion of repetition): all of these criteria are part of the traditional bullying definition. In relation to the new criteria proposed, anonymity and publicity, the results suggest that they are not necessary to label an action as cyberbullying, but they can connote the context.

The Scenarios Study

Cyberbullying Definition Among Adolescents: A Comparison Across Six European Countries by Menesini *et al.* (2012), is a quantitative study conducted in six European countries: Italy, Sweden, Spain, Germany, Estonia, and France. The aim was to evaluate the definition of cyberbullying among adolescents, in relation to the five criteria mentioned above: intentionality, repetition, imbalance of power, anonymity, and public versus private. This was operationalized in terms of applicability of the label to a selection of 32 scenarios displaying situations that might or might not be cyberbullying, on the basis of the five criteria.

These scenarios were created by combining the presence or absence of the criteria. The presence is defined as reported below: for intentionality "…to intentionally hurt…" (vs "…as a joke…"); for repetitiveness "…several times during the last month…" (vs "…once …"); for imbalance of power "…C. was upset and didn't know how to defend himself/herself…" (vs "…C. didn't care…"); for anonymity "…C., who didn't know him/her personally…" (vs "…to C., a familiar boy/girl…"); for publicity "…for other people to see…" and, conversely for privacy, "…only to C…".

In addition, four types of behaviour were covered: written–verbal ("…M. sent to C. a nasty text message…"), visual ("…M. sent C. a compromising photo…"), exclusion ("…M. took C. off their online group…") and impersonation ("…M. has got access to C.'s password or private information…"), resulting in a total number of 128 scenarios.

Eight versions of the questionnaire were created, each comprising 16 scenarios (8 scenarios of one type of behaviour and 8 of another). The eight versions together included the complete set of the scenarios and were administrated randomly to the participants. Analyses took into account two criterion variables: (1) country; and (2) type of behaviours. Participants were 2,257 adolescents from middle to high schools across six European countries: Italy (13 per cent), Spain (27 per cent), Germany (16 per cent), Sweden (14 per cent), Estonia (15 per cent), and France (15 per cent).

Overall, the results across countries and types of behaviour suggested that the cyberbullying definition includes a clear first dimension defined by imbalance of power, which in this study is defined as consequences on the victim who was upset and did not know how to defend him/herself, and a clear second dimension characterized by intentionality and, at a lower level, by anonymity. This shows that when adolescents evaluate a scenario such as cyberbullying they mainly consider the presence of the traditional bullying criteria with an exception: the criterion of repetition. Imbalance of power and intentionality are the two most relevant characteristics to define a cyberbullying act.

In relation to the new criteria proposed, our results suggested that anonymity might change its impact on perception in relation to the other criteria and needs to be considered together with other criteria to be fully understood. Public versus private criterion did not show any relevance for the definition of cyberbullying; it seems that an act is defined as cyberbullying regardless of the fact of whether it is spread to a large audience or not. However, we cannot exclude that this criterion adds something about the cyberbullying definition but at a lower level of relevance (i.e. as third dimension) or in combination with other criteria.

Discussion

Intentionality

Intentionality is the main characteristic of all aggressive acts (e.g. Berkowitz, 1993), and almost all the definitions of bullying and cyberbullying include this attribute (Dooley, Pyzalski, & Cross, 2009). Qualitative research has found that young people consider that a perpetrator must have the intent to harm another person in order to define this behaviour as cyberbullying, otherwise the behaviour is perceived as a joke (Nocentini *et al.*, 2010; Smith, 2009; Spears, Slee, & Owens, 2009; Vandebosch & van Cleemput, 2008). The focus group study also reported an interdependence between the intention and the effects on the victim (Nocentini *et al.*, 2010). This can be explained considering two main points: (1) it has been argued that due to the indirect nature of cyberbullying it is very difficult to identify the intention of this behaviour (Menesini & Nocentini, 2009): Swedish adolescents underlined that since you cannot observe the person behind the screen, this makes it difficult to understand the intention (Berne & Frisén, 2011); (2) unintentional acts – meaning the students are not aware of the harm caused – can also have harmful effects on the victim, thus underlining that only the impact on, or the perpetrator's intention perceived by the victim, should be regarded as a criterion (Nocentini *et al.*, 2010). Intentionality resulted as the second most important criterion to define cyberbullying in the Scenarios Study (Menesini *et al.*, 2012). In line with findings reported above, the intention to harm others is less relevant to define cyberbullying as compared to the consequences on the victim, which was upset and powerless ("didn't know how to defend himself/herself"), albeit still significant.

Overall, we can conclude that the criterion of intentionality needs to be included in the definition of cyberbullying. The problem seems to be how to measure this characteristic: using the perpetrator's or the victim's perspective (e.g. "wants to hurt" vs "felt hurt").

Power imbalance

This criterion describes that bullying and cyberbullying occur when someone who is more powerful in some way targets and attacks a person with less power (Vaillancourt, McDougall, & Hymel, 2008). The imbalance of power causes a feeling of powerlessness for the victim and also makes it difficult to defend oneself (Olweus, 1993; Smith & Brain, 2000). In our view, and also according to other researchers (e.g. Langos, 2012), the meaning of this criterion is not altered in the cyber context, signifying that cyberbullying behaviour must place the victim in a position where he/she cannot easily defend himself/herself; what is different in the cyber context is the way in which someone is powerless in comparison with another.

In traditional bullying, someone is powerless because of his/her physical or psychological weakness, because of his/her rejection status as compared to the popular status of the bully, and/or because of the high number of bullies involved. In cyberbullying, the power imbalance can be defined by other characteristics, although general consent among researchers on this topic has not yet been found. Some researchers argue that a higher ICT literacy and knowledge may contribute to power imbalance (Vandebosch & Van Cleemput, 2008; Ybarra & Mitchell, 2004), but this is not always true because not all the cyberbullying acts need a technological expertise. Also, our qualitative focus group study suggested that imbalance of power cannot be defined in terms of higher levels of media literacy of the perpetrator (Nocentini *et al.*, 2010): adolescents suggested that a cyberbully can be characterized by higher levels of technological skills compared to the victim, but only in the case of more technological sophisticated behaviour such as impersonation, and not in general. Others proposed that power imbalance in the cyber context can be defined by the higher social status of the perpetrator within a virtual community (e.g. Hinduja & Patchin, 2007).

Others assume that anonymity can contribute to a power imbalance (Vandebosch & Van Cleemput, 2008): we will follow up on this issue in a following section related to anonymity. Finally, other researchers assume that the victim feels more powerless because in cyberspace it is hard to defend oneself and to cope with some problems, such as removing or avoiding materials (Dooley, Pyzalski, & Cross, 2009). Similarly a victim may feel less able and even powerless to defend him or herself from an infinite cyber-audience (Langos, 2012). Only the Swedish adolescents claimed that some victims of cyberbullying dared retaliate on the internet, in contrast to traditional bullying, where victims are unable to defend themselves (Berne & Frisén, 2011). This highlights that the criterion of imbalance of power differs partly in cyberbullying as compared to traditional bullying in relation to the tendency to retaliate (Berne & Frisén, 2011).

Although we agree with the difficulty in defining the way(s) by which someone is powerless as compared to another in cyberspace, we think that a general definition of this criterion in cyberspace can follow the one used for traditional bullying: the imbalance of power occurs when someone who is more powerful in some way targets a person with less power, causing a feeling of powerlessness for the victim and also making it difficult for the victim to defend oneself.

Following this assumption, we defined the presence of imbalance of power within the Scenarios Study as: "...*the victim was upset and didn't know how to defend himself/herself...*" (vs the absence "*...the victim didn't care...*"), thus stressing the powerlessness of the victim who is upset and did not know how to defend him/herself. When operationalizing power imbalance as mentioned above we found that this was the strongest criterion for defining cyberbullying, and the relevance of this criterion is confirmed across all the countries involved in the Scenarios Study and across all the types of behaviour (Menesini *et al.*, 2012). This criterion seems to be even more relevant than intentionality.

Our definition of imbalance of power focused on the consequences for the victims and on the interactional micro-processes of action and reaction between bully and victim: if the bully attacks and the victim is upset and does not know how to defend him/herself, then this creates the imbalance within the dyad and, by definition, creates a bullying attack. Our definition of power imbalance did not specify why the victim cannot defend him/herself or why he/she is weaker as compared with the perpetrator, but it gives clear information about the reaction of the victim and about his/her status in the relationship. This definition introduces a more interactional description of imbalance of power criterion which can be applied regardless of the context, virtual or face to face.

Overall, we can conclude that power imbalance remains an essential criterion in order to define cyberbullying: the victim's subjective feeling of powerlessness in comparison with the perpetrator's possession of power is crucial to the definition whatever the source of this subjectively experienced weakness or whatever the motivation of the perpetrator is because the victim cannot defend him/herself. According to other authors, without the power imbalance aspect an act such as cyberbullying cannot be defined (Langos, 2012; Slonje *et al.*, 2012; Ybarra *et al.*, 2012).

Repetition

The presence of repetition in aggressive acts demonstrates a systematic behaviour which is aimed at harming others. In the Focus Group Study, adolescents from the five countries involved agreed that the criterion of repetition can differentiate between a joke and an intentional attack and it can characterize the severity of the action (Nocentini *et al.*, 2010). Repetition and intention are perceived to be related: adolescents from the German focus groups stated explicitly that the behaviour cannot be unintentional if it is repeated. Following these considerations, this criterion needs to be considered to define cyberbullying. Several authors have stated that if this criterion is not included in the measurement instrument, we cannot refer to it as cyberbullying because it is actually cyber-aggression (Slonje *et al.*, 2012; Ybarra *et al.*, 2012).

However, in the virtual context a single aggressive act can lead to an immense number of repetitions of the victimization, without the contribution of the perpetrator (Dooley *et al.*, 2009; Menesini & Nocentini, 2009; Smith,

2012b): a single act may be repeated many times by others, for instance a picture posted online once by a person can be shared with others over and over again or can receive countless "likes" and comments. German adolescents in the focus group well represented this picture using the expression "mass bullying" and "multiple bullying" (Nocentini *et al.*, 2010). Additionally, adolescents in the Swedish focus groups found repetition different in cyberbullying with regards to photo/video clip harassment; e.g. embarrassing photo/video clips could be uploaded to a webpage where each visit might be counted as part of the repetitive act (Berne & Frisén, 2011). Therefore, looking from the victim's perspective, the cyberbully does not need to repeat an act several times to perpetrate a bullying act.

Following this position, Langos (2012) proposed a different definition of repetition in relation to direct and indirect forms of cyberbullying. Direct cyberbullying occurs when the cyberbully directs the electronic communications directly at the victim, as opposed to indirect cyberbullying when communications are posted to more public areas of cyberspace (public forums such as social media sites, blogs, Web pages, and video-sharing Web sites). Repetition is needed in the direct cyberbullying context, where it is defined in the same way as it is defined in the traditional face-to-face bullying context. On the contrary, in indirect cyberbullying, where a perpetrator posts an electronic communication into a public forum, repetition occurs by virtue of the arena in which the behaviour takes place.

It seems that the results from the Scenarios Study are in line with this last consideration: in the Scenarios Study, the criterion of repetition did not appear so relevant to defining cyberbullying. Probably this characteristic is not so important in the virtual context, because the nature of ICT can lead to an immense number of victimizations without the contribution of the perpetrator.

Overall, we can conclude that the criterion of repetition is relevant to define cyberbullying, differentiating between cyberbullying and joking, or between cyberbullying and aggression. At the same time, more caution is needed if it is an indirect cyberbullying attack: in this case we might ask if the single act made by one perpetrator has to be considered as a cyberbullying or not. Slonje *et al.* (2012) suggested that if the repetition is not carried out by the same perpetrator we cannot define it as cyberbullying. However, other authors stated that a picture posted online or a rumour written online and shared with others over time is not so different from a rumour scrawled once on a bathroom wall for many people to see repetitively (Ybarra *et al.*, 2012). Thus, the issue related to the repetition in cyberbullying is still open.

Another major issue concerning repetition is to decide where the cut-off point is; that is to say, what is the number of events and their frequency that leads one to state that the observed victimization is "cyberbullying"? Most of the studies that were completed do not use the same measurement, which makes it difficult to compare results. A better consensus and harmonization seem necessary (Blaya, 2013).

Anonymity

There are contrasting views on whether anonymity can constitute a unique feature of cyberbullying: some authors state that anonymity, occurring when the victim does not know the identity of the bully, is unique to the online world (Spears *et al.*, 2009), since the attack is mediated by the ICT tools. This is supported by a study in which focus-group participants perceived anonymity as an essential aspect of what makes cyberbullying different from traditional bullying (Mishna, Saini, & Solomon, 2009). On the other hand, Ybarra *et al.* (2012) have underlined that, although anonymity can be a relevant feature of cyberbullying (46 per cent who report not knowing who their online bully is), traditional bullying can also have this characteristic: in fact, 12 per cent of youth reporting being bullied at school say they do not "know" who their bully is.

However, anonymity in cyberspace increases feelings of frustration and powerlessness (e.g. Dooley *et al.*, 2009; Slonje & Smith, 2008) and may reduce the need for power imbalance as a criterion (Fauman, 2008). The aggressor's anonymity can have psychological significance, with the offenders often knowing their victims better than the victims know their aggressors (Kowalski & Limber, 2007; Ševcíková & Šmahel, 2009; Ybarra & Mitchell, 2004). This often prevents victims from defending themselves effectively (Vandebosch & Van Cleemput, 2008).

In our studies, both the qualitative and quantitative results suggested that this criterion does not constitute a requisite for labelling an action as cyberbullying, but it is still relevant because it connotes the severity and the nature of the attack and the victims' reaction (Menesini *et al.*, 2012). In particular, in the Scenarios Study it seems that when anonymity is considered without any other criteria, it is perceived as more representative of cyberbullying than when the act is done by a known person; at the same time when the act is anonymous and unintentional, it is less representative of cyberbullying. Our results suggest that anonymity might change its impact on the definition in relation to the presence of other criteria and needs to be considered together with other criteria to be fully understood.

Overall, we conclude that anonymity is not a definitional criterion of cyberbullying, although it adds relevant information on the nature of the situation.

Public vs private

Publicity – as opposed to private exchanges between two parties – characterizes the acts where a large audience is involved (i.e. emails, SMSs, MMSs sent to a large audience, or offences occurring in a public forum, or videos and pictures distributed via social networking sites). In previous studies, students declared cyberbullying acts including a large and public audience as the most severe type of cyberbullying (Slonje & Smith, 2008).

The distinction between direct and indirect cyberbullying proposed by Langos (2012) reflects this criterion: direct cyberbullying occurs in the private domain and indirect cyberbullying occurs within the public cyberspace arena. The concept of the public domain in cyberspace extends to situations where the victim has knowledge of multiple recipients being privy to a personal communication transmitted via ICTs. The nature of this technology is such that the sender has no control over to whom the original communication is forwarded. Following this definition, the author suggested that this criterion (direct vs indirect acts) has implications on whether intentionality and repetition can be criteria needed to define cyberbullying behaviours (see previous sections).

Our Focus Group Study showed that the criterion of publicity was not necessary to define cyberbullying. However, in all countries, students rated public cyberbullying as the most serious incident, because of the role of the bystanders. The victims might worry about what others think about them (Nocentini *et al.*, 2010). Additionally, in the Swedish focus groups the criteria public versus personal was experienced as a bigger problem when many people accessed embarrassing material on the internet than if the target was the only recipient (Berne & Frisén, 2011). In the Scenarios Study, the public versus private criterion did not show any relevance for the definition of cyberbullying; it seems that an act is defined as cyberbullying regardless of the fact of whether it is spread to a large audience or not. However, we cannot preclude that this criterion adds something to the cyberbullying definition often in combination with other criteria and in relation to severity of the situation.

Conclusions

Overall we can conclude that there is a large agreement within the literature about the definition of cyberbullying based on the criteria of intentionality and power imbalance. Therefore, we recommend the inclusion of these two characteristics in the definition and the measurement of cyberbullying. A lower level of agreement characterizes the criterion of repetition: qualitative studies underlined it as very relevant and the literature on general aggression is likely to stress this criterion as specific of bullying and therefore also of cyberbullying. Results from our Scenarios Study did not suggest a relevant role of this criterion as compared to the others. Therefore further studies are needed to understand whether it might be relevant or not also in the virtual context. Finally, the two specific criteria for cyberbullying do not seem to be so relevant to define the phenomenon, although they can add some information in relation to the severity of the acts.

Following these considerations, we can assume that cyberbullying can be defined under the broad banner of bullying, because of the strong relevance of intentionality and power imbalance and the lack of unique and specific characteristics of the cyberspace in its definition. The issue of repetition and of its relevance in relation with private or public virtual context is still open and needs further investigation, taking into account the direct and indirect nature of the attack (Menesini, 2012).

References

Berkowitz, L. (1993). *Aggression: Its causes, consequences, and control*. New York: McGraw-Hill.

Berne, S., and Frisén, A. (2011). *Adolescents' view on how different criteria define cyberbullying*. Symposium at the European Conference on Developmental Psychology, 25 August, Bergen: Norway.

Blaya, C. (2013). *Les ados dans le cyberspace – prises de risque et cyberviolence*. Brusells: De Boeck.

Cassidy, W., Brown, K., and Jackson, M. (2011). 'Moving from cyber-bullying to cyber-kindness: What do students, educators and parents say?' In E. Dunkels, G.-M. Franberg, and C. Hallgreen (eds.), *Youth culture and net culture: Online social practices* (Chap. 15). Pennsylvania: IGI Global Press.

Dooley, J.J., Pyżalski, J., and Cross, D. (2009). 'Cyberbullying versus face-to-face bullying: A theoretical and conceptual review'. *Zeitschrift fur Psychologie/Journal of Psychology, 217*(4), 182–188.

Fauman, M.A. (2008). 'Cyber-bullying: Bullying in the digital age (book review)'. *American Journal of Psychiatry, 165,* 780–781.

Finkelhor, D., Mitchell, J.K., and Wolak, J. (2000). *Online victimization: A report on the nation's youth*. National Center for Missing and Exploited Children.

Fonzi, A., Genta, M.L., Menesini, E., Bacchini, D., Bonino, S., and Constabile, A. (1999). 'Italy'. In P.K. Smith, Y. Morita, J. Junger-Tas, D. Olweus, R. Catalano and P. Slee (eds.), *The nature of school bullying: A cross-national perspective* (pp. 140–156). London: Routledge.

Hinduja, S., and Patchin, J.W. (2007). 'Offline consequences of online victimization: School violence and delinquency'. *Journal of School Violence, 6*(3), 89–112.

——(2010). 'Bullying, cyberbullying, and suicide'. *Archives of Suicide Research, 14*(3), 206–221.

Kowalski, R.M., and Limber, S.P. (2007). 'Electronic bullying among middle school students'. *Journal of Adolescent Health, 41,* S22–30.

Langos, C. (2012). 'Cyberbullying: The challenge to define'. *Cyberpsychology, Behavior and Social Networking, 15*(6), 285–289.

Law, D.M., Shapka, J.D., Domene, J.F., and Gagné, M.H. (2012). 'Are cyberbullies really bullies? An investigation of reactive and proactive online aggression'. *Computers in Human Behavior, 28*(2), 664–672.

Menesini, E. (2012). 'Cyberbullying: the right value of the phenomenon. Comments on the paper "Cyberbullying: An over-rated phenomenon?"'. *European Journal of developmental Psychology, 9*(5), 544–552.

Menesini, E., and Nocentini, A. (2009). 'Cyberbullying definition and measurement: Some critical considerations'. *Zeitschrift fur Psychologie/Journal of Psychology, 217*(4), 230–232.

Menesini, E., Nocentini, A., and Calussi, P. (2011). 'The measurement of cyberbullying: Dimensional structure and relative item severity and discrimination'. *Cyberpsychology, Behavior and Social Networking; 14*(5), 267–274.

Menesini, E., Nocentini, A., Palladino, B.E., Frisén, A., Berne, S., Ortega Ruiz, R., Calmaestra, J., Scheithauer, H., Schultze-Krumbholz, A., Luik, P., Naruskov, K., Blaya, C., Berthaud, J., and Smith, P.K. (2012). 'Cyberbullying definition among adolescents: A comparison across six European countries'. *Cyberpsychology, Behavior and Social Networking, 15*(9), 455–463.

Mishna, F., Saini, M., and Solomon, S. (2009). 'Ongoing and online: Children and youth's perception of cyber bullying'. *Children and Youth Services Review, 31*, 1222–1228.

Monks, C., Smith, P.K., Naylor, P., Barter, C., Ireland, J.L., and Coyne, I. (2009). 'Bullying in different contexts: communalities, differences and the role of theory'. *Aggression and Violent Behavior, 14*, 146–156.

Naruskov, K., Luik, P., Nocentini, A., and Menesini, E. (2012). 'Estonian students' perception and definition of cyberbullying'. *Trames, 16*(4), 323–343.

Nocentini, A., Calmaestra, J., Schultze-Krumbholz, A., Scheithauer, H., Ortega, R., and Menesini, E. (2010). 'Cyberbullying: Labels, behaviours and definition in three European countries'. *Australian Journal of Guidance and Counselling, 20*(2), 129–142.

Olweus, D. (1993). *Bullying in school: What we know and what we can do.* Oxford: Blackwell.

Ortega, R., Del Rey, R., and Mora-Merchán, J.A. (2001). 'Violencia entre escolares: Conceptos y etiquetas verbales que definen el fenómeno del maltrato entre iguales'. *Revista interuniversitaria de formación del profesorado, 41*, 95–113.

Ortega, R., Elipe, P., Mora-Merchán, A.J., Calmaestra, J., and Vega, E. (2009). 'The emotional impact on victims of traditional bullying and cyberbullying'. *Zeitschrift fur Psychologie/Journal of Psychology, 217*(4), 197–204.

Pyżalski, J. (2012). 'From cyberbullying to electronic aggression: Typology of the phenomenon'. *Emotional and Behavioral Difficulties, 17*(3–4), 305–317.

Ševčíková, A., and Šmahel, D. (2009). 'Online harassment and cyberbullying in the Czech Republic: Comparison across age groups'. *Zeitschrift für Psychologie / Journal of Psychology, 217*(4), 227–229.

Slonje, R., and Smith, P.K. (2008). 'Cyberbullying: Another main type of bullying?' *Scandinavian Journal of Psychology, 49*, 147–154.

Slonje, R., Smith, P.K., and Frisén, A. (2013). 'The nature of cyberbullying, and strategies for prevention'. *Computers in Human Behavior, 29*, 26–32.

Smith, P.K. (2009). 'Cyberbullying: Abusive relationships in cyberspace'. *Zeitschrift fur Psychologie/Journal of Psychology, 217*(4), 180–181.

——(2012a). 'Cyberbullying: Challenges and opportunities for a research program – A response to Olweus (2012)'. *European Journal of Developmental Psychology, 9*(5), 553–558.

——(2012b). 'Cyberbullying and cyber aggression'. In R.S. Jimerson, B.A. Nickerson, J.M. Mayer, and J.M. Furlong, (eds.), *Handbook of School Violence and School Safety: International Research and Practice*, pp. 93–103. New York: Routledge.

Smith, P.K., and Brain, P. (2000). 'Bullying in schools: Lessons from two decades of research'. *Aggressive Behavior, 26*, 1–9.

Smith, P.K., Cowie, H., Olafsson, R.F., Liefooghe, A.P.D., and 17 additional authors (2002). 'Definitions of bullying: A comparison of terms used, and age and gender differences, in a fourteen-country international comparison'. *Child Development, 73*(4), 1119–1133.

Smith, P.K., Mahdavi, J, Carvalho, M., Fisher, S., Russell, S.N., and Tippett, N. (2008). 'Cyberbullying: its nature and impact in secondary school pupils'. *Journal of Child Psychology and Psychiatry, 49*, 376–385.

Spears, B., Slee, P., Owens, L., and Johnson, B. (2009). 'Behind the scenes and screens: Insights into the human dimension of covert and cyberbullying'. *Zeitschrift fur Psychologie/Journal of Psychology, 217*(4), 189–196.

Vaillancourt, T., McDougall, P., Hymel, S., Krygsman, A., Miller, J., Stiver, K., and Davis, C. (2008). 'Bullying: Are researchers and children/youth talking about the same thing?' *International Journal of Behavioural Development, 32,* 486–495.

Vandebosch, H., and van Cleemput, K. (2008). 'Defining cyberbullying: A qualitative research into the perceptions of youngsters'. *Cyberpsychology and Behavior, 11*(4), 499–503.

Willard, E.N. (2007). *Cyberbullying and cyberthreats: Responding to the challenge of online social aggression, threats, and distress.* Illinois, USA: Malloy, Inc.

Ybarra, L.M., and Mitchell, J.K. (2004). 'Online agressor/targets, agressors, and targets: A comparison of associated youth characteristics'. *Journal of Child Psychology and Psychiatry, 45*(7), 1308–1316.

Ybarra, M.L., Boyd, D., Korchmaros, J.D., and Oppenheim, J.K. (2012). 'Defining and measuring cyberbullying within the larger context of bullying victimization'. *Journal of Adolescent Health, 51*(1), 53–58.

3   Measurement issues

A systematic review of cyberbullying instruments

Ann Frisén, Sofia Berne, Anja Schultze-Krumbholz, Herbert Scheithauer, Karin Naruskov, Piret Luik, Catarina Katzer, Rasa Erentaite and Rita Zukauskiene

Introduction

As research on cyberbullying has gathered pace, a number of instruments to measure it have been devised in order to assess the nature and prevalence of different kinds of cyberbullying. One working sub-group of the COST Action was dedicated to a study of already existing measures for the assessment of cyberbullying through a systematic review. The systematic review started out with a literature search for publications published prior to October 2010. This generated 636 citations, of which 61 fulfilled the selection criteria we had delineated, and were included in this review, resulting in 44 instruments.

As a first step, we decided to provide an overview of the elements derived from the definitions of the instruments (as specified by the developers/ authors), as well as concepts and number of items for each instrument, and information about the different types of electronic media/devices. We also reported the sample characteristics, description of subscales and, if a factor analysis was conducted, the reliability and types of validity. This information about the included instruments has been published in the journal *Aggression and Violent Behavior* (Berne *et al.*, 2013). In this paper we showed that almost half of the instruments included in the review did not explicitly use the term "cyberbullying". Furthermore, we found that the types of devices/media (e.g. SMS, chatrooms, etc.) assessed varied considerably, with a total of 34 devices/media being assessed by the various instruments. The most common information source was the self-report of respondents, and almost all of the participants in the studies reviewed were in middle school or adolescence. A troublesome finding was that there was a lack of instruments using subscales derived by factor analysis. Finally, we found that most of the instruments had limited reports of reliability and validity testing, and then only internal reliability (internal consistency) and convergent validity had been tested.

In the present chapter we provide additional information from the systematic review that was not included in our previous publication. We report findings regarding the cut-off points and reference periods chosen in the selected studies. Additionally, we present the prevalence rates that have been reported in the studies. We include a focus on how cyberbullying was defined in the selected publications and instruments, although this information has already been presented in Berne *et al.* (2013), as we assume that there is a relationship to prevalence rates of cyberbullying.

We begin the chapter by discussing why systematic reviews are needed. We then review the literature regarding different methodological issues concerning the measurement of traditional and cyber bullying, with a special focus on the topics of this systematic review: definition, cut-off, reference period and prevalence estimation. Finally, we present and discuss the results from our systematic review.

Why are systematic reviews necessary?

Reviews are "required to identify areas where the available evidence is insufficient and further studies are required" (Egger, Smith, & O'Rourke, 2001, p. 4). However, conventional, unsystematic or narrative reviews often show a lack of quality and the generalizability of findings from narrative reviews are limited and often biased. Narrative reviews often use informal and subjective methods to select studies and to collect and interpret information (Egger *et al.*, 2001; Klassen, Jadad, & Moher, 1998). Also, narrative reviews often do not provide detailed information about all the steps of the review process (literature search, selection of literature, inclusion criteria of selected studies) and thus it is usually difficult to replicate their results and to verify or to judge their information and recommendations.

Systematic reviews – in contrast to narrative reviews – can allow for a more objective appraisal of the evidence of research results by synthesizing research results systematically and by rendering the review process transparent (Egger *et al.*, 2001). Meta-analyses are quantitative systematic reviews: "A meta-analysis is the statistical combination of at least two [primary] studies" (Klassen *et al.*, 1998, p. 700). As the scope of this chapter is not to report results from a quantitative meta-analysis, combining statistics "to produce a single estimate of the effect" (Klassen *et al.*, 1998, p. 700), we concentrate on systematic reviews in the sense of a research synthesis or qualitative systematic reviews (cf. Moher, Jadad, & Klassen, 1998).

> A research synthesis can be defined as the conjunction of a particular set of literature review characteristics. (...) research syntheses attempt to integrate empirical research for the purpose of creating generalizations (...) [and to] pay attention to relevant theories, critically analyze the research they cover, try to resolve conflicts in the literature and attempt to identify central issues for future research.
>
> (Cooper & Hedges, 2009, p. 6)

To approach these goals, systematic reviews follow a systematic approach to minimize bias and random errors, e.g. regarding the selection and inclusion of primary studies, coding information and synthesizing singular study results to obtain a more general picture of research findings (Egger *et al.*, 2001). Thus, high quality systematic reviews follow certain principles and procedures (Cooper, Hedges, & Valentine, 2009; Egger & Smith, 2001; Jadad, Moher, & Klassen, 1998; Kitchenham, 2004; Klassen *et al.*, 1998):

- A pre-definition of a review protocol, specifying the research being addressed and the methods that will be used to perform the review to minimize selection bias.
- A clearly and reliably defined search strategy to gather relevant studies to minimize selection bias. In general, electronic searches of the literature identify only about 50 per cent of all relevant articles (Dickersin, Scherer, & Lefebvre, 1994). To avoid publication bias, which refers to the problem that positive results are more likely to be published than negative results, systematic reviews also include the so-called "grey literature" (i.e. unpublished dissertation theses or conference proceedings) and other experts and researchers working in the area are asked if they know of any unpublished results.
- Documentation of the search strategy and search results.
- Definition of fair inclusion and exclusion eligibility criteria respectively to minimize selection bias, including piloting the selection criteria on a subset of primary studies.
- Specification of the information of interest to be obtained from the primary studies by using a well-defined coding manual, including reliability testing, piloting the manual criteria on a subset of primary studies and – if necessary – revisions of the coding manual to minimize rater bias.
- Definitions of quality criteria to evaluate each primary study or publication.

Following these principles and procedures, systematic reviews – in contrast to narrative reviews – reveal an objective, bias-free overview of the evidence of research results.

Literature review

In the following, we continue with a literature review regarding different methodological issues concerning the measurement of traditional and cyber bullying, with a special focus on the topics of this systematic review: definition, cut-off, reference period and prevalence estimation.

Definition

For the most part, researchers provide their participants with a definition of what is meant by cyberbullying when measuring the presence/absence of cybervictims/cyberbullies (Berne *et al.*, 2013). During recent years, considerable research has been directed to whether Olweus' three well-established criteria defining traditional bullying (intention to harm, repetition, imbalance of power) actually are useful to define cyberbullying (Berne *et al.*, 2013; Li, 2005; Menesini & Nocentini, 2009; Menesini, Nocentini, & Calussi, 2011; Menesini *et al.*, 2012; Ortega, Elipe, Mora-Merchán, Calmaestra, & Vega, 2009). Researchers have suggested that repetition and power imbalance might look somewhat different in cyberbullying in comparison to traditional bullying (Berne & Frisén, 2011; Menesini *et al.*, 2012). Additionally, researchers have suggested that there might be three additional characteristics specific to cyberbullying (Menesini *et al.*, 2012; Smith, 2011; Tokunaga, 2010). One such characteristic (the 24/7 nature of it) is that the victim has nowhere to hide, since cyberbullying takes place everywhere, both at home and in school. Another characteristic specific to cyberbullying is that the breadth of the audience might be increased on the internet. Finally, another characteristic is the different aspects of anonymity.

In our previously published paper we reported that researchers in the cyberbullying field operationalize the definition in different ways (Berne *et al.*, 2013). This is troublesome because in order to be able to establish good reliability and validity for instruments researchers need to use the same definition of cyberbullying.

Cut-off

In much of the work on traditional bullying, researchers dichotomize variables with specific cut-off points to establish groups (bullies, victims, bully/victims and different types of witnesses) for statistical purposes (Gradinger, Strohmeier, & Spiel, 2010). For example, one question that is often used to measure experiences of bullying has been obtained from Olweus (1999), namely: "How often have you been bullied in school in the past couple of months?" This is a multiple choice question with the following response alternatives: "I have not been bullied in school in the past couple of months"; "it has only happened once or twice"; "two or three times per month"; "about once per week"; "several times per week". The cut-off point of "two or three times per month" is often used to determine the presence/absence of victims or bullies, when using this question (Solberg & Olweus, 2003).

However, some researchers have chosen to use a lower cut-off point in research about cyberbullying than what is commonly used in research about traditional bullying (Menesini *et al.*, 2011; Menesini *et al.*, 2012; Slonje, Smith, & Frisén, 2012). More specifically, they have chosen to use "it has happened once or more" as a cut-off point. The main reason for using a lower cut-off point in cyberbullying than traditional bullying is the problem with the criterion of repetition in the cyber context (Menesini *et al.*, 2011; Menesini *et al.*, 2012; Slonje *et al.*, 2012). Problems with the criterion of repetition are especially visible in one type of cyberbullying: photo/video clip harassment (Slonje *et al.*, 2012). For example, an embarrassing photo/video clip could be uploaded to a webpage by the cyberbully and each new visit, comment or "like" to the webpage might be experienced as a repetition of the attack from the cyber victim's perspective. Or a photo/video clip can be sent to one person, who in turn transmits it to many others. This leads to the assumption that the use of repetition as a criterion for bullying may be less reliable in the cyber context (Menesini *et al.*, 2011; Menesini *et al.*, 2012; Slonje *et al.*, 2012).

Reference period

In a critical review of traditional bullying research, Monks *et al.* (2009) reported that there is a variety in what time reference period researchers have used when measuring traditional bullying (e.g. last month, last term, last year, ever at school). This is a cause for concern since it hinders researchers from making comparisons, both nationally and cross-culturally. According to Solberg and Olweus (2003) "the past couple of months" is a reference period that is reasonable to use when differentiating traditional victims from non-victims and traditional bullies from non-bullies. Solberg and Olweus (2003) further argue that this time period constitutes a memory unit that is likely to enable the pupils to remember traditional bullying situations. To be more specific, if a questionnaire is given towards the end of a school term, "the past couple of months" represent roughly the time period from the beginning of that term. The reference period "the past couple of months" has been widely used when measuring traditional bullying (Gradinger *et al.*, 2010), but other researchers have used different reference periods (Monks *et al.*, 2009), such as the "past year" or if it "ever" happened.

Prevalence

Solberg and Olweus (2003) have underlined the importance of investigating prevalence of traditional bullying among pupils. One reason for doing this is to see if there are changes in the prevalence of victims/bullies before and after an intervention. Another is to detect time trends about traditional bullying, since that type of knowledge is of importance when making plans for prevention strategies against bullying. Researchers have emphasized that prevalence is affected by which definition, cut-off point and reference period the participants receive, and have provided guidelines in this respect (Monks *et al.*, 2009; Solberg & Olweus, 2003).

However, whilst some authors claim that the traditional and cyber bullying contexts are similar (Mitchell, Ybarra, & Finkelhor, 2007), others argue that they are somewhat different (Menesini *et al.*, 2011). The question thus becomes whether researchers actually use the three well-established criteria (intention to harm, imbalance of power, repetition) and/or the three cyber-specific criteria (24/7 nature, public/private, anonymity) when measuring cyberbullying. Additionally, which cut-off points and reference periods do researchers use when measuring cyberbullying and what prevalence rates do they report?

Methods

Our main aim is to present an overview of information on instruments measuring cyberbullying. The following specific aims guided our investigations: (1) to provide information about what definitions, cut-off points and reference periods the studies have used; (2) to present the prevalence estimations of cyberbullying that are reported in the studies included; (3) to help readers decide which instrument is adequate for their study design and the intentions of their work.

A systematic literature review focusing on instruments developed for cyberbullying assessment was conducted in six steps (see Table 3.1).

1. Literature search/Development of the coding scheme and manual

We searched the literature using the electronic databases EbscoHost, ScienceDirect, OVID, and InformaWorld. Additionally, we contacted different cyberbullying researchers from the European network COST Action IS0801 'Cyberbullying: Coping with negative and enhancing positive uses of new technologies, in relationships in educational settings'. They were asked by email to send us their forthcoming publications and instruments.

The search terms covered were: *chat bullying, chat victimi*ation, cyber mobbing, cybermobbing, cyber bullying, cyberbullying, cyber victimi*ation, cyber aggression, cyber-aggression, cyber harassment, digital bullying, e-bullying, electronic bullying, electronic harassment, electronic victimi*ation, internet bullying, online harassment, online bullying, online victimi*ation, online bullying, phone bullying, sms bullying, text bullying, virtual aggression, virtual mobbing* .(Using the asterisk (*) in a search term ensures that both British and American English spelling will be included in the search; e.g. victimisation and victimization).

Table 3.1 Steps of the systematic literature review

1 Literature search/Development of the coding scheme and manual
2 Selecting relevant publications and instruments
3 First rater training and revision of the coding scheme and manual
4 Second rater training and revision of the coding scheme and manual
5 Coding of relevant publications and instruments
6 Analyses

The search of the databases was limited to publications that were advance published online or published in a journal prior to October 2010. This search generated 636 citations. We developed a coding scheme to assess and value the information deemed relevant concerning the quality of the instruments. It included the subsections: general information (e.g. authors, type of publication, country), details of the study (e.g. timeframe of data, method of data collection), details of the cyberbullying instrument (e.g. name, language, information source, design of items), and psychometric properties (e.g. subscales, reliability, validity, and statistical information). Simultaneously, we developed an accompanying coding manual with definitions, descriptions and guidance for the decisions of the raters. The raters were the nine authors of this chapter.

2. Selecting relevant publications and instruments

We examined the abstracts of all of the 636 publications and, when required/ uncertain, gathered further information from the full publications and by contacting the authors. The criteria for inclusion were that: (1) the publication was in English, and that the instruments received from the authors were translated into English for purpose of analysis; (2) the instrument incorporated at least one of the following topics; cyberbullying, cybervictimization, cyber harassment, or cyberaggression; (3) the study used questionnaires, surveys, vignettes, or qualitative measures with a standardized coding scheme; (4) information on psychometric properties was provided; and 5) the items of the instruments were available in publications or received from the author(s). Non-empirical studies, those not using specified measures, and studies only reporting a global question about cyberbullying or cybervictimization (i.e. single-item instruments), were excluded. We also did not include research exclusively dedicated to sexual harassment online. Furthermore, we excluded publications or instruments from the present review when contacted authors did not provide us with the necessary information. A total of 61 studies (44 instruments) fulfilled the delineated selection criteria and were included in the review.

3. First rater training and revision of the coding scheme and manual

For the first rater training, five of the 61 studies were randomly selected and rated by the nine authors. This step revealed some weaknesses and misunderstandings of the coding scheme and manual, resulting in a first revision.

4. Second rater training and revision of the coding scheme and manual

In the second step, nine further studies of the 61 were randomly selected, and rated by all the authors to test the quality of the revised coding scheme and manual. Inter-rater reliability was assessed by computing the agreement rates

(Orwin & Vevea, 2009) for all of the variables, which were between 60 per cent and 100 per cent. The items with a value of 60–80 per cent were considered a problem. These problems all concerned how to rate subscales and validity. This was addressed by investigating the reasons for this discrepancy and coordinating the rating procedures by further training. Additional revisions were made both for the coding scheme and the manual.

5. Coding of relevant publications and instruments

Finally, the remaining 52 publications were equally distributed among the nine authors to be rated individually.

6. Analyses

Multiple publications using the same instrument (including revised versions) were combined for the analyses, leaving 44 of 61 instruments to be analysed.

Results and discussion

In our previously published paper we showed that almost half of the instruments included in the review did not use the concept cyberbullying (Berne *et al.*, 2013). The concepts measured by the instruments ranged from internet harassment behavior to electronic bullying behavior to cyberbullying. Even though many of the authors used concepts other than cyberbullying they claimed that their instruments did measure it. This could be considered representative of the field of cyberbullying; therefore, we chose to include those instruments in our review. In this chapter we have chosen to categorize all the included instruments into two different groups: (1) cyberbullying instruments; and (2) related instruments, when reporting the details of the studies in tabular formats. We describe our major findings for both groups (cyberbullying instruments and related instruments) jointly in the text. To begin with, we account for and discuss the instruments' definitional basis. Then, we provide information about what cut-off points and reference periods the studies have used. Finally, we present the prevalence estimations of cyberbullying as reported in the studies.

Both Table 3.2 (cyberbullying instruments) and Table 3.3 (related instruments) outline the titles of the selected instruments; they provide an overview of the elements derived from the definitions of the instruments (as specified by the developers/authors), as well as cut-off points and the reference periods the studies have used, and information about the prevalence estimations of cyberbullying and of cybervictimization. The main purpose of both the tables and the written information is to help researchers select the instrument best corresponding to their needs.

Table 3.2 Cyberbullying instruments, elements in the definition[a], cut-off points, reference period and prevalence estimation of cyberbullying[b]

Cyberbullying instrument	Definition	Cut-off	Reference period	Prevalence[c]	Reference
Cyberbullying and Cybervictimization Questionnaire	E, I, R	Infrequent: At least once or twice Frequent: At least about a few times every week	Current school year	Infrequent CB males = 19.9% Infrequent CB females = 14.2% Frequent CB males = 3.7% Frequent CB females = 0.9%	Ang and Goh (2010)
Questionnaire of Cyberbullying (QoCB)	E, I, R	Yes	Ever	CV = 36.1%	Aricak, Siyahhan, Uzunhasanoglu, Saribeyoglu, Ciplak, Yilmaz, and Memmedov (2008)
Cyberbullying questionnaire	E, I, R	CB & CB/V: At least one time CV: At least once in their lifetime	Ever	CB = 2% CB/V = 17.7% CV = 36.7%	Aricak (2009)
–	E, I	–	Ever: IM Mobile phone email Last year: Chatrooms	–	Brandtzaeg, Staksrud, Hagen, and Wold (2009)

Table 3.2 continued

Cyberbullying instrument	Definition	Cut-off	Reference period	Prevalence[c]	Reference
The Cyberbullying Questionnaire (CBQ)	E, I, R, IP	At least sometimes	Ever	CB = 44.1%	Calvete, Orue, Estévez, Villardón, and Padilla (2010)
Cyber Bullying and Victimization Questionnaire	E, I, R, IP	At least once or twice	Past 6 months	CB = 11.9% CV = 19.2% CB/V = 37.4%	Campfield (2006)
The victimization of self (VS) scale with cyber-aggression questions	E, I	At least one time in the past 30 days	Last month	CV = 14%	Dempsey, Sulkowski, Nicols, and Storch (2009)
School Crime Supplement	–	Yes	During the school year	CV = 4% (during the school year)	Dinkes, Kemp, and Baum (2009)
		Once/twice		CV = 73% (once/twice)	
		Once/twice a month		CV = 21% (once/twice a month)	
		Once or twice a week		CV = 5% (once or twice a week)	
Revised cyberbullying inventory (RCBI)	E, I, R	At least once	Last 6 months	–	Erdur-Baker (2010) Topcu and Erdur-Baker (2010) Topcu, Erdur-Baker, and Capa-Aydin, (2008)
Mental health and Violence dimensions survey	E, I	Yes	Last 12 months	CV = 57.3% (Filipino) CV = 48.8% (Native Hawaiian) CV = 48.8% (Samoan) CV = 62.2 (Caucasian)	Goebert, Else, Matsu, Chung-Do, and Chang (2011)

Instrument	Types	Experience	Time	Results	Citation
Cyberbullying Survey	E, I, R	–	Ever	CB = 19% CV = 32%	Harcey (2007)
Cyber Bullying Victimization Scale	E, I	–	Previous 12 months	–	Hay and Meldrum (2010)
Cyberbullying and Online Aggression Survey instruments 2009 version	E, I, R	At least one experience with the behavior	2007 & 2008: Ever	2007: CV (male) = 32.5% CV (female) = 36.3% 2008: CB (male) = 18% CB (female) = 15.6% CV (male) = 32.7% CV (female) = 36.4%	Hinduja and Patchin (2007; 2008; 2010); Patchin and Hinduja, (2006)
			2006 & 2010: Previous 30 days	2006 & 2010: CB ranged from 9.1% to 23.1% CV ranged from 9.1% to 29.4% Witness = 47.1%	
–	E, I, R	At least one cyberbullying experience	–	CB = 20.4% CV = 34.9% Witnessed or being aware of cyberbullying = 63.4%	Huang and Chou (2010)
SURVEY	E, I, R, IP	Yes	–	CB ranged from 14.5% to 17.8% CV ranged from 24.9% to 28.9%	Li (2005, 2006, 2007a, 2007b, 2008)

Table 3.2 continued

Cyberbullying instrument	Definition	Cut-off	Reference period	Prevalence[c]	Reference
Cyberbullying student survey	E, I	–	–	Witness = 56.8%	Li (2010)
Cyberbullying Scale (CS)	E, I, R, IP	Only once or twice 2/3 times a month Once a week Several times a week	Past 2 months	CB = 14% (only once or twice) CB = 2% (2/3 times a month) CB = 0% (once a week) CB = 1% (several times a week) CV = 6% (only once or twice) CV = 2% (2/3 times a month) CV = 0.3% (once a week) CV = 0.7% (several times a week)	Menesini, Nocentini, and Calussi (2011)
Checking In On-Line: What's Happening in Cyberspace?	E, I	At least once or twice	Past 3 months	CB = 33.7% CV = 49.5%	Mishna, Cook, Gadalla, Daciuk, and Solomon (2010)
European Cyberbullying Research Project (ECRP)	E, I, R, IP	At least two or three times a month	Last 2 months	CV = 5%	Ortega, Elipe, Mora-Merchán, Calmaestra, and Vega (2009)
Peer aggression / Victimization Questionnaire	–	At least seldom	Last 6 months	CB = 31.5% CV = 56.2%	Pornari and Wood (2010)

Instrument	Type	Frequency	Time frame	Prevalence	Reference
Text and email bullying	E	At least once	Ever	2002: CV = 13% 2004: CV = 16.4%	Rivers and Noret (2009)
Cyberbullying Survey	E, I	–	Past 2 months	–	Salvatore (2006)
The Berlin Cyberbullying – Cybervictimisation Questionnaire (BCyQ)	E, I, R, IP	At least twice or three times a month	During the last term	CB = 16.9% CV = 15.5 %	Schultze–Krumbholz and Scheithauer (2009a; 2009b)
Cyberbullying Questionnaire	E, I, R, IP	At least once or twice	Past couple of months	CB = 10.3% CV = 11.7 %	Slonje and Smith (2008)
Cyberbullying Questionnaire	2005: E, I, R, IP	2005: At least once or twice	2005: Past 2 or 3 months	2005: CV = 15.6% (once/twice) CV = 6.6% (often)	Smith, Mahdavi, Carvalho, Fisher, Russell, and Tippett, N (2008)
	2006: E, I, R, IP	2006: Last week/month This term Last school year Over a year ago	2006: Last week/month This term Last school year Over a year ago	2006: CB = 6.5% (Last week/month) CB = 2.8% (This term) CB = 1.8% (Last school year) CB = 1.4% (Over a year ago) CV = 5.3% (Last week/month) CV = 5.1% (This term) CV = 3.7% (Last school year) CV = 3.1% (Over a year ago)	

Table 3.2 continued

Cyberbullying instrument	Definition	Cut-off	Reference period	Prevalence[c]	Reference
The Student Survey of Bullying Behavior – Revised 2 (SSBB-R2)	E, I, R	Once/twice a year Monthly	–	–	Varjas, Heinrich, and Meyers (2009)
Cyberbully poll	E, I, R, IP	At least once over the past year	Past year	CB = 24% CV = 30%	Walker (2009)
Cyberbullying Survey for Middle School Students	E	Less than 4 times	–	CB = 14.4% CV = 29.8%	Wright, Burnham, Inman, and Ogorchock (2009)

Note

A dash (–) is used in the table to indicate when no data was reported in the publications.

All publications that are referred to as published 2011 were included because they were also advance published online before October 2010.

a   These elements have been generated from the cyberbullying literature (Tokunaga, 2010). Following letters represent elements in the definitions of cyberbullying (as specified by the developers): Electronic device/media = E; Intentionality = I; Repetition = R; Imbalance of Power = IP; Anonymity = A; Public/Private = P.

b   There is a divergence as to what studies base their prevalence estimations on, in this systematic review prevalence estimations for being cyberbullied and having cyberbullied others are reported.

c   Following letters represent different roles: CB = Cyberbullies; CV = Cybervictims; CB/V = Cyberbully-victims.

Table 3.3 Related instruments, elements in the definition[a], cut-off points, reference period and prevalence estimation of cyberbullying[b]

Cyberbullying instrument	Definition	Cut-off	Reference period	Prevalence	Reference
Cyber-Harassment Student Survey	E, I, R, IP	At least once or twice	–	Cyber-harassment perpetrator = 26% Cyber-harassment victimization = 58%	Beran and Li (2005)
Online (survey) Questionnaire	E, I, R, IP	At least monthly	Last 12 months	Experienced griefing = 38%	Coyne, Chesney, Logan, and Madden (2009)
–	E, I, R	Any reported frequency	–	Online harassment = 10 to 15%	Finn (2004)
Victimization in chatroom and bullying in chatroom	E, I, R, IP	At least every few months	–	–	Katzer, Fetchenhauer, and Belschak (2009)
The survey of Internet Risk and Behavior	E, I, R	Agreement	–	Internet bullying behavior = 10% Cybervictimization = 10%	Kite, Gable, and Filippelli (2010)
Survey of Internet Mental Health Issues (SIMHI)	E, I	Yes	Last 5 years	Internet harassment ranged from 5% to 30% Internet victim ranged from 18% to 70%	Mitchell, Becker-Blease, and Finkelhor (2005) Mitchell, Finkelhor, and Becker-Blease (2007)
Internet harassment/Youth Internet Safety Survey YISS 1	E, I	Yes to at least one of the two questions	Past year	Harasser ranged from 12% to 15% Target ranged from 3% to 6%	Mitchell, Ybarra and Finkelhor (2007) Ybarra (2004) Ybarra and Mitchell (2004a) Ybarra and Mitchell (2004b)

Table 3.3 continued

Cyberbullying instrument	Definition	Cut-off	Reference period	Prevalence	Reference
–	E, I	At least once	Past 6 months	Mobile phone aggression = 70% Mobile phone victimization = 67%	Nicol and Fleming (2010)
Cyber Stalking Survey	E, I	–	Past year	Cyber stalking/harassment = 13%	Paullet (2010)
Lodz Electronic Aggression Prevalence Questionnaire (LEAPQ)	E, I, R, IP	Once in the last 12 months Few times in the last months Frequently in the last months	Last 12 months Last months	Perpetrator of electronic aggression = 20% Victim of electronic aggression = 16.3%	Pyżalski (2009)
Measure of text message victimization	E, I	At least three incidents	Since the start of the school year (5–6 months)	Text message victimization = 23%	Raskauskas (2010) Raskauskas and Prochnow (2007)
The Internet Experiences Questionnaire	E, I, R	Yes	Last school year	Electronic bullying = 21.4% Electronic victimization = 48.8%	Raskauskas and Stoltz (2007)
American Life Survey's Online Teen Survey	E, I	Yes	Ever	Some kind of cyberbullying = > 25%	Sengupta and Chaudhuri (2011)

Scale	Elements[a]	Frequency	Timeframe	Prevalence	References
The Online Victimization Scale–21 items	E, I, R	–	Ever	–	Tynes, Rose, and Williams (2010)
Internet harassment/Youth Internet Safety Survey YISS 2	E, I	At least once	Past year	Limited perpetration of harassment = 17% Occasional perpetration = 6% Frequent harasser = 6% (Ybarra and Mitchell, 2007)	Ybarra and Mitchell (2007) Ybarra, Mitchell, Finkelhor, and Wolak (2007) Ybarra, Mitchell, Wolak, and Finkelhor (2006)
				Internet victim ranged from 9% to 27.7% (Ybarra, Mitchell, Wolak, and Finkelhor, 2006; Ybarra, Mitchell, Finkelhor, and Wolak)	
Growing up with Media (GuwM): Youth-reported Internet harassment	E, I	At least once	Last year	At least once: Harasser = 35% Victim = ranging from 34% to 35%	Ybarra, Diener-West, and Leaf (2007) Ybarra, Espelage, and Mitchell (2007)
		At least monthly		At least monthly: Harasser = 4% Victim = 8%	Ybarra and Mitchell (2008)

Note
A dash (–) is used in the table to indicate when no data were reported in the publications.
All publications that are referred to as published 2011 were included because they were also advance published online before October 2010.
a These elements have been generated from the cyberbullying literature (Tokunaga, 2010). Following letters represent elements in the definitions of cyberbullying (as specified by the developers): Electronic device/media = E; Intentionality = I; Repetition = R; Imbalance of Power = IP; Anonymity = A; Public/Private = P.
b There is a divergence as to what studies base their prevalence estimations on, in this systematic review prevalence estimations for being cyberbullied and having cyberbullied others are reported.

Definition

In our previously published paper we reported about how cyberbullying was defined in the publications and instruments (Berne *et al.*, 2013). We outline the most important findings here as well in order for the reader to have this information parallel to other information about the measurements such as the prevalence rates reported. In summary, the systematic review showed that the developers of the instruments operationalized cyberbullying in different ways. We found that the majority of the definitions emphasized that cyberbullying behavior occurs through electronic devices/media (42 of the 44). Additionally, 40 of the 44 definitions included the criterion that the perpetrator must have the intention to harm. It was less often that the repetition criterion was included in the definitions (25 of the 44). Notably, only 13 of the 44 definitions contained the criterion imbalance of power. Finally, none of the suggested three characteristics specific to cyberbullying (the 24/7 nature of it, the broader audience, and the aspects of anonymity) were included in any of the 44 instruments' definitions of cyberbullying.

Cut-off

The cut-off point "at least once or twice" was used in 19 of the 44 instruments, and 10 of the 44 instruments used the cut-off point "yes" (i.e. at least once). This illustrates that there are many researchers who use a lower cut-off point than is usually used in research about traditional bullying where the cut-off "two or three times per month or more" is often used. Here, only four of the 44 instruments used the cut-off point "two or three times per month or more". Additionally, four of the 44 used arbitrary cut-off points, such as "experience with the behaviors", "sometimes and often", "seldom and over" and "three/more incidents". Finally, in seven out of the 44 instruments, there were no cut-off points reported.

Reference period

Out of the 44 instruments, 35 included some reference period. However, the instruments differed with regard to the reference period used. The two most often included reference periods were "last year" (11 of the 44), and "ever" (nine of the 44). Other reference periods ranged from "last month" to the "previous thirty days" to "since the start of the school year". Only five of the 44 included the reference period "past two or three months" and four of the 44 used "past six months". Thus, it appears that most researchers do not use the same reference period as recommended when measuring traditional bullying, that is "the past couple of months". One possible explanation for this could be the notion that nasty or offensive text messages or unfriendly information (photos, videos, text) that have been uploaded might remain on the internet for a long time and thus a longer time period might be more adequate. Surprisingly, in some of the instruments no information about the time period is provided at all.

Prevalence

Many of the studies in this review have presented some prevalence data (50 of the 61 studies). However, only five of the 61 studies have reported prevalence data for cyberbullying victims and cyberwitnesses. The concept of cyberbullying of others (or related concepts) is measured in 37 of the 61 studies with prevalence rates that vary between 3 and 70 per cent; and 50 of the 61 studies measured the concept of cybervictimization (or related concepts) with prevalence rates that vary between 0.9 and 73 per cent!

This great variability in reported prevalence rates may have several reasons. First, the developers of the instruments operationalized the concept "cyberbullying" in varied ways. Different concepts and a vague definition leave room for subjective interpretation by the participant who is to respond to the questionnaire "what is meant by cyberbullying" (Solberg & Olweus, 2003). By extension, this can increase variability in prevalence rates. Second, instruments used different cut-off points for differentiating cybervictims from non-cybervictims and cyberbullies from non-cyberbullies. It is well known that the use of different cut-off points makes prevalence vary greatly in research about traditional bullying (Monks *et al.*, 2009; Scheithauer, Hayer, Petermann, & Jugert, 2006). Finally, instruments differed with regard to the reference period used in measuring cyberbullying.

Conclusions

The systematic review showed that the developers of the instruments operationalized the concept and definition for cyberbullying in different ways. This is troublesome because in order to be able to advance understanding of cyberbullying, researchers need to use the same definition of cyberbullying. Additionally, researchers have often used the cut-off point "two or three times per month" to measure traditional bullying (Gradinger *et al.*, 2010); but, this review showed that researchers in the cyberbullying field have rarely used the cut-off point "two or three times per month" to measure cyberbullying. Instead, a majority has used the cut-off points "at least once or twice" or "yes" to determine the presence/absence of cybervictims or cyberbullies. Additionally, almost half of the instruments did not provide their participants with a definition that included the repetitive element in a cyberbullying situation. Thus, it appears that many researchers in the cyberbullying field use a more lenient cut-off point, and they do not put much emphasis on the criterion of repetition in comparison to traditional bullying. However, one must be careful to interpret this as a sign that the repetition criterion is not valid in research about cyberbullying; instead, some researchers have argued that the criterion appears differently in cyberbullying.

For example, with regard to photo/video clip harassment, embarrassing photo/video clips could be uploaded to a webpage where each visit might be counted as part of the repetitive act.

Furthermore, we found that instruments differ with regard to the "reference period" used in measuring cyberbullying. Finally, prevalence rates vary greatly, possibly due to different concepts, definitions, cut-offs and reference periods when measuring the prevalence of cyberbullying. Thus, in order to move this area of research forward it might be beneficial to focus on reaching agreements among researchers about which concepts, definitions, cut-offs, and reference periods to use.

One of our aims with this systematic review was to help readers decide which instrument is adequate for their own study design and the intentions of their work. This can hopefully be done with the help of our previously published paper (Berne *et al.*, 2013) and this chapter, which provides the reader with a systematic overview of the current instruments designed to assess cyberbullying. To be more specific, researchers can find information in the tables about the different cyberbullying roles the included instruments cover, and thus can choose an instrument that covers the roles of interest for a particular study. Furthermore, as presented previously and in this chapter, the definitional bases for the instruments vary to a great degree and few instruments include all aspects of the definition of cyberbullying. However, for different research aims, different aspects of the definition might be more or less important to cover. Additionally, there is information in the tables that can be helpful for future studies to choose the relevant instrument regarding cut-offs and reference periods. Caution should be taken, however, in using instruments with no cut-off or no reference period. Finally, in our previously published paper (Berne *et al.*, 2013), the reader will find information about psychometric properties of the instruments, such as validity and reliability that can guide researchers in their choice of instrument to use.

References

* *References marked with an asterisk indicate studies used in the systematic review.*

*Ang, R.P., and Goh, D.H. (2010). 'Cyberbullying among adolescents: The role of affective and cognitive empathy and gender'. *Child Psychiatry and Human Development, 41*, 387–397. doi: 10.1007/s10578-010-0176-3

*Aricak, T.O. (2009). 'Psychiatric symptomatology as a predictor of cyberbullying among university students'. *Eurasian Journal of Educational Research, 34*, 167–184.

*Aricak, T.O., Siyahhan, S., Uzunhasanoglu, A., Saribeyoglu, S., Ciplak, S., Yilmaz, N., and Memmedov, C. (2008). 'Cyberbullying among Turkish adolescents'. *Cyberpsychology and Behavior, 11*, 253–261. doi: 10.1089/cpb.2007.0016

*Beran, T., and Li, Q. (2005). 'Cyber-harassment: A study of a new method for an old behavior'. *Journal of Educational Computing Research, 32*(3), 265–277.

Berne, S., and Frisén, A. (2011). *Adolescents' view on how different criteria define cyberbullying*. Symposium at the European Conference on Developmental Psychology, 25 August, Bergen: Norway.

Berne, S., Frisén, A., Schultze-Krumbholz, A., Scheithauer, H., Naruskov, K., Luik, P., Katzer, C., Erentaite, R., and Zukauskiene, R. (2013). 'Cyberbullying assessment instruments: A systematic review'. *Aggression and Violent Behavior, 18*(2), 320–334. doi:10.1016/j.avb.2012.11.022

*Brandtzaeg, P.B., Staksrud, E., Hagen, I., and Wold, T. (2009). 'Norwegian children's experiences of cyberbullying when using different technological platforms'. *Journal of Children and Media, 3*(4), 350–365. doi: 10.1080/17482790903233366

*Calvete, E., Orue, I., Estévez, A., Villardón, L., and Padilla, P. (2010). 'Cyberbullying in adolescents: Modalities and aggressors' profile'. *Computers in Human Behavior, 26*, 1128–1135. doi: 10.1016/j.chb.2010.03.017

*Campfield, D.C. (2006). *Cyberbullying and victimization: Psychosocial characteristics of bullies, victims, and bully/victims*. (Doctoral dissertation), The University of Montana. Available from ProQuest Dissertations and Theses database.

Cooper, H., and Hedges, L.V. (2009). 'Research synthesis as a scientific process'. In H. Cooper, L.V. Hedges, and J.C. Valentine (eds.), *The handbook of research synthesis and meta-analysis* (2nd ed., pp. 3–16). New York: Russell Sage Foundation.

Cooper, H., Hedges, L.V., and Valentine, J.C. (eds.) (2009). *The handbook of research synthesis and meta-analysis*, 2nd ed. New York: Russell Sage Foundation.

*Coyne, I., Chesney, T., Logan, B., and Madden, N. (2009). 'Griefing in a virtual community: An exploratory survey of second life residents'. *Zeitschrift für Psychologie/Journal of Psychology, 217*(4), 214–221. doi: 10.1027/0044-3409.217.4.214

*Dempsey, A.G., Sulkowski, M.L., Nicols, R., and Storch, E.A. (2009). 'Differences between peer victimization in cyber and physical settings and associated psychosocial adjustment in early adolescence'. *Psychology in the Schools, 46*(10), 960–970. doi: 10.1002/pits.20437

Dickersin, K., Scherer, R., and Lefebvre, C. (1994). 'Identifying relevant studies for reviews'. *British Medical Journal, 309*, 1286–1291.

*Dinkes, R., Kemp, J., and Baum, K. (2009). *Indicators of School Crime and Safety: 2008* (NCES 2009–022/NCJ 226343). National Center for Education Statistics, Institute of Education Sciences, U.S. Department of Education, and Bureau of Justice Statistics, Office of Justice Programs, U.S. Department of Justice. Washington, DC.

Egger, M., and Smith, G.D. (2001). 'Principles of and procedures for systematic reviews'. In M. Egger, D.D. Smith, and D.G. Altman, (eds.), *Systematic reviews in health care. Meta-analysis in context* (pp. 23–42). London: BMJ Books.

Egger, M., Smith, G.D., and O'Rourke, K. (2001). 'Rationale, potentials, and promise of systematic reviews'. In M. Egger, D.D. Smith, and D.G. Altman (eds.), *Systematic reviews in health care. Meta-analysis in context* (pp. 3–19). London: BMJ Books.

*Erdur-Baker, Ö. (2010). 'Cyberbullying and its correlation to traditional bullying, gender and frequent and risky usage of internet-mediated communication tools'. *New Media and Society, 12*(1), 109–125. doi: 10.1177/1461444809341260

*Finn, J. (2004). 'A survey of online harassment at a university campus'. *Journal of Interpersonal Violence, 19*, 468–483. doi: 10.1177/0886260503262083

*Goebert, D., Else, I., Matsu, C., Chung-Do, J., and Chang, J.Y. (2011). 'The impact of cyberbullying on substance use and mental health in a multiethnic sample'. *Maternal and Child Health Journal, 15*, 1282–1286. doi: 10.1107/s10995-010-0672-x

Gradinger, P., Strohmeier, D., and Spiel, C. (2010). 'Definition and measurement of Cyberbullying'. *Cyberpsychology: Journal of Psychosocial Research on Cyberspace, 4*(2). Retrieved August 12, 2011 from http://cyberpsychology.eu/view.php?cisloclanku =2010112301&article=1.

*Harcey, T.D. (2007). *A phenomenological study of the nature, prevalence, and perceptions of cyberbullying based on student and administrator responses.* (Doctoral dissertation), Edgewood Collage. Available from ProQuest Dissertations and Theses database.

*Hay, C., and Meldrum, R. (2010). 'Bullying victimization and adolescent self-harm: Testing hypotheses from general strain theory'. *Journal of Youth Adolescence, 39*, 446–459. doi: 10.1007/s10964-009-9502-0

*Hinduja, S., and Patchin, J. W. (2007). 'Offline consequences of online victimization'. *Journal of School Violence, 6*(3), 89–112. doi: 10.1300/J202v06n03 06

*——(2008). 'Cyberbullying: an exploratory analysis of factors related to offending and victimization'. *Deviant Behavior, 29*, 129–156. doi: 10.1080/01639620701457816

*——(2010). 'Bullying, cyberbullying, and suicide'. *Archives of Suicide Research, 14*(3), 206–221. doi: 10.1080/13811118.2010.494133

*Huang, Y.-Y., and Chou, C. (2010). 'An analysis of multiple factors of cyberbullying among junior high school students in Taiwan'. *Computers in Human Behavior, 26*, 1581–1590. doi: 10.1016/j.chb.2010.06.005

Jadad, A.R., Moher, D., and Klassen, T.P. (1998). 'Guides for reading and interpreting systematic reviews II. How did the authors find the studies and assess their quality?' *Archives of Pediatrics and Adolescent Medicine, 152*, 812–817.

*Katzer, C., Fetchenhauer, D., and Belschak, F. (2009). 'Cyberbullying: Who are the victims? A comparison of victimization in internet chatrooms and victimization in school'. *Journal of Media Psychology, 21*(1), 25–36. doi: 10.1027/1864-1105.21.1.25

Kitchenham, B. (2004). *Procedures for performing systematic reviews.* Keele University Technical Report TR/SE-0401 & NICTA Technical Report 0400011T.

*Kite, S.L., Gable, R., and Filippelli, L. (2010). 'Assessing middle school students' knowledge of conduct and consequences and their behaviors regarding the use of social networking sites'. *The Clearing House, 83*, 158–163. doi: 10.1080/ 00098650903505365

Klassen, T.P., Jadad, A.R., and Moher, D. (1998). 'Guides for reading and interpreting systematic reviews – I. Getting started'. *Archives of Pediatrics and Adolescent Medicine, 152*, 700–704.

*Li, Q. (2005). *Cyberbullying in schools: Nature and extent of Canadian adolescents' experience.* Paper presented at the Annual meeting of the American Educational Research Association, Montreal, Canada.

*——(2006). 'Cyberbullying in schools: A research of gender differences'. *School Psychology International, 27*(2), 157–170. doi: 10.1177/01430343060xxxxx

*——(2007a). 'Bullying in the new playground: Research into cyberbullying and cyber victimization'. *Australasian Journal of Educational Technology, 23*(4), 435–454.

*——(2007b). 'New bottle but old wine: A research of cyberbullying in schools'. *Computers in Human Behavior, 23*, 1777–1791. doi: 10.1016/j.chb.2005.10.005

*——(2008). 'A cross-cultural comparison of adolescents' experiences related to cyberbullying'. *Educational Research, 50*(3), 223–234. doi: 10.1080/00131880802309333

*——(2010). 'Cyberbullying in high schools: A study of students' behaviors and beliefs about this phenomenon'. *Journal of Aggression, Maltreatment and Trauma, 19*, 372–392. doi: 10.1080/10926771003788979

Menesini, E., and Nocentini, A. (2009). 'Cyberbullying definition and measurement: Some critical considerations'. *Zeitschrift für Psychologie/Journal of Psychology, 217*(4), 230–232. doi: 10.1027/0044-3409.217.4.230

*Menesini, E., Nocentini, A., and Calussi, P. (2011). 'The measurement of cyberbullying: Dimensional structure and relative item severity and discrimination'. *Cyberpsychology, Behavior, and Social Networking, 14*(5), 267–274. doi: 10.1089/cyber.2010.0002

Menesini, E., Nocentini, A., Palladino, B.E., Frisén, A., Berne, S., Ortega, R., Calmaestra, J., Scheithauer, H., Schultze-Krumbholz, A., Luik, P., Naruskov, K., Blaya, C., Berthaud, J., and Smith, P.K. (2012). 'Cyberbullying definition among adolescents: A comparison across six European countries'. *Cyberpsychology, Behavior and Social Networking, 15*(9), 455–463. doi: 10.1089/cyber.2012.0040

*Mishna, F., Cook, C., Gadalla, T., Daciuk, J., and Solomon, S. (2010). 'Cyber bullying behaviors among middle and high school students'. *American Journal of Orthopsychiatry, 80*(3), 362–374. doi: 10.1111/j.1939-0025.2010.01040.x

*Mitchell, K.J., Becker-Blease, K.A., and Finkelhor, D. (2005). 'Inventory of problematic internet experiences encountered in clinical practice'. *Professional Psychology: Research and Practice, 36*(5), 498–509. doi: 10.1037/0735-7028.36.5.498

*Mitchell, K.J., Finkelhor, D., and Becker-Blease, K.A. (2007). 'Linking youth internet and conventional problems: Findings from a clinical perspective'. *Journal of Aggression, Maltreatment and Trauma, 15*(2), 39–58. doi: 10.1300/J146v15n02_03

*Mitchell, K.J., Ybarra, M.L., and Finkelhor, D. (2007). 'The relative importance of online victimization in understanding depression, delinquency, and substance use'. *Child Maltreatment, 12*(4), 314–324. doi: 10.1177/1077559507305996

Moher, D., Jadad, A.R., and Klassen, T.P. (1998). 'Guides for reading and interpreting systematic reviews III. How did the authors synthesize the data and make their conclusions?' *Archives of Pediatrics and Adolescent Medicine, 152*, 915–920.

Monks, P.C., Smith, P.K., Naylor, P., Barter, C., Ireland, L.J., and Coyne, I. (2009). 'Bullying in different contexts: Commonalities, differences and the role of theory'. *Aggression and Violent Behavior, 14*, 146–156.

*Nicol, A., and Fleming, M.J. (2010). '"i h8 u": The influence of normative beliefs and hostile response selection in predicting adolescents' mobile phone aggression - a pilot study'. *Journal of School Violence, 9*(2), 212–231. doi: 10.1080/15388220903585861

Olweus, D. (1999). 'Sweden'. In P.K. Smith, J.M. Junger-Tas, D. Olweus, R. Catalano, and P. Slee (eds.), *The nature of school bullying: A cross-national perspective* (pp. 7–27). London: Routledge.

*Ortega, R., Elipe, P., Mora-Merchán, J.A., Calmaestra, J., and Vega, E. (2009). 'The emotional impact on victims of traditional bullying and cyberbullying: A study of Spanish adolescents'. *Zeitschrift für Psychologie/Journal of Psychology, 217*(4), 197–204. doi: 10.1027/0044-3409.217.4.197

Orwin, R.G., and Vevea, J.L. (2009). 'Evaluating coding decisions'. In H. Cooper, L.V. Hedges and J.C. Valentine (eds.), *The handbook of research synthesis and meta-analysis* (pp. 177–206). New York: Russell Sage Foundation.

*Patchin, J.W., and Hinduja, S. (2006). 'Bullies move beyond the schoolyard: A preliminary look at cyberbullying'. *Youth Violence and Juvenile Justice, 4*(2), 148–169. doi: 10.1177/1541204006286288

*Paullet, K.L. (2010). *An exploratory study of cyberstalking: Students and law enforcement in Allegheny county, Pennsylvania.* (Doctoral dissertation), Robert Morris University. Available from ProQuest Dissertations and Theses database.

*Pornari, C.D., and Wood, J. (2011). 'Peer and cyber aggression in secondary school students: The role of moral disengagement, hostile attribution bias, and outcome expectancies'. *Aggressive Behavior, 36*, 81–94. doi: 10.1002/ab.20336

*Pyżalski, J. (August 18–22, 2009). *Poster in workshop.* XIV European Conference on Developmental Psychology. Vilnius, Lithuania.

*Raskauskas, J. (2010). 'Text-bullying: Associations with traditional bullying and depression among New Zealand adolescents'. *Journal of School Violence, 9*(1), 74–97. doi: 10.1080/15388220903185605

*Raskauskas, J., and Prochnow, J.E. (2007). 'Text-bullying in New Zealand: A mobile twist on traditional bullying'. *New Zealand Annual Review of Education, 16, 89–104).*

*Raskauskas, J., and Stoltz, A.D. (2007). 'Involvement in traditional and electronic bullying among adolescents'. *Developmental Psychology, 43*(3), 564–575. doi: 10.1037/0012-1649.43.3.564

*Rivers, I., and Noret, N. (2010). '"I h8 u": findings from a five-year study of text and email bullying'. *British Educational Research Journal, 36*(4), 643–671. doi: 10.1080/01411920903071918

*Salvatore, A.J. (2006). *An anti-bullying strategy: Action research in a 5/6 intermediate school* (Doctoral dissertation), University of Hartford. Available from ProQuest Dissertations and Theses database.

Scheithauer, H., Hayer, T., Petermann, F. and Jugert, G. (2006). 'Physical, verbal and relational forms of bullying among students from Germany: Gender-, age-differences and correlates'. *Aggressive Behavior, 32*, 261–275.

*Schultze-Krumbholz, A. and Scheithauer, H. (2009a). *Measuring Cyberbullying and Cybervictimisation by Using Behavioral Categories – The Berlin Cyberbullying Cybervictimisation Questionnaire (BCyQ).* Poster presented at the Post Conference Workshop 'COST ACTION IS0801: Cyberbullying: Coping with negative and enhancing positive uses of new technologies, in relationships in educational settings', 22–23 August 2009, Vilnius.

*——(2009b). 'Social-behavioral correlates of cyberbullying in a German student sample'. *Zeitschrift für Psychologie/Journal of Psychology, 217*(4), 224–226. doi: 10.1027/0044-3409

*Sengupta, A., and Chaudhuri, A. (2011). 'Are social networking sites a source of online harassment for teens? Evidence from a survey data'. *Children and Youth Services Review, 33*, 284–290.

*Slonje, R., and Smith, P.K. (2008). 'Cyberbullying: Another main type of bullying?' *Scandinavian Journal of Psychology, 49,* 147–154. doi: 10.1111/j.1467-9450.2007.00611.x

Slonje, R., Smith, P.K., and Frisén, A. (2012). 'Cyberbullying: Processes of cyberbullying, and feelings of remorse by bullies: A pilot study'. *European Journal of Developmental Psychology, 9*(2), 244–259. doi: 10.1080/17405629.2011.643670

Smith, J.D., Schneider, B.H., Smith, P.K., and Ananiadou, K. (2004). 'The effectiveness of whole-school antibullying programs: A synthesis of evaluation research'. *School Psychology Review, 33*(4), 547–560.

Smith, P.K. (2009). 'Cyberbullying: Abusive relationships in cyberspace'. *Zeitschrift für Psychologie/Journal of Psychology, 217*(4), 180–181. doi: 10.1027/0044-3409.217.4.180

——(2012). 'Cyberbullying and cyber aggression'. In R.S. Jimerson, B.A. Nickerson, J.M. Mayer, and J.M. Furlong (eds.), *Handbook of School Violence and School Safety: International Research and Practice* (pp. 93–103). New York: Routledge.

Smith, P.K., Cowie, H., Olafsson, F.R., Liefooghe, P.D.A. and 17 additional authors (2002). 'Definitions of bullying: A comparison of terms used, and age and gender differences, in a fourteen-country international comparison'. *Child Development, 73*(4), 1119–1133.

*Smith, P.K., Mahdavi, J., Carvalho, M., Fisher, S., Russell, S., and Tippett, N. (2008). 'Cyberbullying: Its nature and impact in secondary school pupils'. *Journal of Child Psychology and Psychiatry, 49*(4), 376–385. doi: 10.1111/ j.1469-7610.2007.01846.x

Solberg, M.E., and Olweus, D. (2003). 'Prevalence estimation of school bullying with the Olweus bully/victim questionnaire'. *Aggressive Behavior, 29*, 239–268. doi: 10.1002/ab.10047

Spears, B., Slee, P., Owens, L., and Johnson, B. (2009). 'Behind the scenes and screens: Insights into the human dimension of covert and cyberbullying'. *Zeitschrift für Psychologie/Journal of Psychology, 217*(4), 189–196.

Streiner, D.L., and Norman, G.R. (2008). *In health measurement scales: A practical guide to their development and use.* New York: Oxford University Press.

Tokunaga, R.S. (2010). 'Following you home from school: A critical review and synthesis of research on cyberbullying victimization'. *Computers in Human Behavior, 26*, 277–287. doi: 10.1016/j.chb.2009.11.014

*Topcu, C., and Erdur-Baker, Ö. (2010). 'The revised cyber bullying inventory (RCBI): validity and reliability studies'. *Procedia Social and Behavioral Sciences, 5*, 660–664. doi: 10.1016/j.sbspro.2010.07.161

*Topcu, C., Erdur-Baker, Ö., and Capa-Aydin, Y. (2008). 'Examination of cyberbullying experiences among Turkish students from different school types'. *Cyberpsychology and Behavior, 11*(6), 643–648. doi: 10.1089/cpb.2007.0161

*Tynes, B.M., Rose, C.A., and Williams, D.R. (2010). 'The development and validation of the online victimization scale for adolescents'. *Cyberpsychology: Journal of Psychosocial Research on Cyberspace, 4*(2). Retrieved August 10, 2011 from http://cyberpsychology.eu/view.php ?cisloclanku=2010112901&article=2

*Varjas, K., Heinrich, C.C., and Meyers, J. (2009). 'Urban middle school students' perceptions of bullying, cyberbullying and school safety'. *Journal of School Violence, 8*(2), 159–176. doi: 10.1080/15388220802074165

*Walker, J. (2009). *The contextualized rapid resolution cycle intervention model for cyberbullying.* (Doctoral dissertation), Arizona State University. Available from ProQuest Dissertations and Theses database.

*Wright, V.H., Burnham, J.J., Inman, C.T., and Ogorchock, H.N. (2009). 'Cyberbullying: Using virtual scenarios to educate and raise awareness'. *Journal of Computing in Teacher Education, 26*(1), 35–42.

*Ybarra, M.L. (2004). 'Linkages between depressive symptomatology and internet harassment among young regular internet users'. *Cyberpsychology and Behavior, 7*(2), 248–257. doi: 10.1089/109493104323024500

*Ybarra, M.L., and Mitchell, K.J. (2004a). 'Online aggressor/targets, aggressors, and targets: a comparison of associated youth characteristics'. *Journal of Child Psychology and Psychiatry, 45*(7), 1308–1316. doi: 10.1111/j.1469-7610.2004.00328.x

*——(2004b). 'Youth engaging in online harassment: associations with caregiver-child relationships, internet use, and personal characteristics'. *Journal of Adolescence, 27*, 319–336. doi: 10.1016/j.adolescence. 2004.03.007

*——(2007). 'Prevalence and frequency of internet harassment instigation: Implications for adolescent health'. *Journal of Adolescent Health, 41*, 189–195. doi: 10.1016/j.jadohealth.2007.03.005

*——(2008). 'How risky are social networking sites? A comparison of places online where youth sexual solicitation and harassment occurs'. *Pediatrics, 121*, 350–357. doi: 10.1542/peds.2007-0693

*Ybarra, M.L., Diener-West, M., and Leaf, P.J. (2007). 'Examining the overlap in internet harassment and school bullying: Implications for school intervention'. *Journal of Adolescent Health, 41,* 42–50. doi: 10.1016/j.jadohealth.2007.09.004

*Ybarra, M.L., Espelage, D.L., and Mitchell, K.J. (2007). 'The co-occurrence of internet harassment and unwanted sexual solicitation victimization and perpetration: Associations with psychosocial indicators'. *Journal of Adolescent Health, 41*(6), 31–41. doi: 10.1016/j.jadohealth.2007.09.010

*Ybarra, M.L., Mitchell, K.J., Finkelhor, D., and Wolak, J. (2007). 'Internet prevention messages: Targeting the right online behaviors'. *Archives of Pediatrics and Adolescent Medicine, 161,* 138–145.

*Ybarra, M.L., Mitchell, K.J., Wolak, J., and Finkelhor, D. (2006). 'Examining characteristics and associated distress related to internet harassment: Findings from the second youth internet safety survey'. *Journal of the American Academy of Pediatrics, 118,* 1169–1177. doi: 10.1542/peds.2006-0815

Part 3

Regulation and the media

4   Should cyberbullying be criminalized?

Marilyn Campbell and Ales Završnik

Introduction

Society's attitudes towards all forms of bullying have changed in the last 30 years from considering it to be a normal part of childhood, a rite of passage and character building to regarding bullying as a behaviour to be prevented and condemned (Rigby, 2008; Žižek, 2008). This has been brought about by the research into the consequences of bullying during this time, revealing bullying to be detrimental not only to students who have been victimized but also to students who perpetrate the bullying and the bystanders who witness such behaviour. These consequences include increased levels of depression, anxiety and psychosomatic symptoms (Fekkes, Pijpers, Frediks, Vogels, & Verloove-Vanhorrick, 2006; Kim, Leventhal, Koh, Hubbard, & Boyce, 2006; Reijntjs, Kamphuis, Prinzie, & Telch, 2010) for those students who have been victimized. Different detrimental associations have been found for girls and boys who had been bullied in one longitudinal study (Carbone-Lopez, Esbensen, & Bick 2010); girls who had been indirectly bullied increased their drug use whereas boys did not, and while victimized girls showed lower self-esteem, this did not occur for boys.

Researchers have also found poorer psychosocial relationships for children who engage in bullying perpetration (Sourander *et al.*, 2007). Kaltiala-Heino, Rimpela, Rantanen, and Rimpela (2000) found increased anxiety, depression and psychosomatic symptoms in students who bullied, while psychosomatic problems (Gini & Pozzoli, 2009) increased risk for difficulties at school and behaviour maladjustment (Andreou, Vlachov, & Didaskalour, 2005; Carlson & Cornell, 2008; Hampel, Manal, & Hayer, 2009; Murray-Harvey & Slee, 2010; Wei & Chen, 2011), and substance abuse (Sourander *et al.*, 2007) are all associated with students who bully. These students have a greater risk of criminal conviction and substance abuse in early adulthood (Stassen Berger, 2007). The detrimental associations are not confined to students who actively bully or are victimized as it has been shown that witnesses are also prone to mental health risks when a bystander to bullying (Hutchinson, 2012; Rivers, Poteat, Noret, & Ashurst, 2009).

The particular form of cyberbullying has been shown to be even more harmful to students who have been victimized. This had been hypothesized because of the effect of the medium of technology on bullying, including a wider audience, anonymity of the bully, the more enduring nature of the written word and images, and the ability to reach the target at any time and in any place, including the target's home (Campbell, 2005). Cyberbullying has been found to impact on the bullied student's mental health in the form of depression (Gradinger, Strohmeier, & Spiel, 2009; Raskauskas, 2010). In addition, this predictor was found to be over and above that of being victimized by traditional bullying (Perren, Dooley, Shaw, & Cross, 2010). Moreover, students who have been cyberbullied have also been shown to have significantly lower self-esteem than those who were not cyberbullied (Patchin & Hinduja, 2010). In a large Australian study, cyber victims reported significantly more social difficulties, higher anxiety levels and depression than traditional victims. Importantly, those who were bullied in both ways had similar anxiety and depression scores to cyberbullying victims, suggesting the power of cyber victimization to impact over and above traditional victimization (Campbell, Spears, Slee, Butler, & Kift, 2012).

While the general public has not called for changing laws to prevent and punish students who bully face to face, there have been many calls for the laws to change concerning cyberbullying in youth populations. There could be three reasons for this. The first is that adults in Prensky's words are "digital immigrants" to the cyber world in which we now live, while young people who have been born into the world with this technology are deemed the "digital natives" (Prensky, 2001). Therefore, this creates some panic amongst adults as they do not fully understand this world and have no examples from their own childhood to deal with it. The second reason could be that with increasing media attention, cyberbullying has become synonymous with students committing suicide. The inventing of the word "bullicide", the prominence given to students with mental health problems who are cyberbullied and then commit suicide, alarms adults in our society (Hinduja & Patchin, 2010). Third, after the shootings at several high schools in the late 1990s in the US, and the subsequent reports that the perpetrators of these shootings had felt bullied by their peers (Limber & Small, 2003), calls for legislation were rife and thus it is not surprising that some US states have already enacted legislation to make cyberbullying either a crime or at least a misdemeanour (Snakenborg, Van Acker, & Gable, 2011).

Purposes of the law

In considering the law as a prevention and intervention measure against cyberbullying we must look at the purposes for which the law is used. First, we will discuss the law as punishment and retribution, as a deterrent, as a vehicle for compensation, as a moral standard for society and finally its influence on policy.

The law as punishment and retribution

The most common view in society is that the law exists to punish people; its purpose is to provide a clear rule to punish behaviour that is obviously wrong; there being a clear distinction between right and wrong. This invokes the criminal justice system. In relation to cyberbullying criminal laws could be remedial, retributive or used as a deterrent for young people (Chan, 2009). A difficulty in the criminal laws concerning cyberbullying is that the term bullying is often absent from laws and often cyberbullying is not mentioned in Canadian (Stanton & Beran, 2009), in UK (Marczak & Coyne, 2010) or in Australian laws (Campbell, Butler, & Kift, 2008).

The law as a deterrent

If a behaviour, such as bullying, is criminalized by law, it is with the intention to both prevent and manage incidents. The fear of punishment is deemed to deter individuals from engaging in the behaviour. The difficulty with this purpose of the law for cyberbullying is that if applied to impulsive young people it might not act as a deterrent, first, because the perpetrators do not believe they can be caught as they are able to bully anonymously and they believe adults do not understand technology and second, because they are often unaware of the law (Paul, Smith, & Blumberg, 2012). Third, the criminal laws against underage sexual relations and graffiti have not had the deterrent effect that the public would like. Thus it would seem that young people's behaviour in these circumstances of cyberbullying, sexual relations and graffiti do not have the extensive surveillance needed to enforce the law or severe enough sanctions to deter some young people in engaging in these behaviours (Svensson & Larsson, 2012).

The law as a vehicle for compensation

While criminal law may be seen as retribution by the victim or where a victim suffers an injury as a result of a criminal offence against that person, the victim can seek criminal injuries compensation (Butler, Kift, & Campbell, 2009). However, more likely the civil law is invoked in such cases to pay damages or compensation to a victim.

The law as a social norm

The law in each country formalizes what society believes are its social norms, generally reflecting that society's morals and values (Vago, 2009). However, the law and social norms also impact on each other (Svensson & Larsson, 2012) and the law can also be used to modify behaviour and influence social norms and values in society (Evan, 1965). That is, the law can compel people to change their behaviour by sanctions and punishment and cause people to revise their view of what is right and wrong (Droback, 2006). Sometimes legislation can be enacted for this purpose and may not even be enforced. The law could convey a normative, educative message "symbolically announcing what society deems good and valuable" (Limber & Small, 2003, p. 448) similar to the laws against corporal punishment of children by their parents in Sweden and New Zealand (Campbell *et al.*, 2008). Legislation about cyberbullying could serve to codify that cyberbullying is wrong and unjustified and could influence young peoples' social norms so that cyberbullying would be seen as being unacceptable by their peers. Regardless of how they behave, bystanders are the social consensus: that is, how they choose to act will sustain the social norm (Craig, Pepler, & Atlas, 2000).

The law informing policy

Legislation can require all schools within its jurisdiction to develop and maintain a school policy about a particular behaviour such as cyberbullying amongst its students (Ananiadou & Smith, 2002). Schools in England have been legally required to have an anti-bullying policy (Samara & Smith, 2008) as have many states in America (Surdin, 2009).

In general, invocation of the law in cases of cyberbullying may be seen as an extreme response to a behaviour because the perpetrator could not be ascribed the amount of subjective "guilt" for bullying due to the lack of non-verbal, immediate and visible reaction of the alleged victim (Willard, 2006). The communication limited to written text (sometimes called "cockpit effect", Lievens, 2012) can sometimes allow only legal construction of negligence. But many crimes can only be prosecuted if committed with a perpetrator's "direct intent" or even only with a higher degree of intent (such as *dolus coloratus*), but never with "indirect intent" or any type of negligence. This may in turn have a chilling-effect on free speech (King, 2010; Ruedy, 2008; Schwartz, 2009). However, with the realization through research of the detrimental consequences of cyberbullying for both students who are victimized and those who perpetrate, then the seriousness of the situation could warrant legal remedies. However, which legal remedy and for what purpose should the law be invoked for cyberbullying?

Diversity of the law

Every daily activity in contemporary western society is governed by at least one type of law. Visiting web pages and using email, for instance, are regulated by the contract between a user and the Internet Service Provider (ISP) providing access to the internet. An ISP's "contractual power" over the internet encapsulates the ultimate power in cyberspace, i.e. the power to disconnect a user from the grid in cases agreed upon in the contract. Similarly, the use of social networking sites (SNS) is governed by another type of law. When opening an account, users have to accept the usually very lengthy terms of use and agree, typically, not to "harass or advocate harassment of another person... [and] ...violate or attempt to violate the privacy rights, publicity rights, copyrights, trademark rights, contract rights or any other rights of any person" (Myspace, 2013).

Discussions about legal aspects of cyberbullying are thus inevitably discussions about particular (legal) subjects that are (in legal parlance) "holders of rights and duties" in a particular jurisdictional setting. The law relevant for a cyberbullying case can thus range from contractual law such as social networking sites' terms of use to law governing school curriculum or school library's terms of computer use and even criminal law, which is the most coercive power in a modern democratic state reinforced, if needed, by the police and military. Discussion about legal aspects of cyberbullying can only be exercised within a particular legal discipline (e.g. the law of obligations, criminal law), within a particular jurisdiction (e.g. for a specific country or countries that adopted treaties of particular international organization) and with regard to a particular subject (e.g. child, parent, internet service provider, school, state as a legal person).

The literature has examined rights and duties of different subjects, particularly of schools (Campbell, Cross, Spears, & Slee, 2010), ISPs (Ahlert, Marsden, & Yung, 2004; Durant, 2010; Lievens, Dumortier, & Ryan, 2006) and individual users in general (King, 2010; Ruedy, 2008; Schwartz, 2009). The general approach taken by the legal research has been a focus on a specific country, most intensively on legislation in Australia (Kift, Campbell, & Butler, 2010), Belgium (Lievens, 2012), the US (Hinduja & Patchin, 2010; Ruedy, 2008; Schwartz, 2009), the UK (Marczak, & Coyne, 2010; Paul *et al.*, 2012), and international organizations' treaties (e.g. Lievens, 2012). The focus of this research has been on selected legal disciplines, especially criminal law and civil law (Kift *et al.*, 2010; Lievens, 2012), or constitutional law and hate law (King, 2010).

The most important limitation of the existing research on legal aspects of cyberbullying is that there is an exclusive focus on one, typically the authors' domestic, jurisdiction (e.g. Kift *et al.*, 2010; Lievens, 2012). One of the reasons may be attributed to the fact that Anglo-American countries have been pioneers in legislating cyberbullying. The other is the diversity of legal disciplines and legal systems that are based on varying cultural and legal traditions. The main point here is that every discussion about the legal aspects of cyberbullying has to focus on a particular jurisdiction, a particular legal discipline and analyse the law in terms of particular substantive and procedural provisions contained either in legislation (civil law) and/or judicial decisions (common law) adopted at the national or international level.

In the most general sense, the first significant division that exists between the Anglo-Saxon (common law) legal system and the continental (civil law) legal system is that each developed their own taxonomies of legal disciplines and sub-disciplines. Legal disciplines are themselves composed of different sub-areas of law. For example, compensation for damages is part of the law of obligations in civil law countries while the law of torts is considered a private law and not a criminal law within a wider conception of private law in common law countries. Typically, substantial criminal law provisions are scattered in a plethora of bills and not just one (central) codification in common law countries. For example, cyberbullying could be a criminal offence under a number of laws in the US, including the Computer Fraud and Abuse Act, and Criminal Codes at the federal and state levels. Similarly, criminal offences are scattered in numerous laws in the UK including the Protection from Harassment Act (1997), the Malicious Communications Act (1988), Communications Act (2003), Public Order Act (1986), and the Obscene Publications Act (1959), the Computer Misuse Act (1990) and the Defamation Acts (1952 and 1996). Such "side legislation" is atypical for civil law countries. Similar to criminal law, private law is regularly codified in a single systemic law in civil law countries.

Other differences between common law systems and continental systems include: (1) evolution either through judiciary and cases ("case law") or through large legislative projects ("statute law"); (2) the influence of legislation (parliament or other legislative body) on the one hand and judicial decisions (judiciary) on the legal system as a whole on the other hand; and (3) the focus on procedures in common law countries and legal rights and duties (substantive law) in civil law countries. Not only are there these differences in the two major systems of common law and continental law but cyberbullying can be examined also from the point of view of substantive law or from a procedural law perspective. In criminal law, for instance, substantive aspects encompass definitions of crimes that define the scale of prohibited activities in a given jurisdiction (e.g. what is "harassment" or "identity theft"), general rules on criminal responsibility (e.g. about modalities of intent and insanity defence), taxonomies of criminal sanctions and rules for special groups (e.g. minors). Procedural criminal law on the other hand encompasses rules on evidentiary thresholds or standards of proof, investigating measures, police access to traffic and location data saved at public telecommunications providers, notice and takedown procedure, jurisdiction of courts, hearing procedures, and measures to ensure the presence of the accused, to name a few.

Should cyberbullying be criminalized?

Parents, teachers and the wider community are increasingly inclined to expect that the criminal law will provide an appropriate legal response to cyberbullying in educational settings (Kift et al., 2010). According to professionals providing training for parents, school staff and young people in the field of cyberbullying, the factors promoting the emergence and development of cyberbullying relate to the lack of appropriate laws and reporting mechanisms (Jäger, Amado, Matos, & Pessoa, 2010). These experts claim that there are few mechanisms that allow monitoring and controlling of online activities. In regard to the perception of sources of cyberbullying, experts and trainers claim that more adequate rules, monitoring mechanisms and sanctions are important tools to tackle this problem. The law could be an important remedy as cyberbullying incidents often slip through the cracks: parents claim they do not have the technical skills to keep up with children, teachers are reluctant to intervene as it often takes place beyond schools premises, and law enforcement agencies want to see clear evidence of a crime or significant threat to someone's (regular) physical safety before intervention (Hinduja & Patchin, 2010).

There is clearly a gap between expectations of the general public, parents, teachers, experts, trainers and law enforcement personnel on the one hand and legislative efforts to draw clear rules on boundaries of accepted and unaccepted online behaviour on the other hand. Educational measures and non-disciplinary action may be the most effective way to respond to cyberbullying but may sometimes fail to prevent the incidents as they lack the stronger deterrent effect of cyberbullying law that prohibits and punishes (King, 2010). Laws should therefore support a proactive approach with education, training and counselling for dissuading others who might consider cyberbullying. The primacy of educational measures and non-disciplinary action over (criminal) law is also in line with the very cornerstone ultima ratio principle of criminal law that requires that criminal law is used only as the last resort to address deviant and otherwise harmful behaviour. Or as one commentator said: "The most effective way to deal with cyberbullying is in classrooms, not courtrooms" (King, 2010, p. 848).

The current legal situation and cyberbullying

The US v. Lori Drew case in 2009 showed how the absent definition of cyberbullying can lead to shoe-horning this behaviour into existing laws and the resultant legal decisions. This case involved Missouri teenager Megan Meir who committed suicide after a flirtatious relationship which turned vicious with a fellow teen Josh Evans through the social networking site Myspace. Megan, who suffered from clinical depression, took her own life. Only after her death it was discovered by her parents that Josh Evans never existed. Instead Lori Drew, a mother of Megan's friends, created the profile in order to learn Megan's opinion of her daughter that eventually lead to insults and the final posting by "Josh": "The world would be a better place without you" (Maag, 2009). Drew and her accomplices were initially charged with crimes as diverse as conspiracy, cybercrime and inflicting emotional distress. In the absence of specific provisions for the prosecution about cyberbullying they later focused on violations of Myspace's Terms of Service that prohibit creating accounts with false personal data, and charged Drew with serious violations of the Computer Fraud and Abuse Act. For cybercrime experts, the final judicial decision was more or less expected (Kerr, 2005). District court could not but acquit Drew of crimes associated with computers. The breach of the Myspace Terms of Service could not amount to a crime, or as one commentator said: "What used to be small-stakes contracts become high-stakes criminal prohibitions" (Grossman, 2008, p. 2). The judge granted the defence motion to dismiss, ending the prosecution against Drew and overturning her misdemeanour convictions by saying: "Whatever unauthorized access means, it cannot mean mere violation of Terms of Service". According to Kerr (2005), any other decision "would give the government almost unlimited power to prosecute any Internet user and wouldn't give citizens sufficient notice as to what of their Internet conduct was criminal".

The case of Tyler Clementi caused a similar criminal substantive law conundrum. Clementi was a 20-year-old student at Rutgers University who committed suicide after being spied on by his roommate Dharun Ravi who had installed a webcam in his room in order to watch gay Clementi in intimate moments and tweeted about this to friends by inviting them to join "the show". In the absence of an offence tailored specifically for this type of cyberbullying, Ravi was charged with 36 counts against him (Hu, 2010) and convicted of 15 counts which included, more appropriately, bias intimidation and invasion of privacy (Cheng, 2012).

A precise legal definition of cyberbullying is thus a *sine-qua-non* for preventing unjustified criminal prosecution that can cause additional harm to victims and/or their families and devastate lives and affect acquitted defendants. The prosecution pushed the Drew case through the judicial system too eagerly. Despite the nastiness of Drew's acts, it was pretty clear already in investigation that "whatever Drew intended to do, hacking Myspace was not it" (Grossman, 2008).

Thus the law is struggling to catch up with rapid developments of information technology (IT). It can adapt, either by applying new social situations to existing rules or by creating new rules. Firstly, the legislators should look at possibilities offered by the existing laws and only create new rules if needed, and prevent over-regulation ("juridisation") of everyday life. The other starting point legislators should consider in the process of legislating against cyberbullying is that the law needs to be abstract to some degree. Legal theory offers various interpretation methods to extend the meaning of existing rules to new situations. If there is no other way, new rules should be created in line with the existing legal principles codified in the constitution and international human rights law. Legislation against cyberbullying should be created in a balancing act which would take into account the obligation of states to ensure security of the person from physical and psychological harm on the one hand, and fundamental treaty-based rights such as the right to freedom of expression on the other hand. The principle of legality should be understood as having a double meaning: it is both a tool to fight harmful conduct with criminalization (as a "sword") and a tool for the protection against unjustified prosecutions (as a "shield"). The country can proscribe acts as crimes but this power is not unbounded. It should encompass oversight of the international human rights law as clearly stated by the Chair of the United Nations Committee on Crime Prevention and Control: "Crime is what is defined by law as such. On the other hand, the definition must take into account the existence of, and respect for human rights and not merely be the expression of arbitrary power." (López-Rey, 1978, p. 11 in UNODC 2013).

Legal challenges in drafting criminal cyberbullying legislation

Definitional challenges

Clear definitions of crimes are one of the fundamental cornerstones of modern (post-Enlightenment) criminal law. The *Lex certa* principle of criminal law demands that crimes are expressed in clear and precise language. Imprecise definitions or imperfect language in statutes may render provisions unconstitutional for vagueness or for being over-broad. Legal definitions of cyberbullying are thus of prominent importance in setting clear boundaries between what is legal and illegal. Anti-cyberbullying legislation would not only limit fundamental liberties (e.g. freedom of expression) but would secure (other) rights protected by national constitutions and international human rights law at the same time.

One problem in the definition of cyberbullying relates to the mixture of notions such as cyberstalking, cyberharassment and cyberbullying that are common terms used to describe similar behaviours in the English language. These cyber-victimizations carry slight distinctions, primarily with the ages of the parties and the severity and sophistication of the activity involved. Schwartz (2009) notes that cyberbullying is typically defined in the US legislation only in reference to juveniles or students, but it is unclear exactly which party must be a minor for the situation at issue to constitute cyberbullying, i.e. the culprit and the victim (Ottenweller, 2007), only the victim (Ruedy, 2008) or the culprit regardless of the victim's age (Erb, 2008). Others claim that the terms cyberharassment, cyberstalking, and cyberbullying are used interchangeably and synonymously, although each of the terms is subtly distinct (Jameson, 2008). Some even use a more general notion of "cyber targeting" because it both reflects more accurately what is going on and indicates that it can include many potential legal courses of action (Meyers, 2006).

Additionally, the confusion with definition of cyberbullying increases because the majority of non-English speaking countries do not incriminate either stalking or cyberstalking (e.g. France, Spain, Greece, France, Czech Republic, Slovenia). Legal discussions about stalking are predominantly taking place in English-speaking countries and to a much lesser extent in civil law countries. Finally, a single word for "cyberbullying" exists only in English and some Nordic languages and this makes international comparisons even more confusing. Having said that, linguistic difficulties should not obscure the fact that harms occur and are recognized as legally relevant in all the above-mentioned countries regardless of the different labels used to describe the harmful act. Comparative research on the nature of cyberbullying can still be of high value as usage of notions similar to cyberbullying are stabilizing in other languages. For instance, Nocentini *et al.* (2010) persuasively showed that German adolescents most often use "cyber-mobbing", Italian adolescents "bullismo virtual" and Spanish "acoso". However, as others have pointed out, all these terms accentuate some specific aspects of bullying that vary culturally (Fonzi *et al.*, 1999). In legal discourse, definitional challenges of cyberbullying open the legal landscape of constitutional rights, especially freedom of expression and its legitimate (constitutional) restrictions (King, 2010; Lievens, 2012; Ruedy, 2008; Schwartz, 2009) that will be discussed below.

Challenge of national borders

In the age of the global span of the Internet, one of the most pressing criminal procedural questions is how to obtain digital evidence across national borders. International law enforcement cooperation is increasingly regulated by international organizations as existing criminal procedures were tailored for domestic affairs and the pre-digital environment. For example, who should prosecute a cyberbullying case, if a German perpetrator used an American SNS platform to intimidate an Austrian victim from an internet café computer in Switzerland (Kerr, 2005)? For the European region, the European arrest warrant has been developed as a tool to facilitate prosecution of cross-border crime, new institutional support has been offered for internet-related offences in the form of the CERT-EU and the new European Cybercrime Centre (EC3) has been established at the Europol in January 2013. On the regional level members of the Council of Europe (CoE) established points of contact available 24/7 to facilitate international cooperation in the prosecution of cybercrime.

Challenges of balancing cyberbullying and free speech

Cyberbullying is, in most cases, an action intended to hurt or harass another person over whom they have power, with some sort of speech. In legal terms freedom of "expression" has been understood broadly, in terms of not only speech, but also expressions with drawings, pictures, caricatures and film. Regulation of online speech thus treads on delicate constitutional territory (King, 2010; Lievens, 2012; Ruedy, 2008; Schwartz, 2009). Freedoms of speech, expression and thought are fundamental rights included in the constitutional order of every democratic state either directly and through amendments to the constitution (e.g. First Amendment to the Constitution of the US) or through signed international conventions (e.g. the Universal Convention of Human Rights of 1948 that obliges signatories to enforce these freedoms, Articles 18 and 19).

But there are also limitations of free speech that are either allowed by the international human rights law or by case law of the highest human rights bodies. As freedom of expression is not an absolute right, countries enjoy a broad "margin of appreciation" that allows them leeway in determining the boundaries of acceptable expression in line with their culture and legal traditions. Prohibitions of cyberbullying should be in line with the more general restrictions of freedom of expression allowed for the protection of "public safety and prevention of disorder and crime", "public order", "public health" and "public morals", and also more specific limitation such as "breach of confidentiality", "defamation", "threat to person" or "inducement to crime". The focal question is then how to tailor the definition of cyberbullying so that it would not infringe upon the existing definitions of freedom of expression as codified in the universal human rights treaties and interpretations by the highest national and international judicial bodies. Let us turn to two examples, the US Supreme Court and the European Court of Human Rights (ECtHR).

On a general level the scope of freedom of speech is very different in the US and Europe. While the US Supreme Court has chartered a territory of free speech very broadly and allowed the right to be limited in only exceptional cases, the Constitutional Courts of the EU member states and the ECtHR have allowed much broader limitations of freedom of speech. The ECtHR asserted in *Handyside v. UK* (1976) the magnitude of the freedom of expression in the following way: the freedom is applicable not only to information or ideas that are "favourably received or regarded as inoffensive or as a matter of indifference, but also to those that offend, shock or disturb" (para. 49). Negative comments on someone's Facebook "wall" would thus most probably be considered as a protected speech (Lievens, 2012). Having said that, the freedom of expression is not an absolute right (such as prohibition of torture) and limitations may be imposed, if they are: (1) prescribed by the *law*; (2) introduced with a view to *specified interests* such as the protection of health or morals or the protection of the reputation or the rights of others; and (3) *necessary* in a democratic society (para. 2, Art. 19 of the ECtHR).

The US Supreme Court has been more reluctant in limiting the scope of the freedom of expression. This allows a much narrower "margin of appreciation" for the federal states in designing anti-cyberbullying legislation. The leading cases dealing with criteria for limiting freedom of speech in a cyberbullying case are the US Supreme Court case *Watts v. US* and the case *Brandenburg v. Ohio* (King, 2010; Ruedy, 2008). In *Watts*, the Court recognized that "true threats" should not be afforded the protection of the First Amendment (guaranteeing protection of freedom of expression). But the Court did not offer any criteria applicable for determining when a concrete speech was raised to the level of a "true threat". What cumulates into "true threat" has been interpreted very differently across the US lower (states) courts, using varying criteria including: (1) whether a *reasonable* person; (2) would foresee that the statement would be interpreted *by those to whom the* statement is communicated; (3) as a *serious* expression of intent to *harm or assault*; (4) in the light of *entire factual context*; (5) whether the speaker had the *intent or the ability* to carry out the threat; (6) whether the speaker *intentionally or knowingly* communicated the threat; (7) the *proximity or location* of source of the threat.

So for instance, if we apply the *Watts* test to the Megan Maier case, where the statement caused "emotional distress", it seems that it would be very difficult to claim that the last statement by the offender pushed the victim into committing suicide, i.e. "The world would be a better place without you", would amount to a "true threat". A reasonable person would not very likely foresee that the statement would be perceived as a threat to inflict harm. It is not very likely to pass the "true threat" test (Ruedy, 2008). The *Brandenburg* case deals with "inciting speech" that is not protected by the First Amendment. It requires that three criteria are met for a speech to be qualified as "inciting" and thus unprotected by the First Amendment: "(1) express advocacy of *law violation*; (2) the advocacy must call for *immediate* law violation; and (3) the immediate law violation must be *likely to occur*." (Schwartz, 1994). For instance, in the Megan Maier case there was no speech directed to incite an imminent violation, "only" a statement about her character and "wishes" that she disappears.

The examples from Europe and the US show how limitations of freedom of expression are very country specific. The ECtHR has allowed more limitations of the free speech than the US Supreme Court. Advocacy of violence has to call for immediate action and it must be likely that violence will actually occur. Posting nasty messages about someone's character very likely does not call for *immediate* law violation. Similarly, inciting to violence by posting messages on Facebook against a teacher or schoolmate (e.g. "burn him") may not be very likely to occur and would thus enjoy the protections granted by freedom of expression.

Challenges to upholding the law and cyberbullying

Frequently only very high profile cyberbullying cases such as those ending with a suicide of a cyberbullying victim raise law enforcement "radars". Discrepancies in defining cyberbullying (e.g. in the US) or the complete lack of definitions (e.g. in European countries) often leave law enforcement agencies reluctant to react. They may simply claim that a case may be nasty but not up to the level of crime that would deserve their focus, resources and time.

From this point of view, cyberbullying to a great extent shares the difficulties of cybercrimes. Research on cybercrime and techno-policing has shown that the police still share values originating from the forces' inception in the nineteenth century. The reality of the majority of police work is that it is still very low-tech. The police perceive themselves as an agency that needs to be on the streets more than in the offices in front of computer screens (Manning,

2008). Technology is all too often perceived as unreliable and online messages posted on SNS as not really "real". There are also struggles between different educational professions within the police, forcing cyber units to occupy peripheral roles with police organizations. Sometimes police officers do not show any interest for the technology, but when they do, the technological tools are not compatible and are generating more work than they are trying to solve. Hinduja and Patchin (2013) report that almost one quarter of school resource officers did not know if their federal state (in the US) had a cyberbullying law, although their most visible responsibility involves responding to actions which are in violation of law (e.g. harassment, threats, stalking). Similarly, a survey conducted amongst Slovenian students showed that frequent victims of email or social networking site bullying are much more reluctant to turn to the police than users without cyberbullying experience (Završnik & Sedej, 2012). This might be as a result of disillusionment with the police's response to their personal cyberbullying victimization.

While police are hesitant to intervene unless there is a clear violation of criminal law (Hinduja & Patchin, 2011), they can assist in preventative actions such as in class education for students or user notification detection of cyberbullying (Vandebosch et al., 2012). Even applying the law could be difficult with cyberbullying as perpetrators can disguise themselves with pseudonyms and well-disguised IP addresses. This ability to remain anonymous makes it difficult to apply legal remedies; as Meyers (2006) in explaining *Zeran v. America Online*, where the case resulted in no one legally accountable for injuries caused by anonymous postings on the Internet. Another difficulty is that if reactive laws are promulgated against cyberbullying amongst young people then the courts could be overrun with complaints. In the state of Victoria, Australia, students were barred from taking out a restraining order on another student who was bullying them because of the extreme workload this put on the judicial system. Instead they had to attend mediation (Johnston & Masanauskas, 2010). Shariff and Hoff (2007) also contend that often legislative initiatives are designed to "avoid the floodgates of litigation on cyberbullying" (p. 79).

One difficulty is that of young people's legal literacy. Few young people seem to appreciate their potential for attracting criminal liability, as shown by Grade 8 children in the US who were found guilty of threatening classmates online and sentenced to community service. They maintained that they thought their instant messages were private and fleeting and that no one would find out (Kift et al., 2010). The low levels of legal literacy and the fact that most students who cyberbully believe adults do not supervise cyberspace and therefore do not fear punishment mitigate against laws against cyberbullying being a deterrent to that behaviour (Dempsey, Sulkowskil, Nicols, & Storch, 2009). Even with the present laws such as the Telecommunications Act in Australia, and the Protection of Privacy of Young Persons (Section 111) in Canada, many students do not know which laws apply to their behaviour when they cyberbully (Paul et al., 2012).

Conclusions

There have been calls from the public to amend the laws for cyberbullying because of the detrimental outcomes associated with this behaviour for both the student who is a victim and the student who bullies. The law however has many purposes such as punishment and retribution, a deterrent, a vehicle for compensation, a moral standard for society and an influence on policy. It is an interesting notion that cyberspace does not recognize geographical boundaries yet the law has traditionally been based on these boundaries. Most laws were also tailored before the Internet's widespread use and for the offline environment, with tangible evidence being the centre of regulation of law enforcement agencies' activities. This creates problems in applying the law to cyberbullying as discussed earlier. There is continuing tension between those who advise more regulation and control and those who believe that the Internet should remain censorship free. Many want to live in a "free world" in which not every annoyance is prohibited by criminal law. There is therefore, a reluctance to pass special laws to criminalize cyberbullying. Additionally, there is a debate as to whether we want to criminalize children, or if cyberbullying should be considered a disciplinary matter to be dealt with in schools using non-punitive approaches, to educate our youth. Some researchers argue whether educational measures may be the most effective way to respond to cyberbullying, but they may sometimes fail in preventing incidents as they lack the stronger deterrent effect of cyberbullying laws that prohibit and punish such behaviour (King, 2010). Future research will be needed to investigate whether it is more effective to use non-punitive approaches with children or whether cyberbullying should be criminalized.

References

Ahlert, C., Marsden, C., and Yung, C. (2004). *How 'liberty' disappeared from cyberspace: The mystery shopper tests Internet content self-regulation.* Oxford: Oxford University Press.

Ananiadou, K., and Smith, P.K. (2002). 'Legal requirements and nationally circulated materials against school bullying in European countries'. *Criminal Justice, 2,* 471–449.

Andreou, E., Vlachou, A., and Diaskalou, E. (2005). 'The roles of self-efficacy, peer interactions and attitudes in bully-victim incidents: Implications for intervention policy-practices'. *School Psychology International, 26,* 545–562.

Butler, D., Kift, S., and Campbell, M.A. (2009). 'Cyber bullying in schools and the law: Is there an effective means of addressing the power imbalance?'. *eLaw Journal: Murdoch Electronic Journal of Law, 16,* 84–114.

Campbell, M.A. (2005). 'Cyber bullying: An old problem in a new guise?'. *Australian Journal of Guidance and Counselling, 15,* 68–76.

Campbell, M.A., Butler, D., and Kift, S. (2008). 'A school's duty to provide a safe learning environment: Does this include cyberbullying?' *Australian and New Zealand Journal of Law and Education, 13*(2), 21–32.

Campbell, M.A., Cross, D., Spears, B., and Slee, P. (2010). *Cyberbullying: Legal implications for schools*. East Melbourne, Victoria: The Centre for Strategic Education.

Campbell, M.A., Spears, B., Slee, P., Butler, D., and Kift, S. (2012). 'Victims' perceptions of traditional and cyberbullying, and the psychosocial correlates of their victimisation'. *Emotional and Behavioural Difficulties, 17,* 389–401.

Carbone-Lopez, K., Esbensen, F., and Brick, B. (2010). 'Correlates and consequences of peer victimization: Gender differences in direct and indirect forms of bullying'. *Youth Violence and Juvenile Justice, 8,* 332–350.

Carlson, I., and Cornell, D. (2008). 'Differences between persistent and desistant middle school bullies'. *School Psychology International, 29,* 442–451.

Chan, P.C. (2009). 'Psychosocial implications of homophobic bullying in schools. A review and directions for legal research and the legal process'. *The International Journal of Human Rights, 13,* 143–175.

Cheng, J. (2012, March 13). 'Rutgers "cyberbully" found guilty of privacy invasion, hate crimes'. *ArsTechnica.*

Craig, W.M., Pepler, D., and Atlas, R. (2000). 'Observations of bullying in the playground and in the classroom'. *School Psychology International, 21,* 22–36.

Dempsey, A.G., Sulkowski, M.L., Nichols, R., and Storch, E. (2009). 'Differences between peer victimization in cyber and physical settings and associated adjustment in early adolescence'. *Psychology in the Schools, 46,* 962–972.

Drobak, J.N. (2006). *Norms and the law.* Cambridge: Cambridge University Press.

Durrant, P. (2010). *Cyberbullying: The legal and technical constraints for ISPs.* PowerPoint slides presented at the International COST-workshop on legal issues regarding cyberbullying amongst youngsters, Antwerp.

Erb, T.D. (2008). 'A case for strengthening school district jurisdiction to punish off-campus incidents of cyberbullying'. *Arizona State Law Journal, 49,* 257–259.

Evan, W.M. (1965). 'Law as an instrument of social change'. In A.W. Gouldner and S.M. Miller (eds.), *Applied sociology: Opportunities and problems* (pp. 285–293). New York: Free Press.

Fekkes, M., Pijpers, F., Fredriks, A., Vogels, T., and Verloove-Vanhorick, S. (2006). 'Do bullied children get ill, or do ill children get bullied? A prospective cohort study on the relationship between bullying and health-related symptoms'. *Pediatrics, 117,* 1568–1574.

Fonzi, A., Genta, M.L., Menesini, E., Bacchini, D., Bonino, S., and Constabile, A. (1999). 'Italy'. In P.K. Smith, Y. Morita, J. Junger-Tas, D. Olweus, R. Catalano, and P. Slee (eds.), *The nature of school bullying: A cross-national perspective* (pp. 140–156). London: Routledge.

Gini, G., and Pozzoli, T. (2009). 'Social support, peer victimisation, and somatic complaints: A mediational analysis'. *Journal of Paediatrics and Child Health, 45,* 358–363.

Gradinger, P., Strohmeier, D., and Spiel, C. (2009). 'Traditional bullying and cyberbullying: Identification of risk groups for adjustment problems'. *Journal of Psychology, 217,* 205–213.

Grossman, A.M. (2008). 'The MySpace suicide: A case study in overcriminalization'. *Legal Memorandum, 32,* 1–11.

Hampel, P., Manhal, S., and Hayer, T. (2009). 'Direct and relational bullying among children and adolescents: Coping and psychological adjustment'. *School Psychology International, 30,* 474–490.

Hinduja, S., and Patchin, J.W. (2010). 'Bullying, cyberbullying, and suicidal ideation'. *Archives of Suicide Research, 14,* 206–221.

——(2011). 'Cyberbullying: A review of the legal issues facing educators'. *Preventing School Failure: Alternative Education for Children and Youth, 55*(2), 71–78.

——(2013). 'State cyberbullying laws: Brief review of State cyberbullying laws and policies'. Retrieved February 20, 2013 from http://www.cyberbullying.us/Bullying_and_Cyberbullying_Laws.pdf

Hu, W. (2010). 'Legal debate swirls over charges in a student's suicide'. *The New York Times*, October 1.

Hutchinson, M. (2012). 'Exploring the impact of bullying on young bystanders'. *Educational Psychology in Practice: Theory, Research and Practice in Educational Psychology, 28,* 425–442.

Jäger, T., Amado, J., Matos, A., and Pessoa, T. (2010). 'Analysis of experts' and trainers' views on cyberbullying'. *Australian Journal of Guidance and Counselling, 20,* 169–181.

Jameson, S. (2008) 'Cyberharassment: Striking a balance between free speech and privacy'. *Commlaw Conspectus, 17,* 231–236.

Johnston, M., and Masanauskas, J. (2010, June 9). 'Netbullying sparks boom in court orders against children'. *Sydney Morning Herald*, p. 3.

Kaltiala-Heino, R., Rimpela, M., Rantanen, P., and Rimpela, A. (2000). 'Bullying at school – an indicator of adolescents at risk for mental disorders'. *Journal of Adolescence, 23,* 661–674.

Kerr, O.S. (2005). 'Digital evidence and the new criminal procedure'. *Columbia Law Review, 105,* 279–308.

Kift, S., Campbell, M.A., and Butler, D.A. (2010). 'Cyberbullying in social networking sites and blogs: Legal issues for young people and schools'. *Journal of Law, Information and Science, 20*(2), 60–97.

Kim, Y.S., Leventhal, B., Koh, Y., Hubbard, A., and Boyce, A. (2006). 'School bullying and youth violence: Causes or consequences of psychopathology?' *Archives of General Psychiatry, 63,* 1035–1041.

King, A.V. (2010). 'Constitutionality of cyberbullying laws: Keeping the online playground safe for both teens and free speech'. *Vanderbilt Law Review, 63,* 845–884.

Lievens, E. (2012). *Bullying and sexting in social networks from a legal perspective: Between enforcement and empowerment,* ICRI Working Paper 7/2012, Interdisciplinary Centre for Law and ICT, K.U. Leuven.

Lievens, E., Dumortier, J., and Ryan, P.S. (2006). 'The co-protection of minors in new media: A European approach to co-regulation'. *UC Davis Journal of Juvenile Law and Policy, 10*(1), 97–151.

Limber, S., and Small, M. (2003). 'State laws and policies to address bullying in schools'. *School Psychology Review, 32,* 445–455.

Maag, C. (2007). 'A hoax turned fatal draws anger but no charges'. *New York Times, 28,* p. 23.

Manning, P.K. (2008). 'A view of surveillance'. In S. Leman-Langlois (ed.), *Technocrime, technology, crime and social control* (pp. 209–242). Cullompton: Willan Publishing.

Marczak, M., and Coyne, I. (2010). 'Cyberbullying at school: Good practice and legal aspects in the United Kingdom'. *Australian Journal of Guidance and Counselling, 20,* 182–193.

Murray-Harvey, R., and Slee, P. (2010). 'School and home relationships and their impact on school bullying'. *School Psychology International, 31,* 271–295.

Myers, D.A. (2006). 'Defamation and the quiescent anarchy of the internet: A case study of cyber targeting'. *Pennsylvania Law Review, 110,* 667–668.

Nocentini, A., Calmaestra, J., Schultze-Krumbholz, A., Scheithauer, H., Ortega, R., and Menesini, E. (2010). 'Cyberbullying: Labels, behaviours and definition in three European countries'. *Australian Journal of Guidance and Counselling, 20,* 129–142.

Ottenweller, C.J. (2007). 'Cyberbullying: The interactive playground cries for a clarification of the Communications Decency Act'. *Valparaiso University Law Review, 41,* 1285–1334.

Patchin, J.W., and Hinduja, S. (2010). 'Cyberbullying and self-esteem'. *Journal of School Health, 80,* 614–621.

Paul, S., Smith, P.K., and Blumberg, H.H. (2012). 'Investigating legal aspects of cyberbullying'. *Psicothema, 24,* 640–645.

Perren, S., Dooley, J., Shaw, T., and Cross, D. (2010). 'Bullying in school and cyberspace: Associations with depressive symptoms in Swiss and Australian adolescents'. *Child and Adolescent Psychiatry and Mental Health, 4,* 1–10.

Prensky, M. (2001). 'Digital natives, digital immigrants'. *On the Horizon, 9*(5), 1–6.

Raskauskas, J. (2010). 'Text-bullying: Associations with traditional bullying and depression among New Zealand adolescents'. *Journal of School Violence, 9,* 74–97.

Reijntjes, A., Kamphuis, J., Prinzie, P., and Telch, M. (2010). 'Peer victimization and internalizing problems in children: A meta-analysis of longitudinal studies'. *Child Abuse and Neglect, 34,* 244–252.

Rigby, K. (2008). *Children and bullying: How parents and educators can reduce bullying at school.* Oxford: Blackwell.

Rivers, I., Poteat, V.P., Noret, N., and Ashurst, N. (2009). 'Observing bullying at school: The mental health implications of witness status'. *School Psychology Quarterly, 24,* 211–223.

Ruedy, M.C. (2008). 'Repercussions of a MySpace teen suicide: Should anti-bullying laws be created?' *North Carolina Journal of Law and Technology, 9,* 323–346.

Samara, M., and Smith, P.K. (2008). 'How schools tackle bullying, and the use of whole school policies: Changes over the last decade'. *Educational Psychology, 28,* 663–676.

Schwartz, B. (1994). 'Holmes versus Hand: Clear and present danger or advocacy of unlawful action?' *The Supreme Court Review,* 209–240.

Shariff, S., and Hoff, D. (2007). 'Cyberbullying: Clarifying legal boundaries for school supervision in cyberspace'. *International Journal of Cyber Criminology, 1,* 76–118.

Snakenborg, J., Van Acker, R., and Gable, R.A. (2011). 'Cyberbullying: Prevention and intervention to protect our children and youth'. *Preventing School Failure: Alternative Education for Children and Youth, 55*(2), 88–95.

Sourander, A., Jensen, P., Ronning, J., Niemala, S., Helenius, H., and Almqvist, F. (2007). 'What is the early adulthood outcome of boys who bully or who are bullied in childhood? The Finnish "From a Boy to a Man" study'. *Pediatrics, 120,* 397–404.

Stanton, L., and Beran, T. (2009). 'A review of legislation and bylaws relevant to cyberbullying'. *McGill Journal of Education, 44,* 245–260.

Stassen Berger, K. (2007). 'Update on bullying at school: Science forgotten?' *Developmental Review, 27,* 90–126.

Surdin, A. (2009, January 1). 'In several states, a push to stem cyber-bullying: Most of the laws focus on schools'. *The Washington Post.*

Svensson, M., and Larsson, S. (2012). 'Intellectual property law compliance in Europe: Illegal file sharing and the role of social norms'. *New Media and Society, 14,* 1147–1163.

United Nations Office on Drugs and Crime (2013). *Comprehensive study on cybercrime. Draft – February 2013.* Vienna: UNODC.

Vago, S. (2009). *Law and society.* Upper Saddle River, NJ: Pearson Prentice-Hall.

Wei, H., and Chen, J. (2011). 'The moderating effect of Machiavellianism on the relationships between bullying, peer acceptance, and school adjustment in adolescents'. *School Psychology International, 33,* 345–363.

Willard, N.E. (2006). *Cyberbullying and cyberthreats: responding to the challenge of online social cruelty, threats, and distress.* Champaign, Illinois: Center for Safe and Responsible Internet Use.

Završnik, A., and Sedej, A. (2012). 'Spletno in mobilno nadlegovanje v Sloveniji [Internet and mobile phone bullying in Slovenia]'. *Revija za kriminalistiko in kriminologijo* [The Journal of Criminalistics and Criminology], *63,* 263–280.

Žižek, S. (2008). *Violence: Six sideways reflections.* London: Profile books.

5   The role of the industry in reducing cyberbullying

Iain Coyne and Vasiliki Gountsidou

Introduction

Any discussion and debate on cyberbullying has to consider the voice of the industry and what its responsibilities are in reducing cyberbullying. However, we must first preface the chapter by acknowledging that it is simplistic to bracket all organisations under one heading, "the industry". We will do so here, for ease, but "the industry" comprises a variety of different organisations including Internet Service Providers (ISPs), mobile phone companies (MPCs), social networking sites (SNS), music/video file sharing sites, online virtual worlds, online gaming sites, developers of computer games/computer hardware and software, providers of chat and instant messaging facilities etc. Although in some cases, the same organisation provides a number of these services, each will differ in what actions they may be able or even are legally allowed to undertake to reduce cyberbullying. Therefore, while generic "best practice" may well cover a large proportion of these various services, there is likely a need to have some specific guidance and action tailored to the service being offered.

Specifically, the chapter will consider three questions: What can industry do to prevent and reduce cyberbullying? What do technology organisations actually do to reduce cyberbullying? How effective are their actions? The chapter will guide the reader through examples of actions organisations undertake to control and reduce cyberbullying and consider whether what is currently offered is actually effective. The chapter will debate the notion of industry self-regulation and will outline the UK Centre for Child Internet Safety's (UKCCIS) approach, the European Framework for Safer Mobile Use by Younger Teenagers and the EU Safer Social Networking Principles as a guide to evaluating the effectiveness of industry action.

What can industry do to prevent and reduce cyberbullying?

It could be argued that the answer to this question is simple: industry can eliminate cyberbullying and provide a fully safe online experience for children and adults. However, this is very much a naïve request to make, especially as real life cannot ever be said to be truly safe. Byron (2008) posits that no silver bullet exists to make the internet completely safe and policies that advocate this are not only impractical, but are potentially dangerous as they may lull children and parents into a false sense of security. This does not mean that we should subscribe to the view that the internet is a dangerous place that children should avoid. The benefits afforded by technology are wide ranging (see Chapter 10 this volume) and access to the internet from an early age has become part and parcel of the development of our "digitally native" children.

Banning access to technology for children is not only impractical but potentially damaging to the educational and social development of children. We are therefore looking for a medium between these two impractical extremities – one where risks are minimized and where users have the confidence and technical know-how to control their own experience of technology and reduce incidents of cyberbullying.

When debating the requirements of industry in reducing cyberbullying, we are often faced with media hype (see Chapter 6 this volume) of extreme cases and the subsequent backlash against the particular ISP, MPC or SNS on which the incident occurred. Often following such cases there is a strong movement towards wanting the introduction of legislation to stop cases ever happening again. The legal framework within cyberbullying has been discussed in more detail in Chapter 4 of this volume. However, specifically in relation to SNSs, Lievens (2011) critiques the adoption of a traditional legislative framework due to: it being territory-specific where SNSs are global in nature; it being slow and unable to keep pace with changes in technology; and a lack of expertise in addressing issues. Similarly, Durrant (2010) argues that while there is an EU E-Commerce Directive (The European Parliament and the Council of the European Union, 2000) which requires an ISP to remove illegal content once notified, cyberbullying in many cases may not be illegal and hence not subject to this directive.

Further, both authors illustrate the paradox of the law in noting that ISPs, SNS etc., are restricted in what they can do by telecommunication, privacy and data protection laws as well as the right to freedom of speech, privacy and competition rules. This means that an ISP cannot engage in any unauthorized monitoring or interception and cannot provide private data held about an individual (e.g. ISP address) to a third party – unless the offence is illegal or the request has been made by a court order/police warrant. As Durrant (2010) details, the primary legal imperative for an ISP is customer data protection and privacy and text and images which may be deemed to be bullying cannot be removed unless the ISPs terms and conditions have been breached. While an initial reaction of the need to legislate may be an understandable one, the actual ability of the law to offer an effective solution is limited and alternative solutions need to be found. Lievens (2011) promotes the adoption of an Alternative Regulatory Instrument (ARI) in terms of industry self-regulation or a combination of state and industry co-regulation. We will return to this notion later in the chapter.

Additional to the legal restrictions, another problem for the industry is that the different classes of service providers create a complex chain that makes tracing and obtaining data difficult (Durrant, 2010). For example, an SNS could be in a different legal jurisdiction to the user, an SNS may not be certain who the ISP is for a particular user as this data is not visible on the SNS site, and the perpetrator of cyberbullying may not be a customer on the same ISP as the victim or even may access the internet via a cybercafé. Legally, an ISP may not be able to engage in some forms of actions and practically, it is not always possible to trace the perpetrator and ban them from a site. Yet, even though there are legal and practical difficulties for the industry in trying to reduce cyberbullying, they are still required to engage in actions which manage the cyberbullying risk.

One way to consider the question of what industry could do is to look at research on user perspectives in terms of what they do to combat online abuse and what they would like industry to do. In a series of eight focus groups with 36 New Zealand children (aged 13–15 years), Fenaughty and Harré (2013) found three themes which captured participants' perspectives on responding to cyberbullying. The "social support theme" indicated most would not communicate with parents, but would prefer to use peer support, as this group were not "out of touch" and less likely to overreact. The "resolve problems directly theme" clearly indicated participants would engage with technical solutions in terms of blocking, changing privacy controls etc. Finally, an "ignoring theme" perhaps captured a less productive form of responding. Therefore, implications for the industry include the setting up or supporting of peer-support networks (for example, the CyberMentors project from BeatBullying, beatbullying.org) and the development of and education in technical solutions to control abusive behaviour.

Interestingly, a subsequent survey of 1,673 New Zealand school children by the same authors, illustrated only 7.9 per cent used a technical solution to combat mobile phone bullying and 27.5 per cent used technology to reduce internet bullying. Despite the fact that specific actions included reporting the behaviour to the MPC or ISP and blocking and banning the perpetrator, technical solutions did not actually predict subsequent resolution of the bullying. It is not clear here if the reason for the lack of resolution was a result of technical solutions being ineffective or incorrect use of the solutions by the user. This research suggests that the industry not only should consider technical solutions, but also monitor their effectiveness in resolving cyberbullying complaints.

The UK's Department for Education (2012) canvassed opinions (on internet safety more broadly and not solely cyberbullying) of over 3,500 individuals from various backgrounds (of which 22 per cent nominated themselves as parents) on the use of filtering/blocking parental controls as technical solutions for internet safety. Only 35 per cent of the sample actually wanted default blocking, 30 per cent disagreed with what was perceived as an "enforced approach" and 40 per cent felt it should be removed. In fact, 71 per cent of the sample felt that parents have the main responsibility for keeping children safe online (for the parent sub-sample alone, 61 per cent felt it was their responsibility for keeping children safe online). Despite the fact that 47 per cent of the parent sub-sample stated bullying worries their children, only 23 per cent actually wanted help in protecting children from this. Nonetheless, 28 per cent of the total sample and 37 per cent of the parent sub-sample viewed the responsibility for keeping children safe online as a shared one between parents and the industry.

The notion of a shared community response also emerged from analysis of four online synchronous focus groups examining cyberbullying (specifically "griefing") in Second Life (Chesney, Coyne, Logan, & Madden, 2009). When asked to discuss how griefing should be controlled in Second Life, Second Life residents advocated a shared approach between the developer of the virtual world, the individual residents and the Second Life resident community. A follow-up survey of 86 residents also supported the notion of a shared community response, although specific actions emerged within each group (Coyne, Chesney, Logan, & Madden, 2009). Participants suggested individuals could report behaviour (19 per cent), attend in-world training on how to combat griefing (19 per cent) and use technical features to stop griefing (12 per cent). A community response included banning avatars and sharing the details across the community (22 per cent), reporting abuse (18 per cent) and community-based neighbourhood watches (17 per cent). Banning avatars (22 per cent) and providing technical features (27 per cent) featured highly on the responsibilities of the developer, but other actions included ensuring there are consequences to griefing (6 per cent), educating residents (7 per cent) and monitoring abuse (4 per cent).

The latter two studies point to the industry playing a shared role in making the internet a safer place for children and, hopefully, as a result reducing the levels of cyberbullying. The Byron review (Byron, 2008) in the UK strongly advocates this perspective stating:

> In relation to the internet we need a shared culture of responsibility with families, industry, government and others in the public and third sectors all playing their part to reduce the availability of potential harmful material, restrict access to it by children and to increase children's resilience.
>
> (Byron, 2008, p. 2)

In relation to this, Byron argues for a national self-regulatory strategy in which parents and the industry have more or less of a role to play. Reducing access is largely the responsibility of industry, increasing resilience is mostly actioned by the family and restricting access requires industry and family action in equal measure. Industry is not expected to work in isolation or come up with all the answers, even though it may take the lead on some actions. The previous research and the Byron review all point to a joint problem-solving approach with representatives from all relevant stakeholders having a voice in developing a national-level code of practice.

This initiative will be discussed in more detail later when we debate how effective the industry is in relation to cyberbullying. However, one question still remains: Why should the industry sign up to such a code of practice? The answer lies in framing the code within the concept of Corporate Social Responsibility (CSR). Brown and Dacin (1997) state: "Corporate social responsibility associations reflect the organisation's status and activities with respect to its perceived societal obligations" (p. 68). Porter and Kramer (2006) suggest four reasons for CSR:

- Moral – industry has a duty to be good citizens.
- Licence to operate – in order to operate an organisation needs approval from relevant stakeholders (e.g. clients, customers, investors etc.).
- Reputation – ensuring a positive image and enhancing the organisation's brand.
- Sustainability – stewardship of the environment and the community.

Therefore, using a CSR framework, a national self-regulatory voluntary code would provide an organisation with a benchmark of what it means to be a responsible member of the industry and potentially enhance their reputation (Byron, 2008). Such a code would place expectations on industry of how society expects it to behave in terms of reducing cyberbullying (a moral duty) as well as enhancing the image of the ISP, MPC, SNS etc. This brand enhancement not only attracts new users to the organisation, but it also would appeal to advertisers who want to ensure that their brand is associated with a responsible organisation. Clearly, in addition to the moral imperative to act, there is a commercial/business case for organisations to engage with stakeholders in reducing cyberbullying. To some extent this is already happening with Durrant (2010) acknowledging that ISPs within EUROISPA want to ensure CSR in relation to cyberbullying and to do the right thing. Also, in a survey of the UK's ten leading ISPs, Jones, Comfort and Hiller (2012) reported that seven ISPs had posted CSR reports/policies on their websites with the majority of these having a focus on safe and responsible use. They forecast that as stakeholders become more interested in CSR (perhaps through the introduction of a national self-regulatory framework), ISPs will need to publicly report their CSR agendas – although they do caution that currently these agendas tend to be based on a commercial imperative.

So far we have discussed the problems of legislation, the complexity of the technology industry and individual perspectives of what industry could do to reduce cyberbullying. We have introduced the notion of self- or co-regulation and suggested if framed within CSR, there may be an incentive for industry to conform. In the next section we will outline some of the actions being taken by different organisations to address cyberbullying. However, perhaps a fitting way to end this section is to provide a quote from a child from the Byron review: "Kids don't need protection, we need guidance. If you protect us you are making us weaker, we don't go through all the trial and error necessary to learn what we need to survive on our own ... don't fight our battles for us, just give us assistance when we need it." (p. 13).

What is the industry doing?

This section outlines the main features adopted by the industry for safer technology use and provides some specific examples of how organisations deal with cyberbullying. We have restricted the analysis to eight operators (ISPs and SNSs) and three mobile phone companies. This is not a comprehensive or systematic review, but it allows us to provide a flavour of what is going on in the industry at the present time.

Industry action (see Table 5.1) appears to focus on education and empowerment for parents/educators and the user (child). Features attempt to teach the various stakeholders about safe technology use by providing the technical features which allow the user and parents to have some control over their mobile phone and internet use. It suggests that the industry is adopting a joint problem-solving approach as advocated in the Byron review, which includes a reactive (e.g. to reports of abuse) and pro-active (e.g. filtering) approach to managing risks online. Industry provides the tools and information and the expectation is for parents/educators/users to make informed decisions on whether and when they wish to use them.

Table 5.1 Outline of industry solutions for safer technology use

Empowering Parents/Educators	*Empowering the User*
Providing advice + videos + guides + technology which support parents:	Providing advice + videos + guides + technology which supports the user:
• Discuss with children about safe internet use • Develop clear rules on usage • Web/video/SNS/image/keyword filtering • Ability to block or monitor sites • Ability to screen material • Provision of activity reports to monitor use • Ability to change mobile number • Disable features on a phone • Instant alerts when sites are viewed	• Guidance on safe internet use • How to block content • How to control privacy settings • How to report abuse • How to remove content • Social reporting • What to do if you are cyberbullied

Specific examples related to cyberbullying

Vodafone have a dedicated section of their website offering information and advice to parents on cyberbullying (http://www.vodafone.com/content/index/parents/get_involved/cyberbullying.html). Across four sections information is provided on what cyberbullying is, what actions parents can take if their child is a victim or perpetrator of cyberbullying, links to other sites providing information and support as well as a video clip from Teachtoday (www.teachtoday.eu) illustrating examples of cyberbullying. Examples of actions parents can take include:

- Reassuring their child that they have done the right thing by telling they are being bullied.
- Sitting down with their child to compose a written record of the cyberbullying and to gather evidence.
- Making the most of built-in tools on their child's internet or mobile phone services to prevent further cyberbullying.
- Contacting their child's internet, mobile phone or social networking provider – especially if the behaviour contravenes their "Terms of Use".

Additionally, if the parent thinks their child may be bullying others, advice includes:

- Talking to them about cyberbullying and explaining why it's unacceptable and has to stop.
- Talking to their teacher about what's been going on and let them know that you're willing to work with the school to ensure it doesn't happen again.

Virginmedia have a section of their Yourspace community forum focused on cyberbullying (http://www.virginmedia.com/yourspace/guidesandrules/dealing-with-online-bullying.php). Information on what cyberbullying is, along with definitions of terms such as "trolls" and "flaming" is provided, as well as behaviours to watch out for in relation to cyberbullies. A series of "golden rules" are then presented centred on ignoring (ignoring posts from a user), reporting (via the report violation link or email) and informing (telling others in the community). There is also a link to other ways to report abuse which sends the user to another site detailing Virginmedia's approach to internet security. Here, further advice, links and videos are provided.

Subsumed within its online Safety Centre, Facebook has developed a site detailing how to prevent bullying (http://www.facebook.com/safety/bullying). Two videos clips are presented – one showing a cyberbullying incident and how the community responded to support the victim and the other explaining how Facebook has developed reporting tools to resolve conflicts between individuals. A link is provided for users detailing how a user can check the status of something which they reported and links to organisations dedicated to child safety online are also presented. Further, the Facebook user can sign up to an online pledge to stop bullying (as of March 2013, 140,000 users have signed up with over 1.4 million likes). It should be noted that the Safety Centre site (http://www.facebook.com/safety/) offers a lot more information, support and guidance for parents, teachers, teens and law enforcement agencies about wider safety on Facebook.

Therefore, evidence suggests that the industry is providing solutions to promote safer technology use and to help prevent cyberbullying. What we have not yet resolved is how effective all these features are in reducing cyberbullying.

How effective are the industry's actions?

Earlier we introduced the notion of self/co-regulation as an approach to engage industry in playing a role in reducing cyberbullying. In this section we discuss three initiatives, aimed at internet safety more widely (but that include features relevant for reducing cyberbullying) and consider their effectiveness so far. The overarching tenets of all three initiatives are: (1) Self-regulation (or co-regulation) in relation to set codes/principles, developed in conjunction with industry and which would thus obtain industry buy-in; (2) Multi-stakeholder engagement between industry, parents, children and other relevant parties; (3) A proactive approach to assessing the risks to children using the particular technology with the implementation of actions to minimise the risks. As expressed earlier, conforming to such a code would potentially fulfil part of an organisation's CSR agenda and hence provide an incentive for an organisation to engage in reducing cyberbullying – even if the driver is more business rather than morally focused.

The Byron Review (2008)

In an independent review covering the use of technology widely (cyberbullying is only briefly mentioned) sponsored by the UK government, Tanya Byron considered the risks of exposure to potentially harmful or inappropriate material on the internet and in video games. In her review (Byron, 2008), that argued a national strategy was needed involving better self-regulation which focused on: reducing the availability and prevalence of harmful content; restricting access to such content and empowering parents and children to deal with such content; and increasing resilience to such content.

The review recommended the development of a UK council for child internet safety facilitated by representatives from industry, the third sector, children services, parents, young people and the UK government (chaired by relevant government ministers). Working with industry, this council should draw up a voluntary code of practice, reflecting both minimum standards to which all organisations must comply and safety principles which indicate actions beyond minimum standards. Industry should subscribe to the code(s) and there should be a developed independent monitoring system based on self-assessment and independent review. This assessment should not only promote positive actions by organisations in relation to how they are doing in respect of the code, but also result in public censure when the code is breeched (Byron, 2008).

The Department for Children, Schools and Families (DCSF), Department for Culture, Media and Sport (DCMS) and the Home Office (2008) produced an action plan to implement the recommendation from the Byron Review and in September 2008 the UK Council for Child Internet Safety (UKCCIS) was launched (http://www.education.gov.uk/ukccis). The council includes over 180 organisations and individuals representing various stakeholders, with some of the main technology-based organisations and ISPs involved in working with the council. UKCCIS promotes some progress to date including:

- The development, and large scale media coverage of their "Zip it", "Block it", "Flag it" digital code.
- The four main UK ISPs signing up to a code of practice which gives customers the choice whether or not to apply parental controls.
- Working with hardware and laptop manufacturers to include active choice at first switch on.
- Working with MPCs and public Wi-Fi providers to block access to adult material in public places.
- High street retailers introducing in-store promotion of safety messages and on-screen demonstrations.

On the face of it, the approach adopted within the UK in creating the UKCCIS, which is supported by relevant government departments, suggests industry is motivated to manage the problem of internet safety (and potentially cyberbullying), and the UKCCIS has certainly made some steps forward in achieving some of its aims. However, a review of progress since the 2008 Byron review implied that while the creation of the UKCCIS and the agreement by industry to be reviewed against a code of practice were positive outcomes, the industry has been slower than anticipated to act (Byron, 2010). Specifically, at the time of the update review no codes of practice had been developed, no process for independent review has been identified and there was no progress on industry signing up to a public commitment on how quickly inappropriate content is removed once flagged.

Following the Byron update review, a project group within UKCCIS focused on the self-regulation of industry developed industry guidance on chat/instant messaging (2010a), search (2010b), social networking (2010c) and moderation (2010d). Within each of these documents, a series of good practice actions are articulated with a recommendation that industry adopt the principles. Actions across the codes include providing information on how to keep safe online; educating users in privacy settings and encouraging them to use them; including and highlighting tools to reduce or report inappropriate behaviour; and appropriate selection and training of human moderators. Although it could be argued that guides developed for internet safety more generally should provide some security against cyberbullying, only the social networking guidance specifically addresses cyberbullying. Guidance includes:

- Providing prominent messages to users on the importance of behaving responsibly online, the right of providers to remove inappropriate content, the role of users in contributing to a respectful community.
- Informing users on how to block individuals, use ignore functions and remove unwanted content from personal pages.
- Ensure community guidelines are clearly displayed.
- Make users aware that online content is not anonymous and that reports of cyberbullying will be taken seriously with appropriate actions enforced.
- Ensure robust, effective, simple and timely reporting of abuse process.

Certainly, the development of codes of practice is a step in the right direction, especially as industry itself was heavily involved in their creation. However, at the time of writing there is still no robust, independent monitoring process in place which assesses an organisation's performance in relation to the code(s). This is really important as in the current climate various high-profile cases where self-regulation has appeared to have failed (e.g. the global banking crisis and the phone hacking scandal and review of media self-regulation in the UK) have left the wider public with a "...current general 'malaise' with respect to self-regulation or regulation by the market or the sector" (Lievens, 2011, p. 49). Real actions need to be undertaken, coupled with some way of being able to judge the extent of an organisation's engagement with these actions.

European Framework for Safer Mobile Use by Younger Teenagers (2007)

Explicitly targeted at the use of mobile devices and operating at European level, the European Framework for Safer Mobile Use by Younger Teenagers and Children (cited in GMSA Europe, 2009) was proposed by leading mobile operators and content providers. This framework provided a foundation for the creation and/or revision of national-level self-regulatory codes pertaining to mobile device safety. Similar to the previous initiative, cyberbullying is not detailed directly, although the four broad areas covered by the code could have implications for reducing cyberbullying. These areas are:

- Access control mechanisms – the need to provide appropriate means to control access to material unsuitable for children.

- Raising awareness and education – providing safety information to parents and children to develop safer use of mobile devices.
- Classification of commercial content via national standards.
- Working with law enforcement agencies in dealing with illegal content.

Implementation review reports by GSME (2008, 2010) and PriceWaterhouseCoopers (2009) based on documentary evidence and in the case of the 2009 review, analysis of questionnaires and interviews, indicate support from mobile operators for the framework. In 2008, there were 24 industry signatories to the code, with self-regulatory codes covering 21 EU member states. In 2009 this increased to 81 mobile operators operating across 26 EU member states and in 2010, 83 companies signed up to the code covering 25 EU member states. Overall, this represents 96 per cent of all mobile subscribers in the EU benefitting from the framework (GSME, 2010). Further, reviews illustrate a high level of compliance with the requirements of the framework in national level codes of practice (in 2009 this was 90 per cent) and support for the industry's engagement in the initiative from other relevant stakeholders. Although, while stakeholders appreciated and acknowledge the work of mobile operators, there was a sense that they can do more in relation to the rapid development of new mobile technologies.

Different to the UKCCIS initiative, this approach is focused at the European level and additionally, there have been attempts to monitor compliance with the framework. Monitoring suggests that European mobile providers are actually doing a good job in terms of ensuring safer mobile use by young people. However, we do not know specifically how effective this framework is in actually ensuring safer mobile use and what impact these requirements will have on cyberbullying rates. Although the reviews provide some useful and positive data, they lack a robust testing of the framework carried out by independent users of such devices. They tend to rely on documentation provided by the organisation on how they conform to the code. No information is provided on how consistently these requirements are actually implemented in practice.

The Safer Social Networking Principles for the EU (2009)

Again developed at a European level with multi-stakeholder and cross-industry collaboration, the European Commission developed seven principles aimed at social networking providers. They represent: "...principles by which SNS providers should be guided as they seek to help minimise potential harm to children and young people and recommends a range of good practice approaches which can help achieve those principles" (p. 1). Table 5.2 outlines each of the seven principles.

Although aimed at broader internet safety, principles 1, 3, 4 and 6 have direct relevance to cyberbullying. Akin to the other initiatives, these principles promote a joint problem-solving approach between industry and

Table 5.2 The seven Safer Social Networking Principles for the EU (2009)

Principle	Main features
1. Raise awareness of safety education messages and acceptable use policies to users, parents, teachers and carers in a prominent, clear and age-appropriate manner.	Provision of information on acceptable/inappropriate behaviour and guidance/education materials to children/parents/teachers on how to use the SNS site safely.
2. Work towards ensuring that services are age-appropriate for the intended audience.	Limiting exposure to age-inappropriate content and promoting parental controls to reduce access to age-inappropriate content.
3. Empower users through tools and technology.	Providing solutions to allow children to manage their own network especially in relation to inappropriate behaviour (e.g. privacy settings, reporting functions, pre-moderation of content).
4. Provide easy-to-use mechanisms to report conduct or content that violates the Terms of Service.	Developing a system for reporting abuse and for responding appropriately and in a timely manner.
5. Respond to notifications of illegal content or conduct.	Developing a process for reviewing and removing offending illegal content and how information can be shared with law enforcement agencies.
6. Enable and encourage users to employ a safe approach to personal information and privacy.	Providing a range of privacy settings to allow the user to make an informed choice on which settings they want.
7. Assess the means for reviewing illegal or prohibited content/conduct.	Assess services used to identify potential risks, determine appropriate procedures for reviewing reports of illegal content.

users, parents and school staff. They recommend that industry provide technical features and educational instructions to allow safer social networking, but coupled with this, they also endorse the view that these solutions are there to help to empower users or parents to take control of their or their children's social networking activities.

At the time of their launch, 21 social networking companies signed up to the principles, suggesting support and endorsement by the industry. Additionally, built into the principles was a commitment by signatories to provide the European Commission with self-declarations of commitment to the principles, to make available non-confidential information for publication in relation to consideration of the principles, to review and revise the document with relevant stakeholders after 18 months, and to encourage other social networking organisations to add their support for the principles. This initiative supports the implementation of a number of robust and independent programmes of evaluation to assess concordance of the signatories to the principles. Further, company-specific and overall reports on progress are available which allow relevant stakeholders to assess the effectiveness of the industry at large as well as specific organisations in implementing the principles.

Donoso (2011a) reports on an analysis of 14 social networks in terms of how they correspond to the seven principles. The methodology adopted a combination of independent assessment of organisations' self-declarations and user website testing (akin to a mystery shopper approach). In the latter approach, national researchers followed a standard testing scenario and set up a profile in a SNS. Ratings of self-declarations illustrated three judged to be very satisfactory, nine satisfactory and two unsatisfactory. Only one organisation was rated as very satisfactory in all seven principles. The most favourable ratings were obtained for principles 5 and 7 (both focused on illegal content) and the least positive ratings emerged for principle 6. In terms of ratings of implementation of principles on respective websites, four were judged very satisfactory, six rather satisfactory and four unsatisfactory – none were judged as very satisfactory in all seven principles. Principles 1 and 4 were rated the most positive, with principle 3 the least well evaluated (six sites judged to be unsatisfactory). Principles 5 and 7 were not tested via website evaluation.

In relation to cyberbullying, all websites provided safety information on inappropriate behaviour (including bullying) which was easy to understand (principle 1) and all provided some mechanism for reporting inappropriate content or contact on their website (principle 4). However, a bullying scenario test of principle 4 demonstrated that seven sites acknowledged the abuse report within 24 hours, but in six there was no reply within the testing period. In six cases the abusive material was removed, but in only four was some action taken towards the perpetrator.

A further survey using the same methodology on nine additional platforms, such as video-sharing, virtual world and gaming platforms, was conducted (Donoso, 2011b). Analysis of self-declarations resulted in only two SNS being judged as very satisfactory in all seven principles with all rated as very satisfactory in four or more of the principles. Website evaluations were less positive as none of the sites were rated as very satisfactory in all seven principles, though seven were very satisfactory in four or more principles. Focusing on cyberbullying once again, eight of the sites provided specific information on bullying and all provide terms of use (principle 1). In all services an individual could block users, reject friends and in eight the user could delete unwanted content (principle 3). All provided a mechanism to report inappropriate content (principle 4) while seven responded to the fake bullying scenario test within 48 hours (two did not respond at all). Only one SNS warned the offender, asked him/her to remove the content and reminded him/her of the terms and conditions. However, the perpetrator in the scenario exercise did not remove the material and was not warned further.

These independent assessments appear to be what Byron (2008) called for in her report and suggest that industry signatories here have moved a little faster than those supporting the UKCCIS (although some will be represented in both initiatives). The upshot of these evaluations is that there is evidence of good practice in SNS, but it is by no means universal and consistent. The specific bullying scenario exercise highlights the disparity between what is reported in self-assessments and what actually goes on in practice.

The question still remains: to what extent are these principles actually effective in ensuring safer social networking and in preventing and reducing cyberbullying? There is publicly available evidence on the level of commitment by organisations to the principles, what we know less about is the extent that users/parents are adopting the tools provided and the extent that they are effective. Arguably, it is not the industry's responsibility to monitor user engagement with the tools, but as part of their social responsibility they may start to think about engaging with relevant organisations (e.g. researchers, charities, etc.) in supporting research on such issues.

Conclusions

The expectation on the industry is not one of "sort the problem out for us". Far from it, it is one of joint responsibility in which their role is to provide technical features to manage risks in the use of technology and to educate children, parents and teachers in safe technology use. Evidence suggests that many are doing this, with various solutions being reported in this chapter illustrating that industry is providing the technical features which allow the user and parents to have some control over mobile phones and the internet. National and European-level initiatives have been developed providing codes of best practice and evidence here suggests a high level of buy-in by technology-based organisations.

However, there is limited independent evidence of actual conformity to such codes (with the exception being the Safer Social Networking Principles) and where some evidence exists it appears the outcome is "could do better" – especially in relation to cyberbullying. The situation is not one where the industry at large is doing nothing, there is no doubt that many organisations are working towards safer use of technology and in some cases are actually taking the lead. The debatable issues are how quickly and how effectively are they doing this. As Cohen-Almagor (2010) posits, ISPs and other web providers need to have transparency on the internet and are responsible for gaining and maintaining trust in the Net. Through supporting and conforming to national/European self-regulatory codes of practice as part of its corporate social responsibility agenda, organisations will engender the trust of relevant stakeholders and will be perceived as part of a responsible industry.

References

Brown, T.J., and Dacin, P.A. (1997). 'The company and the product: Company associations and corporate consumer product responses'. *Journal of Marketing, 61*(1), 68–84.

Byron, T. (2008). *Safer Children in a Digital World. The Report of the Byron Review.* Retrieved June 1, 2012 from http://webarchive.nationalarchives.gov.uk/20130401151715/http://dcsf.gov.uk/byronreview/index.shtml.

——(2010). *Do we have safer children in a digital world? A review of progress since the 2008 Byron Review.* Retrieved from June 1, 2012 from http://webarchive.nationalarchives.gov.uk/20130401151715/http://dcsf.gov.uk/byronreview/index.shtml

Chesney, T., Coyne, I., Logan, B., and Madden, N. (2009). 'Griefing in virtual worlds: causes, casualties and coping strategies'. *Information Systems Journal, 19*(6), 525–548.

Cohen-Almagor, R. (2010). 'Responsibility of and trust in ISPs'. *Knowledge, Technology & Policy, 23*(3–4), 381–397.

Coyne, I., Chesney, T., Logan, B., and Madden, N. (2009). 'Griefing in a virtual community: An exploratory survey of Second Life residents'. *Zeitschrift fur Psychologie/Journal for Psychology, 217*(4), 214–221.

DCSF, DCMS & Home Office (2008). The Byron Review Action Plan. Retrieved January 21, 2013 from https://www.education.gov.uk/publications/standard/_arc_Childrensworkforce/Page1/DCSF-00521-2008.

Department for Education (2012). 'The government's response to the consultation on parental internet controls'. Retrieved February 19, 2013 from http://www.education.gov.uk/ukccis/news/a00218633/parental-internet-controls-consultation.

Donoso, V. (2011a). *Assessment of the implementation of the Safer Social Networking Principles for the EU on 14 websites: Summary Report.* European Commission, Safer Internet Programme. Luxembourg.

——(2011b). *Assessment of the implementation of the Safer Social Networking Principles for the EU on 9 services: Summary Report.* European Commission, Safer Internet Programme. Luxembourg.

Durrant, P. (2010). 'Cyberbullying (CB)'. *The legal and technical constraints for ISPs.* Paper presented at the COST workshop on legal issues surrounding cyberbullying. University of Antwerp, Belgium.

Fenaughty, J., and Harré, N. (2013). 'Factors associated with young people's successful resolution of distressing electronic harassment'. *Computers & Education, 61*, 242–250.

GMSA Europe (2008). 'European Framework for Safer Mobile Use by Younger Teenagers and Children: One Year after Implementation Report'. Retrieved February 19, 2013 from http://www.gsma.com/gsmaeurope/safer-mobile-use/implementation-review.

——(2009). 'European Framework for Safer Mobile Use by Younger Teenagers and Children'. Retrieved February 19, 2013 from http://www.gsma.com/ gsmaeurope/safer-mobile-use/european-framework.).

——(2010). 'Third implementation review of the European Framework for Safer Mobile Use by Younger Teenagers and Children'. Retrieved February 19, 2013 from http://www.gsma.com/gsmaeurope/safer-mobile-use/implementation-review.).

Jones, P., Comfort, D., and Hiller, D. (2012). 'Corporate social responsibility and the UK's leading internet service providers'. *World Review of Entrepreneurship, Management and Sustainable Development, 8*(3), 308–318.

Lievens, E. (2011). 'Risk-reducing regulatory strategies for protecting minors in social networks'. *Info, 13*(6), 43–54.

Porter, M., and Kramer, M. (2006). 'Strategy and society: The link between competitive advantage and corporate social responsibility'. *Harvard Business Review*, December, 1–13.

PricewaterhouseCoopers (2009). 'European Framework for Safer Mobile Use by Younger Teenagers and Children, Implementation Report'. Retrieved February 19, 2013 from http://www.gsma.com/gsmaeurope/safer-mobile-use/implementation-review.

The European Commission (2009). 'Safer Social Networking Principles for the EU'. Retrieved January 31, 2012 from https://ec.europa.eu/digital-agenda/en/safer-social-networking-principles-eu.

The European Parliament and the Council of the European Union (2000). 'Directive 2000/31/EC of the European Parliament and of the Council'. Retrieved March 4, 2013 from http://ec.europa.eu/internal_market/e-commerce/directive/index_en.htm.

UK Council for Child Internet Safety (2010a). 'Good practice guidance for the providers of chat services, instant messaging (IM) and internet connectivity content and hosting'. Retrieved June 1, 2012 from http://www.education.gov.uk/ukccis/groups/a0075834/self-regulation-of-industry.

——(2010b). 'Good practice guidance for the providers of search'. Retrieved June 1, 2012 from http://www.education.gov.uk/ukccis/groups/a0075834/self-regulation-of-industry.

——(2010c). 'Good practice guidance for the providers of social networking and other user-interactive services'. Retrieved June 1, 2012 from http://www.education.gov.uk/ukccis/groups/a0075834/self-regulation-of-industry.

——(2010d). 'Good practice guidance for the moderation of interactive services for children'. Retrieved June 1, 2012 from http://www.education.gov.uk/ukccis/groups/a0075834/self-regulation-of-industry.

6 The role of the media

*Heidi Vandebosch, Roma Simulioniene,
Magdalena Marczak, Anne Vermeulen and
Luigi Bonetti*[1]

Background

Previous research (Haddon & Stald, 2009) reveals that news media pay considerable attention to stories on internet-related risks and children, especially those involving sex and aggression. With regard to the way news media portray ICT related risks, there are some indications of a moral panic framing (Burger & Koetsenruijter, 2008): News media tend to focus on youngsters, not only in the role of "victims" but also as "perpetrators" (e.g. in the case of "sexting") and often refer to very severe consequences of online risks (e.g. those associated with suicide or suicidal attempts of the victim). Several factors can explain why mass media pay considerable attention to online risks and why they tend to portray the issue in a certain way, such as the external reality, the availability of (official) news sources, news selection processes (e.g. news values) and news construction practices. With regard to the potential effects of the amount of news media coverage on online risks, the agenda setting theory (McCombs & Shaw, 1972) suggests that the media determine what people think about. Issues that are high on the media agenda will also be high on the public's agenda and consequently on policymakers' agenda. The way the media frame the issue may have an impact on how people think about the issue, and on their knowledge, attitudes and actions with regard to a problem (de Vreese, 2005).

Until now, very little was known about the way cyberbullying (as a specific contact or conduct risk) is portrayed in the mass media. As suggested, this knowledge is important because it helps to understand the potential positive or negative effects of the media on the awareness of and actions on cyberbullying of several parties (e.g. youngsters, their parents and teachers, ISPs, e-safety organisations, anti-bullying organisations, policymakers, the

1   The authors would like to thank the other members of COST Working Group 2 for their help with the development of the coding scheme, the selection of newspapers and the search for and coding of the articles. For the UK: Iain Coyne. For Australia: Marilyn Campbell. For Slovenia: Ales Završnik, Nika Skvarča, Nerlisa Osmičević and Cyndi Ovsec. For Greece: Vasiliki Gountsidou.

police, researchers, and so on). In this chapter we will report the findings of a first, large-scale content analysis designed to explore the amount and nature of the coverage on cyberbullying in 43 national, daily newspapers in eight countries (Australia, Belgium, Greece, Italy, Lithuania, Poland, Slovenia, United Kingdom).

Trends in media coverage of children and the internet

Content analyses reveal that mass media pay a considerable amount of attention to the internet (Rössler, 2001) or to specific internet applications such as social networking sites (Arceneaux & Weiss, 2010; Vincze, 2011) in their news. Moreover, this coverage is mainly positive. The internet is framed as a new technology associated with positive outcomes in most domains of political, social and individual life and with particularly great potential for economic progress (Rössler, 2001).

Content analyses that focus on how the media report on youngsters and the internet, however, seem to reveal a predominantly negative news perspective. Haddon and Stald (2009) reported the results of a cross-national research on the media coverage of children and the internet, conducted within the framework of the EU Kids Online project. In this study, the content of 72 popular and quality newspapers, published in October and November 2007, was investigated. The results indicated that the newspapers, on average, published 20 articles per month on the internet and children during this specific time period. In 19 per cent of the articles the tone of the articles was "positive", in 37 per cent it was "negative", and in the remaining articles neither or mixed. The relative high percentage of negative coverage was related to the high degree of reporting on the internet and children in sections about legal changes, crimes, court cases, and police actions. Turning specifically to risks and opportunities, nearly two-thirds of all stories (64 per cent) referred to risks, whereas nearer a fifth (18 per cent) referred to opportunities. There was a considerable variation between countries with regard to the levels of coverage of content risks (e.g. advertising aimed at children, problematic sexual content or violence), contact risks (e.g. children being tracked by advertising, being harassed, groomed or supplied with false information) and conduct risks (e.g. children making illegal downloads, publishing porn, cyberbullying other children). Cyberbullying was in the Haddon and Stald study either classified as a contact risk or a conduct risk, depending on the perspective (child as victim or child as actor). The study did not mention any specific information about the coverage of this phenomenon.

A more in-depth, qualitative analysis of the news coverage in Italy, Spain and Portugal by Mascheroni, Ponte, Garmendia, Garitaonandia, and Murru (2010; within the EU Kids Online framework) revealed that in the two investigated months, cyberbullying and "happy slapping" (the practice of slapping or embarassing an unsuspecting passer-by and filming it with a mobile camera phone, the footage of which is then circulated to others) were receiving most media attention, apart from two other main topics, namely pornography and paedophilia. The authors stated that sexual content and aggressive conduct seemed to have the highest news values, and that youngsters were repeatedly being portrayed as acting outside normal social values, which contradicted the impression of vulnerability and innocence associated with risks on contents and contacts.

The notion of a moral panic, focusing on youngsters as perpetrators, was also the starting point for a study on the media coverage of sexting (i.e. the dissemination of sexually explicit images using cellular phone cameras and multimedia message technology; Lynn, 2010). Using an online archive of more than 700 major US newspapers, these authors detected 93 articles on sexting in the period from November 2008 to April 2009. Although articles appeared on sexting in all of the months investigated, there was a peak of 58 articles in March and April 2009. The results indicated that the media often reported on a sexting "epidemic" based on the results of one study. Teens were consistently framed as lacking the ability to use technology responsibly. Parents too, were negatively stereotyped. Nearly half of the articles presented parents as ignorant of the risks of cell phone use, technologically inept, or incapable of controlling their children's behaviours. To address these supposed parental deficiencies, 60 per cent of articles presented parenting advice for concerned readers, citing law enforcement officials, members of advocacy groups, other experts, and the opinion of the author.

A further aspect reflecting the negative framing of youngsters and the internet, relates to the seriousness of these "online risks": Which consequences are being mentioned in the press? A qualitative study by Thom, Edwards, Nakarada-Kordic, McKenna, O'Brien, and Nairn (2011) suggests that cyberbullying might be associated with suicide. More specifically these authors cited the "Myspace 'Cyber-Bullying'" (or Megan Meier) case, as an illustration of the media coverage of three website-related suicides. In these three cases the technology provided the "X-factor" for journalists to write about these suicides. The primary focus of the news reporting was not on the detail of the individual suicides, but rather on the enabling function of the technology. The news articles also marginalised the potential role of the victim's mental wellbeing in the suicide event.

Predicting the media coverage on cyberbullying

Few researches have dealt specifically with the media coverage on cyberbullying. In this section, we will combine the insights generated by content analyses on the internet and youngsters (see above) with insights related to journalism in general, to predict to what extent and how media report on cyberbullying. In particular, we focus on four factors: the reality of cyberbullying; the availability of (expert) news sources; the newsworthiness of cyberbullying; and the construction of news stories.

News refers to an *external reality*. The occurrence of events related to cyberbullying (such as concrete cases of cyberbullying, studies on this phenomenon, policy initiatives and concrete sensibilisation campaigns), thus influences how often (and how) media (can) report on cyberbullying. The first scientific studies on cyberbullying (or closely-related phenomena such as cyber stalking and cyber harassment) appeared from 2002 on (see, for instance, Finn, 2004; O'Sullivan & Flanagin, 2003; Spitzberg & Hoobler, 2002; Ybarra, 2004; Ybarra & Mitchell, 2004a, 2004b). Since that time, the amount of scientific research on this topic has grown explosively (for overviews, see Slonje, Smith, & Frisén, 2013; Tokunaga, 2010). The results of these studies indicate that the prevalence figures for cyberbullying have risen in the period from 2000–2005, and afterwards appear to have remained fairly constant (Olweus, 2012; Smith, 2012). The main changes relate to the applications or media that are being used to cyberbully. While Instant Messaging was a popular application amongst youngsters a few years ago (Livingstone & Helsper, 2007; Valkenburg & Peter, 2007), social networking sites have come to be the highest in rank (Brandtzæg, Staksrud, Hagen, & Wold, 2009; Wilson, Fornasier, & White, 2010). Although there are no detailed data about the amount of initiatives against cyberbullying over time, it seems necessary to assume that when individual cases or research findings on cyberbullying get media attention, this also leads to (a call for) action(s).

To keep informed about this external reality, journalists are often highly dependent of their news sources. The number and nature of the available sources will have an impact on the amount and type of media coverage on cyberbullying. News studies show that journalists, who generally work under strong time pressure (Prenger & Van Vree, 2004), often rely on routine channels such as professional, elite or expert sources (Burger & Koetsenruijter, 2008; McQuail, 2005; Vasterman & Aerden, 1995). These sources provide a constant flow of information (Vasterman & Aerden, 1995) and can be cited (which is an important aspect of the objectivity routine of journalists). In the case of cyberbullying, these professional sources consist of policymakers, scientists, the police, ISPs, e-safety and anti-bullying organisations.

The availability (and use) of sources also influences the way an issue is framed. For instance, when only the police are being cited by journalists, this may create the perception of cyberbullying as a crime. When journalists mainly rely on e-safety organisations, this may create the impression that cyberbullying is a pure online risk with little connection to traditional bullying. To get a more balanced view of the problem, journalists thus have to present a wide range of perspectives (Burger & Koetsenruijter, 2008). Apart from the abovementioned professional sources, other media are often used as sources by journalists. This trend to follow and copy what other media do, is also known as the intermedia-agenda setting effect (Danielian & Reese, 1989; Mathes & Pfetsch, 1991). This multiplication effect may also partly explain the peaks in the cross-media coverage on a news issue or a particular story (Vasterman, 2005).

Not all information that is available to journalists in the media organisation can become "news". Newspapers, radio and television broadcasts, have a fixed format and have to select the events they think are most newsworthy (cfr. The gatekeeping role of news media; Shoemaker & Reese, 1991). To do this, news organisations rely on a set of news values, such as negativity, threshold (Galtung & Ruge, 1965; Harcup & O'Neill, 2001), proximity (Stephens, 1980) and immediacy (Herbert, 2000; Stephens, 1980). These values can, for instance, explain why sex and aggression related online risks get more media attention, especially when they happen close to home and have serious consequences. The news values have been mentioned as an explanation for fluctuations in the (amount and type) of news coverage over time, as in the case of media hypes around a certain news story (Ruigrok, Scholten, Krijt, & Schaper, 2009; Vasterman, 2005; Wien & Elmelund-Præstekær, 2009) and (more general) issue cycles (Downs, 1972; Waldherr, 2009).

More in particular, the novelty and sensational character of a trigger event or key event, would explain why the news media but also the public and the news sources first pay attention to an event or issue. Through the creation of a moral panic and a call for solutions, this attention can even increase. After a while, the story or issue loses its attractiveness. There is also a growing insight that there are no simple solutions to the problem. These factors would explain the eventual decline in media coverage. In the case of media hypes around specific news events this cycle would typically take place within the time frame of several weeks. In the case of Issue Attention Cycles, on the other hand, issues gain and lose attention over years. The few studies that have examined the media coverage over several years seem to suggest that the media attention for the internet and internet-related risks is relatively constant (Rössler, 2001). An explanation for this is the fact that the internet constantly reinvents or reshapes itself through the development of new applications, and in this way stays new. However, within each year, there seem to be smaller specific events-related peaks.

After an event has come to the attention of a news organisation and has been judged as newsworthy, journalists start to reconstruct the story from a certain angle. This process has been described as framing:

> To frame is to select some aspects of a perceived reality and make them more salient in a communicating text, in such a way as to promote a particular problem definition, causal interpretation, moral evaluation, and/or treatment recommendation for the item described.
>
> (Entman, 1993, p. 52)

The way a story is framed by a journalist depends on his or her ideological or political convictions; pressures and routines within news organisations; external pressures from specific groups; and general social norms and values (Scheufele, 2000). We indicated how the availability of different news sources (cfr. news routines, external pressure) could influence the representation of cyberbullying in the news media. Apart from this, the specific audience that a news medium tries to target influences the framing of issues. Quality news media would mostly rely on thematic framing focusing on general trends, addressing topics on a more abstract level, and looking at external causes of social problems; while popular media would mostly use episodic frames focusing on isolated, concrete events, and looking at internal causes (Iyengar, 1991; Manssens & Walgrave, 1998). With regard to the influences of social norms and values, ideological or political convictions on framing, we refer to the concept of moral panic. In case of a moral panic, framing a (sexual, aggressive, or criminal) phenomenon is being represented (disproportionally and without proper evidence) as a problem in the media. The perpetrators are very negatively portrayed (as folks devils) (Burger & Koetsenruijter, 2008; Thompson, 1998; Welch, Price, & Yankey, 2002).

Statement of the problem and purpose of the study

The literature review shows that the available information on the amount and nature of the media coverage on cyberbullying is scarce. On the basis of the findings of earlier content analyses of news reports on the internet and online risks and children, combined with general insights in news production, we formulate a few general hypotheses and research questions.

Because: a) the prevalence of cyberbullying has first risen (period before 2005) and then remained constant (Smith, 2012); b) there are a lot of professional sources dealing with "cyberbullying"; c) the subject meets several news criteria (e.g. negativity); and d) renews itself constantly (parallel with technological evolutions), we expect that the news media's attention for cyberbullying, after an initial take-off period, has remained constant throughout the years. This does not exclude the existence of certain smaller, event-based peaks during the years. Based on the media hypes theory, we test whether there is a logic in the news coverage on cases, research and actions: do media reports on individual cases stimulate and precede both media reports on research initiatives and policy actions?

With regard to the nature of the media coverage on cyberbullying we expect that most news reports will focus on national cyberbullying related events (cfr. the news value of geographical proximity). Cyberbullying can be the main topic of the news reports or it can be framed within the context of wider phenomena (e-safety or bullying). If cyberbullying is the main topic, the focus will be on cases, research or actions. We expect that most of the cases will deal with cyberbullying amongst youngsters and will focus on negative outcomes for victims such as suicide. Media coverage on research on cyberbullying is expected to mention several types of research initiators (i.e. professional news sources). Initiatives and actions are hypothesised to originate from a large range of actors, and to be aimed at youngsters and their parents. Overall, we expect the tone of the news reports on cyberbullying to be neutral or negative.

In line with other cross-national content analyses on online risks, we explore whether there are differences in the amount and nature of the media coverage on cyberbullying in different countries, and between popular and quality newspapers.

Method

Content analysis was the research technique used to analyse 43 national daily newspapers published throughout the period of 1 January 2004 until 31 December 2011 in eight countries collaborating within the COST Action on cyberbullying. These included Australia, Belgium, Greece, Italy, Lithuania, Poland, Slovenia and the United Kingdom. The list of newspapers included in the search for each country is shown in Table 6.1. Since there is no universally-agreed definition of what constitutes a quality or a popular newspaper (Russ-Mohl, 1992), we relied on what the coders in each country assumed to represent the most commonly agreed categorisation of the newspapers in their country.

The initial coding scheme was developed in Belgium and, after a pretest utilising Flemish newspapers, a second version of a coding scheme was prepared following discussions amongst the research members. The discussions included the clarification of coding problems, mainly the shortening of the original coding scheme and newspapers selection (for example, discussions on what constitutes a "national newspaper" in the various countries). The adjusted coding scheme was tested in the participating countries and readjusted.

All articles containing the search terms cyberbullying or a combination of the words bullying and cyber, digital, online, virtual, internet, mobile, electronic or mobile phone (or, if the term bullying does not exist in a certain language, it was substituted by aggression and harassment) were included in the analysis. However, within the Italian sample the search terms used included only cyberbullismo, cyber bullismo and cyber-bullismo as the other terms already mentioned yielded very limited results (for an overview of the specific terms used in each country, see Table 6.1).

The article search was conducted using available electronic databases (Australia, Belgium, Italy, Lithuania, Poland and the United Kingdom), print copies or microfiches of the newspapers (Greece and Slovenia) or a combination of both methods (Lithuania). All non-relevant articles were omitted (for example, an article on traffic controls which stated that the police used speed cameras, but that they did not do this with the purpose of bullying the drivers and that some of these controls were announced online; or an article reporting on a computer virus infecting computers presented as a sophisticated cyber war attack on nuclear arms programme). An article was considered as relevant when the term cyberbullying was mentioned to describe an incident even if it did not meet the scientific definition of cyberbullying, for instance because there was no repetition or imbalance involved.

Table 6.1 List of newspapers per country

Country	Search terms used	Type of newspaper	
		Popular	Quality
Australia	Cyberbullying Cyber-bullying; Digital + bullying Online + bullying Virtual + bullying Internet + bullying Mobile + bullying Electronic + bullying Mobile phone + bullying	The Age	The Australian
Belgium	Cyberpesten Cyber + pesten Digitaal + pesten Online + pesten Virtueel + pesten Internet + pesten Gsm + pesten Elektronisch + pesten Mobiel + pesten	Het Belang van Limburg Het Laatste Nieuws Het Nieuwsblad Gazet van Antwerpen	De Morgen De Standaard
Greece	Ηλεκτρονικός εκφοβισμός Σχολικός εκφοβισμός Ενδοσχολική βία κυβερνοτραμπουκισμός		ΤΑ ΝΕΑ ΕΛΕΥΘΕΡΟΤΥΠΙΑ ΕΘΝΟΣ ΡΙΖΟΣΠΑΣΤΗΣ ΒΗΜΑ ΚΑΘΗΜΕΡΙΝΗ ΑΥΓΗ ΑΓΓΕΛΙΟΦΟΡΟΣ ΑΚΡΟΠΟΛΗ ΜΑΚΕΔΟΝΙΑ ΑΔΕΣΜΕΥΤΟΣ ΤΥΠΟΣ 24 ΩΡΕΣ
Italy	Cyberbullismo Cyber-bullismo Cyber bullismo		Corriere della Sera La Repubblica La Stampa Il Sole 24 Ore Il Giornale L'Unità
Lithuania	Elektroninės patyčios Elektroninis + patyčios Skaitmeninis + patyčios Internetas + patyčios Virtualus + patyčios Mobilus + patyčios Mobilus telefonas + patyčios		Lietuvos rytas Lietuvos zinios Respublika

Country	Search terms used	Type of newspaper	
		Popular	Quality
Poland	Cyberbullying Cyber przemoc Przemoc elektroniczna Przemoc wirtualna Przemoc online Cyber agresja Agresja elektroniczna Agresja online Agresja wirtualna Cyber szykany Szykany elektroniczne Szykany online Szykany wirtualne Telefon komórkowy + przemoc Telefon komórkowy + agresja Telefon komórkowy + szykany	Gazeta Wspolczesna	Dziennik Rzeczpospolita Gazeta Wyborcza Gazeta Prawna
Slovenia	Nasilje + vrstniško Nasilje + vrstniki Nasilje + internet Medvrstniško nasilje Vrstniško nasilje Medosebno nasilje Elektronsko nasilje Kibernetsko nasilje Mladi + nasilje Digitalno nasilje Nasilje preko telefona Nasilje v spletnih socialnih omrežjih Nasilje na internetu Sexting Mobbing Bullying Bulizem	Slovenske novice	Dnevnik Vecer Primorske Novice Delo
United Kingdom	Cyberbullying Cyber-bullying Digital + bullying Online + bullying Virtual + bullying Internet + bullying Mobile + bullying Electronic + bullying Mobile phone + bullying	The Sun The Mirror The Express Daily Mail Daily Star	The Guardian The Times The Daily Telegraph The Independent
Total:		12	31

All relevant articles were coded using the final coding scheme. First, every article was assigned its own ID–number. Then, the title of the article, the name of the newspaper, the type of newspaper (quality or popular), the publication date and whether cyberbullying was the main topic of the article were registered. If cyberbullying was not the main topic, the context in which it was mentioned was coded. If cyberbullying was the main topic, the article was coded on a series of variables, such as: its text size, geographical focus, general tone and main scope (case, research, action/intervention/policy, other). For each scope, specific additional variables were created, referring, for instance, to the type of actors mentioned in the articles on cyberbullying research or actions, or the (negative) outcomes of cyberbullying mentioned in the articles on cases (suicide or suicidal attempt?). These different variables made it possible to examine the nature of the media coverage.

Results

Overall data analysis

In the search conducted throughout the eight countries, 1,599 articles containing the agreed search terms have been found. The number of articles published throughout the years differed. A general upward trend can be observed starting with 34 articles published on cyberbullying in 2004, with a peak in 2007 with 254 articles, a slight decrease in 2008 (191 articles) and again a steady rise until 2011 when 295 articles on the topic were published (as shown in Figure 6.1).

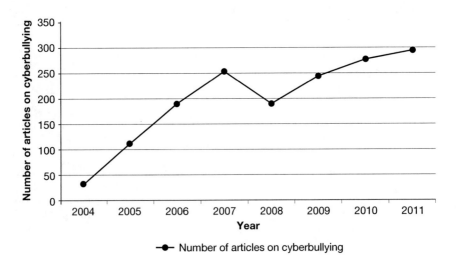

Figure 6.1 Difference in the number of articles on cyberbullying throughout 2004–2011

However, in only 703 articles (44 per cent) was cyberbullying the main topic. These articles focused on a case example ($n = 210$ | 29.5 per cent), outline of research ($n = 177$ | 24.9 per cent), policy, action and/or intervention against cyberbullying ($n = 202$ | 28.4 per cent) or other ($n = 123$ | 17.2 per cent). An article from the "other" category would, for example, explain what cyberbullying was and give a few examples or an announcement of a TV programme on cyberbullying or a call for research participants. Most of the newspaper articles in which cyberbullying was the main topic, reported on cyberbullying events within the newspapers' own country. Almost one quarter (22.5 per cent) of the 703 articles had a local focus (focus on a village, municipality or province for example). In addition, 61.6 per cent of articles had a national focus. Only 12.9 per cent of the articles reported on an event that took place in another country (usually Australia, the United States, the United Kingdom or the Netherlands, Belgium and Germany) and 3 per cent focused on supranational news about European initiatives. The general tone of the articles in which cyberbullying was the main topic was in most instances alarming ($n = 362$ | 52.5 per cent) or neutral ($n = 283$ | 41 per cent), and only in 6.5 per cent ($n = 45$) of the cases was it reassuring.

When the articles' main focus was not on cyberbullying ($n = 899$), it provided information on cyberbullying in the context of bullying in general (34.7 per cent), e-safety (38.3 per cent) or another cyberbullying related issue (27 per cent). This last category contains anything that is not within the categories of bullying and e-safety and as such the articles within it report information on cyber police, cyber addiction, school rules or survey results of young people's internet behaviours, etc.

When looking at articles in which cyberbullying was the main topic, some trends in the reporting of cases, research and actions can be observed (as shown in Figure 6.2). For the articles on cyberbullying cases, for instance, a steady rise with three peak moments can be discerned. These correspond with the press coverage on the circumstances of Megan Meier's suicide in 2006, Tyler Clementi's in 2008 and Phoebe Prince's in 2010, all of which were classed as cases of cyberbullying portrayed in the media. The number of articles reporting on the outline of conducted research on cyberbullying also increases over time, but this rise is less outspoken and the fluctuations are bigger: starting in 2004 ($n = 5$) with a peak in 2006 ($n = 30$), then a decline until 2008 ($n = 18$), a rise in 2009 ($n = 32$), a decline in 2010 ($n = 18$) and again a peak in 2011 ($n = 38$). For the articles reporting on policy, action and/ or interventions against cyberbullying starting from 2004 ($n = 1$), there was a steady rise with a peak in 2007 ($n = 35$), followed by a decrease in articles in 2008 ($n = 22$) and then again a steady rise which continued to 2011 ($n = 41$). As illustrated in Figure 6.2, it does appear that the peaks in articles reporting on the outline of research (in 2006 and 2009) preceded the peaks in articles on policy/action and/or intervention (in 2007 and 2010). It can also be noted that the peak in articles on case examples (in 2006) preceded the peak in the articles on the policy/action and/or intervention (in 2007).

However, this was not the case with a peak in reported case examples in 2008 and 2010 as the number of articles on the policy/action and/or intervention has not outnumbered it.

The articles on cyberbullying cases (*n* = 208) mostly dealt with cyberbullying amongst youngsters. Considering who was involved in the perpetration and victimisation of cyberbullying, the analysis showed that 55 per cent of the articles reported cases regarding kid(s) on kid(s) cyberbullying, 14.8 per cent adult(s) on adult(s), 14.8 per cent kid on adult, 12.9 per cent adult on kid (in 2.4 per cent of the cases the perpetrator was unknown or classed as mixed). Most of the articles (65.7 per cent) mentioned a negative impact on the victim. In 32.7 per cent of the case articles, cyberbullying was associated with suicide or a suicidal attempt.

The articles on cyberbullying research (*n* = 180) reported the results of studies initiated and conducted by various organisations. The biggest initiator of research were governmental actors and organisations (for example, the Ministry of Education) (*n* = 79 | 43.9 per cent). The research had been conducted mainly by universities and/or colleges (*n* = 103 | 56.9 per cent), other non-profit and/or governmental research organisations (*n* = 43 | 23.8 per cent) and private research organisations (such as market research companies) (*n* = 11 | 6.1 per cent). Twenty-four articles reported on research conducted by other organisations (13.3 per cent).

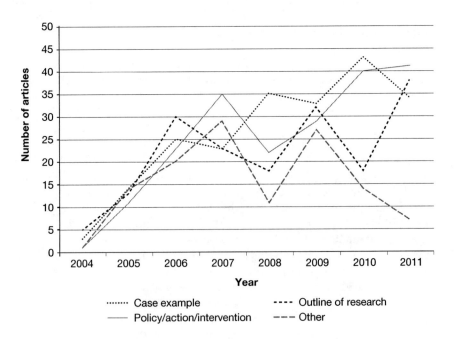

Figure 6.2 Article focus if cyberbullying was the main topic

The articles on policy, actions and interventions with regard to cyberbullying (*n* = 202 | 28.4 per cent) were also conducted by a wide variety of actors. The local, regional, national or supranational government was the most frequently identified actor (*n* = 100 | 49.8 per cent), followed by schools (*n* = 23 | 11.4 per cent), police/law enforcement agencies (*n* = 19 | 9.5 per cent), private organisations (*n* = 14 | 7 per cent), non-profit organisations (*n* = 27 | 13.4 per cent) and others (*n* = 18 | 9 per cent).

Comparison across countries and newspaper types

Across the participating countries, a total of 43 newspapers were taken into account. The average number of articles on cyberbullying (between 2004 and 2011) per newspaper equalled 38.07. There were, however, significant differences in the amount of media attention for cyberbullying across countries (see Figure 6.3), which may be partly explained by the different search approaches (i.e. while in some countries articles on cyberbullying could be searched for using electronic databases, in other countries this had to be done manually). The most articles on cyberbullying were found in newspapers from the UK, Belgium and Australia; the least in Greece and Lithuania.

When the newspaper type was taken into account the analysis revealed that the popular newspapers published more articles related to cyberbullying than the quality newspapers, respectively: 70.6 articles per popular newspaper versus 24.3 articles per quality newspaper. Analysis of the tone of the articles in both types of newspapers revealed that the quality newspapers published more articles of the neutral and reassuring tone in comparison with the popular type (*n* = 133 | 43.5 per cent and *n* = 27 | 8.8 per cent versus

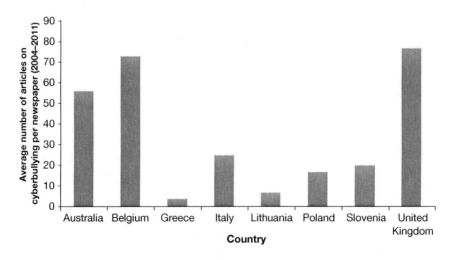

Figure 6.3 Differences between countries

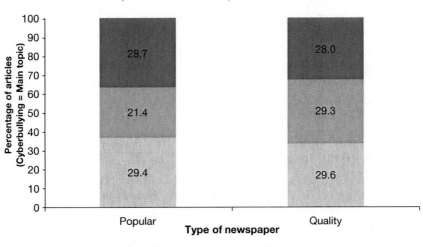

Figure 6.4 Popular versus quality newspapers

n = 156 | 39.3 per cent and n = 23 | 5.8 per cent). The comparison between the popular and the quality papers further showed that both types of newspapers paid almost equal attention to cases, research results and policy/ actions; see Figure 6.4. Quality papers only differed from popular papers with regard to the coverage on research results (29.3 per cent versus 21.4 per cent).

Discussion

The aim of this study was to explore the extent and nature of the coverage on cyberbullying in national daily newspapers in seven European countries and Australia. On the basis of a content analysis, we described general trends and made comparisons across countries and between types of newspapers.

The results of the study revealed that the number of articles on cyberbullying increased in the investigated period (starting from 2004). However, the articles in which cyberbullying was the main topic comprise only less than a half (44 per cent) of the total number of analysed articles. This could be due to the perception of cyberbullying as an aspect of wider phenomena related to e-safety and bullying in general.

In the articles where cyberbullying was the main topic, the case examples received most attention, followed by almost the same amount of articles focusing on policy, action and/or interventions, and research-focused articles in third place. In regard to the changes of coverage over time, the articles on cyberbullying cases demonstrate the most steady rise. These findings do not fit into the context of recent research stating that cyberbullying is a low-prevalence phenomenon, which has not increased over time and has not created many new victims and bullies (Olweus,

2012). This increased interest of media could be interpreted as an indicator of community awareness about the issue, as well as the result of a growing amount of scientific research and policy initiatives, related not only to cyberbullying, but to bullying in general, as well as e-safety issues (Safer Internet Programme, EU Kids Online, etc.). Most of the articles on cases of cyberbullying show a negative impact on the victim including suicide and suicidal attempt. Apart from negativity, the geographical focus or relevance appears to be an important news value, with a high amount of articles reporting events within their own country. We also found a certain logic in the news coverage on cyberbullying with no clear pattern of articles on the outline of research preceding the peaks in the articles on policy/action and/ or intervention, but no clear pattern of the reported cases preceding reports on research and actions. Governmental organisations were the most frequently identified actors as the initiators of research and actions.

Significant differences in the amount of articles on cyberbullying per newspaper were found across participating countries. The most attention to cyberbullying is paid in the newspapers of the UK, Belgium and Australia, and the least in Greece and Lithuania. We can hypothesise that these differences might be partially due to the methodological differences related to the newspaper search term method (e.g. electronic or not) and the fact that not all daily newspapers were included in the analysis because of time constraints (e.g. in Italy). On the other hand, there are many other possible factors that can account for the differences in media representations of risks (Mascheroni *et al.*, 2010), such as the actual prevalence of cyberbullying in each of these countries. Based on the results of EU Kids online survey (Livingstone, Haddon, Görzig, & Olaffson, 2011) about children's online use and risks, the participating countries were classified into four categories. The analysed countries represent three of them: Belgium, Greece and Italy are classified as lower use, lower risk; Poland and Slovenia as lower use, some risk; Lithuania and the UK as higher use, higher risk. Though the latter countries fall into the same category in terms of use and risks, the differences between them in media coverage of cyberbullying are the greatest. The same trend is observed in the first group of countries. Only the newspapers from Poland and Slovenia pay almost equal attention to cyberbullying. In other words, the actual risk level (i.e. with regard to cyberbullying), although perhaps the most logical explanation for differences in the amount of coverage across countries, does not seem that important. Other factors seem to play a role as well, such as the availability of (expert) sources on cyberbullying, who might also use the media to influence policy and defend their own activities.

A few differences in the coverage of cyberbullying were found in regard to the type of newspaper. Though popular newspapers published more articles on cyberbullying than quality newspapers, they were almost equally interested in the cases and policy/actions, with slightly greater attention paid to the coverage of research by quality papers. The major differences were observed in the tone of the articles with more articles of neutral and reassuring tone in quality papers. The results of this research provide some indications of moral panic framing only in popular newspapers.

Implications for future research and practice

We conducted the first large scale international study on cyberbullying coverage over an extensive period. Our focus was rather general and descriptive: we tried to provide data on the amount of coverage on cyberbullying in different types of newspapers in eight countries; and their geographical/thematic focus. Departing from our findings, future content analyses might try to give a more detailed picture of this news coverage on cyberbullying (e.g. Which recommendations are given to parents and teachers?; How are cases actually portrayed?; Which pictures and words are being used?, etc.). New research initiatives might further explore why news media (don't) cover cyberbullying related events (in a certain way), by interviewing journalists in different countries. Apart from further research on the "causes" of the media coverage, studies on its "effects" are also needed. As the agenda-setting (McCombs & Shaw, 1972) and framing theory (de Vreese, 2005; Scheufele & Tewksbury, 2007) suggest, the media coverage can influence people's thinking, knowledge, attitudes and behaviours with regard to the problem.

In regard to the practices of reporting cyberbullying, it should be acknowledged that increased attention and an alarming tone may lead to a moral panic. This is especially important in the context of scientific studies suggesting that cyberbullying is an overestimated phenomenon. Inducing fear might lead to a call for repressive measures focusing on criminalising cyberbullying and cyberbullies (e.g. by adopting new laws), or a call for restrictive and controlling measures from parents and schools (e.g. limiting youngsters' time spent online), while a more educational, nuanced and trusting approach would probably be better-suited. Creating a balanced view of cyberbullying is not only the task of journalists. Different types of professional sources (e.g. governments, e-safety organisations, ISPs, etc.) also battle for the media's attention to influence the public (and political) agenda in directions that suit them best. Scientists too might be tempted to especially focus on the serious consequences of cyberbullying so as to create public awareness and stimulate youngsters, parents, schools, the police, governments to take action. They should be made aware of the media logic that operates and which tends to further emphasise or even single out the very negative aspects and to focus especially on the newness of the phenomenon (i.e. the technology also appears to represent the "X-factor").

Conclusions

Several conclusions can be drawn from this study. First, the increase of articles on cyberbullying published since 2004 shows that the media has helped to place cyberbullying on the agenda.

Second, a logic can be observed in the media representation of cyberbullying-related articles. The hypothesis that the media reports on individual cases stimulate and precede media reports on research as well as policy actions was partially confirmed. We did not find evidence for the coverage of cases preceding reports on research and actions.

Third, the extent and the way the media report about cyberbullying are affected by the availability of news resources, reliance on news values and news construction practices.

The fourth conclusion we can draw is that only a few indications of moral panic framing can be identified. These are related to the negativity aspect of reported cases in the articles where cyberbullying was the main topic, and where a less reassuring and neutral tone is used in the articles on cyberbullying in the popular press.

Fifth, considerable differences among countries were found in the extent of media coverage of cyberbullying with most articles found in the UK, Belgian and Australian newspapers, and the least in Greece and Lithuania.

Sixth, popular newspapers published more articles on cyberbullying than quality newspapers. These newspapers are almost equally interested in the cases and policy/actions, with slightly greater attention paid to the coverage of research by quality papers.

References

Arceneaux, N., and Weiss, A.S. (2010). 'Seems stupid until you try it: press coverage of Twitter, 2006–9'. *New Media and Society, 12*(8), 1262–1279. doi: 10.1177/1461444809360773

Brandtzæg, P.B., Staksrud, E., Hagen, I., and Wold, T. (2009). 'Norwegian children's experiences of cyberbullying when using different technological platforms'. *Journal of Children and Media, 3*(4), 349–365. doi:10.1080/17482790903233366

Burger, J., and Koetsenruijter, W. (2008). *Loverboys: the media construction of a new crime. Content analysis of Dutch news coverage (1995–2005).* Paper presented at the annual meeting of the International Communication Association, TBA, Montreal, Quebec, Canada.

Danielian, L.H., and Reese, S.D. (1989). 'A closer look at intermedia influences on agenda setting: The cocaine issue of 1986'. In P.F. Shoemaker (Ed.), *Communication campaigns about drugs: Government, media, and the public* (pp. 47–66). Hillsdale, NJ: Lawrence Erlbaum.

de Vreese, C.H. (2005). 'News framing: Theory and typology'. *Information Design Journal + Document Design, 13*(1), 51–62.

Downs, A. (1972). 'Up and down with ecology – The "Issue-Attention Cycle"'. *Public Interest, 28*(Summer), 38–50.

Entman, R.M. (1993). 'Framing: Toward clarification of a fractured paradigm'. *Journal of Communication, 43*(4), 51–58.

Finn, J. (2004). 'A survey of online harassment at a university campus'. *Journal of Interpersonal Violence, 19*(4), 468–483. doi: 10.1177/0886260503262083

Galtung, J., and Ruge, M.H. (1965). 'The structure of foreign news. The presentation of the Congo, Cuba and Cyprus crises in four Norwegian newspapers'. *Journal of Peace Research, 2*(1), 64–91.

Haddon, L., and Stald, G. (2009). 'A comparative analysis of European press coverage of children and the internet'. *Journal of Children and Media, 3*(4), 379–393. doi: 10.1080/17482790903233432

Harcup, T., and O'Neill, D. (2001). 'What is news? Galtung and Ruge revisited'. *Journalism Studies, 2*(2), 261–280. doi: 10.1177/1464884904044941

Herbert, J. (2000). *Journalism in the digital age.* Oxford: Focal Press.

Iyengar, S. (1991). *Is anyone responsible? How television frames political issues.* Chicago: University of Chicago Press.

Livingstone, S., and Helsper, E. (2007). 'Taking risks when communicating on the Internet: The role of offline social-psychological factors in young people's vulnerability to online risks: teenagers' use of social networking sites for intimacy, privacy and self-expression'. *Information, Communication and Society, 10*(5), 619–644. doi: 10.1177/1461444808089415

Livingstone, S., Haddon, L., Görzig, A., and Olafsson, K. (2011). *EU Kids Online final report.* LSE, London: EU Kids Online.

Lynn, R. (2010). *Constructing parenthood in moral panics of youth, digital media, and 'sexting'.* Paper presented at the 105th Annual Meeting of the American Sociological Association, Atlanta, Georgia.

Manssens, J., and Walgrave, S. (1998). 'Populair en/of kwaliteit? De Vlaamse pers over de zaak-Dutroux'. *PSW-papers* (pp. 35). Antwerpen: UIA.

Mascheroni, G., Ponte, C., Garmendia, M., Garitaonandia, C., and Murru, M.F. (2010). 'Comparing media coverage of online risks for children in southern European countries: Italy, Portugal and Spain'. *International Journal of Media and Cultural Politics, 6*(1), 25–43. doi: 10.1386/macp.6.1.25/1.

Mathes, R., and Pfetsch, B. (1991). 'The role of the alternative press in the agenda-building process: Spill-over effects and media opinion leadership'. *European Journal of Communication, 6*(1), 33–62. doi: 10.1177/0267323191006001003

McCombs, M.E., and Shaw, D.L. (1972). 'The agenda-setting function of mass media'. *Public Opinion Quarterly, 36*(2), 176–187. doi: 10.1086/267990

McQuail, D. (2005). *Mass communication theory.* London: Sage.

O'Sullivan, P.B., and Flanagin, A.J. (2003). 'Reconceptualizing "flaming" and other problematic messages'. *New Media & Society, 5*(1), 69–94. doi: 10.1177/1461444803005001908

Olweus, D. (2012). 'Cyberbullying: An overrated phenomenon?' *European Journal of Developmental Psychology, 9*(5), 520–538. doi: 10.1080/17405629.2012.682358

Prenger, M., and Van Vree, F. (2004). *Schuivende grenzen. De vrijheid van de journalist in een veranderend medialandschap.* Amsterdam: Nederlandse Vereniging van Journalisten.

Rössler, P. (2001). 'Between online heaven and cyberhell'. *New Media and Society, 3*(1), 49–66. doi: 10.1177/14614440122225985

Ruigrok, N., Scholten, O., Krijt, M., and Schaper, J. (2009). 'Fitna in de media: een brongerichte mediahype'. *Tijdschrift voor Communicatiewetenschap, 37*(3), 238–253.

Ruß-Mohl, S. (1992). 'Am eigenen Schopfe...Qualitätssicherung im Journalismus – Grundfragen, Ansätze, Näherungsversuche'. *Publizistik, 37*(1), 83–96.

Scheufele, D.A. (2000). 'Agenda-setting, priming, and framing revisited: Another look at cognitive effects of political communication'. *Mass Communication and Society, 3*(2), 297–316.

Scheufele, D.A., and Tewksbury, D. (2007). 'Framing, Agenda setting and priming: the evolution of three media effects models'. *Journal of Communication, 57*(1), 9–20. doi:10.1111/j.1460-2466.2006.00326.x.

Shoemaker, P.J., and Reese, S.D. (1991). *Mediating the message. Theories of influences on mass media content*. New York: Longman.

Slonje, R., Smith, P.K., and Frisén, A. (2013). 'The nature of cyberbullying, and strategies for prevention'. *Computers in Human Behavior, 29*(1), 26–32. doi: http://dx.doi.org/10.1016/j.chb.2012.05.024

Smith, P.K. (2012). 'Cyberbullying: Challenges and opportunities for a research program – A response to Olweus'. *European Journal of Developmental Psychology, 9* (5), 553–558.

Spitzberg, B.H., and Hoobler, G. (2002). 'Cyberstalking and the technologies of interpersonal terrorism'. *New Media and Society, 4*(1), 71–92. doi: 10.1177/14614440222226271

Stephens, M. (1980). *Broadcast news*. New York: Holt, Rinehart & Winston.

Thom, K., Edwards, G., Nakarada-Kordic, I., McKenna, B., O'Brien, A., and Nairn, R. (2011). 'Suicide online: Portrayal of website-related suicide by the New Zealand media'. *New Media and Society, 13*(8), 1355–1372. doi: 10.1177/1461444811406521

Thompson, K. (1998). *Moral panics*. New York: Routledge.

Tokunaga, R.S. (2010). 'Following you home from school: A critical review and synthesis of research on cyberbullying victimization'. *Computers in Human Behavior, 26*(3), 277–287. doi: 10.1016/j.chb.2009.11.014

Valkenburg, P.M., and Peter, J. (2007). 'Preadolescents' and adolescents' online communication and their closeness to friends'. *Developmental Psychology, 43*(2), 267–277.

Vasterman, P.L.M. (2005). 'Media-hype. Self-reinforcing news waves, journalistic standards and the construction of social problems'. *European Journal of Communication, 20*(4), 508–530. doi: 10.1177/0267323105058254

Vasterman, P.L.M., and Aerden, O. (1995). *De context van het nieuws*. Groningen: Wolters-Noordhoff.

Vincze, H.O. (2011). 'Social networking in the news (Romanian news media representations of online social networking)'. *Journal of Media Research, 4*(3), 3–18.

Waldherr, A. (2009). *Media attention dynamics in complex societies: A conceptual framework*. Paper presented at the annual meeting of the International Communication Association, Marriott, Chicago, IL.

Welch, M., Price, E.A. and Yankey, N. (2002). 'Moral panic over youth violence: Wilding and the manufacture of menace in the media'. *Youth and Society 34*(3), 3–30. doi: 10.1177/0044118X02034001001

Wien, C., and Elmelund-Præstekær, C. (2009). 'An anatomy of media hypes: Developing a model for the dynamics and structure of intense media coverage of single issues'. *European Journal of Communication, 24*(2), 183–201. doi: 10.1177/0267323108101831

Wilson, K., Fornasier, S., and White, K.M. (2010). 'Psychological predictors of young adults' use of social networking sites'. *Cyberpsychology, Behavior, and Social Networking, 13*(2), 173–177.

Ybarra, M.L. (2004). 'Linkages between depressive symptomatology and internet harassment among young regular internet users'. *CyberPsychology and Behavior, 7*(2), 247–257. doi: 10.1089/109493104323024500

Ybarra, M.L., and Mitchell, K.J.K. (2004a). 'Online aggressor/targets, aggressors, and targets: A comparison of associated youth characteristics'. *Journal of Child Psychology and Psychiatry, 45*(7), 1308–1316.

——(2004b). 'Youth engaging in online harassment: Associations with caregiver-child relationships, internet use, and personal characteristics'. *Journal of Adolescence*, 27(3), 319–336.

Part 4

Coping and guidelines

7   Coping with cyberbullying

How can we prevent cyberbullying
and how victims can cope with it

*Conor McGuckin, Sonja Perren, Lucie
Corcoran, Helen Cowie, Francine Dehue,
Anna Ševčíková, Panayiota Tsatsou and
Trijntje Völlink[1]*

Introduction

This chapter explores current knowledge on coping with cyberbullying. We
define coping strategies as responses (behaviors, but also emotions/cognitions)
that are successful (or not) against cyberbullying and against its impact on
victims. We differentiate between two domains of responses to cyberbullying:
(a) how parents and schools can prevent cyberbullying through the reduction
of risks; and (b) how victims can cope with cyberbullying in order to combat
the problem and buffer its negative impact. In 2012, we published an extensive
report on coping strategies based on a systematic literature review (Perren *et
al.*, 2012a). The current chapter provides a summary of these findings and
integrates most current literature on the topic.

Responses to cyberbullying

One of the aims of the COST Action IS0801 was to review the available
research evidence regarding how children, families, and schools cope with
cyberbullying, so as to better inform those with an interest in developing
guidelines for cyberbullying, and to detail the issues that would require
further research exploration. Towards this aim, we specifically aimed to
explore the empirical (scientific) literature regarding coping strategies against
cyberbullying at the: (a) personal level; (b) family level; and (c) school level.
The work has been published in an extensive report describing methods and

1   The authors would like to extend their grateful thanks to the following for their help and
     assistance with the original work that formed the basis of the chapter: Françoise Alsaker,
     David Šmahel, Georg Spiel, Monika Finsterwald, and D'Jamila Garcia. The authors
     would also like to acknowledge the support of the VITOVIN project
     (CZ.1.07/2.3.00/20.0184), which is co-financed by the European Social Fund and the
     state budget of the Czech Republic.

results in detail (Perren *et al.*, 2012a) as well as in an article reporting and discussing the question of successful responses with cyberbullying (Perren *et al.*, 2012b).

As outlined in Perren *et al.* (2012a, 2012b), we systematically explored empirical findings related to reducing risk, combating cyberbullying and buffering the negative impact on victims (see Figure 7.1).

First, from a preventive perspective, students, parents and schools may try to cope with the emerging problem of cyberbullying by means of reducing known risks. As cyberbullying is strongly associated with traditional bullying (Dooley, Pyzalski, & Cross, 2009; Gradinger, Strohmeier, & Spiel 2009; Sticca, Ruggieri, Alsaker, & Perren, 2013), we may assume that taking action against traditional bullying and associated risk factors through such interventions as whole-school approaches and policies, social skills training or improvement of the school climate could also reduce the risk of cyberbullying. As cyberbullying occurs via the Internet or mobile phone use, it is also associated with general online risks such as risky online contacts or seeing inappropriate content (Livingstone, Haddon, Görzig, & Ólafsson, 2011). Therefore, strategies such as parental mediation or Internet safety measures might also be effective in reducing cyberbullying.

Second, when cyberbullying occurs, a different set of coping strategies to stop these negative behaviors may be applied by students, parents or schools. These strategies include technical solutions (e.g. blocking contact), confronting

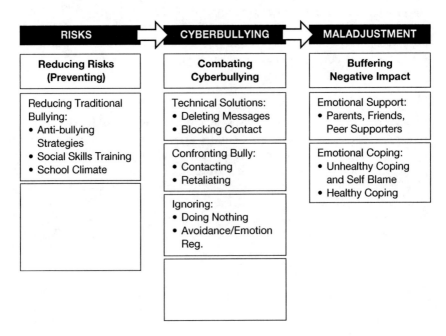

Figure 7.1 Conceptualization of responses to cyberbullying. (Adapted from Perren *et al.*, 2012b)

the bully (e.g. constructive contact or retaliation), ignoring (e.g. doing nothing, avoidant behavior or emotion regulation) and instrumental support (e.g. asking someone else for help).

Third, as cyberbullying has negative consequences for victims (Gradinger *et al.*, 2009; Juvonen & Gross, 2008; Perren, Dooley, Shaw, & Cross, 2010; Sourander *et al.*, 2010), specific coping strategies might also be applied to enhance victims' well-being and to buffer the negative impact. Victims themselves may try to cope emotionally with the problem by adopting individual strategies, which may be healthy or unhealthy strategies. Parents, friends or peers may offer emotional and instrumental support (see also Perren *et al.*, 2012b).

What are "successful" responses?

Our literature review specifically addressed the question of what responses are successful and which coping strategies are used (Perren *et al.*, 2012a, 2012b). Various methodological approaches have been applied, using different study designs and assessment methods and targeting different populations. From a purely methodological point of view, these approaches may range from subjective evaluations to experimental designs. In reviewing the selected studies, we have identified the following taxonomy:

a) What do people, in general, think is effective?
b) Retrospective accounts of cybervictims regarding the success of chosen coping strategies.
c) Cross-sectional studies investigating associations between certain preventive strategies or coping strategies, cybervictimization and victim's well-being.
d) Longitudinal studies investigating whether certain preventive strategies or coping strategies are related to decreasing levels of cybervictimization or victim's well-being.
e) Experimental studies investigating the impact of selected preventive strategies or coping strategies on changes in cybervictimization and victim's well-being.

In our review involving empirical findings published up to the end of 2010, we had to conclude that there is a clear lack of evidence concerning successful responses (Perren *et al.*, 2012a). A few studies reported perceived success, and very few measured the success of the strategies in relation to risks and outcomes. In the meantime, some further studies have been published, which have expanded our knowledge, but still only a few of them yield a strong evidence base. However, awareness of effective and ineffective strategies is essential if schools are to develop programs that are informed by the most up-to-date research findings.

Preventing cyberbullying

In this section, we focus specifically on the research addressing preventive strategies against cyberbullying. The literature on prevention of cyberbullying seems to be broad. However, it predominantly puts forward conclusions about, and implications for, prevention measures rather than actual empirical evidence on the usage and success of such measures (Perren *et al.*, 2012a). There are two different approaches on how to address the issue of cyberbullying prevention. The first one argues that prevention measures should draw upon experience from the prevention of face-to-face bullying (Campbell, 2005; Gradinger, Yanagida, Strohmeier, Stefanek, Schiller, & Spiel, 2012). Specifically, some scholars argue these measures can be extended to prevent cyberbullying without structural changes (Slonje, Smith, & Frisén, 2013). The second approach expands the first one by putting an emphasis on the distinctive nature of the cyberbullying phenomenon and on the need to address this (Tangen & Campbell, 2010). Prevention measures such as parental mediation strategies and education of safe Internet use have been suggested.

General anti-bullying strategies

The prevention strategies used for traditional bullying stress the role of school, specifically teachers who consider the school environment to be important for pupils' protection (DiBasilio, 2008). Several researchers argue that many suggestions concerning teaching, curriculum, and policies which were originally developed for preventing traditional bullying, might be useful for stopping cyberbullying. The main argument for this comes from the fact that cyberbullying is very strongly associated with traditional bullying and only very few students engage only in online forms of bullying and not also in offline bullying (Dehue, Bolman, Völlink, & Pouwelse, 2012; Gradinger *et al.*, 2009; Raskauskas & Stoltz, 2007; Smith, 2011; Smith & Slonje, 2010; Sticca *et al.*, 2013).

Especially, there is an agreement among scholars on the need to train students in developing social skills, which can be done through curriculum programs or special intervention programs (Campbell, 2005; Dranoff, 2008; Mason, 2008). For instance, Gradinger and colleagues (2012), who found support for this approach in their study, provided evidence that a general social competence program to prevent aggressive behavior was also effective in preventing cyberbullying and cybervictimization. Similarly, the evaluation of one general anti-bullying program, KiVa, primarily designed for preventing traditional bullying, showed its positive effect in reducing cyberbullying (Salmivalli, Kärnä, & Poskiparta, 2011).

Media education for young people and parental mediation

But other recent studies have come to a different conclusion – that addressing traditional bullying may not be sufficient for tackling cyberbullying and special attention should be paid to specifics of the phenomena, including technologies used (Campbell, 2005). Students often express their need to see that adult authorities such as parents or teachers understand new technologies and are familiar with cyberbullying (Mishna, Saini, & Solomon, 2009). This goes hand-in-hand with the first recommendation – to heighten awareness of cyberbullying and its consequences among teachers, parents and students (Campbell, 2005; Juvonen & Gross, 2008; Li, 2007; Wright, Burnham, Inman, & Ogorchock, 2009; Young, Young, & Fullwood, 2007). In the literature, there is an emphasis on all the actors and their responsibility for Internet/mobile phone safety (i.e. preventing cyberbullying). This concern is related to results showing that some occurrences of cyberbullying have features (especially the huge audience and anonymity) which may make cyberbullying worse than traditional bullying (Sticca & Perren, 2013).

Specifically, parents should be encouraged to play a greater role in supervising their children's use of technology (Rosen, Cheever, & Carrier, 2008). Some scholars also point out that it is important to take into consideration where the home computer is located (Rosen *et al.*, 2008). On the other hand, the recent large-scale project, EU Kids Online II, did not find any effect of computer location on reducing cyberbullying (Livingstone *et al.*, 2011). Regarding teachers and school education, school curriculum and policy should implement a range of preventive strategies such as direct teaching of values and empathy along with "netiquette" (Campbell, 2005; Dranoff, 2008; Mason, 2008; Stacey, 2009). The term "netiquette" arises from the combination of the words "network" and "etiquette" (Scheuermann & Taylor, 1997) and describes appropriate personal judgment about interpersonal Internet communication (Kumazaki, Suzuki, Katsura, Sakamoto, & Kashibuchi, 2011). Many guidelines on safe Internet use emphasize the role of privacy and warn young people not to publish potentially embarrassing photos or videos on the Internet. Whereas this recommendation is certainly an important cybersafety measure, we have to be aware that it cannot protect children from being bullied. As we have seen that many victims blame themselves for bullying and that self-blame may increase the negative impact of cybervictimization (Machmutow, Perren, Sticca, & Alsaker, 2012), we have to be aware that these kinds of recommendations may even have adverse side effects.

Furthermore, schools should adopt programs for motivating all students, including bystanders, towards taking action against cyberbullying (Campbell, 2005; Stacey, 2009). Finally, the cyberbullying literature stresses the need for empowering children and young people, and making them the key actors in terms of deciding about and implementing prevention strategies and relevant psychosocial interventions (Ybarra & Mitchell, 2004; Young *et al.*, 2007).

To conclude, it seems that traditional anti-bullying programs aimed at systematically tackling cyberbullying, including the participation of students and their parents, might yield fruitful results in terms of preventing cyberbullying or handling it. However, special programs which take into account the specific characteristics of cyberbullying also seem to be needed.

Victims' coping with cyberbullying

This section explores successful and unsuccessful strategies that students use to cope with bullying in general. It also takes account of the impact of the contexts in which such strategies are adopted.

Research evidence indicates that children and young people who are already vulnerable in some way are likely to need support in building up the personal resilience necessary for coping with being bullied by their peers (Frydenberg *et al.*, 2004). Parents and educators need to be sensitive to the young person's feelings of being trapped in a downward spiral in which low self-esteem and interpersonal difficulties can undermine the ability to defend oneself against social exclusion, rejection and intimidation. One outcome is likely to be that the bullied student comes to expect negative treatment from the peer group. Behavior that more resilient students might brush off is therefore experienced even more negatively leading to further victimization, and so the cycle continues (Escobar, Fernández-Baena, Miranda, Trianes, & Cowie, 2011).

It can be difficult to differentiate among the range of possible ways of addressing the problem since the success can be strongly influenced by such factors as the age of the student, their developmental needs and their gender, as well as by the form that the bullying takes, whether it involves social exclusion, physical attacks or online intimidation. Furthermore, the coping mechanism adopted cannot be viewed in isolation from its social context. For example, the response of bystanders can be critical, whether they display indifference to the plight of the victim, actively join the bully or intervene to defend. Younger students are more likely to seek support from adults while adolescents are more likely to seek support from peers. In comparison to girls, adolescent boys prefer to manage the problem themselves in order to enhance their status in the eyes of the peer group (Kochenderfer-Ladd & Skinner, 2002).

Combating cyberbullying through technical and communicative means

Combating cyberbullying covers a wide scale of coping strategies that victims of cyberbullying apply. They range from technical solutions, confronting a bully – including retaliation – and avoidance strategies through seeking instrumental support (Perren *et al.*, 2012b).

Starting with technical solutions, the cyberbullying literature provides evidence that deleting or blocking threatening messages are generally used and considered to be helpful (Aricak *et al.*, 2008; Juvonen & Gross, 2008; Kowalski, Limber, & Agatston, 2008; Livingstone *et al.*, 2011; Smith, Mahdavi, Carvalho, Fisher, Russell, & Tippett, 2008; Stacey, 2009). However, qualitative research on coping with cyberbullying questions the long-term effect of technical solutions. Specifically, victims and students did not consider them helpful in terms of stopping cyberbullying, since the aggressor who wants to bully always find ways to bypass them (Parris, Varjas, Meyers, & Cutts, 2012; Šléglová & Černá, 2011).

Confronting a bully, and mainly retaliation, have received great attention, as characteristics of the Internet, such as anonymity, were thought to encourage victims to retaliate or seek revenge (Perren *et al.*, 2012a). However, Juvonen and Gross' (2008) study showed that, whereas 60 per cent of the cybervictims defended themselves against the bully with traditional face-to-face methods, 12 per cent retaliated only in cyberspace, and 28 per cent used both traditional and cyber forms of retaliation. In contrast to retaliation, non-aggressive confronting of a bully is considered to be constructive and may contribute to reducing cyberbullying. Research seems to be inconsistent regarding the effectiveness of this strategy. While some studies have shown that this strategy could bring about positive outcomes (Huang & Chou, 2010; Parris *et al.*, 2012), Price and Dalgleish (2010) found in their study that confrontation was the least effective. Therefore, greater effort is needed to understand in which context confronting cyberbullying may be effective and helpful.

Doing nothing, or ignoring, is another action that victims may take against cyberbullying. This comprises reactions such as stop looking at websites where the events happened, staying offline or just ignoring (Price & Dalgleish, 2010). Even though this form of response seems to be passive, it was a relatively often-used strategy and was generally proposed by students (Dehue, Bolman, & Völlink; 2008; Hoff & Mitchell, 2009; Livingstone *et al.*, 2011; Price & Dalgleish, 2010; Smith *et al.*, 2008; Wright *et al.*, 2009). Therefore, not surprisingly, the effectiveness of these types of responses has become a subject of several studies. In general, it can be concluded that there is a lack of evidence regarding the success of doing nothing or ignoring what is happening. The cyberbullying research literature documents its ineffectiveness – or rather the fact that many victims do not know what else to do besides adopting this avoidance strategy (Hoff & Mitchell, 2009; Price & Dalgleish, 2010; Šléglová & Černá, 2011).

Emotional coping and seeking support

In addition to (or instead of) problem-oriented coping strategies, victims may use emotion-focused coping strategies which buffer the negative impact as they reduce strong negative emotions such as anger, fear, sadness, helplessness or guilt and other internalizing difficulties (e.g. depression or suicidal ideation) that cybervictimization may evoke (Beran & Li, 2005; Černá, Dědková, Macháčková, Ševčíková, & Šmahel, 2013; Dehue *et al.*, 2008; Hinduja & Patchin, 2010; Livingstone *et al.*, 2011; Perren *et al.*, 2010; Price & Dalgleish, 2010; Völlink, Bolman, Dehue, & Jacobs, 2013).

Seeking support has been generally found to be a very helpful strategy irrespective of the people whom victims confide in (Aricak *et al.*, 2008;

Livingstone *et al.*, 2011; Macháčková, Dědková, Černá, & Ševčíková, 2013; Smith *et al.*, 2008; Stacey, 2009; Topçu, Erdur-Baker, & Capa-Aydin, 2008). However, the cyberbullying literature does not distinguish what kind of support was studied, whether it dealt with instrumental or emotional support, or which type of support victims asked for (Perren *et al.*, 2012a).

To buffer the negative impacts of cyberbullying, victims have been found to seek emotional support, blame themselves or use other unhealthy coping strategies. Machmutow and colleagues (2012) provide sufficient evidence that seeking support from peers and parents is also effective in buffering depressive symptoms that cybervictims report. However, seeking support needs to be a part of the repertoire of coping strategies that individuals use when facing different stressful situations. Specifically, it is apparent that using ineffective coping strategies in daily life leads to their reproduction when facing cyberbullying, which in turn exacerbates depression and health complaints (Völlink *et al.*, 2013). Apart from internalizing difficulties, some cybervictims also incline to externalizing behaviors such as drinking alcohol (26 per cent) and smoking cigarettes (23 per cent) (Ybarra & Mitchell, 2004). Therefore, Völlink and colleagues (2013) stress the need for training children to employ more effective coping strategies which, in addition, should be followed by supportive and close relationships within peer groups and family.

Despite the perceived effectiveness of this coping strategy, the prevalence (and preference) of this behavior has been shown to vary considerably across studies. For instance, cyberbullying research has shown that there are victims who, for various reasons, refrain from seeking support (Juvonen & Gross, 2008). If they do confide in others about cyberbullying incidents, they prefer their peers (Aricak *et al.*, 2008; DiBasilio, 2008; Stacey, 2009; Topcu *et al.*, 2008) to adult authorities such as parents or teachers (Hoff & Mitchell, 2009; Juvonen & Gross, 2008; Li, 2006, 2007; Mishna *et al.*, 2009) who, according to them, lack knowledge about ICT and cyberbullying, or might prefer a simple solution to stop bullying such as banning Internet access or mobile phones (Hoff & Mitchell, 2009; Kowalski *et al.*, 2008; Mishna *et al.*, 2009; Smith *et al.*, 2008; Stacey, 2009). Therefore, according to Livingstone and colleagues (2011), caregivers and teachers should be encouraged to communicate with their children or students about ICT use and safety issues instead of restricting an access to the Internet. Regarding the peer context, Macháčková and colleagues (2013) would add the recommendation that instead of waiting for bystanders' help, victims should try to directly ask onlookers for support. This action has been found to trigger their supportive behaviors towards targets.

As Murray-Harvey, Skrzypiec, and Slee (2012) indicate in their study of coping strategies adopted by 1,223 bullied adolescents in three Australian high schools, students were more likely to try to solve the problem themselves rather than involve another person. One reason for this under-use of available support may have been the students' lack of awareness of the school's anti-bullying policies, poor lines of communication between school and students, and feelings on the part of victims that it would be unsafe to disclose through fear of retaliation by the bully and shaming in the eyes of the peer group. Bullied students reported that they were not likely to use relationship-based interventions, despite the strong advocacy of relationship-based interventions on the part of the informed professionals who were also surveyed in this study about their opinions on the relative effectiveness or ineffectiveness of interventions (for example, restorative justice, peer mediation, peer support, counselling and assertiveness training). The authors concluded that there is a need for much greater dissemination of information about the range of interventions on offer and a need for more training opportunities on how to use them.

Discussion

This chapter has drawn upon a systematic review and analysis of the cyberbullying literature, which was conducted for an extensive two year period (2010–2012). It reports findings in relation to how cyberbullying can be tackled and it specifically discusses evidence on prevention measures and coping strategies.

The literature on prevention appears to be rather prescriptive, making recommendations for prevention measures and foreseeing implications for the future course of cyberbullying. However, there appears to be a lack of evidence on the use of prevention measures and results delivered. This seems to create a gap in the amount of evidence and knowledge available with respect to which measures really work and prevent cyberbullying, in what contexts and circumstances under which conditions, if any. In this sense, the measures suggested by the literature rely either on descriptive, abstract accounts of the individual researcher or on involved actors' subjective and often biased perceptions, and they mostly originate from lessons and experiences of preventing traditional bullying. Regarding the latter, existing accounts offer some limited evidence on the applicability of traditional bullying prevention measures to bullying events in cyberspace. At the same time, the literature points out the challenges that new technologies pose to attempts to apply such traditional measures to new or emerging forms of technologically-mediated bullying. Hence, the literature aiming to make concrete proposals on prevention of cyberbullying appears to be trapped in a relentless struggle to account for and balance between the commonalities and differences of traditional bullying and cyberbullying.

For future research, we recommend that there is a need for a strong evidence base. That is, we need more experimental studies which investigate the impact of specific intervention and prevention strategies on the occurrence of cyberbullying (and at the same time considering that specific cyberbullying prevention does not increase traditional bullying).

As far as victims' coping strategies are concerned, the literature offers evidence on a range of solutions employed by victims to combat cyberbullying, such as technical solutions, retaliation or confronting a cyberbully, seeking support, ignoring, and buffering the negative impact. The available evidence informs us about the effectiveness of such coping strategies and paves the way for examining new, emerging means to combat cyberbullying, and for assessing associated challenges. However, there appears to be a degree of inconsistency and inconclusiveness in the existing evidence, especially with respect to the long-term effects of such solutions and coping strategies. Specifically, the literature does not provide sufficient support to answer questions regarding the long-term effectiveness of technical measures and the ability of technology itself to ensure lasting effects against bullying incidents in cyberspace. Likewise, accounts of strategies such as "doing nothing" or "ignoring" lack evidence on their degree of success and impact. Also, research that examines attempts of the victim to confront the cyberbully has not offered conclusive findings, and so we require further research to understand in which context confronting a cyberbully may be effective and helpful. Similarly, the strategy of seeking support is approached in rather "clunky" terms, with the literature not clearly distinguishing emotional and instrumental support sought by the victim, nor consistently exploring the prevalence of this coping strategy. Future research in this area should also aim to gain a stronger evidence base, in that we need longitudinal studies investigating whether certain coping strategies are related to decreasing levels of cybervictimization or victims' well-being.

Practical implications

The above findings pose questions regarding the current and future research agenda in this evolving and important area, while also directing our attention towards what practitioners should do to counter current and emerging aspects and harmful effects of cyberbullying.

Regarding prevention of cyberbullying, the identified gap regarding the evidence on which measures actually work and successfully prevent cyberbullying – in what contexts, and under what circumstances – requires empirical research alongside community and policy initiatives on implementing preventative measures, testing their applicability and benchmarking their results. To this end, researchers can set the key questions regarding prevention measures and associated challenges, inform on the effects of available or emerging prevention measures, and largely shape the future agenda of related prevention actions and goals accordingly.

At the same time, significant support from the policy and community (or social) forces (e.g. schools, community bodies, family, domestic groupings) is needed. Policy can offer the necessary financial means, regulatory frameworks and infrastructure for testing and benchmarking prevention measures. Socio-community forces can promote the collaboration and engagement of collective bodies and individual actors who have a vested interest in preventing cyberbullying. In reality, what is required are the concerted efforts of key stakeholders and particularly the joint initiatives of researchers, policymakers and socio-community actors, so that on-going and future challenges in the complex and rapidly evolving field of cyberbullying can be addressed early on, at the stage before cyberbullying occurs and when its harmful effects can be prevented.

The generation of tested applicability and effectiveness of prevention measures will also answer the pending question whether such measures ought to be tailored to the particularities of cyberbullying, or whether they are appropriate to deliver the desired results if associated with, and directly derived from, prevention means and techniques applied to traditional bullying. Specifically, conclusions concerning the results delivered from prevention measures could enable scholars and practitioners to assess whether such measures can be of similar structure, content and orientation to those used for preventing traditional bullying, or whether they should embrace features and elements which largely reflect and address the technological and other particularities of bullying occurring in online communication environments.

Regarding coping strategies, it becomes evident that future research should pursue further study into how victims successfully combat cyberbullying. Specifically, research work should focus on the contexts in which coping strategies apply in, and the effects they can account for when diverse contexts and/or actors are involved. Multiple contexts and actors must be considered when assessing coping strategies and their short- or long-term effects. Thus, it is imperative that policymakers and community initiatives mobilize those contexts and the respective actors (i.e. school, neighborhood, family, etc.), facilitating research to obtain a better understanding of how coping strategies take form, are put into action, and deliver results. Furthermore, and independently of future research activity, non-research actors in the field – spanning from official policymakers, police and other authorities, social bodies, community actors, and even domestic or individual actors – should be committed to their own range of efforts directed towards awareness raising, mobilization, training and knowledge enhancement. Then, they can practically assist the spread, optimization and efficient use of existing and future strategies of coping and combating cyberbullying. Industry (e.g. Internet Service Providers, mobile phone companies, social networking sites) also has an important role in provision of technical features to help with management of risks associated with technology and in the education of young people, parents and educators with respect to safe technology use, and indeed there is evidence that many of those in the industry sector are doing this (e.g. self-regulation, 'Corporate Social Responsibility': Coyne & Gountsidou, see Chapter 5 this volume). However, Coyne and Gountsidou suggest that there is a need for industry to support and conform to national and European guidelines of best practice.

Conclusions

Most of the early findings have been in relation to general prevention strategies (e.g. anti-bullying policies or cybersafety strategies) and the use of victims' coping strategies such as seeking support, reactions towards cyberbullies (retaliation or confronting), technical solutions and avoidant and emotion-focused strategies. Whilst a few studies reported on the perceived success of coping strategies, few actually measured the success of the strategies in relation to cyberbullying, its risks and outcomes. The issues regarding the research agenda in this evolving and important area have been explored in the chapter, and attention is directed towards what is known and to what those interested in the area should focus on for current and future research.

References

Aricak, T., Siyahhan, S., Uzunhasanoglu, A., Saribeyoglu, S., Ciplak, S., Yilmaz, N., and Memmedov, C. (2008). 'Cyberbullying among Turkish adolescents'. *CyberPsychology and Behavior, 11,* 253–261.

Beran, T., and Li, Q. (2005). 'Cyber-harassment: A study of a new method for an old behavior'. *Journal of Educational Computing Research, 32,* 265–277.

Campbell, M.A. (2005). 'Cyber bullying: An old problem in a new guise?' *Australian Journal of Guidance and Counselling, 15,* 68–76.

Černá, A., Dědková, L., Macháčková, H., Ševčíková, A., and Šmahel, D. (2013). *Kyberšikana: Průvodce novým fenoménem* [Cyberbullying: a guidebook of the new phenomenon]. Prague: Grada publishing.

Coyne, I., and Gountsidou, V. (2013). 'The role of the industry in reducing cyberbullying'. In P.K. Smith and G. Steffgen, (eds.), *Cyberbullying through the new media: Findings from an international network* (pp. 83–98). Hove: Psychology Press.

Dehue, F., Bolman, C., and Völlink, T. (2008). 'Cyberbullying: Youngsters' experiences and parental perception'. *CyberPsychology and Behavior, 11,* 217–223.

Dehue, F., Bolman, C., Völlink, T., and Pouwelse, M. (2012). 'Cyberbullying and traditional bullying in relation with adolescents' perception of parenting'. *Journal of CyberTherapy and Rehabilitation, 5,* 25–34.

DiBasilio, A. (2008). *Reducing bullying in middle school students through the use of student-leaders.* Unpublished M.A. dissertation, Saint Xavier University, Chicago, Illinois.

Dooley, J.J., Pyżalski, J., and Cross, D. (2009). 'Cyberbullying versus face-to-face bullying: A theoretical and conceptual review'. *Zeitschrift für Psychologie/Journal of Psychology, 217*(4), 182–188.

Dranoff, R. (2008). *Teacher and student perceptions of bullying and victimization in a middle school.* Unpublished Ph.D. dissertation, Dowling College, New York.

Escobar, M., Fernández-Baena, F.J., Miranda, J., Trianes, M.V., and Cowie, H. (2011). 'Low peer acceptance and emotional/behavioural maladjustment in school children: Effects of daily stress, coping and sex'. *Anales de Psicologia, 27,* 412–417.

Frydenberg, E., Lewis, R., Bugalski, K., Cotta, A., McCarthy, C., Luscombe-Smith, N., and Poole, C. (2004). 'Prevention is better than cure: Coping skills training for adolescents at school'. *Educational Psychology in Practice, 20,* 117–134.

Gradinger, P., Strohmeier, D., and Spiel, C. (2009). 'Traditional bullying and cyberbullying: Identification of risk groups for adjustment problems'. *Zeitschrift für Psychologie/Journal of Psychology, 217*(4), 205–213.

Gradinger, P., Yanagida, T., Strohmeier, D., Stefanek, E., Schiller, E.-M., and Spiel, C. (2012). *Prevention of cyberbullying: the evaluation of the ViSC Social Competence Program.* Poster presented at the International Conference: Bullying and Cyberbullying: The Interface between Science and Practice, Vienna, Austria.

Hinduja, S., and Patchin, J. (2010). 'Bullying, cyberbullying, and suicide'. *Archives of Suicide Research, 14*, 206–221.

Hoff, D.L., and Mitchell, S.N. (2009). 'Cyberbullying: Causes, effects, and remedies'. *Journal of Educational Administration, 47*, 652–665.

Huang, Y.Y., and Chou, C. (2010). 'An analysis of multiple factors of cyberbullying among junior high school students in Taiwan'. *Computers in Human Behavior, 26*, 1581–1590.

Juvonen, J., and Gross, E.F. (2008). 'Extending the school grounds? Bullying experiences in cyberspace'. *Journal of School Health, 78*, 496–505.

Kochenderfer-Ladd, B., and Skinner, K. (2002). 'Children's coping strategies: Moderators of the effects of peer victimization?' *Developmental Psychology, 38*, 267–278.

Kowalski, R.M., Limber, S.P., and Agatston, P.W. (2008). *Cyber bullying: Bullying in the digital age.* Malden, MA: Blackwell.

Kumazaki, A., Suzuki, K., Katsura, R., Sakamoto, A., and Kashibuchi, M. (2011). 'The effects of netiquette and ICT skills on school-bullying and cyber-bullying: The two-wave panel study of Japanese elementary, secondary, and high school students'. *Procedia-Social and Behavioral Sciences, 29*, 735–741.

Li, Q. (2006). 'Cyberbullying in schools: A research of gender differences'. *School Psychology International, 27*, 157–170.

——(2007). 'New bottle but old wine: A research of cyberbullying in schools'. *Computers in Human Behavior, 23*, 1777–1791.

Livingstone, S., Haddon, L., Görzig, A., and Ólafsson, K. (2011). 'EU Kids Online final report'. Retrieved March 25, 2013 from http://www2.lse.ac.uk/media@lse/research/EUKidsOnline/EU%20Kids%20II%20(2009-11)/EUKidsOnlineIIReports/Final%20report.pdf

Macháčková, H., Dědková, L., Ševčíková, A., and Černá, A. (2013). 'Bystanders' support of cyberbullied schoolmates'. *Journal of Community and Applied Social Psychology, 23*, 25–36.

Machmutow, K., Perren, S., Sticca, F., and Alsaker, F.D. (2012). 'Peer victimisation and depressive symptoms: Can specific coping strategies buffer the negative impact of cybervictimisation?' *Emotional and Behavioural Difficulties, 17*, 403–420.

Mason, K.L. (2008). 'Cyberbullying: A preliminary assessment for school personnel'. *Psychology in the Schools, 45*, 323–348.

Mishna, F., Saini, M., and Solomon, S. (2009). 'Ongoing and online: Children and youth's perceptions of cyber bullying'. *Children and Youth Services Review, 31*, 1222–1228.

Murray-Harvey, R., Skrzypiec, G. and Slee, P.T. (2012). 'Effective and ineffective coping with bullying strategies as assessed by informed professionals and their use by victimised students'. *Australian Journal of Guidance and Counselling, 22*, 122–138.

Parris, L., Varjas, K., Meyers, J., and Cutts, H. (2012). 'High school students' perceptions of coping with cyberbullying'. *Youth and Society, 44*, 284–306.

Perren, S., Corcoran, L., Cowie, H., Dehue, F., Garcia, D., McGuckin, C., Ševčíková, A., Tsatsou, P., and Völlink, T. (2012a). *Coping with cyberbullying: A systematic literature review* (Unpublished Final Report of the COST IS0801 Working Group 5). Retrieved March 25, 2013 from https://sites.google.com/site/costis0801/books-and-publications-1.

——(2012b). 'Tackling cyberbullying: Review of empirical evidence regarding successful responses by students, parents and schools'. *International Journal of Conflict and Violence, 6*, 283–293.

Perren, S., Dooley, J., Shaw, T., and Cross, D. (2010). Bullying in school and cyberspace: Associations with depressive symptoms in Swiss and Australian adolescents. *Child and Adolescent Psychiatry and Mental Health, 4*, 1–10.

Price, M., and Dalgleish, J. (2010). 'Cyberbullying: Experiences, impacts and coping strategies as described by Australian young people'. *Youth Studies Australia, 29*, 51–59.

Raskauskas, J., and Stoltz, A.D. (2007). 'Involvement in traditional and electronic bullying among adolescents'. *Developmental Psychology, 43*, 564–575.

Rosen, L.D., Cheever, N.A., and Carrier, L.M. (2008). 'The association of parenting style and child age with parental limit setting and adolescent MySpace behavior'. *Journal of Applied Developmental Psychology, 29*, 459–471.

Salmivalli, C., Kärnä, A., and Poskiparta, E. (2011). 'Counteracting bullying in Finland: The KiVa program and its effects on different forms of being bullied'. *International Journal of Behavioral Development, 35*, 405–411.

Scheuermann, L., and Taylor, G. (1997). 'Netiquette'. *Internet Research, 7*, 269–273.

Šléglová, V., and Černá, A. (2011). 'Cyberbullying in adolescent victims: Perception and coping'. *Cyberpsychology: Journal of Psychosocial Research on Cyberspace, 5*. Retrieved March 25, 2013 from http://cyberpsychology.eu/view.php?cisloclanku =2011121901&article=4

Slonje, R., Smith, P.K., and Frisén, A. (2013). 'The nature of cyberbullying, and strategies for prevention'. *Computers in Human Behavior, 29*, 26–32.

Smith, P.K. (2011). 'Why interventions to reduce bullying and violence in schools may (or may not) succeed: Comments on the special section'. *International Journal of Behavioral Development, 35*, 419–423.

Smith, P.K., and Slonje, R. (2010). 'Cyberbullying: The nature and extent of a new kind of bullying, in and out of school'. In S.R. Jimerson, S.M. Swearer, and D.L. Espelage (eds.), *Handbook of bullying in schools: An international perspective* (pp. 249–262). New York: Routledge.

Smith, P.K., Mahdavi, J., Carvalho, M., Fisher, S., Russell, S., and Tippett, N. (2008). 'Cyberbullying: Its nature and impact in secondary school pupils'. *Journal of Child Psychology and Psychiatry, 49*, 376–385.

Sourander, A., Brunstein Klomek, A., Ikonen, M., Lindroos, J., Luntamo, T., Koskelainen, M., Ristari, T., and Helenius, H. (2010). 'Psychosocial risk factors associated with cyberbullying among adolescents: A population-based study'. *Archives of General Psychiatry, 67*, 720–728.

Stacey, E. (2009). 'Research into cyberbullying: Student perspectives on cybersafe learning environments'. *Informatics in Education, 8*, 115–130.

Sticca, F., and Perren, S. (2013). 'Is cyberbullying worse than traditional bullying? Examining the differential roles of medium, publicity, and anonymity for the perceived severity of bullying'. *Journal of Youth and Adolescence, 42*, 739–750.

Sticca, F., Ruggieri, S., Alsaker, F., and Perren, S. (2013). 'Longitudinal risk factors for cyberbullying in adolescence'. *Journal of Community and Applied Social Psychology, 23*, 52–67.

Tangen, D.J., and Campbell, M.A. (2010). 'Cyberbullying prevention: One primary school's approach'. *Australian Journal of Guidance and Counselling, 20*, 225–234.

Topçu, Ç., Erdur-Baker, Ö., and Capa-Aydin, Y. (2008). 'Examination of cyberbullying experiences among Turkish students from different school types'. *CyberPsychology and Behavior, 11*, 643–648.

Völlink, T., Bolman, C.A.W., Dehue, F., and Jacobs, N.C.L. (2013). 'Coping with cyberbullying: differences between victims, bully-victims and children not involved in bullying'. *Journal of Community and Applied Social Psychology, 23*, 7–24.

Wright, V.H., Burnham, J.J., Inman, C.T., and Ogorchock, H.N. (2009). 'Cyberbullying: Using virtual scenarios to educate and raise awareness'. *Journal of Computing in Teacher Education, 26*, 35–42.

Ybarra, M.L., and Mitchell, K.J. (2004). 'Online aggressor/targets, aggressors, and targets: A comparison of associated youth characteristics'. *Journal of Child Psychology and Psychiatry, 45*, 1308–1316.

Young, A., Young, A., and Fullwood, H. (2007). 'Adolescent online victimization'. *Prevention Researcher, 14*, 8–9.

8 Guidelines to prevent cyberbullying

A cross–national review

Mona O'Moore, Donna Cross, Maritta Valimaki, Ana Almeida, Sofia Berne, Gie Deboutte, Hildegunn Fandrem, Dorit Olenik-Shemesh, Tali Heiman, Marjo Kurki, Marta Fulop, Efthymia (Efi) Sygkollitou and Gitte Stald

Introduction

Today, younger and younger users have direct access to the Internet from personal computers and mobile devices, whether at home, school or in public places. As a result, teachers, parents and others who work with children and young people face new challenges in protecting young people from harm. In recent years, a variety of programs and policies have been developed and implemented in an effort to prevent and reduce the problem of cyberbullying in the school environment. These policies and programs have highlighted the use of technology to bully, harass, and intimidate and identified this as unacceptable behaviour. While such initiatives have been helpful, many policy and practice challenges remain, given that cyberbullying can occur both at school and off school premises, as well as overlap with more traditional bullying behaviours, making cyberbullying difficult to address solely by teachers, schools or families.

A working group in COST Action IS0801 investigated how 27 countries are responding to these challenges. A sample of existing guidelines related to ICT use and cyberbullying was surveyed and analyzed. Specifically, the aim was to examine existing national guidelines addressing cyberbullying and safer ICT use in participating COST countries with a view to determine the quality of the guidelines, including an evaluation of their strengths and weaknesses. It was intended that this analysis would reveal and guide good practice for school communities, including teachers, parents and students, to prevent cyberbullying and maintain school safety.

Review of the literature

Given the complexity of bullying behaviours and the social contexts in which they arise, school-based efforts to reduce bullying and cyberbullying are enhanced by using a whole-school approach/health promoting schools model which targets all levels and members of the school community. This approach aims to build a positive and supportive school culture; implement policy and practice to consistently and effectively address bullying behaviour; enhance school staff and students' understandings and skills in relation to these behaviours; and form partnerships between staff, students, families and the wider community to address them.

Student involvement

The active involvement of students enables them to take ownership of school community efforts to prevent bullying, increases the likelihood of their compliance with school policies, ensures that strategies are relevant and engaging for students, and acknowledges that they play a critical role in maintaining a positive school environment and in establishing social norms that discourage bullying and cyberbullying.

While a majority of students do not usually agree with bullying behaviour, many who are aware of bullying or observe it occurring do not take action to support the target or to try and stop the bullying. Instead, student bystanders may directly or inadvertently encourage or support the bullying behaviours of others (Craig, Pepler, & Atlas, 2000; O'Connell, Pepler, & Craig, 1999). Students may choose to not help a target of bullying because of a lack of knowledge or uncertainty about what action to take (Craig et al., 2000; Hazler, 1996), or a fear of becoming the next target of the bullying (Craig & Pepler, 1998; Hazler, 1996). Engaging students to provide peer support is particularly important given that adults' responses to bullying are often felt by targets to be inappropriate or ineffective. Smith and Shu (2000) found that of those students who told a teacher they were bullied, approximately 80 per cent reported the teacher attempted to stop the bullying, while the remainder indicated the teachers took no action.

Improving students' key understandings, skills and competences to prevent and respond to bullying, especially as a bystander, should therefore be an essential element of school action to support students, especially those who do not seek help from school staff. Student response to bullying is associated with their self-esteem (Salmivalli, Kaukiainen, Kaistaniemi, & Lagerspetz, 1999), attitudes towards bullying (Salmivalli & Voeten, 2004), empathy (Gini, Albiero, Benelli, & Altoe, 2007), moral perceptions of bullying (Salmivalli & Voeten, 2004) and social skills (Fox & Boulton, 2005), as well as their expectancies about the outcomes arising from bullying others (Hall, Herzberger, & Skowronski, 1998).

Accordingly, it is recommended that teaching and learning can raise students' awareness about bullying and its harmful effects (Olenik-Shemesh, Heiman, & Eden, 2012), and the rights and responsibilities of all students involved in bullying incidents. Curricula need to provide students with opportunities to develop their social skills and enhance self-esteem. Teaching students strategies to overcome and prevent cyberbullying is an important focus of school action to reduce all types of bullying behaviour. Educating students about technical and cyber safety strategies to prevent, respond to and report cyberbullying is essential, as much cyberbullying behaviour occurs out of sight of adults. A meta-analysis of interventions to prevent cyber abuse found psycho-educational Internet safety programs were effective in increasing students' Internet safety knowledge (Mishna, Cook, Saini, Wu, & MacFadden, 2011).

Students need to be educated about their rights and responsibilities in cyberspace, and encouraged to adopt positive attitudes towards technology and develop good "digital citizenship" skills. Involving students in partnerships with knowledgeable and supportive staff and education services, as well as enhancing student–parent communication about social conflict and bullying issues, will also enable and promote students' ability to prevent and respond to bullying situations.

Families

Given cyberbullying has generally been found to occur more often outside of school hours than during school time (Slonje & Smith, 2008; Smith *et al.*, 2008), developing families' awareness of and skills to address cyberbullying is crucial. Hence opportunities for parents, carers and other family members to increase their knowledge and skills to prevent and respond to all forms of bullying will support schools' efforts to address bullying.

Family functioning and bullying behaviour is closely linked. Students with higher parental support (Wang, Iannotti, & Nansel, 2009) and a good relationship with parents (Aman-Back & Björkqvist, 2007) are less likely to be involved in bullying. Further, parental involvement, including taking an interest in their child's schoolwork, is associated with less bullying behaviour among adolescents (Flouri & Buchanan, 2003). Conversely, poor supervision and lack of attention in the home (Ary *et al.*, 1999; Oliver & Oaks, 1994), parental acceptance of aggressive behaviour (Olweus, 1993), harsh discipline (Ary *et al.*, 1999) and parent modelling of aggressive behaviour (Baldry, 2002; Espelage, Bosworth, & Thomas, 2000) are all associated with bullying behaviour.

Farrington and Ttofi's (2009) meta-analysis suggested that information for parents, such as information about the bullying prevention initiatives at their school, or general tips about bullying, was an important program element related to a decrease in students' bullying others. Parent training, such as information nights, teacher–parent meetings, was significantly associated with a decrease in both student's bullying others and being bullied. Given that cyberbullying has generally been found to occur more outside of school hours, rather than during school (Slonje & Smith, 2008; Smith *et al.*, 2008), developing parent awareness about cyberbullying is crucial and can assist in preventing and responding to cyberbullying.

The parents of students who engage in potentially offensive Internet and mobile phone behaviours are typically less involved with their children's computer and Internet use (Vandebosch & Van Cleemput, 2009). Perpetrators of Internet harassment are also more likely to report a poor emotional bond with their caregiver, as well as more frequent discipline and more infrequent monitoring on the part of their caregiver (Ybarra & Mitchell, 2004). These findings suggest there is a need to communicate with all caregivers to encourage them to employ appropriate strategies to effectively monitor and talk with their child about all forms of bullying including cyberbullying, at times and in locations which maximize their attendance and understanding.

Schools

Creating and maintaining a school environment which supports students' wellbeing and discourages antisocial behaviour is crucial. A supportive school culture provides safety, encourages open communication and positive relationships, and supports a sense of connectedness to school that reduces the risk of bullying. Student perceptions of a safe, positive school culture are associated with reduced likelihood of bullying others (Burns, Cross, Alfonso, & Maycock, 2008; Lee, 2010), whereas not feeling safe at school is a risk factor for being cyberbullied and/or cyberbullying others (Sourander *et al.*, 2010).

Positive relationships enhance school-connectedness, which both contributes to and is fostered by a positive school climate (Waters, 2009). Students who report greater school-connectedness are less likely to bully and cyberbully others (Williams & Guerra, 2007). In contrast, lower levels of school-connectedness are associated with greater frequency of peer harassment (Eisenberg, Neumark-Sztainer, & Perry, 2003). Moreover, students who are bullied, who bully others, or both, are more likely to report a lack of school-connectedness, compared to students with low or no involvement in bullying (Bradshaw, O'Brennan, & Sawyer, 2008; Glew, Fan, Katon, Rivara, & Kernic, 2005). It is therefore important to build school-connectedness by enhancing positive interactions among students, as well as engaging students in school life through positive school and extracurricular activities (Hamilton, Cross, Hall, & Townsend, 2003; McBride, Midford, & James, 1995; McNeely, Nonnemaker, & Blum, 2002).

A positive and supportive school culture communicates the message that bullying is not tolerated, and is supported by clear school policy and consistent school community action to discourage bullying behaviour. School policy and practices are important in reducing bullying (Farrington

& Ttofi, 2009), as they send a strong message to the whole-school community about the school's commitment to providing a safe and supportive school environment, as well as form a basis for positive action and behaviour change. Policy and practice needs to encourage students to report bullying behaviour and enable staff to respond consistently and effectively to these behaviours, so students have confidence that school staff will follow through on reports of bullying, help the person(s) being bullied, and support students who intervene to stop bullying (Craig *et al.*, 2000; O'Connell *et al.*, 1999).

To enhance understanding of and engagement with school policy and practices, these need to be developed in collaboration with all members of the school community, including teaching and non-teaching staff, students, parents and the wider community (Smith & Sharp, 1994). These policies and practices need to be promoted to the whole-school community, implemented consistently and monitored to be effective. The increasing use of technology by students means policy and practice also need to be relevant to and promoted in both online and offline environments.

Teachers

Teachers and other school staff play an important role in contributing to or discouraging bullying and cyberbullying, particularly through the effectiveness and consistency of their response to bullying behaviour among students. Problematically, when bullying behaviours within a school are not acknowledged nor effectively responded to by school staff, it is likely these behaviours will persist and even increase over time (Espelage & Swearer, 2003).

There is also a need for comprehensive professional learning for school staff to enhance their confidence in assisting students with bullying-related matters. Many staff report they feel other teachers at their school need more training to improve their skills related to covert bullying, including cyber (Cross *et al.*, 2009). This training needs to be part of a whole-school response to bullying where the training is linked to the school's bullying-related policy and response plan.

Aspects of teachers' relationships with students, such as their level of supportiveness and warmth, are also related to students' perceptions of the social climate and have an important influence on the bullying behaviour of students (Eisenberg *et al.*, 2003). Students who engage in the perpetration of bullying and cyberbullying as well as students who are the targets of cyberbullying, are more likely to report negative perceptions of their relationships with their teachers and to feel uncared for by their teachers (Bacchini, Esposito, & Affuso, 2009). Poor teacher management of the class (as viewed by students) is associated with a higher likelihood of students bullying others, whereas more effectively-managed classrooms have lower rates of bullying (Roland & Galloway, 2002).

When providing guidelines and training to enhance teachers' ability and confidence to address bullying, developing their knowledge about the forms and functions of technology is also important to enhance their skill in reducing cyberbullying (Hanewald, 2008). School staff appear to be less able to recognize bullying and are more uncertain about how to address bullying involving technology, compared with other forms of bullying (Cross *et al.*, 2009). Some students also report they do not perceive adults at school as being able to help if they were to report cyberbullying to them (Agatston & Limber, 2007).

Aim of the study

Our aim in this study was to use the framework of a health-promoting school to examine existing national guidelines addressing cyberbullying and safer ICT use in participating COST countries. We wished to determine the quality of the guidelines in terms of how comprehensive they are and how they compare to the literature, such as reviewed above. This evaluation will provide greater insight into the strengths and weaknesses of the guidance available to members of the school community in their efforts to prevent cyberbullying behaviour.

Method

Sample

Fifty-four national guidelines created by Government or Non-Government Organizations (NGOs) were gathered by 27 country-members of the COST action on 'Cyberbullying: Coping with negative and enhancing positive uses of new technologies, in relationships in educational settings'. There were 25 European countries: Austria, Belgium, Czech Republic, Denmark, Estonia, Finland, France, Germany, Greece, Hungary, Iceland, Ireland, Italy, Lithuania, Luxembourg, Netherlands, Norway, Poland, Portugal, Slovenia, Spain, Sweden, Switzerland, Turkey, United Kingdom; plus Israel and Australia. These guidelines were judged by representative(s) from the country concerned, on the COST Action Management Committee, to be the two most comprehensive in their countries which dealt with cyberbullying, cyber-safety or bullying in general and which had been developed by a Government Organization or NGO. Stand-alone/one-page advice/tips, or anything that would not be considered a complete resource in itself, were not considered.

The questionnaire

The questionnaire used for the guideline analysis was adapted from Cross *et al.* (2004) and the Australian National Safe Schools Framework (Ministerial

Council on Educational Employment Training and Youth Affairs, 2003). The online questionnaire included two parts: background information with 18 criteria and an extensive array of 159 criteria which targeted four main groups: schools, teachers, young people and parents. For each group, the criteria were divided into four inter-related domains as follows (Cross *et al.*, 2004):

- *Supportive Social Environment:* this refers to anti-bullying ethos in the school, as well as the promotion of positive relationship values and positive uses of technology in social interaction.
- *Proactive Policies, Plans and Practices:* this refers to strategies for preventing and dealing with cyberbullying through school policy and practice.
- *Staff, Student and Parent Key Understandings and Competences:* this refers to structural/technical advice, school curriculum, and whether the guidelines provide suggestions for opportunities and activities to use technology positively.
- *Collaborative School–Family–Community Partnerships:* this refers to whether the guidelines recognize the need for a collaborative effort between students, parents, schools, sectors to address cyberbullying; how well the guidelines provide information about where additional support and resources can be found.

Each criterion was rated on a three-point scale (not at all, somewhat and mostly) according to how well it was addressed by the guidelines, for each group: schools, teachers, young people and parents. Table 8.1 shows the number of criteria within each of the above domains for each of the target groups.

Table 8.1 The number of domain criteria for each target group

Target group	Supportive Social Environment	Proactive Policies	Understandings and Competences	Partnerships	Total number of criteria
Young people	5	3	14	3	25
Parents	6	10	5	4	25
Schools	13	27	26	9	75
Teachers	8	6	13	7	34
TOTAL	*32*	*46*	*58*	*23*	*159*

Procedure and data analysis

An Internet-based survey software was made available (http://www.webropol.com/) to the representative COST members, who scored the two guidelines they were responsible for. The scores for all 54 guidelines were then collated. A descriptive analysis of frequencies and percentages were performed on the ratings (three-point scale) for each of the domain criteria in order to determine the level of their importance. The mean sum of percentages were calculated for the individual domains and the target groups in order to allow a comparison across the domains and target groups as shown in Tables 8.3, 8.6, 8.8 and 8.11.

Results

In presenting the results, attention will first be given to the background information of the guidelines, and next the findings relating to each domain will be presented with attention being given to how well the criteria belonging to the individual domains were addressed for each of the target groups. Due to the high overall number of criteria (159), only some criteria which gained high or low rankings and which are of particular interest, are shown in the tables.

Background information about the guidelines

Of the 54 national guidelines which were reviewed, the most targeted group was parents (n = 41), followed by young people (n = 35), teachers (n = 32), and schools (n = 23). The majority (70.4 per cent) of the guidelines which were analysed belonged to websites. The others were from written resources (24 per cent), school based curriculum material (4 per cent), and audio/visual resources (2 per cent).

Table 8.2 shows the proportion of guidelines scoring on each of the 18 background information criteria. It can be seen that there was an over-representation of guidelines dealing "mostly" with cyber-safety in contrast to cyberbullying. Over a quarter of the guidelines did not provide any definition of cyberbullying and over one-third provided no information on the prevalence of bullying. Also, over half of the guidelines made no reference to the scientific literature relating to cyberbullying.

Table 8.2 Background information about the guidelines (18 criteria); percentages with specific features mostly present, somewhat present, or not at all present

Criteria, Do the guidelines…	Not at all	Somewhat	Mostly
Mainly focus on cyberbullying (CB)?	10.9	54.5	34.5
Mainly focus on cyber-safety?	9.1	14.5	76.4
Mainly focus on bullying (generally)?	54.5	25.5	16.4
Provide prevalence of CB?	38.2	43.6	18.2
Give information on specific harms of CB?	27.3	43.6	29.1
Address the specific feature of anonymity of CB?	25.5	41.8	32.7
Address the specific feature of infinite audience of CB?	21.8	52.7	25.5
Address the specific feature of unlimited access of CB?	21.8	52.7	25.5
Address the specific feature of the lack of authority in cyber space?	43.6	40.0	16.4
Provide a definition of CB?	27.3	25.5	47.3
Refer to literature and research on CB?	52.7	32.7	14.5
Inform on CB occurring on peer to peer networks?	43.6	34.5	18.2
Address CB issues for schools as main target group?	50.9	12.7	27.3
Address CB issues for teachers as main target group?	40.0	23.6	29.1
Address CB issues for young people (school-aged) as main target group?	25.5	27.3	36.4
Address CB issues for parents as main target group?	20.0	27.3	47.3
Use appropriate language for the target groups?	3.6	14.5	81.8
Use appropriate design and marketing for the target groups?	1.8	29.1	69.1

Table 8.3 Percentage of guidelines which address a supportive social environment for schools, teachers, young people and parents

Do the guidelines help create a supportive social environment?	School	Teachers	Young people	Parents
Not at all	29.7	33.9	42.1	25.3
Somewhat	42.5	30.1	34.6	33.5
Mostly	27.8	36.0	23.3	41.2

Scores on domain criteria in the guidelines

1. Supportive social environment

Table 8.3 indicates that the guidelines tended to place the greatest onus on parents, followed by schools, then teachers and finally young people to create a supportive social environment. While three-quarters of the guidelines relate to parents' roles in preventing cyberbullying, only a little more than half of the guidelines relate to young people, even "somewhat".

*   *Schools*: In an effort to develop a supportive social environment to tackle cyberbullying the most frequently cited method involving schools was the need for them "to raise student awareness about their rights and responsibilities to report and resolve cyberbullying". Frequently addressed also were rewarding and modelling positive use of technology for social interaction and raising student awareness that they have a responsibility to seek help to resolve cyberbullying incidents. See Table 8.4 and the emphasis placed on these recommendations.

    Table 8.4 shows that there was also a lack of strong emphasis on empowering the peer group to prevent and tackle cyberbullying. Over one-third of guidelines made no mention of the encouragement of peer influence to discourage cyberbullying and only one in six did so "mostly". Also frequently omitted was the development of programs or the implementation of strategies to empower students to participate in a positive school culture, for example, through peer support systems. The use of cooperative learning methods to promote pro-social behaviour was omitted by as many as 43.5 per cent of the guidelines, with only 21.7 per cent achieving a rating of 'mostly'.
*   *Teachers:* The most widely cited recommendation relating to the role of teachers (46.9 per cent mostly; 34.4 per cent somewhat) was raising student awareness about their rights and responsibilities to seek help to resolve cyberbullying incidents. Many of the guidelines referred to the role of teachers in modelling appropriate social behaviour for students (31.8 per cent mostly; 43.8 per cent somewhat) and "to promote positive ways of using technology for social interaction" (50.0 per cent mostly; 25.0 per cent somewhat).

Table 8.4 Guidelines for schools: percentage addressing selected criteria of a supportive social environment

Criteria of a supportive social environment	Not at all	Somewhat	Mostly
Reward or encourage the positive use of technology for social interaction	17.4	43.5	39.1
Model the positive use of technology for social interaction	17.4	56.5	26.1
Raise student awareness that they have the responsibility to seek help to resolve cyberbullying incidents	8.7	39.1	52.2
Use the peer group to provide support for students who are cyberbullied	34.8	47.8	17.4
Use encouragement or positive recognition to manage student behaviour	34.8	39.1	26.1
Ensure school leadership is committed to a shared vision of a positive and inclusive school	34.8	47.8	17.4

Less emphasis was placed on "using cooperative learning methods to promote pro-social behaviour" (25.0 per cent mostly; 34.4 per cent somewhat) and "using encouragement and positive recognition to manage student cyberbullying behaviour" (25.0 per cent mostly; 31.3 per cent somewhat). The least cited recommendation for teachers was the need for them to "help the peer group use positive peer pressure to discourage cyberbullying" (25.0 per cent mostly; 28.1 per cent somewhat).

- *Young people*: From Table 8.5, it can be seen that the guidelines gave greater consideration to young people taking responsibility to help resolve cyberbullying incidents than they did to the need to show leadership in addressing the behaviour.

- *Parents*: Analysis of the criteria directed at parents showed that all but 4.9 per cent of the guidelines stated the need for parents to raise their children's awareness that they have the right to seek help to resolve cyberbullying incidents (58.5 per cent mostly; 36.6 per cent somewhat), and positively manage their children's online social behaviours (46.3 per cent mostly; 48.8 per cent somewhat). In contrast, only half the guidelines (22.5 per cent mostly; 27.5 per cent somewhat) cited the need for parents to encourage and help children to support victims of cyberbullying. Least cited was the need for parents to have their children use positive peer pressure to discourage cyberbullying (14.6 per cent mostly; 22.0 per cent somewhat).

Table 8.5 Guidelines for young people: percentage addressing criteria of a supportive social environment

Criteria of a supportive social environment	Not at all	Somewhat	Mostly
Take responsibility to help to resolve cyberbullying incidents	20.0	45.7	34.3
Use positive peer pressure to discourage cyberbullying	41.2	38.2	20.6
Show leadership promoting the positive uses of technology and cyberbullying	45.7	37.1	17.1
Show leadership in addressing cyberbullying	57.1	25.7	17.1
Support young people who are cyberbullied	28.6	37.1	34.3

2. Proactive policies, plans and practices

From Table 8.6, it can be seen that the guidelines placed considerably stronger emphasis on developing and maintaining proactive policies, plans and practices which targeted young people, than on those aimed at parents, teachers and schools.

- *Schools:* Of the 27 criteria which addressed the issue of developing policies emphasizing the role of schools, the most widely cited criterion overall was the need to "promote consistent messages about cyberbullying prevention and management across the home, school and community" (27.3 per cent mostly; 59.1 per cent somewhat). Also widely held was the need to "identify, assess and develop skills required by staff, students and parents to manage cyberbullying behaviour" (13.6 per cent mostly; 68.3 per cent somewhat). Cited as often, although the emphasis differed (36.4 per cent mostly; 45.5 per cent somewhat), was the need for schools to "treat reports of cyberbullying seriously and with clear consistent action". Also included widely with only 22.7 per cent of guidelines omitting reference to them were the first four criteria listed in Table 8.7. However, the last two criteria in Table 8.7 were overlooked by a majority of the guidelines and deemed important by less than one in ten, namely to "conduct a periodic evaluation of survey data to inform future planning" and to provide a "statement about the rights and responsibilities of all members of the school community, including visitors to address cyberbullying prevention".

Table 8.6 Percentage of guidelines which address proactive policies, plans and practices for cyberbullying prevention for schools, teachers, young people and parents

Do the guidelines help...develop and update proactive policies plans and practices?	School	Teachers	Young people	Parents
Not at all	33.3	40.8	18.8	22.2
Somewhat	46.7	33.5	30.2	37.6
Mostly	19.9	25.7	51.0	40.2

Table 8.7 Guidelines for schools: percentage addressing selected criteria for proactive policies, plans and procedures

Criteria for proactive policies, plans and procedures	Not at all	Somewhat	Mostly
Consistently involve and value the participation of the whole-school community to address cyberbullying	22.7	50.0	27.3
Engage support from parents to reduce and manage cyberbullying	22.7	50.0	27.3
Implement procedures to identify cyberbullying incidents early and proactive responses to discourage cyberbullying	22.7	59.1	18.2
Implement procedures to ensure students are able to seek immediate help when cyberbullying is witnessed or experienced	22.7	54.5	22.7
Conduct a periodic evaluation of this survey data to inform future planning	68.2	22.7	9.1
A statement about the rights and responsibilities of all members of the school community, including visitors, to address cyberbullying	57.1	38.1	4.8

- *Teachers*: Examining the six criteria in the domain of policy development, plans and practices for teachers, the most frequently mentioned (45.2 per cent mostly; 25.8 per cent somewhat) was the need "to treat reports of cyberbullying seriously and with clear consistent action". The next most cited criterion for best practice was "providing appropriate monitoring and supervision of students' use of technology". However, overlooked by 40.6 per cent of the guidelines was the recommendation that teachers pursue the development of their own skills to effectively intervene in cyberbullying situations, and 37.5 per cent made no mention of the importance of having teachers evaluate their actions to discourage and manage student cyberbullying. Least cited, and omitted by 56.3 per cent of the guidelines, was the recommended practice of "clearly documenting procedures and outcomes for managing cyberbullying incidents to monitor their effectiveness and inform possible modification". Also omitted by 46.9 per cent of the guidelines was the recommendation "to use positive approval, praise and encouragement to modify cyberbullying behaviours"; only 12.5 per cent gave it adequate attention.

- *Young people*: Guidelines directed at young people dealing with policy issues reflected that building online skills was a top concern. Digital citizenship was cited by 91.5 per cent of guidelines although only 42.9 per cent of them addressed it well. "Developing principles of netiquette when socializing online" in contrast, while not quite so widely cited (82.4 per cent) was given greater emphasis with 60.0 per cent of guidelines addressing it 'mostly'. Yet, a quarter of the guidelines (25.7 per cent) for young people made no reference to the need for them to develop cyberbullying preventative skills.
- *Parents*: Of the ten criteria pertaining to parents the one most widely cited (57.5 per cent mostly; 35.0 per cent somewhat) was "talking with their children about seeking help if they are cyberbullied". This was followed by "learn ways (relational and technical) to prevent and deal with cyberbullying". The criterion least mentioned was "helping their children to deal with cyber incidents involving other agencies/services and relevant specialists as appropriate".

3. Help improve understandings and competences

Table 8.8 shows that the guidelines directed at parents, and then young people, paid the most attention to developing understandings and competences of cyberbullying. The least attention given to this key area were the guidelines directed at teachers, with over one-third omitting to make any reference to it.

Table 8.8 Percentage of guidelines which address understandings and competences for cyberbullying prevention for schools, teachers, young people and parents

Do the guidelines help...provide understandings and competences?	School	Teachers	Young people	Parents
Not at all	29.9	39.7	30.3	28.9
Somewhat	44.8	25.8	31.1	32.1
Mostly	25.3	34.4	38.6	38.9

- *Schools:* All the guidelines directed at schools included reference to the need "to develop protective strategies including help-seeking behaviours". However, the emphasis varied with only 30.4 per cent addressing it "mostly" and 69.6 per cent somewhat. The second most cited criterion, with only 4.3 omissions, was "enabling students to report abuse" (52.2 per cent mostly; 43.5 per cent somewhat). Also frequently cited, with only 13 omissions, was the need for schools to "have students create positive healthy relationships online and to develop cooperativeness, empathy and respect".

  Most overlooked by the guidelines (66.7 per cent), with only 4.8 per cent addressing it "mostly" was the criterion of "helping students who cyberbully others to use their leadership or peer skills in more positive ways". Little consideration was given also to the teaching of conflict resolution (9.1 per cent mostly; 22.7 per cent somewhat) and having students differentiate between assertiveness and aggression (13.6 per cent mostly; 22.7 per cent somewhat).

- *Teachers:* Of the 13 criteria addressing the need for teachers to raise student understanding and competence in preventing and dealing with cyberbullying, the most cited was "encouraging and helping students positively use technology for social interaction" (53.3 per cent mostly; 23.3 per cent somewhat). While different types of online activities were included, the most cited were instant messaging and social networking technology and least mentioned were online gaming and blogs.

  Table 8.9 shows the relatively limited emphasis placed on having teachers use curriculum and classroom activities to foster a greater understanding of cyberbullying among students. The least cited criterion was that of teachers encouraging and helping students who engage in cyberbullying behaviour to use their leadership/peer skills in more positive ways. Over half of the guidelines omitted any reference to the recommendation and only one in six addressed it well.

Table 8.9 Guidelines for teachers: percentage addressing selected criteria of the development of understandings and competences

Criteria of the development of understandings and competences	Not at all	Somewhat	Mostly
Use curriculum activities that foster positive social behaviour among students and between students and teachers	38.7	25.8	35.5
Use learning activities that actively engage students in developmentally appropriate ways to address cyberbullying	41.9	25.8	32.5
Use the classroom situation, the curriculum and their knowledge of students, to help those who are cyberbullied	54.8	22.6	22.6

- *Young people*: The majority of guidelines (88.6 per cent) addressed the development of technical skills and knowledge to prevent cyberbullying and the seeking of support from parents to prevent and/or deal with cyberbullying. Also ranked highly (42.9 per cent mostly; 42.9 per cent somewhat) was the need to develop technical skills and knowledge to help them deal with cyberbullying (e.g. reporting to service providers or site administrators, how to block a person who is bullying, saving evidence of cyberbullying). In addition, most guidelines addressed the need for young people "to develop/practice the skills to manage cyberbullying behaviour" (42.0 per cent mostly; 42.9 per cent somewhat) and also "to seek support from teachers to prevent and/or deal with cyberbullying" (37.1 per cent mostly; 45.7 per cent somewhat). However, less emphasis was placed on seeking support from peers (22.9 per cent mostly; 40.0 per cent somewhat). The emphasis placed on the different online activities was similar for young people as for teachers. Least attention was given to blogs and online gaming, with 48.6 per cent and 54.3 per cent respectively giving no consideration to them.
- *Parents*: Most widely cited by the guidelines directed at parents as with those aimed at young people was that of improving technical skills to prevent cyberbullying; see Table 8.10. This table also shows that much emphasis was placed on the criteria of how to deal with and report incidents of cyberbullying as well as how to act safely online. Least cited of all the criteria and omitted by 45 per cent of guidelines was that of parents helping their children if they cyberbully others to develop more appropriate ways of behaving online.

Table 8.10 Guidelines for parents: percentage addressing selected criteria of the development of understanding and competences

Criteria of the development of understandings and competences	Not at all	Somewhat	Mostly
Parents improving their technical skills about privacy settings on social networking profiles	20.0	32.5	47.5
Dealing with cyberbullying technically and reporting it to service providers	22.5	32.5	45.0
Understanding the modes of technology used to communicate positively and negatively	22.5	35.0	42.5

4. Collaborative school–family–community partnerships

Examination of the criteria which addressed the key area of school–family–community collaborative partnerships showed that the guidelines placed more emphasis on young people to develop positive relationships than they did on parents, teachers and schools; see Table 8.11.

Table 8.11 Percentage of guidelines which address collaborative school–family–community partnerships for schools, teachers, young people and parents

Do the guidelines help…create and maintain collaborative school–family–community partnerships?	School %	Teachers %	Young people %	Parents %
Not at all	36.7	36.5	22.1	40.0
Somewhat	33.5	45.7	30.5	41.3
Mostly	29.8	17.8	47.4	18.7

- *Schools:* While over one-third of the guidelines pertaining to schools made no reference to the need for them to develop collaborative relationships, it was found that of those that did the most cited of the nine relevant criteria were "collaborating with parents to ensure that they are involved in the whole school planning process" (31.8 per cent mostly; 36.4 per cent somewhat), and "seeking further information and resources to develop a whole-school policy and procedures to address cyberbullying" (36.4 per cent mostly; 31.8 per cent somewhat). However, over one-third of guidelines saw no merit in recommending that schools "use many channels of communication to promote parent participation and knowledge of school action to reduce cyberbullying" (22.7 per cent mostly; 40.9 per cent somewhat) or that they "seek further information about cyberbullying professional development opportunities for teachers" (36.4 per cent mostly; 27.3 per cent somewhat). Least cited and omitted from 42.9 per cent of the guidelines was the need for schools to contact parents of students involved in cyberbullying; only 19 per cent of guidelines addressed this criterion well. Critical elements such as those shown in Table 8.12 were also overlooked by 40.9 per cent of the guidelines and with less than a third addressing them 'mostly'.
- *Teachers:* The guidelines aimed at teachers, similar to those aimed at schools, tended to undervalue the importance of developing collaborative school–family–community partnerships. The most cited, but only by 68.7 per cent of guidelines (18.7 per cent mostly; 50.0 per cent somewhat), was the need to "build close cooperation with parents and the school administration". Increasing parent awareness of cyberbullying and ways to prevent or deal with it was cited by 66.7 per cent of guidelines (20.0 per cent mostly; 46.7 per cent somewhat). Overlooked by as many as 40.6 per cent of guidelines was an emphasis on teachers "to seek further information about cyberbullying professional development opportunities for teachers" (15.6 per cent mostly; 43.6 per cent somewhat). Least cited was the need for teachers "to increase community awareness of cyberbullying and ways to prevent and deal with the behaviour" (15.6 per cent mostly, 40.6 per cent somewhat).

Table 8.12 Guidelines for schools: percentage addressing selected criteria of collaborative school–family–community partnerships

Criteria of collaborative school–family–community partnerships	Not at all	Somewhat	Mostly
Provide families with information about school policies and procedures related to cyberbullying	40.9	31.8	27.3
Engage where needed the assistance of community professionals	40.9	27.3	31.8
Provide professional learning for parents and other members of the school community	40.9	36.4	22.7
Ensure parents have access to community-based resources and information to help build effective relationships and other positive social behaviour in their children	40.9	31.8	27.3

Table 8.13 Guidelines for young people: percentage addressing criteria of developing collaborative school–family–community partnerships

Criteria of collaborative school–family–community partnerships	*Not at all*	*Somewhat*	*Mostly*
Report cyberbullying to school staff or trusted adults	20.0	20.0	60.0
Seek further online information or resources	17.1	40.0	42.9
Seek further information or resources through professional services such as a phone helpline	26.5	35.3	38.2

- *Young people*: From Table 8.13 it can be seen that "reporting cyberbullying to school staff or trusted adults", while not the most widely cited of the three relevant criteria overall, was the one most strongly recommended in the guidelines.
- *Parents*: As was shown in Table 8.11, there was little emphasis placed on parents to develop collaborative relationships. However, of the guidelines which did address the four relevant criteria, the most widely cited was that of seeking further information, resources or details through additional cyberbullying website links (24.4 per cent mostly, 53.7 per cent somewhat). Such important criteria as "establishing close cooperation with their children's teachers and school" and "developing positive strategies to deal with cyberbullying in collaboration with teachers/ schools" were mentioned by just 58.6 per cent of the guidelines, with

22.0 per cent and 14.6 per cent respectively addressing them well. Cited least, by only 47.5 per cent of guidelines with just 15.0 per cent emphasizing it strongly, was "seeking out information about school policies and procedures around cyberbullying".

Discussion

This analysis of national European, Australian and Israeli guidelines demonstrates both strengths and weaknesses in their promotion of best practice in relation to school ethos, policies and programs, understandings and competences, and collaborative partnerships; elements which are all key in the prevention of cyberbullying. The greater focus of the guidelines on cyber-safety may account, of course, for some of the differences in emphasis which were found.

Supportive school environment

Clearly recognizing the need for schools to provide a supportive school environment to reduce the risk of bullying (Sourander *et al.*, 2010), overall the guidelines placed considerable emphasis on raising student awareness of cyberbullying across all the target groups, (schools, teachers, young people and parents), but only in relation to the right and responsibility of students to seek help to resolve cyberbullying. The guidelines tended to be deficient in encouraging young people to develop leadership skills to support victims and in using positive peer pressure to discourage cyberbullying. For example, over 63 per cent of guidelines directed at parents failed to mention this. Also one-third of guidelines directed at schools made no reference to the need to develop programs and strategies which empowered young people to participate in a positive school culture. Peer support systems have been questioned for their effectiveness by Farrington and Ttofi (2009); but well-designed systems have been found to increase students' sense of self-responsibility and provide training in the much needed areas of interpersonal, social and conflict resolution skills (Cowie & Smith, 2010; Smith, Salmivalli, & Cowie, 2012). Omitted also by almost half the guidelines was the promotion of cooperative group work, which has been shown to increase levels of acceptance and respect for other students (Farrington & Ttofi, 2009).

Proactive policies, programs and procedures

The complex nature of many bullying incidents, traditional and cyber (Kaltiala-Heino, Rimpela, Rantanen, & Rimpela, 2000), is such that the support from external professional agencies can make a real difference to a school's effort to prevent and reduce the level of bullying (O'Moore, 2004). Yet again over half the guidelines overlooked recommending schools to establish and nurture such links. To seek help from external agencies was also the most overlooked aspect for parents.

Assessing the quality of the guidelines to address the important need to develop and maintain proactive policies, plans and programs showed that there was good endorsement of the need promoted by Mishna *et al.* (2010) to have young people use technology for positive social interaction as well as exercising the principles of "netiquette" when socializing online. Also recognized widely by the guidelines was the need for parents to talk to their children about seeking help when they are cyberbullied and importantly to treat their reports with consistent positive responses. A key challenge for any psycho-educational program is to address the strong reluctance on the part of young people to tell of their own or of their peers' victimization (Livingstone, Haddon, Görzig, & Ólafsson, 2011).

Encouraging also was the attention given to the promotion of a whole school community approach (Farrington & Ttofi, 2009). The need to promote consistent messages about cyberbullying prevention and management across the whole-school community was well addressed. Also highly valued was the recommendation to have schools/teachers treat reports of cyberbullying seriously and with clear consistent action. However, considering the limitations of punitive approaches to address bullying (O'Moore, 2010; Rigby & Bauman, 2009) few guidelines encouraged the use of positive measures to modify cyberbullying behaviour. For example, nearly half the guidelines overlooked the importance of using positive approval, praise and encouragement to modify cyberbullying behaviours. Greater emphasis should be placed on minimizing punitive responses to bullying behaviours (Skiba & Peterson, 2000). Restorative approaches, with an emphasis on recognition of hurt but also on constructive and rehabilitative measures, are increasingly being used in schools and may be more effective than punitive measures when dealing with bullying behaviour (Cowie & Jennifer, 2007).

A further failure of many of the guidelines (40 per cent) was the scant attention given to the need for comprehensive professional training for teachers in order to enhance their skills to effectively manage cyberbullying. In addition, there was little onus placed on schools or teachers to document procedures and outcomes and evaluate the effectiveness of their policies and programs, despite evidence that documentation of cases can reduce bullying of individuals (Flygare *et al.*, 2011).

Understandings and competences

The importance of improving understandings and competences in efforts to combat bullying has been clearly demonstrated by Spiel and Strohmeier (2011). However, the guidelines assessed in this study were somewhat disappointing in their lack of strong emphasis on this key area, tending to push the responsibility more onto the parents to both increase their technical skills as well as their ability to deal with and report negative behaviours to service providers. However, nearly half the guidelines aimed at parents failed to press upon them the need to have their children who cyberbully develop more appropriate ways of behaving online. Of the guidelines aimed at schools, most frequently cited was the need "to develop protective strategies including self-seeking behaviours". However, while schools were encouraged to develop cooperative behaviour, empathy and respect among their students, in a similar vein to the parent guidelines, there was little encouragement to help students who cyberbully to learn new ways of behaving. Valuable opportunities were also lost in not recommending the use of the school curriculum to address prejudice, discrimination and anti-social behaviour (for example, 'Action Plan on Bullying: Report of the Anti-Bullying Working Group to the Minister of Education and Skills', Ruairi Quinn, Department of Education and Skills, Ireland, 20th January, 2013), as well as teaching skills of conflict resolution and indeed the differences between assertiveness and aggression.

School–family community partnerships

In addressing the school, family and community partnerships, the guidelines varied in the emphasis they placed on this key component for schools, teachers, young people and parents. Reviews of anti-bullying programs (Farrington & Ttofi, 2009) have shown the value of engaging fully with parents in order to have a shared understanding of what bullying is, its impact and how to deal with it. As cyberbullying is more prevalent out of school than in school (Smith, 2010) it is to be expected that parents play an important role in reducing this behaviour. However, many guidelines aimed at schools did not live up to "best practice" of involving parents in the whole school planning process. Many of them (over 40 per cent) overlooked the need to: a) provide professional training to parents; b) describe school policies and procedures related to cyberbullying; and c) contact them when their children are involved in cyber-training. This reflects an incomplete understanding of the meaning of a school/community-wide approach to tackling cyberbullying. Similarly, the guidelines directed at parents often failed to recommend that they should seek out relevant information from schools to help them become better informed of school policies and procedures. Instead, parents were faced with a lack of guidance in how to find relevant information about cyber behaviour.

Limitations

One limitation of this cross-national review of guidelines is the lack of qualitative data on the reasons for the omissions or the differences in the emphasis of the different criteria. An area for future research would be to fill this gap in future evaluations of guidelines. With information of this nature it will be easier to develop or promote guidelines which contain criteria which meet evidence based "best practice" and which in addition are culturally sensitive.

Implications for future research and practice

The analysis of available guidelines on cyberbullying in Europe, Israel and Australia, showed that they contain many fitting recommendations for schools, teachers, young people and parents to draw on in order to better prevent and respond effectively to all the risks associated with electronic communication. However, this analysis also indicated that important strategies to prevent and respond to bullying, as suggested by the bullying literature, were omitted from the guidelines, and other strategies would benefit from being given greater emphasis in future guidelines.

In view of the lack of evidence to date of the effectiveness of different strategies to prevent cyberbullying (see also Chapter 7), it was to be expected that the guidelines would suffer from some lack of scientific knowledge. However, they did reflect the need for schools to take a whole school community approach to preventing and countering cyberbullying, although certain elements associated with the approach were omitted or given scant attention, e.g. parent training, teacher training and cooperative group work.

The challenge for future guidelines, as highlighted by this analysis, would be in placing a greater emphasis on all members of the school community, including teachers, parents and students, to collaborate in the prevention of cyberbullying. Rather than one partner having sole responsibility in understanding and addressing online risks, schools need to take a greater leadership role and collaborate with staff, students and parents in developing and implementing appropriate policies, programs and procedures. These need to be communicated to all members of a school community using both face-to-face and online training opportunities. In this way, cyberbullying becomes a shared responsibility, with all members of the school community not only appreciating that they have a role in preventing and dealing with bullying but, importantly, ensuring that they have the necessary understanding and competences to do so effectively.

However, of all the recommendations made, the one that must be included in future guidelines is that schools, teachers and parents encourage and facilitate young people taking their own, active role in discouraging cyberbullying and supporting those who they witness becoming victims of it. Clearly, for this to happen provision will need to be made for young people to develop good Internet safety skills and coping strategies so that they know not only when to intervene but how to do so effectively.

Further recommendations which arose from this analysis and which are directed specifically at schools, teachers, young people and parents have been detailed in our booklet, 'Guidelines for preventing cyberbullying in the school environment: a review and recommendations'. This is available to download at http://sites.google.com/site/costis0801/.

References

Agatston, P.W., and Limber, S. (2007). 'Students' perspectives on cyber bullying'. *Journal of Adolescent Health, 41*, S59–S60.

Aman-Back, S., and Björkqvist, K. (2007). 'Relationship between home and school adjustment: children's experiences at ages 10 and 14'. *Perceptual and Motor Skills, 104*, 965–974.

Ary, D., Duncan, T., Biglan, A., Metzler, C., Noell, J., and Smolkowski, K. (1999). 'Development of adolescent problem behaviour'. *Journal of Abnormal Child Psychology, 27*(2), 141–150.

Bacchini, D., Esposito, G., and Affuso, G. (2009). 'Social experience and school bullying'. *Journal of Community and Applied Social Psychology, 19*, 17–32.

Baldry, A. (2002). 'Bullying in schools and exposure to domestic violence'. *Child Abuse and Neglect, 27*(7), 713–732.

Bradshaw, C.P., O'Brennan, L.M., and Sawyer, A.L. (2008). 'Examining variation in attitudes toward aggressive retaliation and perceptions of safety among bullies, victims, and bully/victims'. *Professional School Counseling, 12*(1), 10–21.

Burns, S., Cross, D., Alfonso, H., and Maycock, B. (2008). 'Predictors of bullying among 10–11 year old school students in Australia'. *Advances in School Mental Health Promotion, 1*(2), 49–60.

Cowie, H., and Jennifer, D. (2007). *Managing violence in Schools: A whole-school approach to best practice.* London: Paul Chapman.

Craig, W., and Pepler, D. (1998). 'Observations of bullying and victimization in the school yard'. *Canadian Journal of School Psychology, 13*(2), 41–60.

Craig, W.M., Pepler, D., and Atlas, R. (2000). 'Observations of bullying in the playground and in the classroom'. *School Psychology International, 21*(1), 22–36.

Cross, D., Pintabona,Y., Hall, M., Hamilton, G., and Erceg, E. (2004). 'Validated guidelines for school-based bullying prevention and management'. *International Journal of Mental Health Promotion, 6*(3),34–42.

Cross, D., Shaw, T., Hearn, L., Epstein, M., Monks, H., Lester, L., and Thomas, L. (2009). 'Australian Covert Bullying Prevalence Study (ACBPS)'. Western Australia: Report prepared for the Department of Education, Employment and Workplace Relations (DEEWR).

Eisenberg, M.E., Neumark-Sztainer, D., and Perry, C.L. (2003). 'Peer harassment, school connectedness, and academic achievement'. *Journal of School Health, 73*(8), 311–316.

Espelage, D.L., and Swearer, S. (2003). 'Research on school bullying and victimization: What have we learned and where do we go from here?' *School Psychology Review, 32*(3), 365–383.

Espelage, D., Bosworth, K., and Thomas, S. (2000). 'Examining the social context of bullying behaviours in early adolescence'. *Journal of Counseling and Development, 78*(3), 326–333.

Farrington, D.P., and Ttofi, M.M. (2009). 'School-based programs to reduce bullying and victimization'. *Campbell Systematic Reviews.* Oslo: The Campbell Collaboration.

Flouri, E., and Buchanan, A. (2003). 'The role of mother involvement and father involvement in adolescent bullying behavior'. *Journal of Interpersonal Violence, 18*, 634–644.

Flygare, E., Frånberg, G.-M., Gill, P., Johansson, B., Lindberg, O., Osbeck, C., and Söderström, A. (2011). *Evaluation of anti-bullying methods.* Stockholm: Swedish National Agency for Education.

Fox, C.L., and Boulton, M.J. (2005). 'The social skills problems of victims of bullying: Self, peer and teacher perceptions'. *British Journal of Educational Psychology,* 75, 313–328.

Gini, G. (2006). 'Bullying as a social process: The role of group membership in students' perception of inter-group aggression at school'. *Journal of School Psychology,* 44(1), 51–65.

Gini, G., Albiero, P., Benelli, B., and Altoe, G. (2007). 'Does empathy predict adolescents' bullying and defending behavior?'. *Aggressive Behavior, 33,* 467–476.

Glew, G., Fan, M., Katon, W., Rivara, F., and Kernic, M. (2005). 'Bullying, psychosocial adjustment and academic performance in elementary school'. *Archives of Pediatric and Adolescent Medicine, 159*(11), 1026–1031.

Hall, J.A., Herzberger, S.D., and Skowronski, K.J. (1998). 'Outcome expectancies and outcome values as predictors of children's aggression'. *Aggresive Behavior, 24,* 439–454.

Hamilton, G., Cross, D., Hall, M., and Townsend, E. (2003). 'The role of extra-curricular activities in reducing smoking among adolescents: Final report'. Western Australian Centre for Health Promotion Research, School of Public Health, Curtin University of Technology: Perth, Western Australia.

Hanewald, R. (2008). 'Confronting the pedagogical challenge of cyber safety'. *Australian Journal of Teacher Education, 33*(3), 1–16.

Hazler, R.J. (1996). 'Bystanders: An overlooked factor in peer on peer abuse'. *Journal for the Professional Counselor, 11*(2), 11–21.

Kaltiala-Heino, R., Rimpela, M., Rantanen, P., and Rimpela, A. (2000). 'Bullying at school – an indicator of adolescents at risk for mental disorders'. *Journal of Adolescence, 23,* 661–674.

Lee, C-H. (2010). 'An ecological systems approach to bullying behaviours among middle school students in the United States'. *Journal of Interpersonal Violence,* 26(8), 1664–1693. *iFirst.* doi: DOI: 10.1177/0886260510370591

Livingstone, S., Haddon, L., Görzig, A., and Ólafsson, K. (2011). *EU kids online: Final report.* London: London School of Economics and Political Science.

McBride, N., Midford, R., and James, R. (1995). 'Structural and management changes that encourage schools to adopt comprehensive health promotion programs'. *Health Promotion Journal of Australia, 5*(1), 17–23.

McNeely, C.A., Nonnemaker, J.M., and Blum, R.W. (2002). 'Promoting school connectedness: Evidence from the national longitudinal study of adolescent health'. *Journal of School Health, 72*(4), 138–146.

Mishna, F., Cook, C., Saini, M., Wu, M-J., and MacFadden, R. (2011). 'Interventions to prevent and reduce cyber abuse of youth: A systematic review'. *Research on Social Work Practice,* 21(1), 5–14. *OnlineFirst.*

O'Connell, P., Pepler, D., and Craig, W. (1999). 'Peer involvement in bullying: Insights and challenges for intervention'. *Journal of Adolescence, 22,* 437–452.

O'Moore, M. (2004). 'Guiding framework for national policy'. In E. Munthe, E. Solli, E. Ytre-Arne, and E. Roland (eds.), *Taking fear out of schools.* University of Stavanger: Centre for Behavioural Research, pp.38–51.

——(2010). *Understanding school bullying: A guide for parents and teachers.* Dublin: Veritas.

Olenik-Shemesh, D., Heiman, T., and Eden, S. (2012). 'Cyber-bullying victimisation in adolescence: relationships with loneliness and depressive mood'. *Emotional and Behavioural Difficulties, 17*(3–4), 361–374.

Oliver, R., and Oaks, I. (1994). 'Family issues and interventions in bully and victim relationships'. *School Counselor, 41,* 199–202.

Olweus, D. (1993). *Bullying at school: What we know and what we can do.* Oxford: Blackwell.

Rigby, K. (1994). 'Psychosocial functioning in families of Australian adolescent schoolchildren involved in bully/victim problems'. *Journal of Family Therapy, 16,* 173–187.

Rigby, K., and Bauman, S. (2009). 'How school personnel tackle cases of bullying: A critical examination'. In S. Jimerson, S. Swearer and D. Espelage (eds.), *Handbook of bullying in schools: An international perspective,* pp.455–467. New York: Routledge.

Roland, E., and Galloway, D. (2002). 'Classroom influences on bullying'. *Educational Research, 44*(3), 299–312.

Salmivalli, C., and Voeten, M. (2004). 'Connections between attitudes, group norms and behaviour in bullying situations'. *International Journal of Behavioral Development, 28*(3), 246–258.

Salmivalli, C., Kaukiainen, A., Kaistaniemi, L., and Lagerspetz, K.M.J. (1999). 'Self-evaluated self-esteem, peer evaluated self-esteem, and defensive egotism as predictors of adolescents' participation in bullying situations'. *Personality and Social Psychology Bulletin, 25*(10), 1268–1278.

Skiba, R.J., and Peterson, R.L. (2000). 'School discipline at a crossroads: From zero tolerance to early response'. *Exceptional Children, 66*(3), 335–396.

Slonje, R., and Smith, P.K. (2008). 'Cyberbullying: Another main type of bullying?' *Scandinavian Journal of Psychology, 49,* 147–154.

Smith, P.K. (2010). 'Cyberbullying: the European perspective'. In J.A. Mora-Merchan, and T. Jaeger (eds.), *Cyberbullying: A cross-national comparison,* (pp. 7–19). Landau: Verlag Empirische Padagogik.

Smith, P.K., and Sharp, S. (1994). *School bullying: Insights and perspectives.* London: Routledge.

Smith, P.K., and Shu, S. (2000). 'What good schools can do about bullying: Findings from a survey in English schools after a decade of research and action'. *Childhood, 7,* 193–212.

Smith, P.K., Mahdavi, J., Carvalho, M., Fisher, S., Russell, S., and Tippett, N. (2008). 'Cyberbullying: Its nature and impact in secondary school pupils'. *Journal of Child Psychology and Psychiatry, 49*(4), 376–385.

Smith, P.K., Salmivalli, C., and Cowie, H. (2012). 'Effectiveness of school-based programs to reduce bullying: A commentary'. *Journal of Experimental Criminology, 8,* 433–441.

Sourander, A., Klomek, A.B., Ikonen, M., Lindroos, J., Luntamo, T., Koskelainen, M., Ristkari, T., and Helenius, H. (2010). 'Psychosocial risk factors associated with cyber-bullying among adolescents'. *Archives of General Psychiatry, 67*(7), 720–728.

Spiel, C., and Strohmeier, D. (2011). 'National strategy for violence prevention in the Austrian public school system: Development and implementation'. *International Journal of Behavioral Development, 35*(5), 412–418.

Vandebosch, H., and Van Cleemput, K. (2009). 'Cyberbullying among youngsters: Profiles of bullies and victims'. *New Media and Society, 11,* 1349–1371.

Wang, J., Iannotti, R.J., and Nansel, T.R. (2009). 'School bullying among adolescents in the United States: Physical, verbal, relational, and cyber'. *Journal of Adolescent Health, 45*(4), 368–375.

Waters, S. (2009). 'Social and ecological structures supporting adolescent connectedness to school: A theoretical model'. *American School Health Association, 79*(11), 516–524.

Williams, K.R., and Guerra, N.G. (2007). 'Prevalence and predictors of Internet bullying'. *Journal of Adolescent Health, 41*, S14–S21.

Ybarra, M., and Mitchell, K. (2004). 'Youth engaging in online harassment: Associations with caregiver-child relationships, Internet use, and personal characteristics'. *Journal of Adolescence, 27*, 319–336.

Part 5

Research challenges

9 Cyberbullying amongst university students

An emergent cause for concern?

Helen Cowie, Sheri Bauman, Iain Coyne,
Carrie Myers, Maili Pörhölä and Ana Almeida

Introduction

To date, research into bullying in educational settings has mainly focused on nursery, primary and secondary school levels, with only a very small number of studies addressing aspects of bullying in higher education colleges and universities. However, forums such as "The Student Room" (www. thestudentroom.co.uk) highlight the growing problem of bullying amongst university students with disturbing accounts of the long-term damage to self-esteem, academic achievement and emotional wellbeing experienced by some students. In this chapter, we begin by reviewing research into traditional bullying amongst university students as well as current studies of cyberbullying in higher education. We then consider the possibility of continuities between bullying at school and at university as well as the social contexts which either promote or discourage cyberbullying. Finally, we discuss the implications for policies, training and awareness-raising and conclude with some suggestions for future research.

Rates of bullying among university students

The National Union of Students' (NUS) (NUS, 2008) "Student Experience Report" provides an overview of students' experiences of university across the United Kingdom, looking at different aspects of their lives. Through an online questionnaire, data were collected from 3,135 students from 146 higher education institutions. Seven per cent of the students had experienced bullying during their time at university, of whom 79 per cent indicated that the bullying was carried out by another student, and 21 per cent identified a member of staff as their bully.

Similarly, the Student Health Survey (Pörhölä & Kunttu, in submission) is a national survey which investigates Finnish university students' physical, mental and social health as well as their health-related behaviour. In the 2008 survey, the representative random sample consisted of 4,969 undergraduate students from all Science and Arts universities as well as universities of Applied Sciences in Finland. During their higher education, 5.6 per cent stated that they had been bullied "relatively much" or "very much" by their fellow students. Another survey (Lavikainen, 2010) of 5,698 students from Finnish universities of Applied Sciences revealed that the most typical form of bullying was being excluded from student groups. International students reported the highest levels of victimization.

Nursing and medical students seem to be particularly at risk of experiencing bullying during their education (e.g. Ahmer *et al.*, 2008; British Medical Association [BMA], 2006; Curtis, Bowen, & Reid, 2007). In the BMA (2006) students' welfare report, 17 per cent of UK medical students reported that they had been a victim of bullying or harassment during their time at medical school. In a survey of final year medical students in six medical colleges in Pakistan, 52 per cent of the respondents reported that they had faced bullying or harassment during their medical education, with 25 per cent of them reporting being bullied less than once a month, 15.9 per cent once a month, 11 per cent once a week, and 6 per cent daily. The forms of bullying varied from verbal abuse, being deliberately ignored or excluded, to physical abuse. Of the respondents who had been bullied, 18 per cent had faced this behaviour from nurses and peers (Ahmer *et al.*, 2008).

Continuities between bullying at school and at university

There is evidence to support the idea that there may be some continuity between bullying at school and bullying at university. Studies among children (e.g. Salmivalli *et al.*, 1998) and adolescents (e.g. Kumpulainen *et al.*, 1999; Sourander *et al.*, 2000) indicate moderate to strong relationships between being nominated by peers as a bully or a victim at different time points, suggesting stability of roles (Isaacs *et al.*, 2008).

For example, the 2008 Finnish Student Health Survey (Pörhölä, 2011) revealed that 51 per cent of those individuals who had bullied their fellow students during their higher education studies had also bullied their schoolmates at school, while 47 per cent of those who had been victimized during their higher education had previously been subjected to school bullying. Similar findings were later reported by Lappalainen *et al.* (2011) based on their study among 2,805 students in one Finnish university. This continuum from school to university was especially prevalent among males in the study. Bauman and Newman (2013) found similar patterns in a sample of 709 university students (25 per cent male) in the US, 3.7 per cent of whom indicated that they had been bullied at the university at least occasionally. Of those who were victimized at university, 84.6 per cent indicated that they had been bullied in junior high school, and 80.8 per cent had been victims in high school; 73 per cent of university victims were bullied in both junior and high school. Examining those patterns by gender, 64.7 per cent of females victimized at university were victimized in both junior and senior high; 100 per cent of males victimized at university reported being bullied at both previous school levels.

Similarly, in a retrospective study in the US, Chapell *et al.* (2006) found a positive relationship between being a child and adult bully and between being an adolescent and adult bully. In this study, it was found that 54 per cent of the adult bully participants had also bullied during childhood and adolescence. In Canada, Curwen *et al.* (2011) surveyed 159 female and 37 male undergraduates who admitted to having bullied a fellow student at least once since coming to university. The survey revealed that most of those who were bullies at university had a history of bullying at school. The bullies tended to target victims who were passive and less likely to retaliate. As the researchers speculate, the fact that many of these young adults had stable bullying characteristics suggests that there are strong benefits to them arising from this kind of behaviour. Furthermore, victims may remain silent through embarrassment and bystanders may reinforce the aggressive behaviour by remaining detached from the target, just as they did at school.

Cyberbullying amongst university students

The preliminary findings of the 2012 National Student Health Survey in Finland (involving 4,403 students in Higher Education) suggest that approximately 1 per cent of university students are cyberbullied at least occasionally (Pörhölä, 2012). In Portugal, Almeida *et al.* (2012) surveyed 311 university students (32.1 per cent male; mean age 23.3 years). With regard to cyberbullying by mobile phone, 89.6 per cent reported that it never happened, 7.5 per cent reported themselves as victims, 2 per cent as perpetrators and 1 per cent as bully-victims. Similarly, in the context of cyberbullying on the internet, 91.1 per cent had no episodes to report, 4.6 per cent were victims, 2.3 per cent were bullies and 2 per cent were bully-victims.

There is also a body of evidence to indicate a substantial overlap between traditional bullying and cyberbullying. Cyberbullies often target peers who are already being bullied in traditional, face-to-face ways (Dooley *et al.*, 2009; Gradinger, Strohmeier, & Spiel, 2009; Perren *et al.*, 2010; Riebel *et al.*, 2009; Sourander *et al.*, 2010). As is the case with traditional bullying, according to Willard (2006), the reported reasons for attacking a person online involve the bullies' need for power and dominance within a group, the perceived vulnerability of the target, perceived provocation on the part of the target (usually as a justification for the aggression on the part of the bully) and interpersonal animosities.

High status/high profile university students in the US (e.g. athletes, student government officers) are often targeted by cyberbullies (Baldasare *et al.*, 2012). In addition, students who are involved in sororities and fraternities (known as "Greek life" in the US) are disproportionately represented among cyberbullies and victims. Those who belonged to "Greek life" organizations were more frequent victims of humiliation and malice than non-members, and perpetrated acts of public humiliation more often as well. They reported significantly more distress from cyberbullying experiences and also indicated that more of the experiences occurred via Facebook than other groups.

Sexual orientation is also a factor that increases risk for victimization. In Australia, Wensley and Campbell (2012) examined heterosexual and non-heterosexual university students' involvement in both traditional and cyber forms of bullying, as either bullies or victims. In a study, 528 first-year university students (mean age 19.5 years) were surveyed about their sexual orientation and their bullying experiences over the previous 12 months. The results showed that non-heterosexual young people reported higher levels of involvement in traditional bullying, both as victims and perpetrators, in comparison to heterosexual students. In contrast, cyberbullying trends were generally found to be similar for heterosexual and non-heterosexual young people. Bauman and Baldasare (under review) surveyed 1,114 students (47 per cent male, 52 per cent White) at a large university in the southwestern US. Almost 8 per cent of participants self-identified as lesbian, gay, bisexual, or transgender (LGBT). The LGBT students were victimized by unwanted online contact more often than their straight peers, but there was no difference between the two groups on the degree of distress experienced from this type of victimization. The LGBT students also used deception online more frequently than their heterosexual peers, and received more anonymous cyberbullying than heterosexual students.

Hoff and Mitchell (2008) invited undergraduates to reflect retrospectively on the causes of cyberbullying in their experience while at school. The main reasons reported were relationship difficulties, such as the break-up of a friendship or romance, envy of a peer's success, intolerance of certain groups on the grounds of ethnicity, sexual orientation, gender or disability, and ganging up on one individual. This is confirmed at university level in a study by Bennett et al. (2011) who found evidence of hostility, humiliation, exclusion and intrusiveness by means of electronic victimization in friendship and dating relationships.

Being a victim of cyberbullying emerges as an additional risk factor for the development of depressive symptoms in adolescents (Aricak, 2009; Perren et al., 2010; Sourander et al., 2010), and this is confirmed in studies at university level. For example, Schenk and Fremouw (2012) found that college student victims of cyberbullying scored higher than matched controls on measures of depression, anxiety, phobic anxiety and paranoia. Similarly, in a sample of Portuguese undergraduates, Texeira et al. (2010) investigated the relationships amongst depression and anxiety and four dimensions of aggressiveness – physical aggression, verbal aggression, rage and hostility – in the context of cyberbullying through mobile phones and the internet. For cyberbullying by mobile phone, there were positive correlations between the depression and anxiety measures and all four dimensions of aggressiveness. For cyberbullying by internet, there were positive correlations with physical and verbal aggression and hostility.

The social context of bullying and cyberbullying

Much research focuses on the individual aspects of bullying by exploring the characteristics of perpetrators and targets, and thus overlooking the powerful influence of its social context, such as membership in a university sorority or fraternity. While an understanding of the personal aspects of the bully–victim relationship is important, it only addresses part of the issue. Bullying involves more than the individuals directly involved since it is experienced within a group of peers who adopt a range of participant roles, whether as active agents, targets, bystanders or defenders, and who experience a range of emotions. Salmivalli *et al.* (1996) proposed a participant role approach to the study of traditional bullying (see also Salmivalli, 2010 for a recent review of the participant role approach). They argued that perpetrators seldom act alone but are usually supported by their immediate group of *assistants* and *reinforcers*. The bullying escalates further as a result of the responses of the bystanders as *outsiders*, whether they react with indifference to the plight of the victim or implicitly condone what is happening. Only a small proportion of bystanders will act in the role of *defenders* who offer emotional support or protection to the victims.

The social context of the institution is also important in influencing the expression of empathy for the victims. Myers and Cowie (2013) carried out a qualitative role-play study of cyberbullying amongst Master's students (*n*=60) in which they found that bystanders tended to blame the victim and were reluctant to intervene, cybervictims felt let down and marginalized by their peers' indifference and hostility, while cyberbullies failed to acknowledge or understand the consequences of their actions.

Research with school-age students may offer insights into the relationship difficulties that bullying exacerbates. For example, Pörhölä (2008) found that in a sample of 872 seventh and eighth graders, the experiences of bullying others and being victimized by school peers were both related to peer integration problems. Victimized students reported the most peer relationship problems, such as having fewer or no close friends, feeling not valued and being actively disliked by peers, having only few contacts with classmates, being unsuccessful in the establishment of peer relationships, and being afraid of peers. Victims were followed by bully-victims, and finally by those who bullied, with each group reporting a decreased association with negative outcomes. Adolescents not involved in bullying – the bystanders – reported the highest quality in their peer relationships and level of peer community integration. Bystanders have the potential to play a key role in intervening to prevent bullying behaviour but there are often powerful social forces that counteract altruism.

Salmivalli (2010, p. 117) proposed that bystanders are "trapped in a social dilemma". Although they understand that bullying is wrong and may even wish that they could do something to stop it, they are acutely aware of their own needs for security and safety within the peer group. Unfortunately, through their inaction, bystanders not only reinforce the bullying behaviour but also threaten the victim's need to belong in the peer group. Many victims lack the social skills to protect themselves. Their feelings of low self-esteem and shame signal to others that they are worthless individuals who somehow deserve the treatment that they receive (Escobar *et al.*, 2011).

The principles of the participant role approach apply equally to the study of cyberbullying. For example, Myers and Cowie (2013) found that university student bystanders reported shame at their inaction. Their reluctance to intervene may be due to their understanding of the risks that may ensue if they offer protection to victims and the pressure that they are under to conform to group norms. Just as at school, altruistic university students who spontaneously act in defence of cybervictims remain a minority and are easily overruled by the majority.

Implications for institutions

Policies

In most universities, specific policies on cyberbullying are often lacking. For example, from a legal perspective in the UK, legislation applies to stalking, defamation and harassment but, to date, cyberbullying per se is not recognized as a crime. This makes it difficult for students to know the university's position. Despite the university's "duty of care", 70 per cent of students in the NUS survey (2008) did not report cyberbullying to anyone; many did not know of any person whom they could inform and 62 per cent reported that the university provided inadequate or no support when they did inform someone. This suggests that staff need training on the dynamics of this problem and potential strategies for managing incidents. There are important implications for university policies on student wellbeing. On the whole, punitive methods tend not to be effective in reducing cyberbullying. In fact, as Shariff and Strong-Wilson (2005) found, zero-tolerance approaches are actually more likely to criminalize young people and add a burden to the criminal justice system. Restorative approaches such as mediation, conciliation and awareness-raising have great potential for reducing the incidence of cyberbullying.

The university counselling service has a crucial role to play here. It is imperative that personnel at university counselling centres are aware of the seriousness of cyberbullying, and that they take care not to trivialize the concerns of victims. Screening for symptoms of depression and anxiety should be routinely undertaken in these cases, and in very severe situations, post-traumatic stress disorder (PTSD) should not be ruled out. Counsellors should be familiar enough with technology to be able to recommend technological strategies (e.g. blocking, reporting) that could be helpful to victims. They also need to be familiar with the law, and know when to inform victims about legal options. Finally, they need to be well-versed in university policies and serve as advocates for effective and accessible mechanisms by which those victimized by cyberbullying can make reports.

Training

For those universities that have student halls of residence, those responsible for handling student issues should be given training on how to intervene when incidents come to their attention, as complaints are more often directed to them than university disciplinary authorities. The counselling services could take on the task of providing education and awareness-raising so that staff know how to respond when they work with students on this issue. Counsellors could also use their therapeutic skills to facilitate change within particular groups of students and so have an impact on bystander apathy. University officials should consider alternatives to punishment, including counselling for all involved parties. In order to prevent bullying problems and to improve students' integration into their studying communities, higher education institutes should offer sufficient opportunities for guided training of communication skills. The focus of the communication courses should be shifted to relationship skills, group communication skills and the ethics of communication. We could argue that these skills are needed also in technologically-mediated communication contexts.

Friends and social support

In the study by Myers and Cowie (2013), students in the role of bystanders demonstrated that they admired altruistic behaviour at a macro level, such as campaigning for justice. However, at the micro level, they showed much less empathy for the feelings of a student who had been bullied by a popular student and, as a consequence, marginalized by his/her peer group. The fact that the bully was an admired figure meant that his unethical request for a fellow-student to write his/her essay for him was perceived in a much more lenient way than would have been expected. The role play restorative conference gave the students the opportunity to explore the others' point of view but also to have their assumptions challenged in public. Despite this, some polarization of views remained and core moral issues were only addressed by the victim group.

Interventions that work with peer group relationships and with young people's value systems have some likelihood of success. For example, peer support systems that involve processes of active listening, conflict resolution and problem-solving have been successful at school level, particularly when they are integrated into the whole-school policy against bullying (Cowie, 2011). Systems like these could be developed much further at university level in order to address bullying/cyberbullying when it occurs and to open up discussion about the moral dilemmas faced by bystanders when they observe someone being bullied. The practice of peer support might give direction to the minority of bystanders' altruistic wishes to address injustices such as cyberbullying in their university community and challenge the moral disengagement of those who bully as well as the silent majority of bystanders.

Student unions could also play a more active role in increasing awareness of traditional and cyber bullying and discouraging bullying behaviour by declaring that such behaviour is strongly disapproved of among students. In addition, student unions could actively work against discrimination and help new students to make friends with other students and integrate into the university peer community. This could be done, for example, by means of organizing social events in which all university students would feel comfortable and safe, regardless of their ethnic and social background or sexual or religious orientation. These kinds of social events would increase cohesion in the student community, and, in this way, prevent social exclusion and bullying.

Implications for future research

Evaluation of strategies

Although research to date indicates how difficult it can be for the bystander group to break the code of silence upheld by the student peer group, students themselves have constructive ideas on how to address the issue through such interventions as netiquette training, guidelines on appropriate behaviour during online teaching sessions, and awareness-raising about the negative impact of cyberbullying on students' self-esteem, academic attainment and peer relationships. For example, in their survey of university students, Bauman and her colleagues investigated students' perceptions about the role of the university in reducing cyberbullying. The items were rated on a five-point scale, from 1 (disagree) to 5 (agree). The highest mean score (4.1) was obtained for the item: "Professors who use online discussions boards should have a section in the syllabus that insists upon respectful communication". The increasing use of online classes suggests that this environment is one that can be appropriated by some for cyberbullying. Participants also believed (M = 3.91) that "All students should receive information about how to protect oneself from harmful digital communications and how to respond if one is victimized", suggesting that the university has a role to play in educating students about cyberbullying. Many respondents (M = 3.82) believed that undergraduate student induction was an appropriate context in which this could occur. Further studies are needed to evaluate which strategies are likely to be most successful and in which contexts.

Exploration of the role of empathy in prevention of cyberbullying

Hoffman (2000) proposes that empathy plays a significant part in the development of morality, with the origins of its development in the earliest relationships within the family, the neighbourhood and at school. Empathy is what one feels as appropriate for another person's situation, not one's own. It involves being aware of others' emotional states, sensing the other's perspective and feeling concern for others' situations. Empathy is especially important in instances that require the ability to restore balance and fairness in social relationships. From this perspective, universities as communities continue to have an important part to play in strengthening students' conceptions of right and wrong and in challenging behaviour that is oppressive and unjust. The potential for altruistic pro-social behaviour seems to be present in some young people but they need frameworks with which to express their dislike of anti-social behaviour such as bullying. The growing popularity of peer-support systems in schools and universities is a sign that these schemes are meeting a need and providing a vehicle through which bystanders might be able to take action against cyberbullying, given the right training (Cowie, 2011; Houlston *et al.*, 2011). Young people who spontaneously defend the victim are to be found in all social groups. However, it must be remembered that even at university level these individuals remain a minority and are easily overruled by the majority. Empathy-based socialization practices might encourage perspective-taking and enhance pro-social behaviour, leading to more satisfying relationships and a greater tolerance of stigmatized outsider groups. A critical way of extending such protectiveness beyond the immediate friendship group is to create contexts where there is a belief that relationships need not be abusive, violent or exploitative (Seligman *et al.*, 1995). Research could investigate the effectiveness of a range of interventions designed to heighten students' sensitivity to the emotional and social impact of cyberbullying on peers and to reduce moral disengagement.

Investigating the social and cultural contexts of cyberbullying

Although the number of studies conducted on bullying in higher education institutions is small, these studies suggest a wide range in the prevalence of bullying in higher education institutions in different cultures. The measures, samples and analyses used vary significantly between the individual studies, making direct comparisons of the results difficult, and further research is needed to assess the extent of bullying in higher education. As we have seen, the research in Finland found more bullying amongst Applied Sciences students (who typically work in groups) than amongst Arts and pure Science students (who are more likely to study alone). Similarly, the study of sororities and fraternities in the US indicated a greater likelihood of cyberbullying in students involved in those societies. Such findings suggest that cyberbullying is embedded in group formulation processes and hierarchies, indicating support for the view that the dynamics of the wider peer group play a significant role in the emergence or otherwise of cyberbullying. Further research could test such ideas by, for example, investigating whether Applied Science students or "Greek life" students were more likely to create in-groups and out-groups.

Theoretical models could also be tested. For example, the Social Identity model of Deindividuation Effects (SIDE), as applied to studies of computer-mediated communication by Reicher *et al.* (1995), suggests that anonymity shifts an individual's awareness from personal identity to social identity so that they become "deindividuated". As a result, such individuals will identify with the group's norms and behave in a manner accepted by the group. In relation to cyberbullying, this could mean, for example, that an individual may compose offensive material about someone online if this behaviour is condoned, or even encouraged, by the group. Therefore, behaviour is guided by social norms rather than by personal codes of morality. How this process of moral disengagement evolves is a topic of great relevance to our understanding of cyberbullying at university level.

Finally, we propose that the study of bullying amongst university students offers a unique opportunity to bridge the research literature on bullying at school level and bullying in the workplace. In working contexts, there is scant evidence on cyberbullying prevalence rates, with the limited research indicating rates of 9 per cent (Baruch, 2005), 10.7 per cent (Privitera & Campbell, 2009) and 20 per cent (Pitch, 2007). Within educational contexts the focus has been at school level and the cyberbullying of teachers, with rates of 15 per cent (Association of Teachers and Lecturers, 2009) and 36 per cent (Phippen, 2011) reported. A recent series of studies comprising a total of 231 UK university employees across academic, administrative, research, management and technical roles (Sprigg, Axtell, Coyne, & Farley, 2012) reported rates of cyberbullying of 80 to 88 per cent (for experiencing at least one negative act in the previous six months) and of 14 to 21 per cent (for experiencing at least one behaviour, at least weekly for six months).

Many young people leaving school make important decisions about whether to take a gap year, or to join the workforce or to go to university. In each of these social contexts there is the risk of being exposed to incidents of cyberbullying. The age at which university students begin their studies could be one factor to investigate and the extent to which students are considered by the authorities (and themselves) to be independent adults rather than young people in need of care and support. The study of cyberbullying amongst university students therefore has the potential to illuminate understanding of social relationships during the transition from adolescence to adulthood, and from higher education to the workplace.

References

Ahmer, S., Yousafzai, A.W., Bhutto, N., Alam, S., Sarangzai, A.K., and Iqbal, A. (2008). 'Bullying of medical students in Pakistan: A cross-sectional questionnaire survey'. *PLoS ONE, 3*(12), e3889. doi: 10.1371/journal.pone.0003889.
Almeida, A., Correia, I., Marinho, S., and Garcia, D. (2012). 'Is virtual less real? A study of cyberbullying and its relations to moral disengagement and empathy'. In Q. Li, D. Cross, and P.K. Smith (eds.), *Bullying goes to the cyber playground: Research*

on cyber bullying from an international perspective (pp. 223–244). Oxford: Wiley-Blackwell.

Aricak, O.T. (2009). 'Psychiatric symptomology as a predictor of cyberbullying among university students'. *Eurasian Journal of Educational Research, 34,* 167–184.

Association of Teachers and Lecturers (2009). '15 per cent of teachers have experienced cyberbullying'. Retrieved January 10, 2013 from http://www.atl.org.uk/Images/Joint%20ATL%20TSN%20cyberbullying%20survey%202009.pdf.

Baldasare, A., Bauman, S., Goldman, L., and Robie, A. (2012). 'Cyberbullying? Voices of college students'. In C. Wankel and L. Wankel (eds.), *Misbehavior in online education* (pp. 127–156). Bingley, UK: Emerald.

Baruch, Y. (2005). 'Bullying on the net: Adverse behavior on e-mail and its impact'. *Information and Management, 42*(2), 361–371.

Bauman, S., and Baldasare, A. (under review). 'Cyberaggression in college: Experiences, reactions, and recommendations for policies'.

Bauman, S., and Newman, M.L. (2013). 'Testing assumptions about cyberbullying: Perceived distress associated with acts of conventional and cyber bullying'. *Psychology of Violence, 3,* 27–38.

Bennett, D.C., Guran., E.L., Ramos, M.C., and Margolin, G. (2011). 'College students' electronic victimization in friendships and dating relationships: Anticipated distress and associations with risky behaviors'. *Violence and Victims, 26*(4), 410–429.

British Medical Association (BMA). (2006). *Medical students' welfare survey report.* Retrieved, from August 28, 2011: http://www.bma.org/ap.nsf/content/WELFARE2006.

Chapell, M.S., Hasselman, S.L., Kitchin, T., Lomon, S.N., MacIver, K.W., and Sarullo, P.L. (2006). 'Bullying in elementary school, high school, and college'. *Adolescence, 41,* 633–648.

Cowie, H. (2011). 'Peer support as an intervention to counteract school bullying: Listen to the children'. *Children & Society, 25,* 287–292.

Curtis, J., Bowen, I., and Reid, A. (2007). 'You have no credibility: Nursing students' experiences of horizontal violence'. *Nurse Education in Practice, 7,* 156–163.

Curwen, T., McNichol, J.S. and Sharpe, G.W. (2011). 'The progression of bullying from elementary school to university'. *International Journal of Humanities and Social Science, 1*(13), 47–54.

Dooley, J., Pyzalski, J., and Cross, D. (2009). 'Cyberbullying versus face-to-face bullying. A theoretical and conceptual review'. *Zeitschrift für Psychologie/Journal of Psychology, 217* (4), 182–188.

Escobar, M., Fernandez-Baen, F.J., Miranda, J., Trianes, M.V., and Cowie, H. (2011). 'Low peer acceptance and emotional/behavioural maladjustment in schoolchildren: Effects of daily stress, coping and sex'. *Anales de Psicologia, 27*(2), 412–417.

Gradinger, P., Strohmeier, D., and Spiel, C. (2009). 'Traditional bullying and cyberbullying: Identification of risk groups for adjustment problems'. *Zeitschrift für Psychologie/Journal of Psychology, 217*(4), 205–213.

Hoff, D.L., and Mitchell, S.N. (2009). 'Cyberbullying: Causes, effects, and remedies'. *SO – Journal of Educational Administration, 47,* 652–665.

Hoffman, M. (2000). *Empathy and Moral Development: Implications for Caring and Justice.* New York: Cambridge University Press.

Houlston, C., Smith, P.K., and Jessel, J. (2011). 'The relationship between use of school-based peer support initiatives and the social and emotional well-being of bullied and non-bullied students'. *Children & Society, 25,* 293–305.

Isaacs, J., Hodges, E., and Salmivalli, C. (2008). 'Long-term consequences of victimization: A follow-up from adolescence to young adulthood'. *European Journal of Developmental Science, 2,* 387–397.

Kumpulainen, K., Räsänen, E., and Henttonen, I. (1999). 'Children involved in bullying: Psychological disturbance and the persistence of the involvement'. *Child Abuse and Neglect, 23*(2), 1253–1262.

Lappalainen, C., Meriläinen, M., Puhakka, H., and Sinkkonen, H-M. (2011). 'Bullying among university students – does it exist?' *Finnish Journal of Youth Research, 29*(2), 64–80.

Lavikainen, E. (2010). 'Opiskelijan ammattikorkeakoulu 2010. Tutkimus ammattikorkeakouluopiskelijoiden koulutuspoluista, koulutuksen laadusta ja opiskelukyvystä'. [Student's university of applied sciences 2010. Research on the study tracks, views on the quality of education, and own ability to study of students in the universities of applied sciences]. Helsinki, Finland: Opiskelijajärjestöjen tutkimussäätiö Otus.

Myers, C., and Cowie, H. (2013). 'An investigation into the roles of the victim, bully and bystander in role-play incidents of cyberbullying amongst university students in England'. *Pastoral Care in Education.* Published online July 2013 http://dx.doi.org/10.1080/02643944.2013.811696

National Union of Students (NUS) (2008). 'Student Experience Report'. Retrieved March 3, 2011 from http://www.nus.org.uk/PageFiles/4017/NUS_Student ExperienceReport.pdf.

Perren, S., Dooley, J., Shaw, T., and Cross, D. (2010). 'Bullying in school and cyberspace: Associations with depressive symptoms in Swiss and Australian adolescents'. *Child and Adolescent Psychiatry and Mental Health, 4*(28), 28–38.

Phippen, A. (2011). *The Online Abuse of Professionals.* Research Report from the UK Safer Internet Centre. Retrieved March 3, 2011 from http://www.swgfl.org.uk/ getattachment/News/Content/News-Articles/Professionals-Online-Safety-Helpline/Professional-Abuse-Survey-March-2011-Final-(2).pdf.aspx.

Pitch, G. (2007). *One in 10 workers experiences cyber-bullying in the workplace.* Retrieved March 3, 2011 from http://www.personneltoday.com/articles/2007/07/26/41707/ one+in+10+workers+experiences+cyber-bullying+in+the+workplace.html.

Pörhölä, M. (2008). 'Koulukiusaaminen nuoren hyvinvointia uhkaavana tekijänä. Miten käy kiusatun ja kiusaajan vertaissuhteille?' [School bullying as a risk factor for the well-being of an adolescent. What happens to the peer relationships of bullies and victims?] In M. Autio, K. Eräranta, and S. Myllyniemi (eds.), *Polarisoituva nuoruus? Nuorten elinolot -vuosikirja 2008* (pp. 94–104). Helsinki, Finland: Nuorisotutkimusverkosto/Nuorisotutkimusseura, Nuorisoasiain neuvottelukunta, & Sosiaali- ja terveysalan tutkimus- ja kehittämiskeskus Stakes.

——(2011). 'Kiusaaminen opiskeluyhteisössä'. [Bullying in university community]. In K. Kunttu, A. Komulainen, K. Makkonen and P. Pynnönen, (eds.), *Opiskeluterveys* (pp. 166–168). Helsinki, Finland: Duodecim.

——(2012, September). 'How experiences of bullying affect the well-being of students?' Paper presented at the 16th Nordic Congress for Student Health, Helsinki, Finland.

Pörhölä, M., and Kunttu, K. (in submission). 'Experiences of bullying and victimization in higher education: Cccurrence rates according to university type and gender'.

Privitera, C., and Campbell, M.A. (2009). 'Cyberbullying: the new face of workplace bullying?' *CyberPsychology and Behavior, 12*(4), 395–400.

Reicher, S., Spears, R., and Postmes, T. (1995). 'A social identity model of deindividuation phenomena'. *European Review of Social Psychology, 6,* 161–198.

Riebel, J., Jaeger, R.S., and Fischer, U.C. (2009). 'Cyberbullying in Germany – an exploration of prevalence, overlapping with real life bullying and coping strategies'. *Psychology Science Quarterly, 51*(3), 298–314.

Salmivalli, C. (2010). 'Bullying and the peer group: A review'. *Aggression and Violent Behaviour, 15,* 112–120.

Salmivalli, C., Lagerspetz, K., Björkqvist, K., Österman, K., and Kaukiainen, A. (1996). 'Bullying as a group process: Participant roles and their relations to social status within the group'. *Aggressive Behavior, 22,* 1–15.

Salmivalli, C., Lappalainen, M., and Lagerspetz, K.M.J. (1998). 'Stability and change of behavior in connection with bullying in schools: A two-year follow-up'. *Aggressive Behavior, 24,* 205–218.

Schenk, A.M., and Fremouw, W.J. (2012). 'Prevalence, psychological impact, and coping of cyberbully victims among college students'. *Journal of School Violence, 11*(1), 21–37. doi: 10.1080/15388220.2011.630310

Seligman, M.E.P., Reivich, K., Jaycox, L., and Gillham, J. (1995). *The Optimistic Child.* New York: Houghton Mifflin.

Shariff, S., and Strong-Wilson, T. (2005). 'Bullying and new technologies: What can teachers do to foster socially responsible discourse in the physical and virtual school environments?' In J. Kincheloe (ed.), *Classroom Teaching: An Introduction* (pp. 219–240). New York: David Lang Publishers.

Sourander, A., Brunstein Klomek, A.B., Ikonen, M., Lindroos, J., Luntamo, T., Koskelainen, M., Ristkari, T., and Helenius, H. (2010). 'Psychosocial risk factors associated with cyberbullying among adolescents'. *Archives of General Psychiatry, 67*(7), 720–728.

Sourander, A., Helstelä, I., Helenius, H., and Piha, J. (2000). 'Persistence of bullying from childhood to adolescence: A longitudinal 8-year follow-up study'. *Child Abuse and Neglect, 24,* 873–881.

Sprigg, C., Axtell, C., Coyne, I., and Farley, S. (2012). 'Punched from the screen. Cyberbullying in the workplace'. Paper presented as part of the ESRC Festival of Social Science, Sheffield, November 7th 2012.

Teixeira, V., Correia, I., Almeida, A., and Lourenço, J. (2011). 'Bullying and cyberbullying in Higher Education students: psychological correlates'. Paper presented at the 1st Developmental Psychology International Congress at ISPA (Instituto Superior de Psicologia Aplicada), Lisbon, Portugal.

Wensley, K., and Campbell, M. (2012). 'Heterosexual and nonheterosexual young university students' involvement in traditional and cyber forms of bullying'. *Cyberpsychology Behaviour and Social Network, 15*(12), 649–654.

Willard, N. (2006). 'Flame retardant'. *School Library Journal, 52*(4), 55–56.

10 Positive uses of new technologies in relationships in educational settings

Barbara Spears, Angela Costabile,
Antonella Brighi, Rosario Del Rey,
Maili Pörhölä, Virginia Sánchez,
Christiane Spiel and Fran Thompson

Introduction

Although much literature has focused on the negative impact that online behavior can have on young people's wellbeing, and the unsafe use of the internet by children and adolescents (e.g. Valcke, De Wever, Van Keer, & Schellens, 2011), Costabile and Spears (2012) emphasized the positive influences of technology on children's and adolescents' social, academic and personal wellbeing and adjustment in their edited book: *The Impact of Technology on Relationships in Educational Settings.* This chapter summarizes the contributions by members of Working Group 6 of the COST Action (see Chapter 1) towards understanding the positive uses of new technologies, and highlights ongoing evidence relevant to it. In doing so, we present a counterpoint to the known, negative consequences of new technologies, such as cyberbullying, and challenge the reader to adopt a holistic view, reflecting on both sides of the ICT "coin" in terms of relationships in educational settings: where positive uses and impacts are not only the converse of negative, but are also closely intertwined.

Background

Young people living in contemporary societies in 2013, who are aged 18 years and under, have never known a world without an online presence. Within two decades of the appearance of the publicly available World Wide Web (Internet), (*circa* 1995), young people are experiencing a rapidly changing social context that is forging new social and legal boundaries (see Chapter 4) and are simultaneously re-configuring how they, and the adults around them, operate relationally. They have a digital footprint that has grown with them; which is intertwined in and around their relationships; and which will follow them into the future. They use social media to communicate directly and indirectly, through sharing videos and images as well as text, and this has enabled young people to represent themselves and see others in ways which were not foreseeable prior to the advent of the internet. The "web" or "touch-screen" generation and their development, attitudes and behavior are different compared to those of their parents: the so-called "millenials" (Ferri, 2011). One key difference relates to how each uses technologies: the wireless and touch-screen generation embrace technologies as an expected and integral part of their daily social and learning worlds, whereas their parents predominantly use ICTs as tools to accomplish tasks. Young people and adults now operate in a truly global communications community, with increasingly mobile technologies which are converging all features to single, hand-held devices, and adopting active roles as: *content creators* and *publishers* (e.g. Wikis); *content sharers* (e.g. YouTube; Instagram); *discussants* (e.g. Skype; Blogs); *social networkers* (e.g. Facebook, bebo; Myspace; LinkedIn); *micro-bloggers* (e.g. Twitter); *LifeStreamers and Livecasters* (e.g. Y!Live); *virtual world inhabitants* (e.g. Habbo; Second Life); *social gamers* (e.g. Angry Birds) and *massively multiplier onliners [gamers]* (MMO) (e.g. World of Warcraft).

The reciprocal influence of this significant information, communication and technological (ICT) revolution on young people, parents, families, school communities, and broader societies cannot be underestimated. On the one hand, young people control, create and drive the innovative uses of these new technologies: on the other hand, they are the recipients of all the positive and negative influences and impacts that it has to offer.

The impact of technology on relationships in educational settings

As this chapter is reporting on the contribution of Working Group 6, it is relevant to summarize the edited book published by this group (Costabile & Spears, 2012). Thirty-eight contributors from the COST Action on cyberbullying shared their cross-cultural understanding and expertise of how positive uses of ICTs were contributing to positive outcomes for young people and the school communities in which they operated. This was an important contribution to the field, as it demonstrated the interplay between the two sides (positive/negative) of the same online "coin".

Part I of the book presented some of the background issues to the impact of technology on relationships in educational settings. Spears, Kofoed, Bartolo, Palermiti, and Costabile (2012) set the scene by directly engaging with youth voice in three countries about the positive contribution that social networks played in their lives; Arnthórsson (2012) noted the bigger picture: the importance of protecting identity and having secure net addresses at a national level; and De Santo and Costabile (2012) highlighted the challenges of creating new academic curricula, so that media education can directly impact on educational practices.

Part II explored scholarly settings, and the role that technology played in enhancing relationships within those contexts. Brighi, Fabbri, Guerra, and Pacetti (2012) discussed the potential of technology to transform educational structures and experiences; whilst Pörhölä and Lahti (2012) reviewed current literature and examined the ways young people established and maintained their peer relationships, specifically reporting on "virtual rooms" created for them; and Del Rey, Sánchez, and Ortega (2012) explored pro-sociality in the internet. Popper, Strohmeier, and Spiel (2012) suggested the use of notebooks and e-learning in schools as examples where technology enhanced learning and learning outcomes; and Pyżalski (2012) reflected on the digital generational divide and the functional and dysfunctional styles of internet use by adolescents. Hayat and Amichai-Hamburger (2012) examined the relationship between internet use and the psychological and psycho-social wellbeing of children; Aouil (2012) discussed the impact of online support/ help; and Glasheen and Campbell (2012) noted how online counselling enhanced relationships and connectedness in school settings.

Part III drew attention to international evidence-based practices which promoted participation, support and learning opportunities, as well as cyberbullying interventions which employed these positive strategies in dealing with cyberbullying. Menesini and Nocentini (2012) reported on the differences between online and face-to-face peer-led education and intervention approaches; and von Kaenel-Flatt and Douglas (2012) presented an innovative model of online and offline peer mentoring (Cybermentoring). Poskiparta, Kaukiainen, Pöyhonen, and Salmivalli (2012) outlined an anti-bullying computer game from the KiVa program, designed to motivate children and enhance their learning processes; similarly, Wolke and Sapouna (2012) examined a virtual intervention game to reduce victimization. Wotherspoon, Cox, and Slee (2012) reported on employing creative storyboarding, freeze-frame methodologies and mobile phone technologies to create and send anti-bullying video messages to students via mobile phones, and Spears (2012) reviewed online programs in Australia which promoted cybersafety and digital citizenship.

Collectively, the authors noted the importance of the contribution from young people as experts in this domain; and advocated for social support and learning opportunities using ICTs directly, through online gaming, explicit teaching and integration in lessons and indirectly, through training of peers, teachers and parents. They also articulated how technologies can enhance learning, relationship skill development, curriculum development and pedagogy, as well as the need to consider online safety and identity growth. Some of these notions are further explored by members of this Working Group in the sections to follow.

Cognition and identity considerations

The rapid increase in ICT use has given rise to a plethora of research on brain development, social impacts and academic outcomes (Greenfield & Yan, 2006) which have direct implications for understanding the positive influences of ICTs on relationships in educational settings, including cyberbullying and the ways in which we might subsequently intervene.

Cognition and Development

In terms of cognition, the use of the internet and social media generally provides more developmental advantages than disadvantages for children. ICT use has also been found to impact on such areas as memory, perception, attention and learning processes and frequent internet users cognitively outperform infrequent users (Greenfield & Yan, 2006; Johnson, 2008, 2010). There is also a downward developmental trend regarding actual use, and Spears (2010) reported that "tech-savvy tots", very young children (aged from 9 months to 3 years), are using iPads and iPhones as interactive, visual, self-reinforcing learning tools, well before they can read or utilize the full range of capabilities of the devices. These tech-savvy tots, who will be in school settings within five years, are learning to press, click, swipe, pinch and expand screens; to multi-task; and to operate across multi-screens. There are learning and social relationship implications arising from all these shifts and researchers will need to consider them, as well as how these children also form and develop their identity in relation to use of ICTs, if prevention and intervention strategies are to be effective with this new "touch-screen" generation, and the positive impacts of future ICTs are to be understood.

Identity

According to classical theories of identity development (Erikson, 1968; Palmonari, 2011; Slee, Campbell, & Spears, 2012), personal identity becomes central around 11–15 years of age. Identity experimentation and exploration by adolescents is essential as they transit from childhood to adulthood. However, until recently, the main influential factors were via offline relationships: parents, peers, and important other adults. The virtual environment: the internet, including convergent mobile devices, and the rise in social media use, is increasingly more significant for this age group and this suggests that there is a need to reconsider classic theories in light of this new online environment.

Affirming autonomy and identity occurs by naturally separating from parents, and simultaneously by testing themselves in peer groups. Recently, however, "real" peer groups have been dramatically supplemented by online social networks and virtual communities: with the consequence that relationships are played out within both real and online contexts. Whilst young people have articulated that there is only one social life which flows seamlessly between on/offline contexts, their online identities impact on their offline contexts, and vice versa (Spears et al., 2012).

Developing identity through public social networking sites (SNSs) such as Facebook, Twitter, Pinterest, Tumblr, YouTube and Myspace, is an active and reflective, cognitive and social process. These sites connect young people in networked spaces where they can publicly and privately meet each other, establish friendship circles and learn about and experience interpersonal relationships. SNSs thus contribute to the development of an adolescent's identity through enabling young people to experiment with different ways of being, including explicitly adopting different personas and identities (Spears et al., 2012).

SNSs also promote identity formation through the different artistic expressions and representations of themselves that they choose to make available to others online. The "photo-voice" of young people is immediately apparent when viewing such sites as Pinterest, Instagram, YouTube and Tumblr, which pictorially/visually reveal their social contexts, their emotions, their perspectives of themselves and their worlds. Exercising some control in how they portray themselves to others online, through for example, the taking and posting of photographs of themselves (so-called "selfies"), is an important component of this representation and is demonstrative of how they create and manipulate their own images: to suit the projection of themselves that they want *others* to have of *them*. SNSs then are as much about image control/management, as they are about having friends and socializing online.

Making choices about how they see themselves, how others see them, and how they want to be seen by others are deliberate, reflective acts in their online environment, and these choices are constantly refined and adjusted in a process of image and impression management, designed to put the best version of themselves forward (Stern, 2008). Valkenburg and Peter (2007) suggest that this control over how they express their online identity enhances adolescents' feelings of security. However, with the ability of others to manipulate images online, there can be a subsequent loss of control, suggesting that there is a tension here for young people at the very time they are trying to establish and stabilize their identity as they progress towards adulthood.

One clear advantage in using the online setting for social purposes, is the opportunity to not only belong to a larger peer group than is reasonably possible offline, but to also experience a unique online identity: with the many hundreds of friends, and friends-of-friends who would not typically be available to individuals in offline situations. Proximity is a key determinant of friendship, and social networking sites create an appearance/illusion of proximity, through the online 24/7 aspect of always having access and being reachable. The tyranny of time and distance however, are mediated through these online SNSs, and friendships which would have naturally faded due to someone moving away, can now be maintained or rekindled, and families too can stay connected when living in different parts of the world, thus contributing to identity formation in ways that were not available before. Identity development is a constant refinement of comparison and contrast, and online groups offer increased opportunities to compare oneself with vast numbers of others, including those who in the past may have not been influential due to time and distance. The role of social comparison theory

(Festinger, 1954; Gruder, 1971) is relevant here, and is worthy of investigation in an online context, particularly when there is such opportunity for commentary by others.

Young people who participated in a three-country cross-cultural qualitative study concerning what was positive for them about being online in SNSs (Spears *et al.*, 2012) reported many impacts including: being able to test different identities; feeling less/lower risk when experiencing strong emotions; and being able to experiment with different kinds of relationships and roles without feeling guilty if they made mistakes or had misunderstandings. Each of these related to learning about themselves as individuals, as well as learning to be members of a group and the dynamic which accompanies it. Identity formation then, in an online context reflects what is known in the offline setting, where it concerns both individual and group aspects. However, due to the expansive and unique nature of the online setting, forging one's identity and determining a sense of self and belonging can be challenging, especially when an individual can choose to pose as and compare oneself to, something/someone that may not be "real". The exposure to many more people through SNSs means that the peer influence from others may also be greater, driving the need to present self-images which either fit in, or stand out as different/unique. Forging a stable identity in relation to an online peer group, where everyone may not be who or what they purport to be, is something that needs to be explored in future research. Spears and Costabile (2012) concluded that the risks, opportunities and challenges of being on SNSs were intertwined, and that the positives they experienced contributed to their identity development through enabling experimentation with how they presented themselves to others.

ICTs have thus influenced the roles, functions and strategies known to build identity and interpersonal relationships, along with young people's cognitive and skills development. Adolescents' and pre-adolescents' psychological development is appearing to be impacted by the pressure of ICTs and Web use, and these influences have to be considered in current and future research on the positive impacts of technology on relationships in educational settings.

Learning from experience to improve cyber-behavior

In recent years important initiatives have been developed to promote positive and secure uses of new technologies, especially in educational settings (Lau, Lau, Wong, & Ransdell, 2011; Richards, 2009). The main thrust of these initiatives however, has been on the prevention of risk-related behaviors such as cyberbullying, with the positive outcomes being achieved through students' involvement in pro-social online behaviors, such as cybermentoring others (Perren *et al.*, 2012).

Taking advantage of all that the internet and social networks have to offer, along with the education required to deal with eventual risks that may arise from its use, are new challenges for schools. However, this does not mean that we must start from scratch when developing positive cyber-behaviors, as cyber-behavior is fundamentally a social activity (Livingstone & Haddon, 2011), albeit one where physical and virtual lives are connected and inter-dependent (Casas, Del Rey, & Ortega-Ruiz, 2013). Indeed, the role of schools in the promotion of safe uses of new technologies has been recognized by primary students, who consider that it is the best context to learn about positive and secure uses of ICTs (O'Connel, Price, & Barrow, 2004).

In order to respond to these challenges, it is pertinent to call upon previous professional and scientific understandings: about how to improve interpersonal relations in school settings; how to deal with interpersonal problems which may affect them, such as bullying; and how to identify the keys for evaluating the effectiveness of such psycho-educational programs (Ttofi & Farrington, 2011).

Programs based on whole-school approaches and policies (Smith, Pepler, & Rigby, 2004), such as the Finnish national school-based anti-bullying program (KiVa) (Salmivalli & Poskiparta, 2012), are recognized as having a positive impact on reducing bullying, but are especially advantageous for improving interpersonal relations, enhancing empathy towards the victims and developing defense strategies for the victims. Likewise, developing any educational action or implementing an existing program should respect evidence-based practices (Eisner & Malti, 2012).

Following these premises, psycho-educational programs evaluated using the criteria of practice based on evidence, that obtain positive results in terms of quality of cyber-behavior and virtual relations of adolescents, are usually those are developed as an extension of, or complement those that obtained positive results when tackling bullying: by enhancing the protection factors and the reduction of risk factors.

Among them, we describe four programs developed and evaluated in different countries: the *ConRed Program* – Knowing, Building and Living Together on Internet and Social Networks (Del Rey, Casas, & Ortega-Ruiz, 2012; Ortega-Ruiz, Del Rey, & Casas, 2012) the *Noncadiamointrappola* Program (Menesini & Nocentini, 2012; Palladino, Nocentini, & Menesini, 2012); and the Medienhelden Program – Media Heroes (Schultze-Krumbholz, Wölfer, Jäkel, Zagorscak, & Scheithauer, 2012). Finally, the Cybermentors program is presented.

1. The ConRed program

The ConRed Program (Ortega-Ruiz, Del Rey, & Casas, 2012) has been developed in secondary education schools in Spain that were already employing a *convivencia* project: which showed improved interpersonal relations between pupils (Ortega-Ruiz & Del Rey, 2004). On the basis of the theory of normative social behavior (Rimal, Lapinski, Cook, & Real, 2005), where individuals' attitudes and behaviors are heavily influenced by perceptions of the social conventions that surround them, the ConRed Program intended: to show adolescents the legal issues related to actions of misconduct in virtual environments; to inform of the risks that certain virtual behaviors may face; and to explain how certain behaviors do not reinforce groups, but stimulate rejection and intimidation. Using pupils, teachers and families, these three objectives were approached from the perspective of positive psychology (Affleck & Tennen, 1996) and were reinforced by a campaign for increasing awareness. The work with the pupils was developed during one-hour sessions per week, over eight weeks. In addition to their presence in the pupils' sessions, the teachers were involved in two sessions. For families, one single evening session was devised. Several videos, virtual spaces and news from the press were analysed during these sessions.

The evaluation showed that, in experimental schools versus controls, not only was it the quality of pupils' virtual interactions was improved, but also their physical/offline lives at school. With regard to the use of social networks and the internet, pupils were more aware about the need to control their private information on the internet; there were lower levels of dependency relating to connecting to the internet; and lower levels of cyber-aggression and cyber-victimization. With respect to face-to-face relations, after the program, pupils perceived fewer security problems in their schools; better quality of school climate; and even lower levels of traditional bullying, particularly with regard to victimization; and higher levels of empathy. Today, the ConRed Program is generally acknowledged in Spanish schools and is considered as a reference/benchmark by certain regional governments of the country.

2. The Noncadiamointrappola program

The *Noncadiamointrappola* Program (Menesini & Nocentini, 2012) is a peer counseling program that was designed and implemented in Italy for the prevention and reduction of bullying, by training pupils to help their friends/mates in their social relations. This approach is based on the assumption that peers are an important influence on each other, not only in terms of social and academic learning, but also with regards to the social norms that students consider as acceptable or unacceptable in their peer relationships. The first edition of the program (Menesini & Nocentini, 2012) included a face-to-face and an online intervention, both led by peer-educators who were previously selected and trained. The focus of the face-to-face intervention followed three components: a meeting with students, in which peer educators explained and discussed cyberbullying with their friends/classmates. The second component involved a meeting with institutions in the city about the problems of youth, and the third involved the preparation of a TV program regarding cyberbullying. The online intervention involved the creation of a school forum, where the peer-educators were the forum moderators.

The first evaluation of the project showed ambiguous results. Specifically, the results showed a decrease in cyberbullying, but only for male educators, and not in the rest of the groups, as expected from previous studies (Ttofi & Farrington, 2011). However, in the second edition of the *Noncadiamointrappola* Program (Palladino *et al.*, 2012) the authors made a considerable effort to enhance the capacity of peer educators to encourage the participation of more friends/mates, in order to improve their respective classes. The authors also considered the mediating effect of coping strategies in the effectiveness of the program. While developing the program, an emphasis was put on effective strategies for the victims and bystanders to deal with cyberbullying episodes. Positive results were obtained at the time of the second evaluation. In terms of behavioral change, the program was effective in the reduction of cybervictimization for the experimental group and, regarding coping strategies, the evaluation showed that the capacity of pupils to deal with problems was increased. The most important results came from the mediating effect of coping strategies in the decrease of bullying and cyberbullying. Results showed that a reduction in the strategy of avoidance predicted a decrease for victimization and, in contrast, an increase in the use of problem solving predicted a decrease in cyber victimization, but only in the peer-educator group.

The second edition of the program seemed to support the efficacy of the peer-model in decreasing bullying and cyberbullying behavior; and enhancing the use of adaptive strategies to cope. Considering that the training was intended for peer-educators, it could also be used for improving interpersonal relationships, not only face-to-face but also those relations which operate across the online medium. Clearly, the importance of learning from what has gone before is noted. Refining the program, based on the evidence gathered previously, has resulted in an effective program. The learning here is that it may not always be necessary to design new approaches, rather, refinement of the practices, based upon evidence, may see change occurring.

3. The Medienhelden–Media Heroes program

The Medienhelden–Media Heroes (Schultze-Krumbholz *et al.*, 2012) is a program based on the Theory of Reasoned Action and cognitive-behavioral methods that intend to improve digital competencies and prevent cyberbullying. Through the use of a specific purpose-designed manual, teachers are trained and supervised to develop the program as an integrated aspect within the existing school curriculum in middle-aged school classes (12–16 years). Teacher training lasts eight hours and the work to be developed with pupils may take either a long or short version. The former lasts seven weeks with 14 sessions and an evening for family training. The latter consists only of a single day with four sessions, and without family training.

In order to achieve change in students' virtual behaviors, the main focuses of the program are: providing information and knowledge; exploring values and norms; and identifying social emotional competencies which are presented in the structured manual as "Media Heroes". The proposed work sequence is as follows: increasing awareness of pupils about possible consequences of their actions on the internet; and looking for change in their behaviors and having positive experiences. Different activities are performed throughout, such as: peer-to-peer tutoring; peer-to-parent monitoring; and role plays. The evaluation aims to determine: involvement in cyberbullying; levels of empathy; perspective taking; self-esteem; and subjective health. Results have shown that control schools were worse with respect to the post-test, than the pre-test and that experimental schools using the short intervention performed the same as control schools. Experimental schools that used the long intervention obtained better results overall. Medienhelden was perceived by teachers as being highly applicable as a school-based program, and about half of the pupils liked the program "a lot" or "mostly". Currently, analysis of third phase data that was collected after six months following the finalization of the implementation, is being undertaken, with a view to improving the materials. A relevant datum to be noted for future interventions: it has been shown that isolated interventions do not seem to have great positive effects and therefore, time and effort need to be invested, in following up and revisiting the materials.

4. Cybermentors

CyberMentors (www.cybermentors.org.uk/) was one of the first forms of virtual peer support launched by BeatBullying, a leading UK anti-bullying charity, in 2009. Students, usually recruited in schools, were trained by BeatBullying staff in two-day training workshops. CyberMentors mentor online in and out of school; have an online identity and are protected from abuse by a software filter called "netmod". They are supported through the CyberMentors' website by a referral team of senior cybermentors and counsellors. The scheme was evaluated by Banerjee, Robinson, and Smalley (2010) who found that the CyberMentor scheme reduced bullying in five intervention schools. BeatBullying's training was highly regarded and the CyberMentors were found to raise awareness of bullying and cyberbullying in schools and were particularly effective at transition for younger students. There was an increase in both the understanding of bullying and reporting of bullying incidents in the student population. Students using the scheme found the CyberMentors easy to contact and helpful to an extent. However, schools varied in their promotion of the schemes and the supervision of mentors; not all school staff was engaged and the scheme needed ongoing monitoring.

A second evaluation of the CyberMentor scheme was carried out by Thompson, Robinson, and Smith (2013) as part of a DAPHNE III project. Cybermentors and cybermentees were asked to complete an online questionnaire on the CyberMentors' website at the end of a mentoring session. Almost all respondents were female aged 15 years. Most Cybermentors had been newly-trained in the last year and thought the training had prepared them well. They found the website easy to use and felt safe and well supported: "You feel that you can help people out and this will make a big difference to their lives, no matter how big or small their problem was".

Cybermentees found it easy to contact and talk to a cybermentor, most finding the cybermentors' advice helpful. They would use the cybermentor scheme again and also recommend it to a friend. Most comments about the scheme were positive: "The good part about the session was being able to tell someone I don't know everything and just let it out without getting criticized".

The main shortcoming of the scheme is the lack of engagement of young males. Although this gender imbalance is evident in most face-to-face peer support schemes (Cowie & Smith, 2010), it is surprising that an online scheme where the cybermentee's identity is anonymous still fails to engage boys and young men. This was the main finding of the evaluation and needs addressing. However, overall, those who used the scheme gave positive feedback.

Summary

It is evident from these interventions/programs that employing the positive aspects of ICTs in order to address the negative is a worthwhile strategy: where the prevention of risk-related behaviors is achieved through involvement in pro-social online activity. That is, it assumes that a form of inoculation takes place when positive ideas, attitudes and behaviors are introduced and reinforced, which grow and spread, so that negative behaviors are reduced.

The role of adults in promoting positive uses of technology

Guidance in ethical peer networking

Greater understanding is needed to find ways in which young people can be encouraged and guided to engage pro-socially in peer networking and to avoid anti-social uses of new technologies. Direct guidance should be provided for young people about how they should act and communicate online, and how they could protect themselves from being hurt by their virtual peers.

According to Pörhölä and Lahti (2012), who summarized the extant literature at the time, children and adolescents use multiple forms of information and communication technology to establish peer relationships and to maintain and enlarge their social networks. They use this technology as a communication channel to expand their physical environments into online "virtual rooms" where they continue sharing their social experiences with their friends and unknown peers at any time of the day or night. Social interaction with peers thus appears to be the most important function of

ICTs for children and adolescents (Kaare, Brandtzæg, Heim, & Endestad, 2007; Pelastakaa, 2009; Subrahmanyam, Greenfield, Kraut, & Gross, 2001), suggesting that a substantial part of their cognitive and emotional experiences – learning, seeking play and having fun, and relationship and identity building – take place online. Being able to interact online is perceived by adolescents to have positive impacts on the quality of their friendships and romantic relationships (e.g. Blais, Craig, Pepler, & Connolly, 2008; Lenhart, Rainie, & Lewis, 2001; Valkenburg & Peter, 2007), and enable them to keep in contact even with long-distance peers (Lenhart *et al.*, 2001; Lenhart, Purcell, Smith, & Zickuhr, 2010). Via the internet, children and adolescents can thus: share concerns and emotions; give and ask for social support; build their identity by, for example, uploading photos and different kinds of texts in web galleries; engage in playing online games; share music, movies, software and other files; join virtual communities and meet new peers with similar interests and hobbies (see Pörhölä & Lahti, 2012, for a review).

Being in these "virtual rooms" however, affects the cycle of real-life relationships: introductions, development and closures. The anonymity provided by these virtual rooms enables harmful communication practices such as cyberbullying, or concealing one's real identity, pretending to be someone else, or adopting an imaginary identity (Kaare *et al.*, 2007; Lenhart *et al.*, 2001; Sjöberg, 2002; Smith, & Curtin, 2001).

The following recommendations are made, premised upon current understanding of the interplay between the online and offline environments for young people, and the need for transferability of pro-social skills. Firstly, pro-social interactions with peers online require similar peer interaction skills as in face-to-face situations. In order to establish and maintain positive peer relationships and join peer groups online, young people should be able to, for example, display initiative and commitment in their online interpersonal and group relationships, acknowledge others equally and be sensitive to their needs and desires, interpret social situations and accommodate others' communications pro-socially, give and receive feedback constructively, as well as possess good conflict management and mediation skills. Explicit training in these skills should be undertaken, consistently, and repeatedly, not only at school and after-school activities, but also at home with parents and siblings.

Secondly, as parents, teachers, and other adults are seldom present in young people's social networking activities, children and adolescents create their own norms and rules for their online interactions. What adults can do is to have discussions with young people about the ethical stance of their norms and rules. In order to be able to discuss the ethical issues of online peer interactions, adults do not need to know the special characteristics of each application used by young people. Instead, they can direct young people's attention towards identifying the violations of ethical practices in their own and others' communications and behaviors when online, together appraising the consequences and finally encouraging them to avoid such violations. Young people should have guided training in ethical online interactions such as taking others into account, showing friendliness, avoiding hurting, encouraging others, and giving support.

Thirdly, parent and student unions as well as non-governmental organizations (NGOs) could take an active role in increasing awareness and understanding of matters related to young people's peer relationships and uses of ICTs, and guide the associated perceptual and learning processes. Children and adolescents should be made aware of social networking services which are safe and appropriate for individuals in their age group, and they should have equal skills and facilities to use these services. At the same time, being aware of the risks associated with online interaction with known and unknown individuals is crucial for their safety and well-being.

Internet social forums such as Habbo Hotel and IRC-Galleria, which have been developed in Finland to promote children's and adolescents' constructive peer networking and support the positive development of their peer relationships, provide platforms where children and adolescents can interact and socialize. As these virtual social forums are very popular amongst children and adolescents, they also provide an arena for online youth work, and many NGOs have extended their work from authentic real-life fields into these online environments, making contact with young people who spend a lot of time online. Policemen, nurses and youth workers are thus available for real-time online chats with young people, answering their questions on different issues such as drugs, alcohol, peer relationships, and bullying. Experiences from these activities have shown that there is a definite need for youth work services online.

These kinds of online services could also help in disseminating information, for example, about the social and legal aspects and consequences of substance abuse, bullying and cyberbullying, and about effective coping methods and support available. These types of websites could also provide an interactive forum for young people for sharing their concerns, ideas and experiences, getting peer and professional support, learning and enlarging their understanding of issues interesting to them, in a safe virtual environment, which would be moderated/monitored by adults. Professionals of different kinds (e.g. youth social workers, communication experts, psychologists, and police and legal experts) could be on call at particular hours, discussing online with youth about their concerns and giving them advice.

Finally, it is worth noting that children and adolescents are also in a key position to transfer knowledge about the internet and its applications to older generations. Attention should be paid to creating more dialogue between young people and adults (e.g. teachers, parents, administrators, politicians) about the use of ICTs among youth. Those who know best are young people who have gained the most up-to-date and diversified knowledge about the digital youth cultures emerging on the internet. Therefore they should be invited and trained to educate parents, teachers, policy makers and other adults who work with young people, and to help these adults to understand what kind of sites and services adolescents use online and why. These kinds of experiments have already been successfully conducted, for example, in Finland (Mediaskooppi, 2007; see Pörhölä & Lahti, 2012, for a review).

Integrating ICTs into teaching and learning

Another positive use of new technologies, and one which specifically requires positive input from adults, concerns the direct use of ICTs in teaching and learning. When used as an educational tool, ICT has the potential to inform changes to teaching and learning strategies in schools and to foster motivation for learning (Rau, Gao, & Wu, 2008). Using ICTs effectively for teaching and learning however, requires that a fundamental re-orientation or at least a reflection of one's teaching and pedagogy has to take place (Schober, Wagner, Reimann, & Spiel, 2008). This process of re-orientation involves consideration of: the learning requirements (active "knowledge construction" by the learner); the qualification and task profile of teachers and students (specific e-learning didactics); a modification of interaction and communication patterns (at least partly computer-based communication); as well as learning styles of the students (predominant self-regulated learning) (Dabbagh & Kitsantas, 2004; Kerr, Rynearson, & Kerr, 2006; Stokes, 2000). However, to date, in Europe there appears to be a lack of concrete advice on how to effectively use ICTs in teaching that takes cognizance of these issues.

The following recommendations are made to support teachers and instructors in effectively integrating ICTs in their teaching and are based on the evaluation results of the project "E-learning and E-teaching in notebook classes" (Dorninger & Horschinegg, 2002), which provides a positive example of ICT use in school contexts (Popper & Spiel, 2010; Popper *et al.*, 2012). Furthermore, findings from the Vienne E-Lecturing (VEL) project are considered (Schober *et al.*, 2008). Recommendations are provided for the preparation of lessons and the implementation of the lessons (= teaching) (for details see Spiel & Popper, 2003).

Recommendations for the preparation of lessons

Preparation of lessons using ICTs are significantly different to preparation of traditional lessons. For the effective use of ICTs the modification of traditional lessons is not recommended, rather, that new concepts are developed and trialled. There are many more learning materials available when considering online teaching and learning, not only books, however, these materials have to be searched for, selected and prepared so as to relate to the teaching and learning context in which they will be employed. Therefore, ensuring that there is enough time allocated for these tasks is important and exchanges with colleagues and support by students are strongly recommended.

In contrast to traditional teaching, more written information has to be given to the students, which also needs advanced preparation. For example, it is strongly recommended that the learning goals will be presented as concretely as possible in written form. To support a collaborative working environment, respective tasks for student teams have to be prepared in detail. Here, is has to be considered, and taken into account, that working in virtual teams might be a new experience for students. Therefore, such tasks have to be supported and carefully prepared by the teachers.

It has been shown that the explicit presentation of pedagogical goals (e.g. working collaboratively) supports learning motivation in students. Consequently, to use ICTs effectively, in the beginning, greater effort and investment in preparation is necessary than may be required for the preparation of traditional lessons. In the long run, a positive return on the investment of time and effort can be expected. Written materials can be used repeatedly and subsequent modifications are simple. Furthermore, in the case of student absence it is much easier for them to comprehend what has been going on in the meantime. Last but not least, an increase in using written tasks, learning materials etc. supports the development of standards and therefore contributes to quality assurances in schools.

Recommendations for the implementation of the lessons (= teaching)

There are also significant changes in teaching required if using ICTs systematically within lessons. For example, it is much easier to explain complex and abstract topics by using internet software to illustrate its practical relevance. Furthermore, there are also positive effects on students' self-regulatory and collaborative work competences. In the beginning, however, students need support in how to work effectively with the ICTs. Consequently, recommendations are especially addressed towards the introduction phase, when both teachers and students are not familiar with this kind of teaching. Here, a decrease in communication among students and between students and teachers is a possible risk. Therefore, one recommendation is to differentiate between time periods when using the internet, and time periods when not. Using ICTs also increases the possibilities of different problems, for example, concerning technical configuration. It is recommended that the establishment of a system of mutual support amongst students is established from the beginning. In particular, it is helpful to integrate support from students who are more advanced in using ICTs, as class mentors, to overcome any possible risk of an increasing gap between "good" and "poor" students in using new technologies in the class. It is also recommended that when doing collaborative work, poorer students are explicitly engaged and expected to contribute. As a specific challenge, learning with ICT needs high levels of concentration. Tasks, such as video–gaming or surfing the internet, reduce concentration on learning, hence it is recommended that an explicit discussion is held to explore these risks with a view to enhancing students' learning.

In sum, it is strongly recommended that ICTs are integrated into teaching in schools, so that adults can act as models and mentors in association with young people. Obviously, effort and engagement is needed in establishing ICTs as educational tools. However, in the long run there are many advantages concerning improved quality standards in teaching and in students' motivation and competencies.

Different sides of the same coin

The risks, challenges and opportunities from using social networking sites and social media were reported, by the young people interviewed by Spears *et al.* (2012, pp. 18–19), to be closely intertwined: the positive uses and impacts of technology were deemed to be the "flip side" of the negative uses and impacts and online and offline behaviors were considered "different sides of the same coin". Technology has thus become more than a transmitter or tool of information: it has become an enabler of young people's relationships, where "being online" means all day, every day, and where both positive and negative aspects of relationships are encountered. For young people, however, on and offline interactions represent a certain "sameness", where friendship-driven practices are the platform for all social interactions: be they positive or negative. These insights by young people relate specifically to the ways in which social media and social networking sites in particular, sustain and influence their friendships, as well as their capacity to manage and maintain them.

The role of disinhibition

These two faces of the same issue, however (i.e. the possibilities of new knowledge, positive social interactions, and emotional experiences versus the risks which are associated with being online, such as cyberbullying) can also be depicted as existing along a continuum where it is very difficult to trace a clear cut-off between the "bright" and the "dark" side of the impact of ICTs. In order to disentangle these two sides of the same coin, it may be helpful to consider the notion of "disinhibition", a process which occurs in online communications.

Prentice-Dunn and Rogers (1982) considered disinhibition as a product of a reduced awareness of one's public self, which led to a minor worry about other people's judgements (Fenigstein, Scheier, & Buss, 1975; Joinson, 1998). Suler (2004) advanced this notion and suggested an "online disinhibitory effect": whereby communicative exchanges are often sent anonymously and are characterized by the lack of face-to-face interactions, with an associated apparent reduction in the worry about presenting oneself in public and others' subsequent judgements: things can be said and done online, with fewer immediate consequences for the perpetrator and, subsequently, less worry.

In this particular context, social signals are easily repressed and very often people behave in a way they never would in the offline experience. This online disinhibition can manifest itself in two apparently opposite directions: a "benign disinhibition" and a "toxic disinhibition" (Suler, 2004; Nicoletti & Gallingani, 2009). Benign disinhibition concerns individuals sharing very personal things about themselves, revealing emotions, desires, fears and showing acts of generosity and kindness to help others, without thought or fear of how others might view them. An example of this, in a positive context, relates to online self-help groups: where people who have never met share deep emotions that they would never share in the context of an offline relationship. Some adolescents may confess their difficulties in socializing with peers, their doubts about sexuality or sexual identity without fear of the consequences to themselves.

Benign disinhibition can thus lead to developed and improved awareness of self, or may foster processes of identification with someone met online, helping to solve intrapsychic problems: thus contributing to the positive side of this online "coin". Benign disinhibition is also the underlying process in online services aimed at providing psychological support and counselling to adolescents, as reported, for instance, by Aoiul (2012). The same mechanism is called into question in services designed to support victims of aggression (both online and offline) as reported by counselling services in schools: "When the written word can be used synchronously, it combines the benefits of immediacy and the online disinhibition effect which has potential to build or repair relationships" (Glasheen & Campbell, 2012, p. 131).

Nicoletti and Gallingani (2009) indicated, however, that discerning between a benign and a toxic disinhibition is not so clear-cut. Toxic disinhibition represents the other side of the so-called "coin", the "dark" side of the disinhibition process online and accounts for the free use of very often bad language, harsh criticisms, and free expression of anger which easily escalates to the point where threats occur. People can also visit online sites relating to violence, crime, pornography which, in the real world, they would never explore. These disinhibitory processes may help to create a separate dimension far from the demands and responsibility of the real world. How young people interact with these forms of disinhibition require further examination, in terms of understanding how they are using ICTs positively.

Real versus virtual self: another two-sided coin

When people enter cyberspace, the real "I" is substituted by the virtual "I" in a psychological dimension, where it is possible to experience a sense of "Self", which is no longer unitary but multiple (Turkle, 1995, 2004). Gergen (1991) describes the impact of this infinite range of options for the Self as "multiphrenia", or rather, the experience in which our identities are defined and modelled by too many choices of self-expression. These multiple identities change the modality of one's relation with oneself and may propose innovative dynamics. The phenomenon of gender switching online, for example, can be one of those "benign" explorations of alternative self.

In adolescence, this behavior may contribute to exploring different dimensions of self-identity not necessarily coinciding with actual sexual identity. The internet, in fact, enables users to search for a sexual identity, as anonymity provides the opportunity to pretend to be a representative of the opposite sex (Kaare *et al.*, 2007). Also, the experiences carried out in virtual contexts (such as Second Life) may help to explore different lifestyles, values, and even rule breaking in a protected environment wherein risky behaviors may be looked at without incurring harmful and dangerous outcomes as would happen in real life. In real life, adolescents rarely have been given the opportunity to exercise power or control, either physically or socially, and virtual worlds may offer the unique opportunity of trialling choices, for instance, designing an Avatar and deciding on a wide range of options: the physical design, the clothing, the items that they buy; they may also test how these factors may affect interactions with other participants of the community. This exposure to a variety of social settings and circumstances may enable adolescents to master the skills required in social situations in the offline world (for instance reflecting on self-presentation strategies), and acquire a broadened view of themselves and the world around them.

Building on this notion of there being two sides of the same coin when it comes to understanding online behaviors, it is evident from the contributors in the previously-mentioned book (Costabile & Spears, 2012) that many of the suggested interventions relied on building the positive side of the "coin": strategies related to individual capacity, skills and positive behaviors, in order to counter the negative side: the impacts associated with engaging in toxic social relationships online and offline.

Young people are using new technologies to forge relationships, to experiment with and challenge identities and constructions of self, as well as practicing new ways of operating in a safe environment. Social networks and other ICTs provide opportunities for both positive and negative interactions, but it is through one, that the other comes to be understood.

Conclusions

Today's adults have never been teenagers in this online context, and cannot therefore fully understand the experience which technology brings to this developmental period. To fully comprehend not only how young people are using technologies and new social media generally, but also the benefits which they perceive flow from their online engagement, young people must be at the centre of any dialogue. However, it is also evident, that they need the counsel and guidance from adults in terms of developing the normal range of social skills, such as peer group entry, making and keeping friends, and conflict management, as applied to the online environment. Further to this, learning to make ethical decisions about behaviors online requires some cognizance of their own development and moral compass, and also that there is an online disinhibition effect in play, which encourages freer commentary than is acceptable in a face-to-face situation.

The so-called "new" sociology of childhood (Corsaro, 1997; James & Prout, 1997) has positioned children and young people as having agency and power, as distinct from being merely passive recipients of adult direction and supervision (see Chapter 11). This is particularly salient for young people's use of ICTs and online behaviors and engagement as they are actively involved in the evolution of their relationships across on/offline boundaries. Spears *et al.* (2012) found from speaking directly with youth from Australia, Denmark and Italy, and examining their individual and collective lived realities, that the challenges of managing personal information online; identity formation; concerns about cyberbullying and cybersafety; and understanding the legal and copyright aspects of being online were largely outweighed by the benefits they derived socially from being online. The role for adults then, in order to ensure that there is balance between the online challenges which face youth and the social outcomes which they find so positive, is to become learners with them, guides as they steer through new experiences, and mentors as they navigate the social benefits, rather than as directors who simply monitor and control their use.

References

Affleck, G., and Tennen, H. (1996). 'Construing benefits from adversity: Adaptational significance and dispositional underpinnings'. *Journal of Personality, 64*(4), 112–124.

Aouil, B. (2012). 'Online support in psychological and pedagogical practices'. In A. Costabile and B. Spears (eds.), *The impact of technology on relationships in educational settings* (pp. 116–127). London: Routledge.

Arnthórsson, H. (2012). 'Secure net addresses: secure internet and responsibility'. In A. Costabile and B. Spears (eds.), *The impact of technology on relationships in educational settings* (pp. 22–29). London: Routledge.

Banerjee, R., Robinson, C., and Smalley, D. (2010). *Evaluation of the Beatbullying Peer Mentoring Programme.* Report for Beatbullying. University of Sussex.

Blais, J., Craig, W., Pepler, D., and Connolly, J. (2008). 'Adolescents online: The importance of Internet activity choices to salient relationships'. *Journal of Youth and Adolescence, 37*(5), 522–536.

Brighi, A., Fabbri, M., Guerra, L., and Pacetti, E. (2012). 'ICT and relationships: promoting positive peer interactions'. In A. Costabile and B. Spears (eds.), *The impact of technology on relationships in educational settings* (pp. 45–54). London: Routledge.

Casas, J.A., Del Rey, R., and Ortega-Ruiz, R. (2013). 'Bullying and cyberbullying: Convergent and divergent predictor variables'. *Computers in Human Behavior, 29,* 580–587.

Corsaro, W. (1997). *The sociology of childhood.* Thousand Oaks, CA: Pine Forge Press.

Costabile, A., and Spears, B.A. (eds.). (2012). *The impact of technology on relationships in educational settings.* London: Routledge.

Cowie, H., and Smith, P.K. (2010). 'Peer support as a means of improving school safety and reducing bullying and violence'. In B. Doll, W. Pfohl, and J. Yoon (eds.), *Handbook of Youth Prevention Science* (pp. 177–193). New York: Routledge.

Dabbagh, N., and Kitsantas, A. (2004). 'Supporting self-regulation in student-centered web-based learning environments'. *International Journal on E-Learning, 3*, 40–47.

De Santo, E., and Costabile, A. (2012). 'Media education: a new academic curriculum'. In A. Costabile and B. Spears (eds.), *The impact of technology on relationships in educational settings* (pp. 30–42). London: Routledge.

Del Rey, R., Casas, J.A., and Ortega-Ruiz, R. (2012). 'The ConRed Program, an evidence based practice'. *Comunicar, 39*, 129–138.

Del Rey, R., Sánchez, V., and Ortega-Ruiz, R. (2012). 'Pro-social use of the internet in adolescence'. In A. Costabile and B. Spears (eds.), *The impact of technology on relationships in educational settings* (pp. 66–76). London: Routledge.

Dorninger, C., and Horschinegg, J. (2002). 'Mobile e-Learning und e-Teaching. Ein Modellprojekt mit Schülernotebooks an Österreichs Sekundarschulen'. [Mobile e-Learning and e-Teaching. A model project with student notebooks at Austrian secondary schools]. *Die Deutsche Schule, 94*(2), 247–256.

Eisner, M.P., and Malti, T. (2012). 'The future of research on evidence-based developmental violence prevention'. *International Journal of Conflict and Violence, 6*(2), 166–175.

Erikson, E. (1968). *Gioventù e crisi di identità*. Armando: Rome.

Fenigstein, A., Scheier, M.F., and Buss, A.H. (1975). 'Public and private self consciousness: Assessment and theory'. *Journal of Consulting and Clinical Psychology, 43*, 522–527.

Ferri, P. (2011). *I nativi digitali*. Milan: Mondadori.

Festinger, L. (1954). A theory of social comparison processes. *Human Relations, 7*(2), 117–140.

Gergen, K. (1991). *The saturated self: dilemmas of identity in contemporary life*. New York: Basic Books.

Glasheen, K., and Campbell, M.A. (2012). 'Online counseling for enhancing relationships'. In A. Costabile and B. Spears (eds.), *The impact of technology on relationships in educational settings* (pp. 128–136). London: Routledge.

Greenfield, P., and Yan, Z. (2006). 'Children, adolescents, and the Internet: A new field of inquiry in developmental psychology'. *Developmental Psychology, 42*, 391–394.

Gruder, C.L. (1971). 'Determinants of social comparison choices'. *Journal of Experimental Social Psychology, 7*(5), 473–489.

Hayat, Z., and Amichai-Hamburger, Y. (2012). 'Kids in the fast lane: achieving wellbeing through online support'. In A. Costabile and B. Spears (eds.), *The impact of technology on relationships in educational settings* (pp. 102–115). London: Routledge.

James, A., and Prout, A. (1997). *Constructing and reconstructing childhood: Contemporary issues in the sociological study of childhood*. London: Falmer Press.

Johnson, G.M. (2008). 'Cognitive processing differences between frequent and infrequent Internet users'. *Computers in Human Behavior, 24*, 2094–2106.

——(2010). 'Young children's Internet use at home and school: Patterns and profiles'. *Journal of Early Childhood Research, 8*(3), 282–293.

Joinson, A. (1998). 'Causes and implications of disinhibited behavior on the Internet'. In J. Gackenbach (ed.). *Psychology and the Internet: intrapersonal, interpersonal, and transpersonal implications* (pp. 43–60). San Diego: Academic Press.

Kaare, B.H., Brandtzæg, P.B., Heim, J., and Endestad, T. (2007). 'In the borderland between family orientation and peer culture: the use of communication technologies among Norwegian tweens'. *New Media & Society, 9*(4), 603–624.

Kerr, M., Rynearson, K., and Kerr, M. (2006). 'Student characteristics for online learning success'. *Internet and Higher Education, 9,* 91–105.

Lau, P.W.C., Lau, E.Y., Wong, D.P., and Ransdell, L. (2011). 'A systematic review of information and communication technology-based interventions for promoting physical activity behavior change in children and adolescents'. *Journal of Medical Internet Research, 13*(3), e48. Retrieved April 19, 2013 from http://www.jmir.org/2011/3/e48/.

Lenhart, A., Purcell, K., Smith, A., and Zickuhr, K. (2010). *Social media and mobile internet use among teens and young adults.* Washington, DC: Pew Internet and American Life Project.

Lenhart, A., Rainie, L., and Lewis, O. (2001). *Teenage life online.* Washington DC: Pew Internet and American Life Project.

Livingstone, S., and Haddon, L. (2011). *Management report EU Kids Online II: enhancing knowledge regarding European children's use, risk and safety online.* EU Kids Online Network, London, UK.

Mediaskooppi (2007). *Mediaskoopin Esittelydiat Englanniksi.* Online. Retrieved April 23, 2010 from http://www.mediaskooppi.net/aineistot/mediascope.pdf.

Menesini, E., and Nocentini, A. (2012). 'Peer education intervention: Face-to-face versus online'. In A. Costabile and B. Spears (eds.), *The impact of technology on relationships in educational settings* (pp. 139–150). London: Routledge.

Nicoletti, S., and Gallingani, F. (2009). 'Behavioural psychopathology online and cyberbullying'. In M.L. Genta, A. Brighi, and A. Guarini (eds.), *Bullying and cyberbullying in adolescence* (pp. 59–76). Rome: Carocci.

O'Connel, R., Price, P., and Barrow, C. (2004). *Emerging trend amongst primary school children's use of the Internet.* Preston: University of Central Lancashire.

Ortega-Ruiz, R., and Del Rey, R. (2004). *Construir la convivencia.* Barcelona: Edebé.

Ortega-Ruiz, R., Del Rey, R., and Casas, J.A. (2012). 'Empowering students against bullying and cyberbullying: Evaluation of an Italian peer-led model'. *International Journal of Conflict and Violence, 6*(2), 313–320.

Palladino, B.E., Nocentini, A., and Menesini, E. (2012). 'Online and offline peer led models against bullying and cyberbullying'. *Psicothema, 24,* 634–639.

Palmonari, A. (2011). *Psicologia dell'adolescenza.* Bologna: Il Mulino.

Pelastakaa, L. (2009). *Lapsen Ääni 2009.* Helsinki, Finland: Pelastakaa Lapset ry.

Perren, S., Corcoran, L., Cowie, H., Dehue, F., Garcia, D., McGuckin, C., Sevcikova, A., Tsatsou, P., and Völlink, T. (2012). 'Tackling cyberbullying: A review of empirical evidence regarding successful responses by students, parents and schools'. *International Journal of Conflict and Violence, 6*(2), 283–293.

Popper, V., and Spiel, C. (2010). 'Entwicklung eines komplexen dreistufigen Evaluationsdesigns unter schwierigen Rahmenbedingungen: Die Evaluation von Notebook-Klassen'. [Development of a complex three-stage evaluation design under difficult conditions: Evaluation of notebook classes]. *Zeitschrift für Evaluation, 9*(1), 7–28.

Popper, V., Strohmeier, D., and Spiel, C. (2012). 'Using the internet positively in schools: The case for notebooks'. In A. Costabile and B. Spears (eds.), *The impact of technology on relationships in educational settings* (pp. 77–90). London: Routledge.

Pörhölä, M., and Lahti, H. (2012). 'The use of interpersonal communication technologies to establish and maintain peer relationships'. In A. Costabile and

B. Spears (eds.), *The impact of technology on relationships in educational settings* (pp. 55–65). London: Routledge.

Poskiparta, E., Kaukiainen, A., Pöyhonen, V., and Salmivalli, C. (2012). 'Bullies' and victims' experiences of the anti-bullying game from the KiVa program'. In A. Costabile and B.A. Spears (eds.), *The impact of technology on relationships in educational settings* (pp. 158–168). London: Routledge.

Prentice-Dunn, S., and Rogers, R.W. (1982). 'Effects of public and private self-awareness on deindividuation and aggression'. *Journal of Personality and Social Psychology, 43*(3), 503–513.

Pyźalski, J. (2012). 'The digital generation gap revisited: constructive and dysfunctional patterns of social media usage'. In A. Costabile and B.A. Spears (eds.), *The impact of technology on relationships in educational settings* (pp. 91–101). London: Routledge.

Rau, P.P., Gao, Q., and Wu, L. (2008). 'Using mobile communication technology in high school education: Motivation, pressure, and learning performance'. *Computers & Education, 50*(1), 1–22.

Richards, D. (2009). 'Features and benefits of online counselling at University: Trinity College Online Mental Health Community'. *British Journal of Guidance & Counselling, 37*(3), 231–242.

Rimal, R., Lapinski, M., Cook, R., and Real, K. (2005). 'Moving toward a theory of normative influences: How perceived benefits and similarity moderate the impact of descriptive norms on behaviors'. *Journal of Health Communication, 10*, 433–450.

Salmivalli, C., and Poskiparta, E. (2012). 'KiVa antibullying program: Overview of evaluation studies based on a randomized controlled trial and national rollout in Finland'. *International Journal of Conflict and Violence, 6*(2), 293–301.

Schober, B., Wagner, P., Reimann, R., and Spiel, C. (2008). 'Vienna E-Lecturing (VEL): Learning how to learn self-regulated in an internet-based blended learning setting'. *International Journal on e-Learning, 7*(4), 703–723.

Schultze-Krumbholz, A., Wölfer, R., Jäkel, A., Zagorscak, P., and Scheithauer, H. (2012). 'Prevention of cyberbullying in Germany – The Medienhelden Program'. Paper presented at the International Conference on Cyberbullying, 28–29 June, Paris.

Sjöberg, U. (2002). *Screen rites: A study of Swedish young people's use and meaning-making of screen-based media in everyday life.* Sweden: University of Lund.

Slee, P., Campbell, M., and Spears, B. (2012). *Child, adolescent and family development.* Cambridge: Cambridge University Press.

Smith, P.K., Pepler, D., and Rigby, K. (eds.) (2004). *Bullying in schools: How successful can interventions be?* Cambridge: Cambridge University Press.

Smith, R., and Curtin, P. (2001). 'Children, computers and life online: education in a cyber-world'. In I. Snyder (ed.), *Page to screen: Taking literacy into the electronic era* (pp. 213–234). London: Routledge.

Spears, B.A. (2010). 'CyberChat #3: Tech-savvy Tots'. *Educational technology solutions, 37*, 20. Retrieved April 19, 2013 from http://www.decd.sa.gov.au/speced2/files/links/Cyber_Chat_ETS37.pdf.

——(2012). 'A review of initiatives using technology to promote cyber-safety and digital citizenship'. In A. Costabile and B.A. Spears (eds.), *The impact of technology on relationships in educational settings* (pp. 188–203). London: Routledge.

Spears, B.A., and Costabile, A. (2012). 'Introduction'. In A. Costabile and B.A. Spears (eds.), *The impact of technology on relationships in educational settings* (pp. 1–4). London: Routledge.

Spears, B.A., Kofoed, J., Bartolo, M.G., Palermiti, A., and Costabile, A. (2012). 'Positive uses of social networking sites: Youth voice perspectives'. In A. Costabile and B.A. Spears (eds.), *The impact of technology on relationships in educational settings* (pp. 7–21). London: Routledge.

Spiel, C., and Popper, V. (2003). 'Evaluierung des österreichweiten Modellversuchs "E-Learning und E-Teaching mit Schueler/-innen-Notebooks". Abschlussbericht'. [Evaluation of the Austrian-wide model test 'E-learning and e-teaching with student notebooks'. Final report]. Vienna: Bundesministerium für Bildung, Wissenschaft und Kultur.

Stern, S. (2008). 'Producing sites, exploring identities: Youth online authorship. Youth, Identity, and Digital Media'. In D. Buckingham (Ed.), *The John D. and Catherine T. MacArthur Foundation Series on Digital Media and Learning* (pp. 95–118). Cambridge, MA: The MIT Press.

Stokes, S. (2000). 'Preparing students to take online interactive courses'. *The Internet and Higher Education, 2,* 161–169.

Subrahmanyam, K., Greenfield, P.M., Kraut, R., and Gross, E. (2001). 'The impact of computer use on children's and adolescent's development'. *Applied Developmental Psychology, 22,* 7–30.

Suler, J. (2004). 'The online disinhibition effect'. *CyberPsychology and Behavior, 7(3),* 321–326.

Thompson, F., Robinson, S., and Smith, P.K. (2013). 'An evaluation of some cyberbullying interventions in England'. In M.L. Genta, A. Brighi, and A. Guarini (eds.), *Cyberbullismo: Ricerche e Strategie di Intervento* (Cyberbullying research and intervention strategies) (pp. 136–153). Milano: Franco Angeli.

Ttofi, M., and Farrington, D.P. (2011). 'Effectiveness of school-based programs to reduce bullying: A systematic and meta-analytic review'. *Journal of Experimental Criminology, 7,* 27–56.

Turkle, S. (1995). *Life on the screen: Identity in the age of internet.* New York: Simon & Schuster.

——(2004). 'Whither psychoanalysis in computer culture?' *Psychoanalytic Psychology, 21*(1), 16–30.

Valcke, M., De Wever, B., Van Keer, H., and Schellens, T. (2011). 'Long term study of safe internet use of young children'. *Computers & Education, 57*(1), 1292–1305.

Valkenburg, P.M., and Peter, J. (2007). 'Preadolescents' and adolescents' online communication and their closeness to friends'. *Developmental Psychology, 43*(2), 267–277.

von Kaenel-Flatt, J., and Douglas, T. (2012). 'Cybermentoring'. In A. Costabile and B.A. Spears (eds.), *The impact of technology on relationships in educational settings* (pp. 151–157). London: Routledge.

Wolke, D., and Sapouna, M. (2012). 'FearNot! An innovative interdisciplinary virtual intervention to reduce bullying and victimization'. In A. Costabile and B.A. Spears (eds.), *The impact of technology on relationships in educational settings* (pp. 169–177). London: Routledge

Wotherspoon, A.J., Cox, G., and Slee, P.T. (2012). 'Using mobile phones to counter cyberbullying: an innovative project'. In A. Costabile and B.A. Spears (eds.), *The impact of technology on relationships in educational settings* (pp. 178–187). London: Routledge.

11 Transgressing research binaries

Youth as knowledge brokers in cyberbullying research

Barbara Spears and Jette Kofoed

Introduction

Researchers from many countries and many fields of enquiry, such as psychology, education, sociology and health promotion have raised the question of how we can best approach the study of cyberbullying. Traditionally, researchers favor one or other of the investigative paradigms: quantitative or qualitative, determined either according to their field of enquiry or their beliefs and ways of interacting with the world. Each brings with it a set of standards and processes which guide researchers' actions. Increasingly, however, mixed methodologies are being employed across many disciplines. Education and sociology, for example, often employ qualitative/interpretive approaches such as: naturalistic enquiry, critical theory, interpretivism, constructivism, or feminist and emancipist enquiry, which are founded upon the notion that human beings are active agents in their social worlds, constructing meaning, which is constantly being created, changed, modified and developed through interaction. This paradigm supports that there are many "truths" and multiple realities. Psychology, on the other hand, traditionally favors empirical methods founded on positivism, with an emphasis on objective reality, where directly observable and measurable behaviors are considered, and theories tested.

As with any new phenomenon, such as cyberbullying, the rush to understand it often centers on how it is defined and subsequently measured, so that its prevalence and nature can inform policy and practice. Cyberbullying has its research roots in earlier studies into school bullying, which, over the past 35 years, has been driven largely by the quantitative paradigm (Jimerson, Swearer, & Espelage, 2010; Mishna, 2012). This chapter argues, however, that the time is right to challenge this methodological dominance of one paradigm over another, contending that qualitative/interpretive enquiry is of equal import if we are to understand this phenomenon fully, and that youth voice is central to that understanding.

In order to situate this argument, we first consider how the view of childhood has changed over time, and with it, the role that children and youth play in society and subsequently in research. With a focus on cyberbullying, a contemporary iteration of traditional school bullying, this chapter argues for transgressing the research binaries which have traditionally accompanied those views. In doing so, it challenges this research community to shift from privileging one paradigm over the other, so that both are valued equally, and to position youth voice and youth-centered methodologies as necessary if we are to more completely and competently enable this new phenomenon to be investigated and understood.

Understandings of childhood

The adoption of the Convention on the Rights of the Child, (UNCRC) by the United Nations General Assembly in 1989, (United Nations Convention on Rights of the Child, UNCRC 1989) is important in this context, for it has changed the way that children are viewed by contemporary society, and hence the view of children within research. This Convention highlighted that children and young people have certain rights which adults need to uphold: (1) the right to participate; (2) the right to have their say in decisions that affect them; and (3) the right to share opinions about matters which are important or impact upon them. In doing so, the Convention shifted earlier perceptions of childhood which ascribed children as passive recipients of knowledge, and as "adults in waiting", towards being social actors and agents, knowledgeable in their own worlds, and with the right to voice that knowledge.

Whilst the UNCRC (1989) extended previously-held views of children's status, rights and their role in society, the shift towards an online society is pertinent in terms of how the current technological and communications upheavals of recent times might again be influencing our views of children, young people, childhood and adolescence. It is important then, to briefly revisit the past, so as to inform the current perspective, understanding the past positions, childhood and youth in a context of social, economic, political, technological and philosophical change. What is of relevance to this chapter is how research has been constructed in relation to these views of childhood and how it might be positioned in the future in relation to understanding online social practices and cyberbullying in particular. How we conceptualize and understand childhood is relevant here, as cyberbullying presents a new and challenging form of bullying: a relationality which requires a contemporary understanding of childhood and adolescence in a wired/ wireless society.

The past

Children in Western societies have been viewed for centuries as having little status or no rights in an adult world. During mediaeval times, they were viewed solely as property (Elkind, 1987), with paternalistic/patriarchic approaches common in the 17th and 18th centuries (Russell, 1974). The

Industrial revolution of the 18th and 19th centuries brought about significant social and economic upheaval, where children were seen in predominantly economic terms, with few rights. However, child labor laws in the 19th century brought about changes, so that children were finally protected from these extremes and abuses. Finally, in the 20th century, through the emergence of the field of psychology and contributions of developmental psychology in particular, childhood came to be considered separate from adulthood: a distinct period of development comprised of several unique stages (early, middle, late and adolescence).

These images of children and childhood presented above, lead us through an understanding of *adult* conceptions of childhood across temporal, social, philosophical and economic upheavals, which reach back through Locke's view of the child at birth as "tabula rasa", to that of Wesley's s*iniquitous* child; Rousseau's *virtuous* child; and Elkind's *competent* child (Slee, Campbell & Spears, 2012). The notion of the *postmodern* child, who has *agency* (the capacity to act and make own free choices) and competence, and who is a social actor, impacting on and being impacted by his/her environment emerged from sociological approaches to understanding childhood in the early-mid 1990s (Corsaro, 1997; James & Prout, 1997).

It is important to consider in more detail, an understanding of the *postmodern* childhood view, for this is the child view which emerged around the time that the Internet appeared in the public domain (viz 1995) and one which subscribes to the socio-cultural view of childhood (see below). Most recently, in the 21st century, childhood can be seen in terms of the "wired" and the "wireless" child (Slee, Campbell, & Spears, 2012), who is directly and indirectly embedded in and intertwined with the online community. This latest view of childhood identifies that technology is ubiquitous in contemporary life and dominates young people's social interactions. In shifting from using PCs which were locked to desktops (the "wired" child) through to the convergence and increasing mobilization of technologies through increasingly smaller devices, the so-called "wireless" child has emerged as one who has independence, agency and operates within a social reality which does not separate online from offline environments.

The transformations above of how childhood has been viewed over time reflect the different social contexts, philosophical, psychological, sociological and technological views relevant to each century. It is these larger world views which have contributed to the ways in which childhood has been understood, and which have subsequently contributed to the research binaries with which we are now so familiar.

Sociocultural approaches to childhood

Whilst the study of childhood and adolescence has been approached differently by different disciplines, psychology and sociology in particular have both contributed significantly to the contemporary view of the child and childhood. Rather than seeking out the differences between these domains, this chapter argues for seeking out the commonalities between these disciplines, so that child/youth voice collectively may contribute to our greater understanding of cyberbullying.

By way of background, in the early 1990s, the sociology of childhood was just emerging as a sub-discipline, but by the late 1990s, several authors posited ways of thinking about childhood, which capitalized on both the United Nations Convention on the Rights of the Child (UNCRC, 1989) through Articles 12 and 13, and the Save the Children Fund submission to the UN Summit on Social Development (1995). The Rights of the Child Convention places a moral and legal imperative upon all adults: to listen to and hear the opinions of children, and to involve them in decision-making, as well as ensuring that children receive and can share information through age appropriate participation. How this document is interpreted, however, will depend on the theoretical and philosophical views one holds regarding development or constructions of childhood. The *postmodern* and now *wireless* view of childhood sits well here: the agentic and technologically-competent child, who can and does make free choices as a social actor, reciprocally interacting with the environment.

The latter document (Save the Children) highlighted several deficits in planning for children that were evident at that time (1995): a failure to collect child-specific information; lack of recognition of children's productive contribution; no participation of children in decision-making; the use of an inappropriate "standard model of childhood"; the pursuit of adult interests that render children passive; and lack of attention to gender and generational relationships. When viewed through the lens of 21st century cyberbullying research, however, these so-called deficits of the mid-1990s planning, highlight opportunities upon which we have not currently capitalized to any great extent and serve to confirm that there is still much to be done: i.e. collection of child-specific information (about cyberbullying); recognition of children's productive contribution (to our understanding of cyberbullying); and participation of children in decision-making (in designing interventions against cyberbullying).

Corsaro's *The Sociology of the Child* (1997), James and Prout's *Constructing and Reconstructing Childhood* (1997), and James, Jenks, and Prout's *Theorizing Childhood* (1998) have all significantly contributed to the movement now recognized as the *new sociology of childhood*, with James and Prout (1997) proposing an emergent paradigm for the study of childhood. The following key tenets from James and Prout (1997, p. viii–xiii), which underpin this proposed paradigm are informative when re-considering cyberbullying and how it interplays with young people's lives in the 21st century. These tenets are that:

- childhood is a social construction;
- childhood is a variable in social analysis;

- children's social relationships and cultures are worthy of study in their own right;
- children should be looked upon as social actors, not as outcomes of social processes;
- ethnography and (more recently) other participatory methods are useful for the study of childhood;
- the study of childhood requires engagement with reconstructing childhood in society.

The notion of children's social relationships and cultures being worthy of study (point 3 above) is a particularly salient one when reconsidering cyberbullying research: as technology has brought a new cultural context for children and youth which is not static, but is entwined with what they actually *do* in their social, technologically-mediated relationships. The other tenets support possible new ways of studying the cyberbullying phenomenon. That is: in order to understand the meaning-making of children and youth in this context, we need to know how *they* are constructing their social relations; also, that there is not "one childhood", but many; and that children and youth are active social agents in their own social processes.

Alongside these understandings of postmodern and wireless childhood, are perspectives which relate to and conform with the dominant paradigms of previous times: from research practices where something was *done to* children and young people (subjects) (Woodhead & Faulkner, 2000); to something that can be *conducted with* them (as informed consenting participants) (Alderson, 2000; Alderson & Morrow, 2004); to contemporary practices which are: *enabling* of young people *as knowledge brokers, co-constructors of knowledge,* and undertaking research co-designed *by* them (Boyden & Ennew, 1997; Spears & Zeederberg, 2013).

Multiple perspectives

The point of continuity being argued is that the child and the child's world are central to understanding key aspects of cyberbullying and that youth are operating within broad and varied socio-cultural contexts. The challenge for cyberbullying researchers is to capture the experience of being a child/young person in an embedded, intertwined sociality of so-called "real" and "virtual" relationalities, when we as adults have no personal experience to draw upon. Whilst we have all *been* children, we can never *be* or *become* children again, as we all now filter the world through our adult experiences and we simply cannot apply our understanding from a previous generation to contemporary childhood.

Children and young people have the so-called *insider* perspective to these worlds and we need to support them as co-researchers, to design, carry out and disseminate research with us, so that our understanding is enhanced and can be used to drive policy and practice for their benefit. Kellett (2005, p. 8) noted that children/youth have different (research) priorities, frame questions differently and collect data in different ways to adults. It is through listening to their expertise, respecting their methods and valuing their insights, and enabling young people to assume responsibility for educating themselves and the adults around them, that greater understanding of cyberbullying can be achieved.

In order to achieve a more complex understanding of cyberbullying from a youth voice perspective, we suggest that contemporary cyberbullying researchers need to recognize the importance and power of the youth perspective and expand their repertoire of methods, to not only transgress beyond the binary of one or the other (qualitative/quantitative) paradigms, but to move towards mixed methods which value both: where one is not privileged over the other, but which simultaneously and systematically move closer to working directly with young people as co-generators of new knowledge.

The new paradigm for the study of childhood as proposed by James and Prout (1997), and others linked with the *new sociology of childhood* (Hallet & Prout, 2003), point to this place and time in cyberbullying research, suggesting the following: it requires a youth view; a blending of the sociological and psychological approaches where children and youth are at the centre of the phenomenon; where their social and cultural practices operate within an online/offline social group context, and where they are social agents in the process.

Bullying and cyberbullying research practices

Traditionally, bullying research has focused on self-report/survey methodologies and the generalizability of findings through quantitative empirical pursuits. This is not surprising, since its inception as a field of research in Scandinavia in the late 1970s (Olweus, 1978), has been largely led by the developmental/psychological domain, which has sought to measure problems and to test/re-test theory-driven hypotheses. Most recently, health domains have contributed to ways of examining issues related to intervention implementation and evaluation. These are entirely valid pursuits, but they are not the only ones we could be considering in the quest to understand this complex phenomenon known as cyberbullying.

This chapter argues that the United Nations Convention on the Rights of the Child (UNCRC, 1989) should be actively acknowledged and engaged when researching into bullying and cyberbullying practices with young people in a technologically rich 21st century. The rights of young people to inform practices which impact upon them should be a fundamental tenet of contemporary cyberbullying research: where young people are not viewed as participants/objects that we "do" research "on" or "to", but rather, as participants/collaborators who are:

- listened to and engaged with, in building and brokering new knowledge: ensuring *their right to participate*;

- co-designers of interventions and tools: ensuring their right *to have their say in decisions that affect them*;
- enabled as co-researchers, to create, carry out and disseminate research alongside adults: ensuring their right *to share opinions about matters which are of import or impact upon them*.

These rights position children and young people beyond simply completing a survey, participating in an interview or focus group, or membership of a committee or advisory group which may be tokenistic and still adult moderated and led, but rather center them in the research process. We are not suggesting that young people should not be asked to fill out questionnaires, nor to participate in interviews or focus groups. Rather, we are proposing that each time, we carefully consider how youth voice can be heard and taken into account in numerous ways. Such centering can be done in a number of ways. One way of doing it can be to take young people's subjective accounts and constructions of their social worlds as potentially enabling of a *youth-centered, user-led approach to research on cyberbullying*, as distinct from responding to a research agenda which is always adult/"expert"-led and driven.

Smith and Brain (2000) in their overview of bullying research over the preceding two decades, summarized the historical research shifts which had occurred across different continents, countries and cultures, together with the different research foci over time, ranging from the individual (target/perpetrator) to the group (participant roles; social dynamic) and to whole-school contexts (school climate; community issue), highlighting a significant body of work undertaken worldwide.

An examination of the methodological approaches employed however, was not undertaken, but what is evident, with even a cursory glance at the literature during that time, is that what has been largely missing in this research trajectory which now spans some 35 years, is the *voice* of young people and the methodologies which allow for carefully listening to, engaging and sharing the research journey with them.

This is not to suggest however, that qualitative/interpretive accounts of bullying experiences have not been noted in the past, indeed they have been (e.g. Bansel, Davies, Laws, & Linnell, 2009; Kofoed, 2009; Kofoed & Ringrose, 2012; Mishna, 2004; Owens, Shute, & Slee, 2000; Ringrose & Reynold, 2011; Spears, Slee, Owens, & Johnson, 2009) but equally, qualitative/interpretive studies have not been afforded the same privileging/emphasis in the cyberbullying literature, as quantitative studies. Crudely speaking, in the cyberbullying research domain, qualitative/interpretive accounts have been conceptualized and identified as non-positivist inquiry: as adjuncts to empirical, scientific studies, which are largely small-sample, subjective, limited in nature and non-generalizable. This position diminishes the importance of this work and the contribution it makes to this field of enquiry.

In other disciplines, however, qualitative/interpretive research is conceptualized as a valid source of enquiry with its own rich history, and which explores not only the lived experiences of individuals or contexts, but the discourses which support power relations contributing to the development of knowledge and theory through those insights. Bansel *et al.* (2009) explored, for example, the experience of bullying through stories generated through a collective biography workshop and fictional accounts of bullying. Rather than examine bullying as individual and family pathology, they explored the everyday relations of power in children's lives, through individuals reflecting on their own memories and stories, in relation to existing texts about bullying: both academic and fictional: Atwood's *Cat's Eye* (1988); Hughes' *Tom Brown's School Days* (1857). The process involved shifting from individual, autobiographical stories, to a collective story, produced by the group which reflected power practices of inclusion and exclusion, and membership maintenance occurring in the broader school setting. This creative methodology unpacked the individual story against what was known collectively, and brought a depth of understanding about normalization process in school settings across all levels of power. This is clearly not research that is driven by the need to know the experiences of how many, or how often, but rather, it explored the phenomenon of the power differential through the lived experiences of those who were present in the situation: through their eyes, their meaning and their voice, triangulated to both academic and fictional literature and reflecting the rights of young people to inform practices which impact upon them.

In sum, research practices from the field of bullying are largely founded in empiricism and have logically contributed to how we have approached researching cyberbullying as it emerged. The studies into bullying which have used alternate methods, are not as visible, yet hold potential insights when applied to cyberbullying practices where the subtleties of a technologically mediated school-life can be unfolded and unpacked in ways that allow us to understand new dimensions of the phenomenon that have hitherto mostly been counted.

Cyberbullying

With the advent of cyberbullying, new ways of enquiry have emerged as they are needed in order to explore this phenomenon which has exploded onto the social radar (Kofoed, 2013a; Kofoed, 2013b; Kofoed & Ringrose, 2012; Spears *et al.*, 2011; Spears & Zeederberg, 2013). Spears *et al.* (2011, p. 9) suggested that young people are change agents and partners, as they are the most experienced stakeholders in a socially mobile context, straddling both on and offline environments and are thus well positioned to assist adults to help them navigate it safely and to research the phenomenon in ways that allows for understanding the complexities of it.

The emergence then, of qualitative studies in relation to cyberbullying, speaks to researchers' awareness of needing different approaches to learn more about this phenomenon. Several studies have employed interviews and focus groups (e.g. Agatston, Kowalski, & Limber, 2007; Grigg, 2010; Kofoed, 2009, 2013a; Mishna, Saini, & Solomon, 2009; Nocentini *et al.*, 2010; Vanderbosch & Van Cleemput, 2008). Others have utilized such methods as ethnographies, case studies, phenomenological approaches, and grounded theory (e.g. Kofoed, 2013a; Maher, 2008; Mishna, McLuckie, & Saini, 2009; Mishna, Saini, & Solomon, 2009). Spears *et al.* (2008, 2009) employed creative pedagogical practices such as using "Y" charts, where students recorded what cyber and covert bullying "looked like, sounded like and felt like" to them in their daily lives, as well as harnessing digital technologies to assist the gathering and recording of stories over time. Kofoed (2013a) employed forwarding of text messages and worked with emerging and flexible research designs (Kofoed, 2007) in order to allow the researcher to move according to the changing field, new technologies and altering processes of becoming, among the children and youth involved.

Most recently, and building upon these earlier qualitative studies, researchers have highlighted the need for new ways of utilizing qualitative enquiry as a means of expanding understanding about cyberbullying, and in particular, the role that youth, through their engagement and voice must play in this endeavor. These include methodologies that take into account transgressing research binaries and of including youth voice in such transgressive methodologies (e.g. Bauman & Cross, 2013; Kofoed & Søndergaard, 2009, 2013; Mishna & Van Wert, 2012; Schott & Søndergaard, 2013; Spears & Zeederberg, 2013; Underwood & Card, 2013).

In addition, Espinoza and Juvonen (2013) draw attention to methods which have been previously employed in school-based bullying which are currently being *underutilized* in the cyberbullying area: e.g. daily diaries, peer informants (bystanders) and longitudinal approaches. Making use of publicly available data to explore the online discourse of youth in chat rooms, blogs, and social networking sites and observational research of interactions online, along with experimental manipulation of the environments, are research opportunities suggested by them that are not yet fully realized. What is still lacking, however, is youth-*centered* and youth-*driven* research.

Transgression and the challenges of the paradigms

The challenge for cyberbullying research concerns whether researchers adhere to the existing binaries of quantitative/qualitative research methodologies or embrace and possibly go beyond a mixed-methods approach, which claims to enable greater diversity of methods to deal with increasingly more complex social challenges: potentially offering diverse solutions to diverse problems.

In choosing to adhere to the existing binaries, inquiry will continue to represent an empiricist/other dichotomy. However, in the case of bullying/ cyberbullying research, maintaining this stance will provide an opportunity for *quantitative* research to be refined and indeed re/constructed to meet the challenges of working alongside the online environment, including consideration of ethical issues when working online (Mishna, Underwood, Milne, & Gibson, 2013). New ways of working empirically with online studies could emerge. Maintaining the binary approach will also enable *qualitative* enquiry in this domain to develop into a strong body of work in its own right, which, to date, has been lacking. In this way, qualitative enquiry into cyberbullying can shift from having "adjunct" status: as a pre-cursor activity to instrument item development, or the follow-up interviews to provide support for findings from survey approaches, and can openly expand to stand alongside quantitative studies, offering an alternate, trustworthy, legitimate, stand-alone approach to studying the lived realities and multiple perspectives of this phenomenon. The recent studies noted above, are beginning to address the dearth of qualitative/interpretive enquiry in this field and are providing much needed rich insights into these negative social practices, along with methodological freshness.

Mixed-methods have been described by Tashakkori and Teddlie (2003) as the "third methodological movement of the 20th century" (p. ix), and if both paradigms are afforded equal status, then this case could be successfully argued. However, Giddings (2006) suggests that mixed methods often fail in this regard, and are actually "positivism dressed in drag" (p. 198), which continue to promote and privilege a predominantly positivist view of research, and only "pay[ing] tokenistic attention to the qualitative contribution". We argue however, for a more equitable view of mixed methods: one where both paradigms enlighten the field of cyberbullying research practices and therefore contribute equally to knowledge development in this field. In so doing, we acknowledge that mixed methods have moved in innovative directions within many fields. However, within the field of cyberbullying research, we caution that these innovations have not yet been made to any great extent.

Adopting a mixed-method approach in the cyberbullying research domain suggests the best of both worlds, in that it offers a bridge between the paradigms, a holistic view of the issue and thus greater certainty in the findings (Henningsen & Søndergaard, 2000; Henningsen *et al.*, 2013). Indeed, Denzin (1978) reported that the combination of quantitative and qualitative studies was a means of ensuring confidence when drawing conclusions. This is an important development as there is promise in transgressing the binaries and employing mixed methods to scrutinize what may already be understood within cyberbullying literature. In developing this field further it is therefore important to pay attention to the power relations between the two paradigms in pursuing equity *between* the paradigms.

Furthermore, the practice of quantifying qualitative data through content analysis, actually serves to diminish its integrity as a qualitative approach, with the ensuing effect that any potential contribution of the approach to understanding the phenomenon, may be lost when individual, information-rich accounts are reduced to numbers for statistical analysis. Employing mixed methods to enhance this field is hence much more than adding qualitative approaches to surveys. It includes reconfiguring and re-tooling methodologies for specific analytic purposes (Henningsen *et al.*, 2013).

Does cyberbullying research, however, need different ways of thinking to go beyond the well-established research boundaries? Cyberbullying is a 21st century iteration of an age-old problem, and in this chapter we argue not only for the need to break away from the unequal dichotomy of qualitative and quantitative approaches, and to embrace diverse mixed methods approaches, but to also shift towards recognition of the new paradigm of childhood as espoused by Corsaro (1997) and colleagues, where the construction of child/childhood is crucial to enquiry, where centralizing youth voice and elevating participants to the roles of co-researchers and co-generators of new knowledge is fundamental to understanding. There are two reasons for this.

First, the insights that can be gained from qualitative/interpretive studies reflect the subtleties of youth life as mediated by evolving, diverse technologies, elevating these methods to greater importance. Kofoed's (2013) study, which followed young people and technologies across a number of sites and involved fieldwork at several locations, "both real and virtual", reveals the complexities of working with youth when text messages circulate within and beyond the classroom. Noting the interplay between material, temporal-discursive and technological space, Kofoed reports that the methods employed required months of participant observations, virtual fieldwork on social networking sites and interviews. Drawings and essays and focus groups were also used to gather data.

This is not "moment in time" research, where a survey can capture these intersecting subtleties. Rather, the narratives bring a thick, rich understanding of the phenomenon, which, in Kofoed's case (Kofoed, 2009, 2013), highlight the affectivity of cyberbullying and particularly the non-simultaneity of cyberbullying, i.e. the "presence of displaced positions and displaced time, their entanglements and interactions" (Kofoed, 2009, p. 117). It also drew out the inherent "messiness" of cyberbullying and these online/offline interactions and therefore the difficulties associated with intervening. The challenge for educators in this, and any school situation where texting and cyberbullying occurs, was how to exert control and enforce discipline when confronted with "traces of evidence which vanished and did not return" (Kofoed, 2009, p. 129).

Similarly, Spears *et al.* (2008, 2009) noted the ephemeral nature of a young girl's cyberbullying experiences: "It's like the wind.... [You] feel the effects, but it is hard to see" (p. 6) and therefore the inherent difficulty in trying to define, measure and deal with cyberbullying in school settings. Adult researchers involved with these examples, were placed into a realm where they have never personally experienced the practices, the situations, the affective tenor of these or the technological context, making it essential that young people find ways of describing their experiences, and equally, ways for all researchers to value those narratives.

Knowledge brokers

Young people are thus the brokers, traders and advisors of this new knowledge and their voice provides a bridge between what they know and understand, and what researchers need to know and understand to properly inform policy and practice. Lomas (2001, p. 131) defined knowledge brokering in the context of health research as the process of linking and facilitating researchers and decision-makers "…so that they are able to better understand each other's goals and professional cultures, influence each other's work, forge new partnerships, and promote the use of research-based evidence in decision-making". Nutley, Walter and Davies (2007, p. 63) sum up knowledge brokers as "effectively construct[ing] a bridge between the research and policy communities".

The notion of young people as *knowledge brokers* in the transmission of understanding about cyberbullying is a new and exciting construct for this field to consider. To broker knowledge is enabling for young people and elevates them to positions where they can assume some power and ownership of the research process and relationship. For example, young people who attended the COST Australian Training School, held in Melbourne, 2010, spoke directly with the researchers who attended, and challenged them to listen and to acknowledge their expertise in this area. Their *Youth Statement on Cyberbullying* (see Chapter 13), which arose from the interface between researchers and these young people, demonstrated that young people not only wanted a voice, but particularly wanted to be acknowledged as having expertise, and to be involved in the education of each other and their parents and teachers. This *Youth Statement* was subsequently included in a submission to the Australian Government Joint Select Committee on Cybersafety (Commonwealth of Australia, 2011), and is a powerful outcome of listening to youth and how they can broker knowledge to inform policy and practice (http://www.aph.gov.au/Parliamentary_Business/Committees/House_of_Representatives_Committees?url=jscc/report.htm).

The work of Danah Boyd is a different example of how listening to and working with youth allows for new insights. In Marwick and Boyd, (2011, p. 1) they argue that

> adults often refer to these practices [of gossip, jokes, and arguments played out through social media like Formspring, Twitter, and Facebook] with the language of "bullying", whereas teens are more likely to refer to the resultant skirmishes and their digital traces as "drama". Drama as used here, is a performative set of actions distinct from bullying, gossip, and relational aggression, incorporating elements of them but also operating quite distinctly.

They argue further that the use of "drama" allows teens to distance themselves from practices which adults may conceptualize as bullying.

Similarly, Spears, Jennifer, and Williams (2011) employed youth voice to explore new insights into girls' understandings and experiences of sexual bullying and verbal sexual harassment. Using different methodologies, girls' voices from two different decades and cultural and contextual settings, revealed a complexity of interactions that intersected with gender and power. Girls' voices from a decade apart told a similar story: little had changed in terms of their experiences of sexual bullying. However, girls in co-educational settings experienced a double-dose: sexual bullying from other girls as well as from boys. With the advent of technology, sexual bullying has taken a new form, through "sexting" and posting of "selfies"/images online, and girls were also spreading sexualized rumors online. Such findings challenge the well-established consensus within the bullying/cyberbullying research community and represent a refreshing and destabilizing contribution from youth voice to the established knowledge regime in this field. In this way, youth are serving as knowledge brokers and advisors, bridging the gap between their lived realities, and researchers' quest for evidence to underpin policy and practice development.

Extending the methodological pool

Second, we argue that in order to transgress the existing binaries, it is imperative to extend the pool of methods employed within the cyber/ bullying research field through diversifying the *range* of qualitative methods used. Qualitative approaches are many and varied and draw from such fields as education, anthropology, sociology, philosophy, and political science, to name but a few. The cross-disciplinary nature of enquiry available to this field is highlighted through existing research methods such as ethnography, grounded theory, phenomenology, interpretivism, hermeneutics, feminist theory, minority research as well as critical and emancipatory theory. Mishna and Van Wert (2012, pp. 390–396), in their review of qualitative studies, outlined the approaches they consider to be the best suited to cyberbullying research: viz focus groups, interviews, vignettes, technology-assisted data collection and multiple-combined approaches. However, this chapter goes further and argues not only for the approaches noted above, but also for consideration of methods developed within what has been termed the *new paradigm of childhood sociology* (Corsaro, 1997; James & Prout, 1997; James, Jenks, & Prout, 1998) as well as methods which spring from online practices amongst the youth themselves: e.g. forwarding text messages; virtual fieldwork on social media; or by experimenting with youth practices of sharing pictures and retooling them as research apparatuses. The current authors thus advocate for methods which highlight the role of youth voice, explore power relations in the research process and create research partnerships with young people, where meaning is co-constructed, and where qualitative methods are equally privileged with other, traditional scientific methods.

Cyberbullying research at this moment, thus presents researchers with a conundrum: we do need to know and understand prevalence, typology, risk and protective factors, relationships and practices, and as Espinoza and

Juvonen (2012) recognize, given the early days of this field of enquiry, it is not surprising that survey methods dominate. At the same time, however, we also need to know what it is like to be a child/young person in this unprecedented social arena: and it is children/young people who have that expert knowledge (Christensen & Prout, 2002; Hallett & Prout, 2003; Kofoed, 2004; Spears *et al.*, 2008, 2009, 2011; Spears & Zeederberg, 2013) and it is alternate methodologies, drawn from multi-disciplines which may help to bring that voice to the fore.

Youth voice

The role of youth voice in this research domain thus becomes one of importance, for the lived realities of young people need constant exploration in a rapidly changing technological environment (Spears *et al.*, 2008, 2009, 2011, 2012; Spears & Zeederberg, 2013), and it is methodological innovation which may subsequently benefit as a result. New relationalities emerge, new terms and languages evolve and it is important that researchers engage with and listen to youth who live their social lives in technologically mediated spheres, if they are to fully understand the phenomenon. Costabile and Spears (2012) noted that there is much that is positive about the online environment, and indeed young people from three countries shared their thoughts and feelings, and reiterated the benefits of being online (Spears *et al.*, 2012). Here is an example of how seeking out youth voice informed not only the field, but also grew the COST researchers' capacity to expand their methodological repertoire through engaging directly with youth, and then sharing across cultural contexts.

This chapter argues for creating new understandings of how qualitative work fits into the cyberbullying research domain: not as an "add-on", but as a methodological approach which positions young people as central to its understanding, so that we may gain new insights into the lives of contemporary youth, which pay respect to the complexities of it in ways that do not "tidy" the "irregularity and messiness" of it. We thus explicitly acknowledge the United Nations Convention on the Rights of the Child (UNCRC, 1989) and the Save the Children submission (1995), by recognizing the rights of young people to be actively engaged in endeavors which matter to them, to listen to and hear their messages, through positioning postmodern, wired/wireless children and youth at the forefront of research practices in this domain.

Emergent methods

Emergent methods, according to Hesse–Biber and Leavy (2008, p. v) "arise as a means of accessing answers to complex research questions ... and for discovering knowledge that lies hidden ... [and which] ... is difficult to tap into because it has not been part of the dominant culture or discourse". Cyberbullying research meets these criteria for needing emergent methods: it is a complex phenomenon that, until recently, was not part of the research discourse or culture associated with bullying. Bullying, however, has been part of the schooling and research landscape/discourse for the past 35 years and whilst there is overlap between bullying and cyberbullying, there is much that is difficult to "tap into" in using conventional self-report/survey methods. Cyberbullying brings us to this crossroads of thinking: where views of contemporary childhood and youth converge with mobilizing technologies, creating a need for broader methodological awareness and innovation.

Kuhn's (1970) suggestion that paradigms are "models of knowledge building" and that scientific knowledge goes through various "paradigm shifts" is relevant here, as cyberbullying has presented the social sciences with the need to recognize and shift to a world view of childhood and youth that reflects operating in a technological diorama. Hesse-Biber and Leavy (2008) suggest that such paradigmatic shifts can create hybrid methodologies, which eventually push discipline boundaries, and challenge researchers to be risk-takers and innovators. For example, the Danish research group eXbus (Exploring Bullying in Schools) proposes that the concept and phenomenon of bullying needs re-thinking, and proposes new ways of conceptualizing the phenomenon (Schott & Søndergaard, 2013, forthcoming). With this in mind, a brief look at one such method, participatory design, is warranted as it may suggest a paradigmatic shift in how researchers engage with young people in the quest to understand cyberbullying practices in a changing technological landscape.

Genuine participation

Reflecting on Hart's (1992, 2008) ladder of participation is useful here, where young people's level of participation in projects is described: from manipulation through to decoration, tokenism that is assigned but correct, consulted and informed; to adult-initiated, shared decisions with children; to child-initiated and directed and finally to child-initiated, shared decisions with adults. Hart (2008) clarified that the ladder metaphor was not meant to suggest sequential stages of development, but rather to represent the varying degree to which *adults enabled* children to participate. Fielding (2001, 2004) also noted that a transformative approach to participation was needed, where change was directed by youth, but enabled by adults. What is important to note, is that Hart recognized that genuine participation cannot occur without some power-sharing, which in turn can only take place when we shift beyond simple consultation and move into shared decision-making, ultimately moving towards the point whereby children and young people become empowered to take the lead on issues which directly affect their lives. Participatory design seems to be a process and series of experiences which naturally lead young people towards this end: towards mutual learning across the research relationship, shared power and ownership where their voice is guiding researchers, brokering knowledge and assisting in transgressing the existing binaries.

Participatory research and design (PD), as distinct from expert-led research, asks the end-users, in this case young people, to participate in the creation and development of products/technologies/interventions that they will eventually employ (Schuler & Namioka, 1993). It is a research/design process, where the context of everyday user-behaviors and practices are embedded and shaped by motivations and feelings. In the case of cyberbullying, this means active, participatory research, where young people engage directly in the creation and review of their own knowledge, as derived from their subjective experiences and narratives of the phenomenon, and where youth are seen as creative agents enabling the research processes and foci to move in new directions. For example, a particular interest in the affective tenor of cyberbullying allows for new insights into details of the lived experiences of cases of cyberbullying (Kofoed, 2009, 2012; Kofoed & Ringrose, 2012).

Participatory design

The particularity of participatory research and design (PD) has been adopted in response to the UNCRC (1989), which advocates for the rights of children, by the proponents of the new sociology of childhood (Corsaro, 1997; James & Prout, 1997; James, Jenks, & Prout, 1998). It draws upon user-centred design, market research and broader qualitative research methods (Heath & Walker, 2011). As with all qualitative work, it seeks to understand the lived experiences of children and youth, but it can also be used to generate new ways of thinking and doing. PD thus extends beyond consultation and tokenistic membership, and seeks to engage youth as co-designers in the creation of proposals and alternative courses of action. Knowledge is generated by both the researcher and the young person, and it employs a process of mutual learning which creates a "shared language" (Schuler & Namioka, 1993). The co-generation of ideas, language and knowledge occurs through experiential and action-based methods that put an emphasis on play, co-operative learning, and creating visions of the future. At a pragmatic level, PD assists in the development of interventions that are authentic and engaging for young people, and therefore more likely to be used. A key facet of this method is that of continuous engagement, which, in the case of cyberbullying research, will ensure the acceptability of proposals as well as keeping pace with fast-moving technological change and shifting social habits online. The *Safe and Well Online* project of the Young and Well Cooperative Research in Australia, led by Spears and her team at the University of South Australia in conjunction with researchers from the University of Western Sydney (Collins) and the Queensland University of Technology (Drennan), is employing such techniques to create and design online social marketing campaigns to address core values which support anti-bullying practices, such as respectful behavior, when online. Young people are involved throughout this iterative process, and participatory design provides a framework to help shift emphasis from expert-led to user-led innovation.

Conclusions

This chapter has argued that the view of childhood has and is undergoing change, and that researchers in the cyberbullying domain need to heed the current view of postmodern and wired/wireless childhood and to pay respect to the rights of the child to participate, to be heard and to be empowered in the research process. In doing so, this chapter argues that researchers can transgress the binaries which have persisted within the field of cyberbullying research, and further argues for a shared lens across the new sociology of childhood, where new theories and conceptualizations of cyberbullying can emerge through the insights which youth voice as a whole, bring.

Cyberbullying is not a neat construct. It is fluid and "messy" as it operates in and around young people, whose peer groups ebb and flow. It works in convoluted and complex ways between and across the off and online settings, yet young people do not differentiate in terms of their social lives (Spears *et al.*, 2012). Part of this "messiness" relates to the ways that it can be conceptualized (Kofoed & Ringrose, 2012; Spears, 2011). Spears (2011, p. 16) posited that the Internet can be considered simultaneously as both a setting and a system: a *setting* when it operates as a "virtual" entity, distinct from what is "real", e.g. an online setting where young people socialize. As a *system*, however, it operates in conjunction with the existing socio-ecological system, acting as a third dimension, surrounding and intersecting individuals, families, schools and workplaces. Johnson and Puplampu (2008) also wrote of a techno-subsystem which impacts on cognition and development and together these conceptualizations can influence how we might approach cyberbullying methodologically.

Youth voice enables researchers to explore that "messiness" from a youth perspective and the challenge for researchers is to move beyond the fixed positions of quantitative/qualitative approaches with their outsider, expert-led design, towards centralizing young people at the heart of enquiry, as co-researchers and co-generators of knowledge, whereby they broker that knowledge *to and with* researchers and policy makers.

In presenting this chapter, the authors challenge researchers within the field of cyberbullying from both paradigms to join a research community which is cross-disciplinary, innovative, open to experimentation and change, but mostly, which is willing to risk co-sharing the responsibility of researching this problem of cyberbullying, with young people at its heart. Youth voice will both challenge and enable empirical and interpretive worlds to come together as they transgress these binaries to grow knowledge and progress the field of cyberbullying enquiry.

References

Agatston, P.W., Kowalski, R., and Limber, S. (2007). 'Students' perspectives on cyberbullying'. *Journal of Adolescent Health, 41*(6), 859–860.

Alderson, P. (2000). 'Children as researchers'. In P. Christensen and A. James (eds.), *Research with children* (pp. 275–288). London: Falmer Press.

Alderson, P., and Morrow, V. (2004). *Ethics, social research and consulting with children and young people* (2nd Ed.). Ilford: Barnado's.

Bansel, P., Davies, B., Laws, C., and Linnell, S. (2009). 'Bullies, bullying and power in the contexts of schooling'. *British Journal of Sociology of Education, 30*(1), 59–69.

Bauman, S., and Cross, D. (2013). 'Methods: Guiding principles'. In S. Bauman, D. Cross, and J. Walker (eds.), *Principles of cyberbullying research: Definition, measure and method* (pp. 233–244). New York: Routledge.

Boyden, J., and Ennew, J. (eds.). (1997). *Children in focus: A manual for participatory research with children*. Stockholm: Radda Barnen.

Christensen, P., and Prout, A. (2002). 'Working with ethical symmetry in social research with children'. *Childhood, 9*(4), 477–497.

Clark, A., and Moss, P. (2001). *Listening to young children: The mosaic approach*. London: National Children's Bureau.

Commonwealth of Australia. 'Joint select committee on cyber-safety and the young'. Wortley, Dana (2011). *High Wire Act: cyber-safety and the young: Interim report*. Canberra: Commonwealth of Australia.

Corsaro, W.A. (1997). *The sociology of childhood*. London: Pine Forge Press.

Costabile, A., and Spears, B.A. (eds.). (2012). *The impact of technology on relationships in educational settings*. London: Routledge.

Denzin, N.K. (ed.) (1978). *Sociological methods: A sourcebook*. New York: McGraw-Hill.

Elkind, D. (1987). 'The child yesterday, today and tomorrow'. *Young Children, 42*(4), 6–11.

Espinoza, G., and Juvonen, J. (2013). 'Methods used in cyberbullying research'. In S. Bauman, D. Cross, and J. Walker (eds.), *Principles of cyberbullying research: Definition, measure and method* (pp. 186–206). New York: Routledge.

Fielding, M. (2001). 'Students as radical agents of change'. *Journal of Educational Change, 2*(2), 123–141.

——(2004). 'Transformative approaches to student voice'. *British Educational Research Journal, 30*(2), 295–312.

Giddings, L.S. (2006). 'Mixed-methods research. Positivism dressed in drag?' *Journal of Research in Nursing, 11*(3), 195–203.

Grigg, D.W. (2010). 'Cyber-aggression: Definition and concept of cyberbullying'. *Australian Journal of Guidance and Counselling, 20*(2), 143–146.

Hallett, C., and Prout, A. (eds.) (2003). *Hearing the voices of children: Social policy for a new century*. London: Routledge Falmer.

Hart, R. (1992). *Children's participation: from tokenism to citizenship*. UNICEF Innocenti Essays, No. 4. Florence, Italy: International Child Development Centre of UNICEF.

——(2008). 'Stepping back from "The Ladder": Reflection on a model of participatory work with children'. In A. Reid, B.B. Jensen, J. Nikel, and V. Simovska (eds.), *Participation and learning: Perspectives on education and the environment, health and sustainability* (pp. 19–31). Dordrecht: Springer.

Heath, S., and Walker, C. (2011). *Innovations in youth research*. Basingstoke: Palgrave MacMillan.

Henningsen, I., and Søndergaard, D.M. (2000). 'Forskningstraditioner krydser deres spor – Kvalitative og kvantitative socio-kulturelle empiriske forskningsmetoder'. *Kvinder, køn og forskning 4*. [Research traditions crossing their tracks – Qualitative and quantitative socio-cultural empirical research]. *Women, sex and research, 4,* 26–38.

Henningsen, I., Hansen, H.R., and Kofoed, J. (2013). 'When classroom culture tips into bullying'. In R.M. Schott and D.M. Søndergaard (eds.), *School bullying: New theories in context*. Cambridge: Cambridge University Press.

Hesse-Biber, S.N., and Leavy, P. (eds). (2008). *Handbook of emergent methods*. New York: The Guilford Press.

James, A., and Prout, A. (1997). (2nd ed.). *Constructing and reconstructing childhood*. Basingstoke: Falmer Press.

James, A., Jenks, C., and Prout, A. (1998). *Theorizing childhood*. Cambridge: Polity Press.

Jimerson, S.R., Swearer, S.M., and Espelage, D.L. (2010). 'International scholarship advances science and practice addressing bullying in schools'. In S.R. Jimerson, S.M. Swearer, and D.L. Espelage (eds.), *Handbook of bullying in schools: An international perspective* (pp. 1–6). New York: Routledge.

Johnson, G.M., and Puplampu, P. (2008). 'A conceptual framework for understanding the effect of the internet on child development: The ecological techno-subsystem'. *Canadian Journal of Learning and Technology, 34,* 19–28.

Kellett, M. (2005). *Developing children as researchers*. London: Paul Chapman Publishers.

Kofoed, J. (2004). 'Elevpli. Inklusion-eksklusionsprocesser blandt børn i skolen'. *Pædagogisk Psykologi*. København, Danmarks Pædagogiske Universitet. Ph.d.-dissertation. [Polished pupilness. Processes of inclusion and exclusion among children in school].

——(2007). 'Ansvar for egen elevhed. Suspensive komparationer på arbejde'. *Magtballader. 14 fortællinger om magt, modstand og menneskers tilblivelse.* D. Staunæs and J. Kofoed. København, Danmarks Pædagogiske Universitetsforlag. [Responsibility of your own pupilness. Suspensive comparisons at work. In: Powertroubles. 14 narratives of power, resistance and subjective becoming].

——(2009). 'Emotional evaluations in activities recognized as cyber bullying'. In B. Sapio, L. Haddon, E. Mante-Meijer, L. Fortunati, T. Turk, and E. Loos (eds.), *The good, the bad and the challenging. Conference proceedings* (Volume 2), (pp. 1048–1055). Slovenia: COST Office.

——(2012) 'Saturated knowledge?' *Affective rhythms as a productive analytical concept.* Paper presented at the 5th Psychosocial Studies Network Conference 2012, Institute of Education, London.

——(2013a). 'Non-simultaneity in cyberbullying'. In R.M. Schott and D.M. Søndergaard (eds.), *School Bullying: New Theories in Context*. Cambridge: Cambridge University Press.

——(2013b). 'Cyberbullying'. In T. Teo (ed.), *Encyclopedia of Critical Psychology*. New York, NY: Springer Publications.

Kofoed, J., and Ringrose, J. (2012). 'Travelling and sticky affects: Exploring teens and sexualized cyberbullying through a Butlerian-Deleuzian-Guattarian lens'. *Discourse: Studies in the Cultural Politics of Education, 33*(1), 5–20.

Kofoed, J., and Søndergaard, D.M. (eds.). (2009). *Mobning. Sociale processer på afveje.* Copenhagen: Hans Reitzels Publisher. [Bullying. Social processes astray].

——(eds.). (2013). *Mobning gentænkt*. Copenhagen: Hans Reitzels Publisher. [Re-thinking Bullying].

Kuhn, T.S. (1970). *The structure of scientific revolutions* (2nd Ed.). Chicago: University of Chicago Press.

Leckie, B.A. (1997). 'Girls, bullying behaviors and peer relations: The double-edged sword of exclusion and rejection'. Paper presented at the Australian Association for Research in Education Conference: November–December: Brisbane, Queensland.

Retrieved March 29, 2013 from http://www.eric.ed.gov/ERICWebPortal/search/detailmini.jsp?_nfpb=true&_&ERICExtSearch_SearchValue_0=ED4604 50&ERICExtSearch_SearchType_0=no&accno=ED460450.

Locke, J. (1690). *An essay concerning human understanding.* London: Tegg & Son.

Lomas, J. (2007). 'The in-between world of knowledge brokering'. *British Medical Journal, 334*(7585), 129–132.

Maher, D. (2008). 'Cyberbullying: An ethnographic case study of one Australian upper primary school class'. *Youth Studies Australia, 27*(4), 49–57.

Marwick, A.E., and Boyd, D. (2011). *The Drama! Teen Conflict, Gossip, and Bullying in Networked Publics.* A Decade in Internet Time: Symposium on the Dynamics of the Internet and Society. Available at SSRN: http://ssrn.com/abstract=1926349. (Accessed July 8, 2013).

Mishna, F. (2004). 'A qualitative study of bullying from multiple perspectives'. *Children and Schools, 26*(4), 234–247.

——(2012). *Bullying: A guide to research, intervention and prevention.* Oxford Scholarship Online. Retrieved March 28, 2013 from http://www.oxfordscholarship.com/view/10.1093/acprof:oso/9780199795406.001.0001/acprof-9780199795406.

Mishna, F., and Van Wert, M. (2013). 'Qualitative studies'. In S. Bauman, D. Cross, and J. Walker (eds.). *Principles of cyberbullying research: Definition, measure and method* (pp. 374–407). New York: Routledge.

Mishna, F., McLuckie, A., and Saini, M. (2009). 'Real world dangers in an online reality: A qualitative study examining online relationships and cyber abuse'. *Social Work Research, 33*(2), 107–119.

Mishna, F., Saini, M., and Solomon, S. (2009). 'Ongoing and online: Children and youth's perceptions of cyber bullying'. *Children and Youth Services Review, 31*(12), 1222–1228.

Mishna, F., Underwood, M., Milne, C., and Gibson, M.F. (2013). 'Ethical issues'. In S. Bauman, D. Cross, and J. Walker (eds.), *Principles of cyberbullying research: Definition, measure and method* (pp. 244–272). New York: Routledge.

Nocentini, A., Calmaestra, J., Schultze-Krumbholz, A., Scheithauer, H., Ortega, R., and Menesini, E. (2010). 'Cyberbullying: Labels, behaviours and definition in three European countries'. *Australian Journal of Guidance and Counselling, 20*(2), 129–142.

Nutley, S.M., Walter, I., and Davies, H.T.O. (2007). *Using evidence: how research can inform public services.* Bristol: The Policy Press.

Olweus, D. (1978). *Aggression in the schools: Bullies and whipping boys.* Washington DC: Hemisphere Press, Wiley.

Owens, L., Shute, R., and Slee, P. (2000). '"I'm in and you're out…"'. *Psychology, Evolution and Gender, 2*(1), 19–46.

Ringrose, J., and Renold, E. (2011). 'Boys, girls and normative violence in schools: A gendered critique of bully discourses'. In C. Barter and D. Berridge (eds.), *Children behaving badly? Peer violence between children and young people* (pp. 181–195) Sussex: Wiley and Sons Ltd.

Russell, B. (1974). *History of western philosophy.* London: Allen & Unwin.

Save the Children Fund. (1995). *Towards a children's agenda.* London: Save the Children Fund.

Schott, R.M., and Søndergaard, D.M. (eds.) (2013). *School bullying: New theories in context.* Cambridge: Cambridge University Press.

Schuler, D., and Namioka, A. (1993). *Participatory design: Principles and practices.* Hillsdale, NJ: Lawrence Erlbaum Associates.

Slee, P.T., Campbell, M., and Spears, B. (2012). *Child, adolescent and family development.* (3rd ed.). Cambridge: Cambridge University Press.

Smith, P.K., and Brain, P. (2000). 'Bullying in schools: Lessons from two decades of research'. *Aggressive Behavior, 26*, 1–9.

Spears, B.A. (2011). 'CyberChat: Using technology to enhance wellbeing'. *Education Technology Solutions*, 40, 16. Retrieved March 20, 2013 from http://www.decd.sa.gov.au/speced2/files/links/Cyberchat_ETS_40.pdf.

Spears, B.A., and Zeederberg, M. (2013). 'Emerging methodological strategies to address cyberbullying: Online social marketing and young people as co-researchers'. In S. Bauman, D. Cross, and J. Walker (eds.), *Principles of cyberbullying research: Definitions, measures and method* (pp. 273–285). New York: Routledge.

Spears, B.A., Jennifer, D., and Williams, S. (2011). 'Girls, verbal sexual harassment and sexual bullying: Implications for wellbeing'. In R. Shute (ed.), *International perspectives on mental health and wellbeing in education* (pp. 103–117). Adelaide: Shannon Research Press.

Spears, B.A., Kofoed, J., Bartolo, M.G., Palermiti, A., and Costabile, A. (2012). 'Positive uses of social networking sites: Youth voice perspectives'. In A. Costabile and B.A. Spears (eds.), *The impact of technology on relationships in educational settings* (pp. 7–21). London: Routledge.

Spears, B., Slee, P.T., Campbell, M., and Cross, D. (2011). *Educational change and youth voice: Informing school action on cyberbullying.* Victoria: Centre for Strategic Education.

Spears, B.A., Slee, P.T., Owens, L., and Johnson, B. (2008). *Behind the scenes: Insights into the human dimension of covert bullying.* Canberra: Department of Education, Employment and Workplace Relations.

——(2009). 'Behind the scenes and screens: Insights into the human dimension of covert and cyberbullying'. *Zeitschrift für Psychologie/Journal of Psychology, 217*(4), 189–196.

Tashakkori, A., and Teddlie, C. (eds.) (2003). *Handbook of mixed methods in social and behavioral research.* Thousand Oaks, CA: Sage.

Underwood, M.K., and Card, N.A. (2013). 'Moving beyond tradition and convenience: suggestions for useful methods for cyberbullying research'. In S. Bauman, D. Cross, and J. Walker (eds.), *Principles of cyberbullying research: Definitions, measures and method* (pp. 208–232). New York: Routledge.

United Nations (1989). *Convention on the rights of the child.* Geneva: United Nations.

Vandebosch, H., and Van Cleemput, K. (2008). 'Defining cyberbullying: A qualitative research into the perceptions of youngsters'. *Cyberpsychology and Behavior, 11*(4), 499–505.

Woodhead, M., and Faulkner, D. (2000). 'Subjects, objects or participants? Dilemmas of psychological research with children'. In P. Christensen and A. James (eds.), *Research with children: Perspectives and practice* (pp. 10–39). London:Routledge.

12 Australian research to encourage school students' positive use of technology to reduce cyberbullying

Donna Cross, Marilyn Campbell,
Phillip Slee, Barbara Spears and
Amy Barnes[1]

Introduction

Information and Communications Technology (ICT) has spread rapidly in Australia. Mobile phones, which increasingly have advanced capabilities including Internet access, mobile television and multimedia storage, are owned by 22 per cent of Australian children aged 9–11 years and 73 per cent of those aged 12–14 years (Australian Bureau of Statistics, 2012b), as well as by over 90 per cent of Australians aged 15 years and over (Australian Communications and Media Authority [ACMA], 2010). Nearly 80 per cent of Australian households have access to the Internet and 73 per cent have a broadband Internet connection, ensuring that Internet access is typically reliable and high-speed (Australian Bureau of Statistics, 2012a). Ninety per cent of Australian children aged 5–14 years (comprising 79 per cent of 5–8 year olds; 96 per cent of 9–11 year olds; and 98 per cent of 12–14 year olds) reported having accessed the Internet during 2011–2012, a significant increase from 79 per cent in 2008–2009 (Australian Bureau of Statistics, 2012b). Approximately 90 per cent of 5–14 year olds have accessed the Internet both from home and from school, with close to 49 per cent accessing the Internet from other places (Australian Bureau of Statistics, 2012b). Young people often make use of borrowed Internet access (e.g. in friends' homes),

1   The Cyber Friendly Schools Project was supported by the Western Australian Health Promotion Foundation (Healthway). The authors wish to thank the many students, parents and school staff who have contributed to the research described in this chapter, as well as research project managers Robyn Garland, Patricia Cardoso, Kate Hadwen and Thérèse Shaw.
    The Safe and Well Online Project is supported by the Young and Well Co-operative Research Centre (CRC) through an Australian Government Initiative administered by the Department of Industry, Innovation, Science, Research and Tertiary Education. The CRC program supports end-user driven research collaborations to address major challenges facing Australia. CRCs pursue solutions to these challenges that are innovative, of high impact and capable of being effectively deployed by the end users.

commercial access (e.g. cybercafés), public access (e.g. libraries), and mobile device access in areas offering free Wi-Fi (Lim, 2009).

Having grown up immersed in a diverse array of readily available technologies, particularly the Internet and mobile devices, young people learn, work and interact in fundamentally different ways compared to their parents' or teachers' experiences as adolescents (Palfrey & Gasser, 2008; Tapscott, 1998). Young people experience the many advantages of ICT, including greater access to information, improved social communication and identity exploration. However, its potential for misuse and harm is also recognized (Bennett, Maton, & Kervin, 2008). The platforms for social interaction provided by mobile phones and the Internet also provide opportunities for bullying behaviour using technology, particularly in Australia, where close to 70 per cent of 12–14 year olds use social networking sites (Australian Bureau of Statistics, 2012b) and where the Internet is one of the most common means by which adolescents bully others (Cross *et al.*, 2009; Sakellariou, Carroll, & Houghton, 2012).

Together, Australia's widespread access to and use of ICT, the relatively recent occurrence of negative online behaviours, and a limited understanding of their manifestation and impact creates a "perfect storm" of online risk for young people. Two Australian studies, one conducted nationally in 2008 and another in the state of Victoria in 2011, confirm the ongoing prevalence of cyberbullying in Australia. The national study involving 7,500 students found that on average 7 per cent of students aged 8–14 years reported being frequently cyberbullied (every few weeks or more often in the last three months), and 3.5 per cent of Australian students reported frequently cyberbullying others (every few weeks or more often in the last three months) (Cross *et al.*, 2009). The Victorian study found that approximately 12 per cent of 14 to 16-year-old students reported cyberbullying others and around 13 per cent reported cyberbullying victimisation during the past 12 months (Hemphill, Tollit, & Kotevski, 2012). These data, plus young Australians' increasing reliance on ICT for work, entertainment and socialising, indicates an urgent need for an evidence-based understanding of what can be done to prevent and manage cyberbullying behaviour among children and young people.

Moreover, in Australia, despite considerable public interest, until 2010 research investigating evidence-based strategies for intervening to reduce and prevent cyberbullying was virtually absent. While many educational materials have been developed to address this issue by the Australian government and non-government agencies, as well as individual authors/publishers, very few have been empirically tested. This lack of evidence, coupled with most Australian teachers reporting that they feel unskilled to address cyberbullying and other covert bullying behaviours amongst their students (Barnes *et al.*, 2012), provides much of the impetus for the conduct of quality research. However, Australia's vast geographical size and considerable distance from Europe and North America, where most research related to bullying and cyberbullying was being conducted, has limited its researchers' intra-national and international opportunities for face-to-face exchange of cyberbullying research ideas, networking and collaboration, especially related to the development of instruments, interventions and analytical methodologies.

To respond to the need for intra-national collaboration, researchers Dr Barbara Spears and Professors Phillip Slee, Marilyn Campbell and Donna Cross, formed the Australian Universities' Anti-bullying Research Alliance (AUARA). This collaboration united the four university-based research teams from the University of South Australia, Flinders University, Queensland University of Technology and Edith Cowan University, who are leading much of the empirical cyberbullying research being conducted in Australia, at this time.

These researchers, led by Professor Donna Cross from Edith Cowan University, secured Collaborative Research Network funding from the Australian government for four years to enable AUARA's research teams to build their collective capacity and evidence-based research outcomes. Importantly, the outcomes of this alliance are currently being used to inform government and school policy and practice; and to reduce harm from cyberbullying among Australian children and young people in schools throughout the country.

AUARA also developed significant international links and membership with the European Co-operation of Science and Technology (COST) Action IS0801, 'Cyberbullying: coping with negative and enhancing positive uses of new technologies, in relationships in educational settings' (http://sites.google.com/site/costis0801/) and other international collaborations. AUARA's membership of COST Action IS0801 has positively influenced and enriched Australian research practices, outcomes and the national and international translation of Australian cyberbullying research outcomes. Equally, this Australian alliance of researchers has also contributed to the COST Action IS0801 through the four-day COST Training School conducted in Melbourne, Australia in 2010 (see Chapter 13). The alliance also actively contributed to five of the six COST Action IS0801 Working Groups (https://sites.google.com/site/costis0801/working-groups) that were most closely aligned with their research programs: Working Groups 1, 2, 3, 5 and 6 (see Chapter 1).

Professor Phillip Slee's contribution to both Working Group 1 (the sharing of developing expertise in knowledge base and measurement techniques across researchers; see Chapters 2 and 3), and Working Group 5 (the sharing of research on coping strategies, in different countries; see Chapter 7), was informed by his research and provided a vehicle for the translation of this research into Greek schools via COST members in Greece. Professor Marilyn Campbell's research, investigating how legal sanctions can influence cyberbullying-related behaviour, formed a significant part of the actions conducted by Working Group 2 (sharing input from outside the research community; from legal experts and from mobile phone companies and

Internet service providers; see also Chapter 4). Professor Donna Cross contributed to Working Group 3 (the investigation and sharing of nationally published guidelines, see Chapter 8); the whole-school criteria developed to evaluate national guidelines were largely the conceptual basis of her Cyber Friendly Schools whole-school research project described later. Finally, Dr Barbara Spears' research involving social media and social marketing online, contributed to and operationalised many of the findings of Working Group 6 (positive uses of new technologies, in relationships in educational settings), through the active engagement of young people.

This chapter describes the major Australian cyberbullying intervention-related research programs conducted since 2009 by the AUARA founding members connected to the COST IS0801 Action. It will also describe how the opportunities provided by the COST Action IS0801, further enabled the research teams associated with AUARA to synergistically enhance their research programs.

Australian cyber-related intervention research involving young people

In this chapter, four AUARA cyber-related intervention research programs will be described. The first, led by Dr Barbara Spears from the University of South Australia, exploits the innovative use of social media to enhance the respectful use of technology; the second, led by Professor Marilyn Campbell from the Queensland University of Technology, investigates the salience of regulatory practices of law and policy development in schools and its influence on cyberbullying behaviour; the third, led by Professor Donna Cross from Edith Cowan University, focuses more broadly on whole-school interventions to reduce cyberbullying; and the fourth, led by Professor Phillip Slee from Flinders University, addresses an intervention developed and tested in Australia and Greece that aims to enhance young people's means of coping with all forms of bullying.

University of South Australia Research Program – Young and Well

Overview

In 2010, the Australian Government announced the establishment of the Young and Well Cooperative Research Centre (Young and Well CRC) (http://www.youngandwellcrc.org.au/), to be funded for five years (2011–2016: $AUD 27.5 million) as part of the national agenda to support end-user driven research collaborations to address major challenges facing Australia (http://www.crc.gov.au/About-Us/CRCs/Pages/default.aspx).

Led by the Inspire Foundation, one of Australia's leading mental health organisations supporting young people to get help when they need it (http://inspire.org.au/our-work/), the Young and Well CRC unites young people with researchers, practitioners, innovators and policy-makers from over 70 partner organisations across non–profit, academic, government and corporate sectors to explore the role of technology in young people's lives and how technology can be used to improve the mental health and wellbeing of young people aged 12–25 years. Three main research programs operate in relation to these aims: *Safe and Supported* (all young people); *Creative and Connected* (those vulnerable to ill mental health); and *User-Driven and Empowered* (those who are experiencing mental health difficulties) and each is comprised of four key research projects (http://www.youngandwellcrc.org.au/research).

The *Safe and Well Online* project (2011–2016), from the *Safe and Supported* program, is led by a consortium of researchers and media industry partners: Barbara Spears (University of South Australia: Research Team Leader: Longitudinal Cohort Study); Philippa Collin (University of Western Sydney: Participatory Design); Judy Drennan (Queensland University of Technology: Social Marketing) and Mike Zeederberg and Val Borbone (Zuni Digital Strategists: Creative and Campaign Development). This project is designed to develop and test a program of online, youth-centred social communications to promote young people's safety and wellbeing online. It aims to develop and evaluate an online social marketing framework; execute at least four marketing campaigns, and use longitudinal tracking and innovative digital data collection to measure reach, outcome and impact of campaign activity, whilst determining the efficacy of attitudinal and behaviour change in young people.

Rationale

Current interventions to reduce cyberbullying in schools are rooted in "traditional" anti-bullying approaches (Spears & Zeederberg, 2013), such as whole-school approaches (Cross, Monks, Campbell, Spears, & Slee, 2011) and more recently, national intervention programs (Spiel, Salmivalli, & Smith, 2011). This is a logical approach, as there is evidence of overlap in terms of bullying and cyberbullying behaviours, crossing from online to offline situations (Beran & Li, 2007; Cross *et al.*, 2009; Hinduja & Patchin, 2008; Raskauskas & Stoltz, 2007; Smith *et al.*, 2008; Vandebosch & Van Cleemput, 2009). The role of youth voice and participation in interventions has also been highlighted in terms of understanding the phenomenon more fully (Spears, Kofoed, Bartolo, Palermiti, & Costabile, 2012; Spears, Slee, Campbell, & Cross, 2011). In a contemporary social-media driven social environment, however, the question needs to be asked: are these the best methods to target new ways of being bullied? Universally, first attempts to harness the online environment and to get messages out to young people about cyberbullying were through a plethora of adult-created websites, but are these sites actually reaching the audience for whom they were intended and are they evidence-based? What is the role of youth voice and participatory design in contemporary cyberbullying research (Boeck & Collin, 2012)?

Building upon a previously successful anti-cyberbullying campaign, developed by NAPCAN and used under license, which utilized YouTube and web platforms to distribute key anti-bullying messages (*Smart Offline: Safe Online;* http://www.soso.org.au/) (Spears & Zeederberg, 2013), *Safe and Well Online* argues for moving directly into the networked spaces in which young people socialize, through the adoption of online social marketing techniques. Social marketing is concerned with changing attitudes and behaviours for social good: it is not "selling" a product. By delivering youth-centred, user-designed, anti-cyberbullying messages directly to young people in the socially mediated network spaces in which they operate online, this project aims to investigate and build safe and supportive online environments and provide strategies and tools that promote cybersafety, mental health and wellbeing.

Research Methods

The *Safe and Well Online* project involves several methods/strands which operate in concert with each other: the development of key messaging and an online social marketing campaign; a youth-centred participatory design model; a longitudinal cohort study to examine attitude and behaviour change over time; and an online panel to track campaign delivery reach and impact.

- *Campaign messaging, creative development and participatory design:* The youth-centred, participatory design model ensures that young people are directly involved in the co-design of the technologies they will use. These collaborative processes build upon utilizing youth voice, through workshops and focus groups, and are driven by those actually affected by the technology being designed; in this case, the design of the messaging and online social marketing campaign concerning respectful behaviour online, *Keep it Tame* (http://www.youngandwellcrc.org.au/news/article/213). Stakeholder/end-user organisations in partnership with the Young and Well CRC also informed the messaging development, through reporting on the key issues that young people were highlighting to their organisations. In addition, the Youth Advisory Group (YAG) to the Australian Government (https://yag.gov.au/) was engaged directly in online dialogue with research team leader, Barbara Spears, as well as the Consultative Working Group (CWG) on cybersafety, which brings together members drawn from community groups, Internet Service Providers, industry associations, business and government. The overarching theme of respectful behaviour online emerged from all informants as a key issue when considering the behaviours associated with cyberbullying, and became the central theme for the first social marketing campaign.
- *Crowd sourcing* was employed to develop the conceptual brief; whereby a diverse group of young people, media partners, Creative Directors and

Agencies, and concept generators, interacted directly with the theme ("Respect"), to establish the best concepts to take to a professional agency for development into an online social marketing campaign.

- *Longitudinal Cohort Study*: A longitudinal cohort is being established to explore attitude and behaviour change over time, in respect of the campaign messaging over the next three years, 2013 to 2015. Using innovative tracking methodologies, the pilot campaign (Campaign 1 2012: *Keep It Tame: Key Message/Respect of Self and Others*) tested opportunities for undertaking a randomized control study in an online environment. Individuals were randomly allocated to control, comparison and exposure groups as they registered for the online study, and were administered pre- and post-campaign surveys. Alongside this testing cohort, the Nielsen group surveyed a comparison group drawn from their online panels, and tested for campaign reach and exposure.

Selected results

The first/pilot online social marketing campaign, *Keep it Tame,* was launched in November 2012 (YouTube, http://www.youtube.com/embed/Ka2GsHqWycQ?fs=1) and ran for four weeks online. It followed the journey of an animated mobile phone that became ugly and turned nasty if the wrong decisions were made. Young people were encouraged to not let the device get out of hand, and to "keep it tame" through using the tools available to them to create safe and respectful online experiences for themselves and their friends: e.g. apologize, block, inform an adult. Rather than being a website-based campaign, it formed part of an interactive "banner ad" (featuring the animated mobile phone), that literally "popped up" all over the Internet. It invited the user to "see what happens next" in response to choosing to post an embarrassing image of a friend, or not. The response chosen, then linked to a social network video experience that highlighted the impact of that action, challenging them to think before they acted, and to treat themselves and their friends with respect.

Through purchasing advertising space in websites where young people in the target age group 12–15 years old were known to visit (e.g. Club Penguin; Star Doll; Facebook), the reach and impact of the campaign could be measured. Over 14 million total impressions were delivered online across all manner of websites (a measure of the number of times an "ad" is displayed) during the four week period. Another analytic was used: the click through rate (CTR). This captures viewers' initial responses to websites and advertising banners, and is a measure of the success of the advertising or website. With a media industry CTR average of 0.02 per cent, a CTR of 0.31 per cent for this campaign is considered impressive by media industry standards for a display campaign, targeting youth.

Other web analytics determined that the type of technology in use by young people when watching the video component, was high-level and sophisticated. The average visit to the video lasted 152 minutes, which indicated that the vast majority of individuals watched the story to the end, suggesting a high level of engagement. In addition, the "rich media (video) manual closes", indicate that after the video had run once automatically (following redirection from the banner ad), it was again opened and closed. In advertising terms, this indicates direct interaction with the campaign.

The pilot sample, randomly drawn from five schools in Adelaide, South Australia, tested the online survey mechanics and the Model of Goal Directed Behaviour (Perugini & Bagozzi, 2001) being employed in this study. Specifically, the model proposes that attitudes, subjective norms, anticipated emotions and control are the antecedents for desires, which in turn provided the direct impetus for intentions which then are a key predictor of behaviour. Preliminary findings revealed that each of the proposed pathways in the model were statistically significant and further explained a significant amount of variance, indicating preliminary support for the Model of Goal Directed Behaviour. In addition, post campaign, deep access interviews also supported the model. Preliminary findings are promising: the profile of the sample reflects the larger national studies being undertaken by Young and Well CRC, including those from stakeholder organisations, such as the Australian Communications and Media Authority; the students indicated that being respectful is the right thing to do; that social norms around respect are positive, and that adults were the stronger source of those norms than peers.

Implications for policy and practice

Cyberbullying seems ubiquitous, and whilst it occurs in the online environment, it impacts on the offline social environments of school settings and families, often affecting an individual's mental health. Introducing a layer of prevention and intervention within the online setting, which is specifically youth-centred and user-designed, using the technologies and methodologies which are employed by young people as they navigate their socially-mediated spaces, deepens and adds to our existing school- and community-based programs. Using technology to promote strong and supportive relationships, good communication and life skills and, in the current case, respectful behaviours on and offline, are all known to enhance a young person's ability to manage, survive and thrive in the face of adversity. The *Safe and Well Online* study will contribute to understanding of how youth-centred and led user-designed technologies and social marketing techniques can change attitudes and behaviours for the social good of the community. Schools are no longer just operating within an offline community but positioned in socially-mediated spaces, and policy and practice must reflect this shift by harnessing the potential of this medium to contribute positively to young people's health and wellbeing.

Queensland University of Technology Research Program – Legally-informed Intervention to Reduce Cyberbullying in Schools

Background

During the last four years, Marilyn Campbell, Barbara Spears, Phillip Slee, Donna Cross, Des Butler and Sally Kift have conducted two large scale research projects on the law and cyberbullying, funded by the Australian Research Council. The first project investigated the incidence and consequences of cyberbullying among both students and teachers in the workplace and examined knowledge of current policy and practice in schools in Australia. The second project, currently in progress, aims to develop and trial a legally-informed intervention in schools to increase knowledge and understanding of the law in order to assist schools in preventing and managing cyberbullying incidents. It will clarify the standards expected of schools and workplaces to meet their legal and social obligations and will highlight the need for educationally proactive responses which will keep students and employees in safe workplaces and schooling settings, and reduce the need for reactive litigious responses, keeping schools and workplaces out of court.

It is now not uncommon for cases of face-to-face bullying in schools to lead to civil claims for compensation or prosecution in the criminal courts. In Australia, there has yet to be a reported case seeking civil compensation specifically for cyberbullying, and there has only been one criminal prosecution arising from a case involving threatening SMS messages (Milovanovic, 2010). However, with the prevalence of cyberbullying among young people, cases of cyberbullying may begin to come before the courts. Cyberbullying represents the potential confluence of a number of areas of law including criminal law, discrimination law, negligence law and other areas of civil liability. However, Australian law on cyberbullying is far from clear and application of existing law has proven problematic (Campbell, Cross, Spears, & Slee, 2010).

Research methods

Using a questionnaire presenting 20 scenarios (developed using a Delphi technique; Hasson, Keeney, & McKenna, 2000), the first project explored understandings of cyberbullying among primary and secondary school students and teachers, particularly relating to the incidence and consequences of cyberbullying. Written anti-bullying policies, programs and other documents were also analyzed. The second project has adopted a repeated measures design to collect data for three years at three time points: pre-, post-intervention and follow-up for students, teachers and parents. The study has two parallel aspects. First, the knowledge and attitudes of the school community to legal responses for cyberbullying will be examined, and second, legally-informed resources (addressing both student and workplace bullying) will be developed in response to these findings. A group randomized control trial, with schools randomly allocated to two conditions with post-measures, will be used to evaluate resource effectiveness.

Selected results

In the first project, we found that understanding of cyberbullying increased with age in students, whereas adults in the older age groups did not identify cyberbullying scenarios as accurately as younger adults. There were no gender differences for either students or adults. The incidence of cyberbullying among students was found to be about 15 per cent (half the number for traditional bullying) and about 8 per cent of students identified themselves as perpetrators (Campbell, Spears, Slee, Kift, & Butler, 2011). The consequences for students who were cyberbullied were found to be more detrimental than for those who were traditionally bullied (Campbell, Spears, Slee, Butler, & Kift, 2012) and the consequences for students who perpetrated the cyberbullying were similar to those who were cyberbullied (Campbell, Slee, Spears, Butler, & Kift, 2013). Anti-bullying policies of schools were examined and found wanting in comparison to legal requirements (Butler, Kift, Campbell, Slee, & Spears, 2011).

Implications for policy and practice

Schools and their communities clearly have diverse understandings of bullying and cyberbullying incidents, as measured by various scenarios of bullying and non-bullying incidents. Both in-service and pre-service teachers would benefit from an enhanced ability to recognise when an incident involves cyberbullying. School policies would benefit from a greater understanding of legal requirements for dealing with online bullying and harassment. School anti-bullying policies should draw on the National Safe Schools Framework (http://deewr.gov.au/national-safe-schools-framework-0) principle that schools be safe and supportive institutions for all members of the school community. Better practice would require, among other things, Australian schools to adopt as a matter of policy that bullying – including cyberbullying – is unacceptable behaviour, and also to provide an inclusive definition of those terms. The policy should describe procedures and prescribe a process by which complaints of such behaviour will be handled. Potential sanctions should be stipulated, including the possibility of police involvement. Policies should also be consistently explained and reinforced for students and the broader school community.

Edith Cowan University Research Program – The Cyber Friendly Schools Project

Background

The earlier Supportive Schools project (Lester, Cross, Dooley, & Shaw, 2013; Lester, Cross, & Shaw, 2012; Lester, Cross, Shaw, & Dooley, 2012; Cross, Hall, Waters, & Hamilton, 2008) had targeted the bullying affecting secondary students, following their transition to secondary school. As part of this, Cross and her colleagues became aware that students and their teachers were referring to forms of bullying perpetrated via students' mobile phones and the Internet. Survey data collected in 2006 from 2,034 12–13 year old students found that 8.5 per cent of students reported being sent a mean and hurtful message via the Internet, and 3.5 per cent had been sent a mean and hurtful text message (Cross *et al.*, 2008).

A comprehensive cross-sectional prevalence study involving over 7,500 students completed in 2008, confirmed the prevalence of cyberbullying among students across Australia, with 25 per cent of the oldest students in the study (14 years of age) reporting experiencing cyberbullying (Cross *et al.*, 2009). Three extensive formative studies were subsequently conducted by the research team from 2007–2009, involving widespread consultation with students, parents and school staff using large student forums, focus groups and interviews, to understand the many concerns and needs of young people and to determine the most effective means to reduce harm from cyberbullying.

Research methods

In 2010, Professors Donna Cross, Clare Roberts, Phillip Slee and Thérèse Shaw received funding to evaluate, using a group randomised control trial, the whole school-based prevention and intervention materials which were developed and pilot tested during 2009 based on data collected from the formative studies (Cross, Brown, Epstein, & Shaw, 2010). This study was designed to compare the effectiveness of this intervention to the standard cyberbullying management practices used in secondary schools. It was hypothesised that the students who received the Cyber Friendly Schools Project (CFSP), which engaged school staff, students, parents and the broader community to enhance whole-school policies and teaching and learning practices to reduce cyberbullying, would report less involvement in cyberbullying behaviour than students in the comparison condition. The main outcome measures were students' reports of involvement in cyberbullying victimisation and cyberbullying perpetration.

Just under 3,500 Grade 8 students (13 years old) from 37 secondary schools were recruited to the three-year study, having been randomly selected from a pool of 53 secondary non-government schools located in Perth, Western Australia metropolitan area, and were randomly assigned to the intervention or comparison condition. Quantitative data were collected from students with consent using an online survey at pre-test (beginning of Grade 8), post-test 1 (end of Grade 9), and post-test 2 at the end Grade 10.

Student involvement in cyberbullying victimisation and perpetration behaviours were measured using two scales of 11 items (for example; "I sent pictures/video clips about someone to others' mobile phones to embarrass, hurt or upset the person") (Shaw, Dooley, Cross, Zubrick, & Waters, in press), based on research conducted by Smith *et al.* (2008).

The whole-school CFSP intervention was based on a socio-ecological approach (1995) targeting the many online contexts in which 13 to 15 year old students interact and the responses they receive from their actions in each context. Intervention school staff were encouraged to integrate the CFSP resources into their current whole-school approaches addressing inappropriate social behaviour, including traditional bullying.

The intervention's conceptual framework recognised the seamless online/offline social context of students' lives and the means by which they engaged with others in these environments. It addressed the proximal and distal ecological, cognitive and psychosocial risk and protective factors, such as feeling connected to school, identified during the previous formative studies that can be regulated or mediated at the school, classroom, family and individual levels to reduce cyberbullying. Accordingly, the intervention targeted the pastoral care staff, teaching staff and students and their parents. The intervention also actively engaged slightly older (Grade 10) trained student "cyber-leaders" to help teachers to plan for and implement the whole-school activities.

The Cyber Friendly Schools' teaching and learning intervention was designed by young people in collaboration with adults to reduce student harm online via "5 Cs": the online *contexts* where students were spending time (such as Facebook, or chat rooms etc); the online *contacts* they made; the extent to which they managed their *confidentiality* (privacy); their own *conduct* and online skills; and the *content* they accessed. The teaching and learning program aimed to enhance online social skills, with a strong emphasis on positive communication, resilience, self-management and social responsibility. Students were provided with information and skills-based strategies to increase pro-victim attitudes to help others; to cope adaptively with cyberbullying should it occur; and to react assertively and not aggressively to cyberbullying.

Selected results

Student self-reported cyberbullying behaviour data were analyzed using two-part random effects growth models. Despite low levels of implementation by intervention teachers, who taught on average two to three 40–60 minute classroom modules (of a total of eight modules), the results of this study indicate the CFSP may have slightly reduced adolescent involvement in cyberbullying after 18 months of intervention. This significant difference however, was not maintained 12 months after the intervention program had ended, when the student cohort were in Grade 10. The findings suggest the CFSP reduced the likelihood of students being involved in bullying as a target or perpetrator from baseline to the first post-intervention data collection, but among those who were a target or perpetrator it did not reduce how frequently they experienced this behaviour (Cross *et al.*, in submission).

Implications for policy and practice

While significant and positive differences were found immediately following the implementation of this whole school intervention in this study, the CFSP may have experienced partial implementation failure. Qualitative data collected from school staff suggests that many teachers felt under-skilled to teach this program, despite intervention training. These low levels of self-efficacy related to teaching cybersafety content had been evident in our early pilot testing also and the program had been modified accordingly. The classroom learning activities in particular were designed to allow the teachers to adopt a facilitator role helping and supporting students to access the self-directed learning materials rather than teaching the content to students. Similarly, many teachers also indicated that cyberbullying prevention (while they felt it was important) was not currently being taught in their programs, as they were too crowded with other content. Consequently, whereas many teachers indicated that they liked the online resources, they could not find the necessary curriculum/classroom time to teach the online modules. Of those modules that were taught however, most teachers provided positive feedback about student use and satisfaction. To be more effective it appears that the CFSP intervention requires far greater teacher professional learning to lift their self-efficacy to teach in this area, and teachers require more assistance to find time in their curriculum to include this content.

In this study, the CFSP student leaders were found to be excellent catalysts for whole-school action within the school, so much so that the school pastoral care staff may not have been prepared sufficiently to support the students' actions. In some cases staff reported subduing the student leaders' enthusiasm for action to improve student cybersafety. Hence, intervention schools also may require more effective preparation for pastoral care staff to allow greater student ownership and engagement in leading whole-school activities to support student behaviour change.

Flinders University Research Program – Cyberbullying through the new media: findings from an international network

Background

In April 2010, AUARA, in collaboration with European Union senior researchers organized a one-week jointly funded COST-DIISR Training

School in Melbourne (see Chapter 13). Arising out of a collaborative relationship established at the COST-DIISR Training School in Melbourne in April 2010, researchers from Flinders University and two Greek universities are currently involved in a joint anti-bullying intervention program based on Flinders University research. Researchers at the University of Thessaly and Aristotle University in Greece are involved, with University of Thessaly researchers leading the project in Greece. The Greek researchers have been working with Professor Slee's team from the Research Centre "Student Wellbeing and Prevention of Violence" (SWAPv) at Flinders University, who have designed an intervention to help students deal with bullying. In 2011, Dr Grace Skrzypiec was funded by Flinders University to visit Greece to help establish the intervention. This was based on the DVD *Coping with School Bullying*, which included scenes of online bullying developed at Flinders University and translated into Greek. In addition, Skype meetings involving the Australian and Greek researchers have been held to coordinate the Greek phase with the Australian research plans for 2012–2013.

Aims and significance of the project

The research literature on coping clearly identifies both productive and non-productive strategies used by adolescents to cope with problems in general. Our own research (Skrzypiec, Slee, Murray-Harvey, & Pereira, 2011) has revealed that unproductive coping is highly correlated with adolescent students' reports of being victimised and with negative effects on their psychological health (including apathy, depression, aggression, somatic symptoms). Coping is no longer conceptualised as a general trait, attribute or style of a person, as current theories propose that coping needs to be understood in terms of a mix of personal and situational variables. The implication is that coping strategy use is likely to vary depending on the context and be employed differently by particular groups such as children, adolescents, or adults. In relation to the proposed research, this is reflected in our focus on how coping strategies are used in the specific context of being bullied (situational variable) and by adolescent males and females in the upper primary and junior years of high school (person variables) where the incidence is highly problematic.

Despite considerable efforts of individual schools to address bullying issues, and national imperatives for schools to put in place policies and procedures to deal with the problem, much of the work undertaken in schools remains at the level of broadly based, and not necessarily research-informed, intervention. With recent advances in knowledge about the indicative elements of effective intervention programs (Dix, Slee, Lawson, & Keeves, 2011) it is now understood that interventions must attend to critical elements including "dosage" (e.g. length and intensity of the program), adherence (e.g. the lessons are taught as intended), and professional development (e.g. teachers are given some PD relating to the topic). From the preliminary but extensive research we have undertaken to date in two Adelaide high schools to assess students' coping with bullying, we have piloted an instrument that identifies effective and ineffective coping strategies to deal with bullying using items adapted from Frydenberg and Lewis' Adolescent Coping Scale (Frydenberg, 2004; Frydenberg *et al.*, 2004; Frydenberg & Lewis, 1996).

Greek schools intervention

Additionally, developing out of the research relationship established at the COST-DIISR Training School in Melbourne (2010), Greek researchers are undertaking a similar intervention in 50 Greek schools in Thessaly in 2012–2013. They are using the piloted "Coping with Bullying" questionnaire and the intervention program piloted in South Australia by Phillip Slee to target bullying generally, including cyberbullying. Their separately-funded project will run in two stages: a pilot in five Greek schools in early 2012, followed by the larger intervention in 50 Greek schools. Data gathered in Greece and Australia will be loaded onto a common SPSS database to enable comparison. Initial pilot study data gathered from three schools in Greece in 2012 indicated that 13.6 per cent of Grade 8 students (aged 12–14 years, $n = 132$) reported being seriously bullied i.e. "once a week or more often" (Andreou *et al.*, 2012). The intervention showed that fewer students reported being "seriously bullied" post intervention. This finding is consistent with findings for Australian students.

Implications for policy and practice

This project brings together the investigators' experience in two related, but until recently separate areas of research interest: coping and bullying. Both areas are connected to research that has focused on improving wellbeing and academic outcomes for children and young people. The results of our investigations have contributed both to the scholarly literature (Murray-Harvey & Slee, 2007; Murray-Harvey, 2001; Murray-Harvey *et al.*, 2000; Murray-Harvey & Slee, 1998; Slee, Murray-Harvey, & Ward, 1996) and to practical resources for use in schools and by other practitioners who work with children and their families (Slee, Murray-Harvey, & Mitchell, 1997). Likewise, recent instructional resources such as "Coping with Bullying" (Slee, Murray-Harvey, & Wotherspoon, 2008), developed to reduce bullying and victimisation in schools, have arisen from research spanning 10 years on the effects of bullying and victimisation on students' lives including the detrimental psychological health and academic performance outcomes at and beyond school (Murray-Harvey & Slee, 2006; Murray-Harvey, Slee, Saebel, & Taki, 2001). The current research builds on collaborative work supported by the COST-DIISR funding.

It will be important to determine longitudinally the extent to which increased technology knowledge, media literacy and access to ICT at a school level, such as the roll-out of school laptop programs (in a structural context), contributes to an increase in cyberbullying behaviour and/or provides a platform for teaching and learning to encourage positive uses of technology.

Conclusions

The major recommendations emerging from the Australian and COST Action IS0801 research collaboration addressing 'Cyberbullying – coping with negative and enhancing positive uses of new technologies, in relationships in educational settings' can be categorised into the importance of engaging:

a) multi-disciplinary national and international (cross-cultural) research collaborators who are willing to exchange methodologies and share research perspectives and findings;
b) young people as active partners in all aspects of research development, implementation and sustainability;
c) early and mid-career researchers to enhance their capacity to sustain and grow research efforts that encourage the positive uses of technology and reduce cyberbullying;
d) practitioners (and parents) as co-researchers who may be responsible for the effective implementation of interventions in educational settings.

Multi-disciplinary research collaborators

The complexity of cyberbullying behaviour clearly demands a highly collaborative multi-disciplinary team which could include but not be limited to experts in: information and communication technology, informatics, behavioural science, law, psychology, education, sociology, anthropology, social marketing and bio-statistics. The COST Action IS0801 provided a vast international network of multi-disciplinary teams which allowed the rapid sharing and exchange of methodologies, findings and insights from a diverse range of cultural representatives. The different perspectives and methodologies provided by these disciplines enriched the completeness, innovativeness and quality of research processes. This approach seems particularly important when investigating *new* behaviours conducted in *new* contexts such as cyberbullying, and where much research is yet to be published. The links between lawyers, psychologists, educators and behavioural scientists are particularly evident for example, in the research conducted by Professor Campbell.

Importantly, communication technology itself also enables faster and more responsive cross-discipline collaboration through online forums and other no/low cost online environments such as Skype, albeit challenging at times to synchronise meetings across different time zones.

Young people as partners

For behaviours that may be relatively unfamiliar to adults, like cyberbullying, which are conducted in rapidly changing online environments, it is essential that the target audience, in this case young people, are engaged as co-researchers and collaborators in all levels of resource development and implementation. As suggested in the research described in this chapter, this collaboration helps to secure a more authentic understanding of young people's interactions in a cyber environment and how these connect with their offline behaviours. Comprehensive formative research − especially qualitative research − with purposeful samples of young people is also necessary, in addition to key student advisors, to validate recommendations and to facilitate a more representative student input from others involved in or associated with this behaviour. This wider engagement of young people helps to create dynamic and responsive interventions that can maintain broad appeal and relevance to young people, as shown in the social media research conducted by Dr Spears.

While it is critical that young people work in partnership with adults in this research process, they may also need support, encouragement and training to effectively contribute. Hence, it will be important to continue to monitor and evaluate the best means to engage "student voice" as a positive catalyst to change in the cyber environment.

Early and mid-career researcher engagement

To maintain and build the momentum and success of research investigating ways to encourage the positive use of technology and to reduce cyberbullying it seems essential to establish and implement longer-term plans across diverse sectors to train, mentor and connect early and mid-career researchers to existing research networks. This process will help to accelerate the career development of these researchers and enhance their range of skills and experience through their involvement in multi-site, multi-disciplinary research. Access to experienced research leaders and mentors, national and international linkages, and their programs and people, is also required. These researchers will therefore be able to experience different styles of guidance from several mentors and supervisors, and learn to apply a range of research methods in different studies at different locations.

The Australian Alliance (AUARA) and European researchers who were also members of the COST Action IS0801 were able to easily use the COST project as a conduit to initiate research together. This was especially true for Australian and European early and mid-career researchers who were fortunate to be involved in the COST Action's Training Schools. These Training Schools and the COST conferences and Working Party meetings were particularly successful in supporting early and mid-career researchers to join collaborative research teams. This COST Action offered these researchers the opportunity to develop within a global research community while focusing on the positive uses of technology and cyberbullying prevention, as was demonstrated by the Greek–Australian research exchange involving early to mid-career researchers.

Practitioner partners

While few would argue against the importance of implementing evidence-based research in schools to prevent harmful behaviours such as cyberbullying, the fidelity and dose of this implementation often rely on the skills, experience, commitment and unique contexts of the practitioners involved. Their implementation may be affected by complex individual, social and cultural factors that impact school communities. Consequently, the intended effects of a program may not be consistently demonstrated across different age groups, schools, locations, cultures and social and economic contexts. As shown in the Cyber Friendly Schools research presented in this chapter, cyberbullying interventions create unique challenges for implementation largely because of the limited self-efficacy, knowledge, skills and experience of many practitioners in educational settings, especially in Australia. It will be important to continue to conduct implementation research to better understand the nature of barriers to program implementation and how best to overcome these, and particularly how to engage practitioners to ensure the intervention meets the strengths and needs of those who will disseminate and implement these programs in education settings.

References

Andreou, E., Roussi-Vergou, C., Zafiropoulou, M., Didaskalou, E., Skrzypiec, G., and Slee, P. (2012). 'Coping with bullying: a pilot intervention study'. Paper presented at the 13th Biennial Conference of the European Association for Research on Adolescence, Isle Spetses, Greece.

Australian Bureau of Statistics (2012a). 1301.0 – Year Book Australia 2012; Information and Communication Technology. Retrieved September 3, 2013 from http://www. abs.gov.au/ausstats/abs@.nsf/Lookup/by%20Subject/1301.0~2012~Main%20 Features~Use%20of%20information%20technology~174.

——(2012b). 4901.0 – Children's Participation in Cultural and Leisure Activities, Australia, April 2012. Retrieved September 3, 2013 from http://www.abs.gov.au/ ausstats/abs@.nsf/Latestproducts/4901.0Main%20Features1Apr%202012?opendocu ment&tabname=Summary&prodno=4901.0&issue=Apr%202012&num=&view=.

Australian Communications and Media Authority (ACMA) (2010). Trends in media use by young people: Insights from the Kaiser Family Foundation's Generation M2 2009 (USA), and results from the ACMA's *Media and communication in Australian families 2007*. Canberra: ACMA.

Barnes, A., Cross, D., Lester, L., Hearn, L., Epstein, M., and Monks, H. (2012). 'The invisibility of covert bullying among students: Challenges for school intervention'. *Australian Journal of Guidance and Counselling, 22*(2), 206–226. doi: 10.1017/jgc.2012.27

Bennett, S., Maton, K., and Kervin, L. (2008). 'The "digital natives" debate: A critical review of the evidence'. *British Journal of Educational Technology, 39*(5), 775–786. doi: 10.1111/j.1467-8535.2007.00793.x

Beran, T.T., and Li, Q. (2007). 'The relationship between cyberbullying and school bullying'. *Journal of Student Wellbeing, 1*(2), 15–33.

Boeck, T., and Collin, P. (2012). 'Youth and adult researcher reflection on participatory research in Australia and the United Kingdom'. In J. Fleming and T. Boeck (eds.), *Involving children and young people in health and social care* (pp. 197–208). London: Routledge.

Bronfenbrenner, U. (1995). 'Developmental ecology through space and time: a future perspective'. In P. Moen, G.H. Elder, and K. Luscher (eds.), *Examining lives in context: perspectives on the ecology of human development* (pp. 619–647). Washington, DC: American Psychological Association.

Butler, D.A., Kift, S.M., Campbell, M.A., Slee, P., and Spears, B. (2011). 'School policy responses to cyberbullying: an Australian legal perspective'. *International Journal of Law and Education, 16*(2), 7–28.

Campbell, M.A., Cross, D., Spears, B., and Slee, P. (2010). 'Cyberbullying: legal implications for schools'. *Occasional Paper 118*. Melbourne: Centre for Strategic Education.

Campbell, M.A., Slee, P., Spears, B., Butler, D., and Kift, S. (2013). 'Do cyberbullies suffer too? Cyberbullies' perceptions of the harm they cause to others and to their own mental health'. *School Psychology International*.

Campbell, M.A., Spears, B., Slee, P., Butler, D., and Kift, S. (2012). 'Victims' perceptions of traditional and cyberbullying, and the psychosocial correlates of their victimisation'. *Emotional and Behavioural Difficulties, 17*(3–4), 389–401. doi: 10.1080/13632752.2012.704316

Campbell, M.A., Spears, B., Slee, P., Kift, S., and Butler, D. (2011). '*The prevalence of cyberbullying in Australia*'. Paper presented at the 5th World conference and IV Iberoamerican congress on violence in school. Investigations, interventions, evaluations and public policies, Mendoza, Argentina.

Cross, D., Brown, D., Epstein, M., and Shaw, T. (2010). 'Cyber Friendly Schools Project: Strengthening school and families' capacity to reduce the academic, social, and emotional harms secondary students' experience from cyber bullying' (Public Education Endowment Trust, PEET). Perth: Child Health Promotion Research Centre, Edith Cowan University.

Cross, D., Hall, M., Waters, S., and Hamilton, G. (2008). 'A randomised control trial to reduce bullying and other aggressive behaviours in secondary schools' (Healthway Final Report). Perth: Child Health Promotion Research Centre, Edith Cowan University.

Cross, D., Monks, H., Campbell, M.A., Spears, B., and Slee, P. (2011). 'School-based strategies to address cyberbullying'. *Occasional Paper 119*. Melbourne: Centre for Strategic Education.

Cross, D., Shaw, T., Hadwen, K., Cardoso, P., Slee, P., and Roberts, C. (in submission). 'Impact of a school-based online program on cyberbullying behaviour in adolescents'.

Cross, D., Shaw, T., Hearn, L., Epstein, M., Monks, H., Lester, L., and Thomas, L. (2009). '*Australian Covert Bullying Prevalence Study*' (ACBPS). Western Australia: Report prepared for the Department of Education, Employment and Workplace Relations (DEEWR).

Dix, K.L., Slee, P.T., Lawson, M.J., and Keeves, J.P. (2011). 'Implementation quality of whole-school mental health promotion and students' academic performance'. *Child and Adolescent Mental Health, 17*(1), 45–51. doi: 10.1111/j.1475-3588.2011.00608.x

Frydenberg, E. (2004). 'Coping competencies: What to teach and when'. *Theory into Practice, 43*(1), 14–22. doi: 10.1207/s15430421tip4301_3

Frydenberg, E., and Lewis, R. (1996). 'Measuring the concerns of adolescents: developing a concise classificatory system'. *Australian Educational Researcher, 23*(1), 47–64.

Frydenberg, E., Lewis, R., Bugalski, K., Cotta, A., McCarthy, C., Luscombe-Smith, N., and Poole, C. (2004). 'Prevention is better than cure: Coping skills training for adolescents at school'. *Educational Psychology in Practice, 20*(2), 117–134. doi: 10.1080/02667360410001691053

Hasson, F., Keeney, S., and McKenna, H. (2000). 'Research guidelines for the Delphi survey technique'. *Journal of Advanced Nursing, 32*(4), 1008–1015. doi: 10.1046/j.1365-2648.2000.t01-1-01567.x

Hemphill, S.A., Tollit, M., and Kotevski, A. (2012). 'Rates of bullying perpetration and victimisation: a longitudinal study of secondary school students in Victoria, Australia'. *Pastoral Care in Education, 30*(2), 99–112. doi: 10.1080/02643944.2012.679953

Hinduja, S., and Patchin, J.W. (2008). 'Cyberbullying: An exploratory analysis of factors related to offending and victimization'. *Deviant Behavior, 29*(2), 129–156.

Lester, L., Cross, D., Dooley, J., and Shaw, T. (2013). 'Developmental trajectories of adolescent victimization: Predictors and outcomes'. *Social Influence, 8*, 107–130. doi: 10.1080/15534510.2012.734526

Lester, L., Cross, D., and Shaw, T. (2012). 'Problem behaviours, traditional bullying and cyberbullying among adolescents: longitudinal analyses'. *Emotional and Behavioural Difficulties, 17*(3–4), 435–447. doi: 10.1080/13632752.2012.704313

Lester, L., Cross, D., Shaw, T., and Dooley, J. (2012). 'Adolescent bully-victims: Social health and the transition to secondary school'. *Cambridge Journal of Education, 42*(2), 213–233. doi: 10.1080/0305764x.2012.676630

Lim, S.S. (2009). 'Home, school, borrowed, public or mobile: Variations in young Singaporeans' internet access and their implications'. *Journal of Computer-Mediated Communication, 14*(4), 1228–1256. doi: 10.1111/j.1083-6101.2009.01488.x

Milovanovic, S. (2010). Man avoids jail in first cyber bullying case. *The Age*. Retrieved September 3, 2013 from http://www.theage.com.au/victoria/man-avoidsjail-in-first-cyber-bullying-case-20100408-rv3v.html.

Murray-Harvey, R. (2001). 'How teacher education students cope with practicum concerns'. *The Teacher Educator, 37*(2), 117–132.

Murray-Harvey, R., and Slee, P.T. (1998). 'Family stress and school adjustment: Predictors across the school years'. *Early Child Development and Care, 145*(1), 133–149.

——(2006). 'Australian and Japanese school students' experiences of school bullying and victimization: Associations with stress, support and school belonging'. *International Journal on Violence in Schools, 2*, 33–50.

——(2007). 'Supportive and stressful relationships with teachers, peers and family and their influence on students' social/emotional and academic experience of school'. *Australian Journal of Guidance and Counselling, 17*(2), 126–147.

Murray-Harvey, R., Slee, P.T., Lawson, M.J., Silins, H., Banfield, G., and Russell, A. (2000). 'Under stress: The concerns and coping strategies of teacher education students'. *European Journal of Teacher Education, 23*(1), 19–35.

Murray-Harvey, R., Slee, P.T., Saebel, J., and Taki, M. (December 2001). '*Life at school in Australia and Japan: the impact of stress and support on bullying and adaptation to school*'. Paper presented at the Annual Conference of the Australian Association for Research in Education, Fremantle, Australia. Retrieved from: http://www.aare.edu.au/indexpap.htm

Palfrey, J., and Gasser, U. (2008). *Born digital: Understanding the first generation of digital natives*. New York: Basic Books.

Perugini, M., and Bagozzi, R.P. (2001). 'The role of desires and anticipated emotions in goal-directed behaviours: Broadening and deepening the theory of planned behaviour'. *British Journal of Social Psychology, 40*(1), 79–98.

Raskauskas, J., and Stoltz, A.D. (2007). 'Involvement in traditional and electronic bullying among adolescents'. *Developmental Psychology, 43*(3), 564–575. doi: 10.1037/0012-1649.43.3.564

Sakellariou, T., Carroll, A., and Houghton, S. (2012). 'Rates of cyber victimization and bullying among male Australian primary and high school students'. *School Psychology International, 33*(5), 533–549. doi: 10.1177/0143034311430374

Shaw, T., Dooley, J.D., Cross, D., Zubrick, S.R., and Waters, S. (in press). 'The Forms of Bullying Scale (FBS): Validity and reliability estimates for a measure of bullying victimization and perpetration in early adolescence'. *Psychological Assessment*.

Skrzypiec, G., Slee, P., Murray-Harvey, R., and Pereira, B. (2011). 'School bullying by one or more ways: Does it matter and how do students cope?' *School Psychology International, 32*(3), 288–311. doi: 10.1177/0143034311402308

Slee, P.T., Murray-Harvey, R., and Mitchell, B. (1997). *Stressed out and coping in families. Video and resource package*. Adelaide, Australia: Flinders University.

Slee, P.T., Murray-Harvey, R., and Ward, H. (1996). 'Stressed out and growing up'. *Every Child, 2*(4), 18–19.

Slee, P.T., Murray-Harvey, R., and Wotherspoon, A.J. (2008). *Coping with school bullying, DVD*. Adelaide, Australia: Flinders University.

Smith, P.K., Mahdavi, J., Carvalho, M., Fisher, S., Russell, S., and Tippett, N. (2008). 'Cyberbullying: Its nature and impact in secondary school pupils'. *Journal of Child Psychology and Psychiatry, 49*(4), 376–385. doi: 10.1111/j.1469-7610.2007.01846.x

Spears, B., and Zeederberg, M. (2013). 'Emerging methodological strategies to address cyberbullying: Online social marketing and young people as co-researchers'. In S. Bauman, D. Cross, and J. Walker (eds.), *Principles of cyberbullying research: Definitions, measures & methodology* (pp. 166–179). New York: Routledge.

Spears, B., Kofoed, J., Bartolo, M.G., Palermiti, A.L., and Costabile, A. (2012). 'Positive uses of social networking sites: Youth voice perspectives'. In A. Costabile and B. Spears (eds.), *The Impact of Technology on Relationships in Educational Settings* (pp. 7–21). New York: Routledge.

Spears, B., Slee, P., Campbell, M.A., and Cross, D. (2011). 'Educational change and youth voice: informing school action on cyberbullying'. *Seminar Paper 208*. Melbourne: Centre for Strategic Education.

Spiel, C., Salmivalli, C., and Smith, P.K. (2011). 'Translational research: National strategies for violence prevention in school'. *International Journal of Behavioral Development, 35*(5), 381–382. doi: 10.1177/0165025411407458

Tapscott, D. (1998). *Growing up digital: The rise of the net generation*. New York: McGraw-Hill.

Vandebosch, H., and Van Cleemput, K. (2009). 'Cyberbullying among youngsters: Profiles of bullies and victims'. *New Media and Society, 11*, 1349–1371. doi: 10.1177/1461444809341263

13   Training researchers

Visits and Training Schools

*Vera Boronenko, Zehra Ucanok,
Phillip Slee, Marilyn Campbell,
Donna Cross, Maritta Valimaki and
Barbara Spears*

Introduction

COST IS0801, like all COST Actions, provided many opportunities for the training of early career researchers and initiation of new research projects. Some of these were supported by short-term visits of usually one or two weeks, up to a maximum of three months, by an Action member to another venue, for purposes that supported the overall aims of the Action. The first part of this chapter provides some description of these, illustrated by a number of case studies. The second part of the chapter overviews the organization and outcome of two Training Schools for early career researchers, one in Australia entitled 'Research to Policy and Practice: Innovation and Sustainability in Cyberbullying Prevention', and one in Finland, entitled 'Adolescents and Social Media: Guidelines and Coping Strategies for Cyberbullying'. The organization of these Training Schools, the educational approaches used, and their evaluation and impact, will be summarized.

Short Term Scientific Missions (STSMs): supporting mobility within the network

Short Term Scientific Missions (STSMs) were a very important part of the COST IS0801 Action throughout the four years. PhD students, professors and practitioners from COST countries participating in the Action were eligible to apply, normally to work with someone on the Management Committee at a host institution of another country from their own. The applicant should normally be engaged in a program of research as a postgraduate student or postdoctoral fellow or be employed in an institution of a COST country participating in the Action. The theme of their visit (within the overall aims of the Action), as well as the duration (minimum one week, maximum three months) and the date of the visit, were chosen by the applicant. An STSM application was overseen by a sub-committee within the Action (Drs Boronenko and Ucanok), and finally approved by the Chair (or in case of any conflict of interest, the Vice-Chair). If approved, the applicant received a grant towards travel and subsistence; they had to provide a final report after the visit was over, and these reports are available on the COST IS0801 website.

STSMs were thus aimed at strengthening existing networks by allowing scientists to go to an institution or laboratory in another country to foster collaboration, to learn a new technique or to take measurements using instruments and/or methods not available in their own institution/laboratory. They were particularly intended for early career scientists, generally taken as those within eight years of their PhD or last degree. It is envisaged in COST Actions that training opportunities for early career researchers through STSMs will facilitate cross-national cooperation, and these researchers will be expected to contribute, via presentation of their work, to the annual workshops and conferences of their Action.

Here we present and analyse some activities, findings and outcomes of STSMs, as realized in COST IS0801. Some main quantitative indicators are summarized in Table 13.1. As can be seen, the most active year was the last year of the COST IS0801, namely 2012; this may reflect an increasing experience amongst Management Committee members and potential applicants of the benefits of STSMs, plus an increased financial allowance for STSMs in the final year. Of the total 56 STSMs, 48 (85.7 per cent) were early career researchers (ECRs), with eight being by more established researchers. In the Action, STSMs proved to be an important instrument for supporting ECRs, helping them to be included in the European scientific arena via meeting personnel in another laboratory, acquiring new skills, carrying out short programs of research, and presenting of the results of their researches.

The average duration of STSMs within COST IS0801 was 13 days (minimum seven days, maximum 89 days). The majority (73 per cent) of participants had STSMs shorter than ten days – usually week-long visits. The average funding for a STSM was €918 (minimum €400, maximum €1,500), with 78 per cent being less than €1,000. For these shorter visits, STSMs participants often took part in a conference activity or Training School, some organized by the Action (see Chapter 1). Longer stays allowed the participant to carry out empirical surveys or compare/analyse already collected data

Table 13.1 Number and financial cost of STSMs realized in COST IS0801, 2009–2012

Year	Number	Total amount, euro
2009	12	12,590
2010	12	10,600
2011	10	9,690
2012	22	17,510
Total	*56*	*50,390*

with results of other surveys. Participants also worked with host institutions on common publications, sharing their research experience, making new scientific contacts, etc.

As a result of these activities, many empirical researches were presented via posters and oral contributions within COST IS0801 workshops, seminars and conferences; STSMs facilitated many scientific papers of an ECR published in collaboration with more senior researchers and professors. In the next section, we present six case studies of STSMs which illustrate the methodological and empirical activities that participants undertook. The source of information about these case studies is drawn from the final scientific reports provided by the STSM participants, revised by them for this chapter.

1. Cyberbullying measurement: a comparison between different strategies

Annalaura Nocentini

Dr Annalaura Nocentini, from the University of Florence, Italy, spent one week in August 2009 visiting Professor Rita Zukauskiene in Vilnius, Lithuania. She writes:

> My STSM was scheduled during the 14th European Conference on Developmental Psychology (ECDP) and the associated COST Workshop (see Chapter 1). The general aim consisted of sharing knowledge, methodologies and competence on cyberbullying relevant for my scientific training as well as to make progress in the discussion within Working Group 1, since definitional and measurement issues were the two main topics of the COST Workshop. Furthermore, there were other relevant oral presentations, symposia and posters on cyberbullying at the ECDP Conference. The Workshop constituted a unique opportunity for me to understand the state of art on cyberbullying across three broad geographic areas, namely Europe, the US and Australia, and also to compare approaches deriving from different professional profiles (psychologists, educators, mental health services, etc). Different theoretical and methodological approaches and an overview of strengths and limitations on cyberbullying research were presented. Overall, the intensive discussions suggested ideas and new research questions.
>
> During the Conference, I presented a poster entitled *Cyberbullying Measurement: A Comparison between Different Strategies*. This case study of 708 Italian adolescents compared different strategies of cyberbullying measurement: multiple-items scale (Cyberbullying Scale: CS) versus a global key question. The CS was composed of ten items for perpetrated and ten items for received cyberbullying behaviors (Menesini, Nocentini, & Calussi, 2011). The comparison between the CS and the global key question showed satisfactory percentages of concordance (92 per cent for victimization and 80 per cent for perpetration). However, we found a

high percentage of adolescents who did not define themselves as a cyberbully or a cybervictim but nevertheless reported to have perpetrated or suffered from a specific behavior (respectively 50 per cent and 56 per cent). In order to understand what we labeled as this "incoherent" group of students, we carried out a specific analysis on the type and frequency of behaviors reported. We found that 78 per cent and 84 per cent of this incoherent group said they had done or received "silent/prank phone calls", while 45 per cent and 35 per cent reported perpetrating or receiving "insults on instant messaging", 13 per cent and 15 per cent reported "insults on websites" and 14 per cent and 15 per cent "insults on blog". In relation to the frequency of behaviors, 10 per cent of the incoherent group said they had perpetrated or received, with a frequency of two or three times a month or more often, "silent/prank phone calls" and "insults on instant messaging", whereas for the other behaviors only 1 per cent said this.

Overall, the results showed differences between measurement via the key question and the scale. The percentages of concordance between adolescents who defined themselves as cyberbullies and who said that they perpetrated at least one behavior, were satisfactory. But we found a high percentage of adolescents who did not define themselves as cyberbullies but who had perpetrated cyberbullying behaviors. We proposed two hypotheses to explain this. First, some adolescents may deny their role while they perpetrate cyberbullying behaviors. Second, there may be difficulties with the scale, in the sense that some acts are not perceived by adolescents as cyberbullying. We concluded that the exclusive use of the key question can underestimate adolescents' involvement in cyberbullying, and the exclusive use of the cyberbullying scale can overestimate the involvement considering some minor acts. Thus, the parallel use of both strategies can offer an added value and improved accuracy of measurement. Part of this work (the Cyberbullying Scale: CS) was published in Menesini, Nocentini, and Calussi (2011).

2. Exploring cyberbullying through Quality Circles

Simone Paul

Dr Simone Paul (Ms Simone Paul at the time of her visit), from Goldsmiths, University of London, U.K., had two STSMs each of one week duration. She writes:

I was fortunate to have participated in COST IS0801 Workshops, Training Schools and Conferences during the four year Action from 2009 to 2012. I considered these events as an invaluable opportunity for an early career researcher with an interest in cyberbullying to develop expertise by meeting academics and industry professionals with specialist knowledge. I shared in my experience as a practitioner researcher by presenting my work in progress at each event in poster format. My second STSM was at the Training School in Melbourne, Australia in April 2010 (described later in this chapter). Here I describe the first STSM.

On my first STSM I visited Professor Rita Zukauskiene in Vilnius, Lithuania in August 2009. The main aim was to attend the 14th European Conference on Developmental Psychology, as well as pre-conference seminars and post-conference events, including the first 'COST Workshop on Cyberbullying: Definition and Measurement Issues'. For the Workshop I prepared a poster of the initial stage of my PhD research, this was later published as part of the *Australian Journal of Guidance and Counselling* special issue on Cyberbullying (Paul, Smith, & Blumberg, 2010).

The poster was about my use and evaluation of the Quality Circle (QC) approach. QCs can be used in many contexts, but I was interested in them as a way of studying cyberbullying and getting ideas for prevention. The QC approach allows explorative analysis of cyberbullying in secondary education to identify issues for further consideration. This approach requires students to establish a small anti-bullying task force, and then with the guidance of a facilitator, embark on a problem solving exercise over a period of time. The process involves identifying key issues and prioritizing concerns, analysing problems and generating solutions.

In my study, the QCs comprised six groups of students representing the secondary educational years of seven, eight and nine (ages about 12, 13, 14 years). An average of five volunteers for each group, from the existing school population, participated in weekly sessions spanning one school term. The group sessions were designed to enable students to express their views in a thoughtful and constructive way. The work produced during the practical activities was documented and discussions recorded to consider the emerging QC themes.

Each group was directed to produce three project proposals for consideration and then collect votes for the most popular idea from other students and teachers. The anti-bullying theme was introduced to identify solutions to the problem of general bullying or cyberbullying, and an additional project relating to antisocial behavior in the Academy. In total, four cyberbullying projects and two general bullying ideas were introduced.

The areas of interest regarding cyberbullying were the perceptions of each representative group and collectively the range of problems identified and solutions generated. Students report the incidence of verbal bullying and cyberbullying as prominent concerns in school. Qualitative analysis showed that the newly established educational institution which I was working in, with a multicultural, technologically literate population, had a traditional bullying problem and that a number of forms of cyberbullying were being experienced. This and subsequent work with QCs resulted in several peer reviewed journal articles: Paul, Smith, and Blumberg (2012a, 2012b, 2012c).

3. Bully/victims problems in school and cyberspace: associations with depressive symptoms in Swiss and Australian adolescents

Sonja Perren

As an established researcher, Professor Sonja Perren from the University of Zurich, Switzerland, made a longer STSM (36 days) to visit Professor Donna Cross at Edith Cowan University, Perth, Australia, in July/August 2009. She writes:

There is a large range of studies showing that students who are bullied by their peers are at risk of internalizing problems. In the following, we differentiate between two types of bullying: traditional bullying (including physical or verbal harassment, exclusion, relational aggression), and cyberbullying (involving the use of some kind of electronic media). Most studies which had been conducted had shown that cyberbullying is an increasingly common phenomenon among adolescents and that there is some overlap between both types of bullying. However, we did not know at that time whether being a victim of cyberbullying had the same negative consequences as being a victim of traditional bullying.

During my STSM I worked with Australian colleagues on a comparative study. The aim was to investigate the associations between both types of bullying and depressive symptoms in two different countries. First, we hypothesized that traditional victims and bully-victims would report higher levels of depressive symptoms. Second, we hypothesized that there is an overlap between traditional bully/victim problems and cyberbullying/-victimization. Third, we investigated whether cybervictimization is an independent risk factor – over and above traditional victimization – for depressive symptoms. Fourth, we investigated whether country moderates the findings.

A total of 371 students from Switzerland (5 schools) and 1,288 students from Western Australia (from four schools) participated in the study. Gender (52 per cent female), age (M=13.8, SD=1.0), and Grade (first to third year of secondary school) composition were comparable in both samples. Students' self-reports regarding the frequency of being a perpetrator or victim of different forms of traditional bullying were used for categorization (cut-off: at least once a week): "traditional" victims (10.4 per cent), bully-victim (3.9 per cent), bullies (9.0 per cent), and non-involved. Students also reported on the frequency of cyberbullying and cybervictimization and completed well-established scales on depressive symptoms. Data analyses were controlled for the nestedness of the data (school/classes).

In both samples, a strong overlap between both forms of bullying was found. Across both samples, traditional victims and bully-victims reported more depressive symptoms than bullies and non-involved children. Importantly, victims of cyberbullying reported significantly higher levels of depressive symptoms, even when controlling for the involvement in traditional bullying/victimization. This association was not moderated by country. The findings are very similar in both countries, despite different assessment and sampling methods, and emphasize the robustness of the reported results.

In sum, cybervictimization seems to be an overlapping risk factor for depressive symptoms in adolescents. The findings were discussed regarding methodological and educational implications. The draft of the paper was worked out during my STSM, and was subsequently published (Perren, Dooley, Shaw, and Cross, 2010).

In addition to the research collaboration reported above, I had the chance to gain some insights into a series of applied work performed by the research team, e.g. regarding challenges and opportunities of participatory prevention work with youths and parents. During this five-week stay in Australia, I also visited Adelaide for a scientific exchange with Phillip Slee and Barbara Spears. In sum, the STSM was an excellent opportunity to share my knowledge as well as gain expertise and take inspiration from renowned researchers in Australia.

4. Cyberbullying and face-to-face bullying among adolescents in Israel

Tamar Tarablus

Ms Tamar Tarablus, from the Open University in Israel, had a STSM of one-week duration, hosted by Professor Maritta Valimaki at the University of Turku, Finland, in May 2011. The primary aim was to attend the second Training School (see later in this chapter) and associated COST activities. She writes:

During my STSM I presented part of a large study (carried out with Dr Tali Heiman and Dr Dorit Olenik-Shemesh) on cyberbullying in Israeli adolescents. This examined the similarities and differences between cyberbullying and face-to-face bullying among junior high school students, and the connections between cyberbullying and social-emotional factors as well as academic achievement. A total of 458 students, aged 13–14 years, filled out four questionnaires: a cyberbullying questionnaire, a multidimensional scale for social support, a children's depression's inventory questionnaire and a loneliness questionnaire.

The results showed significant correlations between involvement in cyberbullying and social-emotional factors such as mood, loneliness and social support. In terms of social-emotional implications, the settings of cyberbullying enabled distribution of damaging material to a wider audience than in the settings of face-to-face bullying, therefore causing greater damage to the victims of cyberbullying. Contrary to expectations, involvement in cyberbullying did not correlate with decrease in academic achievement or other changes in academic function.

Our results illustrated that there are no boundaries between the "cyber" world and the "real" world. Cyberbullying and regular bullying have similar effects and most of the teenagers who are involved in cyberbullying are also involved in regular bullying. The findings suggest a strong correlation between victims of cyberbullying and victims of face-to-face bullying. These findings were presented with my thesis supervisors at the *Research Center for Innovation in Learning Technologies 6th Conference*: Tarablus, Heiman, and Olenik-Shemesh (2012).

The goal of my STSM was to inform the participants of the Training School about the study that we have conducted in Israel among teenagers in junior high school and to learn about other studies that have been conducted in Western countries. The Training School was beyond my expectations. I learned about new research methods, interesting researches and it has enriched my knowledge on the subject of cyberbullying; and I met wonderful researchers from around the world.

5. Cyberbullying and exceptional pupils

Piotr Plichta

Dr Piotr Plichta, from the Pedagogical Academy in Lodz, Poland, made a one-week STSM in July 2012, hosted by Professor Catherine Blaya, at the Université de Bourgogne, France. The visit was made to Paris. He writes:

The main aim of the STSM was to attend the International Conference on Cyberbullying, organized by the COST Action in collaboration with the Observatoire International de la Violence Scolaire, under the patronage of the French Ministry of Education (see Chapter 1).

During the STSM, I also partook in some activities facilitating the preparation of the conference, together with other STSM beneficiaries and the host, Professor Blaya.

At the conference, I presented a poster entitled 'Bullying and Cyberbullying among Intellectually Disabled Students'. This discussed the results of examining prevalence of bullying and cyberbullying among 100 adolescents with mild intellectual disability (ID) learning in special education settings in Poland. This phenomenon is not well recognized in Polish or foreign literature (nor in the domain of special education, nor in the literature on general ICT usage). The relation between involvement in cyberbullying and in traditional bullying was also examined.

Intellectually disabled children are often isolated or rejected by their peers. They tend to have fewer friends both at school and outside and become "easy targets" of aggression. The risk for intellectually disabled students of becoming an aggression victim is at least twice that for students falling within the normal intellectual range. Intellectually-disabled pupils often have limited social skills, which may also enhance the risk of their aggressive behavior towards their peers (Plichta, 2010). The data for my poster was obtained using the Lodz Electronic Aggression Prevalence Questionnaire (LEAPQ; Pyżalski, 2009), adjusted to the respondents' intellectual abilities. Many similarities to the results obtained for non-disabled students (e.g. time of ICT usage, cyberbullying prevalence) were found. The research revealed considerable involvement in traditional bullying as well as in cyberbullying: 53 per cent of the respondents with ID had performed at least one act of electronic aggression; 65 per cent had become victims of electronic aggression at least once; 45 per cent were involved in traditional bullying (12 per cent bullies, 16 per cent victims, 17 per cent bully-victims); and 27 per cent were involved in cyberbullying (13 per cent cyberbullies, 8 per cent cybervictims, 6 per cent cyberbully-cybervictims). Moreover, a significant relationship between traditional bullying and cyberbullying was found.

Another advantage of the STSM was increasing awareness of higher risk of peer victimization (including cybervictimization) among special needs students and the steps that should be taken to protect them. This goal was reached by familiarizing conference participants with the outcomes of a Polish–Norwegian project "ROBUSD", namely educational materials entitled *Bullying and Special Needs. A Handbook*, edited by Jacek Pyżalski and Erling Roland. This is available for free download from http://www.robusdproject.wsp.lodz.pl/en_materialy.htm. A part of this is devoted to the issue of cyberbullying. Their content and possible application was discussed with anyone who was interested.

During the STSM period I had many opportunities to share my knowledge as well as gain expertise and take inspiration from renowned researchers from all over the world, which can result in further scientific collaboration, especially in the field of cyberbullying research and protecting the vulnerable ICT users from potential harm. An article concerning issues presented during the conference has been published (Plichta, 2012).

6. Cybergrooming – risk factors, coping strategies and associations with cyberbullying

Sebastian Wachs

Mr Sebastian Wachs, from the University of Bremen, Germany, took a one-week STSM in October 2012, hosted by Professor Catherine Blaya, at the Université de Bourgogne, France. The visit was made to Paris. He writes:

The main purpose of my STSM was active participation in the International Conference on Cyberbullying held in Paris 2012 and organized by the COST Action in collaboration with the Observatoire International de la Violence Scolaire, under the patronage of the French

Ministry of Education (see Chapter 1). There, I gave an oral presentation entitled "Cybergrooming – risk factors, coping strategies and associations with cyberbullying".

While the use of information and communication technologies has become ubiquitous among adolescents, new forms of cyber aggression have emerged. Cybergrooming and cyberbullying are only two of them. Cybergrooming can be defined as the establishing of a trust-based relationship between an adult using ICTs to systematically solicit and exploit minor(s) for sexual purposes. Until now, little was known about the nature and extent of cybergrooming. Therefore, the aims of this study were to investigate risk factors of being cybergroomed, to identify various coping strategies on cybergrooming and to explore the associations between being cyberbullied and cybergroomed.

The sample consisted of 518 students from Northern Germany attending fifth to tenth grades (approximately 12–18 years old). The study was conducted in school computer labs during school hours. The Mobbing Questionnaire for Students by Jäger *et al.* (2007) was further developed to assess cybergrooming in this study.

Concerning risk factors of cybergrooming, victimization was significantly higher for girls than for boys (8.7 per cent vs. 4.3 per cent). No age differences were found. Further, specific online behavior seemed to be protective: students who were not willing to meet strangers had lower levels of being cybergroomed (4.4 per cent vs. 15.5 per cent). The same applies for students who were not willing to discuss problems online with strangers (5.6 per cent vs. 11.4 per cent).

A further research question was how students cope with cybergrooming victimization. Three types of coping strategies could be identified: aggressive/assertive, cognitive-technical and helpless coping. In general, boys tended to cope more aggressively/assertively than girls, and girls coped more cognitive-technically than boys; no gender differences were found in helpless coping. Interestingly, the applied coping strategy influenced the risk of being cybergroomed. Students who applied aggressive/assertive coping strategies decreased the risk of becoming a victim of cybergrooming, whereas using cognitive-technical coping strategies increased the risk. In sum, the findings of this study not only shed light on understanding cybergrooming, but also suggest noteworthy associations between various forms of cyber aggression and resulting multiple cyber-victimization. The research presentation can be found at http://de.slideshare.net/sebastianwachs. This study was published with my supervisor Professor Karsten Wolf and a colleague Dr Ching-Ching Pan in a special issue of the Spanish journal *Psicothema*: Wachs, Wolf, and Pan (2012). This is on Open Access: http://www.psicothema.com/pdf/4064.pdf.

Aside from presenting my current study at the conference, I expected the STSM to provide further opportunities for an exchange of ideas between researchers and allow for extended discussion on the topic of cyberbullying and cybergrooming that might lead to joint initiatives in the future.

Having attended the 2nd COST Workshop in Antwerp, the COST Training School in Turku and an STSM for a stay as visiting researcher at Goldsmiths, University of London, I had already benefitted by establishing networks with other PhD students working in similar research fields from different countries. During that time we had an amazing exchange of research ideas, methodology issues and current studies, but also discussions about conditions, challenges and advantages in the dissertation process and additionally, some informal discussions about the economic crisis and the effects on PhD students' lives.

These networks were used in Paris, in order to start a research project to gain more information about cybergrooming and its association with other forms of cyber aggression (such as cyberbullying). The main study is planned for late Summer 2013 in the Netherlands, Thailand, Spain, US and Germany. This cross-national study will be a major outcome of the STSM and gives an example of how STSMs can have long-term impact on an early stage researchers' career. In sum, realization of STSMs during this COST Action contributed to achieving its aim effectively through more "inclusive" and more "personal" networking and more "targeted" sharing of knowledge.

The organization and outcome of Training Schools

The other major training activity in COST IS0801 was the organization of two Training Schools. These events were specifically designed and funded to give early career researchers the opportunity to listen to and interact with leading researchers in the area, develop their skills and knowledge base, interact and network with others, and present their own research plans and activities.

The Australian Training School

The first COST IS0801 Training School was held in Melbourne, Australia, from 11–16 April, 2010. It was particularly distinctive and innovative as it was the first venture to be held jointly between COST in Europe and the Australian Department of Innovation, Industry and Science Research; it attracted extra financial support on this basis. As well as COST funding, further financial support was successfully sought from the Australia–Europe Research Collaboration Fund.

The Training School was jointly organized by senior Australian and European Union researchers involved in the COST IS0801 project. Applications were invited from ECRs through the COST website and through extensive personal and professional email networks. Following a selection procedure, 30 ECRs from Europe and 18 from Australia attended;

in addition there were nine faculty members – five from Europe and four from Australia. On behalf of Professor Francesco Fedi, President of the CSO (http://www.cost.eu/service/glossary/CSO), COST was represented by Dr Michel Gorlicki, COST CSO delegate for France.

The stated aims of the Australian Training School were:

1. To foster collaboration between Australian and European senior and early career researchers.
2. To share scientific and professional knowledge and expertise in multi-disciplinary areas of study related to cyberbullying.
3. To make links from research expertise and findings to evidence-based practice and policy.
4. To disseminate the outcomes of the Training School to the global community of researchers, practitioners and policy-makers.

The program

Using a dedicated section of the COST website, pre-reading materials were provided by the keynote speakers, to be read before arriving in Australia. The Training School itself involved an intensive five-day schedule of lectures, workshops, roundtable discussions and presentations (see Table 13.2). The event was held in conference rooms at the Melbourne Cricket Ground (MCG) an iconic sporting venue. The venue and some of the participants and activities can be seen by accessing the DVD of the Training School at http://www.flinders.edu.au/ehl/educationalfutures/groups-and-centres/swapv/dvd.cfm.

The Training School had a strong social focus on welcoming people to Australia and to this end a social event was held at the Melbourne Zoo in the "Rainforest Room" with introductions, games and activities, all part of the "getting to know you" process to provide a basis for the coming week's activities. The following day started with an indigenous "Welcome to the Country", made by a representative of the local aboriginal community from Reconciliation Australia, a not-for-profit organization that builds relationships between indigenous and non-indigenous Australians. A "Welcome to the Country" is where an Aboriginal, Torres Strait Islander custodian or elder from the local region welcomes people to their land. Despite the absence of fences or visible borders, Aboriginal and Torres Strait Islander groups had clear boundaries separating their country from that of other groups. Crossing into another group's country required a request for permission to enter – like gaining a visa – and when that permission was granted the hosting group would welcome the visitors, offering them safe passage. This is done through speech, song, dance or ceremony. In this instance the speaker also alerted the audience to the difficult past when Aboriginal children were taken away from their families while their parents were often deprived of their land. Other social activities during the week were provided to enable continuations of informal discussions between participants with sharing of meals. One such memorable occasion was the Training School dinner held at a Chinese restaurant in Melbourne's Federation Square, highlighting one aspect of the multicultural nature of Australian society.

The Training School was planned to be very interactive and to use innovative techniques for enhancing learning. All presenters were conscious that many of the participants had English as an additional language. One way to enhance learning was the establishment of "Buddies" where an Australian participant was linked with a European counterpart to help them navigate the mysteries of the Australian culture and language. Also, multiple modes of teaching were used. For example, a traditional slide show with lectures was used to explain some of the intricacies of the law in relation to cyberbullying. The same information was then presented by the two lecturers taking different roles: the lawyer and a teacher asking legal questions, followed by a parent, then a principal and a student. This was followed by the "Great Debate", where participants were divided into two teams: one for the government and one for the opposition on the topic, "Cyberbullying should be criminalized". Each team had four "speakers" with five minutes each. Each "speaker" had five participants who could choose to speak for one minute or any other combination of times. Many participants gave excellent feedback that they had come to the Training School with their mind made up on the legal issues but left with a different view.

A feature of the Training School was that young people were invited to address the researchers on the opening day, and challenged them to use their research to better support young people in general and to help them understand this new phenomenon. They then chaired and led roundtable discussions, and activities, engaging the researchers in dialogue as to what cyberbullying really meant to them. Young people also spoke during organized visits to schools. This focus on "youth voice" was a feature of the week and a Youth Statement was developed by the young people, which captured what it was that they wanted from researchers in this area:

- a clear definition of what cyberbullying is, including consequences and effects;
- clarity around policy, what do we mean by inappropriate behaviors?
- education and to educate parents and peers in cybersafety: how to use Facebook, privacy settings and what they really mean;
- adults to acknowledge the importance of how children and young people cope with cyberbullying;
- research in every country to figure out the nature of the problem, which feeds into addressing the issues;
- increased communication between students and teachers;
- to promote the notion that it is OK to talk about experiences of cyberbullying, to help those who are victimized in the future;
- to identify the strategies for parents to give support/advice to their children.

A visit to an Australian school was organized. The Training School members were met by student representatives of the schools and taken on a tour of the school. Some of the trainees had an opportunity to develop their sporting skills and learnt about "Aussie Rules" football, which is a very different game to that of other football codes. After the tour of the school the students conducted a small lecture touching on how their school addressed the issue of bullying and cyberbullying.

As for any good teaching and learning activity there was a lot of fun and rewards. The inaugural "Bilby" awards helped introduce Training School participants to aspects of Australian culture. A bilby is a desert-dwelling marsupial omnivore – very cute and cuddly. Chocolate bilbys often replace the more traditional European chocolate rabbits in Australian shops at Easter. Each day a Training School participant could "win" a chocolate bilby if they could answer a penetrating question regarding some aspect of Australian culture; for example, what does the phrase "*fair dinkum*" mean (it means: true, real, genuine, as in "I'm a dinkum Aussie"; "is he/she fair dinkum"). Finally, the Training School was rounded off with a recognition of all the Bilby award winners, a rousing Australian bush ballad and the presentation of a small gift by the Australian "buddies" to their European counterpart. An outline of the program is given in Table 13.2. On completion of the Training School, participants received a certificate which detailed the content of their work.

Table 13.2 The Australian Training School schedule of activities

Day	The programme of lecturing and other activities
Sunday	**Registration:** Welcome to delegates Australia by Australian Faculty **Social Event:** Melbourne zoo – 'Rainforest Room'
Monday	**Indigenous 'Welcome to the Country' and Launch** **Roundtable: Guests and Audience.** Convenor: Phillip Slee; Michel Gorlicki, Julia Stamm (COST Office); DIISR representative, Peter Smith (COST IS0801) **The Challenges For Research: From Policy to Practice.** Chair: Tom Woods; Maritta Valimaki (COST); Peter Smith (COST); Alastair Nichols (NCAB); Greg Cox (SSSC–Australia); Sharon Trotter (ACMA); Student Representative of the Victorian Youth Affairs Council **Presentation and Question Time:** Keynote speakers: Ersilia Menesini and Phillip Slee – Definition and Measurement of Cyberbullying **Breakout Discussion Groups:** Using presentation information and pre-reading **Reflection** and reporting on personal learning from the whole day: in Buddy Groups **Social event:** Aussie BBQ, Melbourne Cricket Ground

Table 13.2 continued

Day	The programme of lecturing and other activities
Tuesday	**Presentation and Question Time:** Keynote speakers: Georges Steffgen and Barbara Spears – Risk and Protective Factors **Breakout Discussion Groups:** Using presentation information and pre-reading **Presentation and Question Time:** Keynote speakers: Sally Kift and Marilyn Campbell – Legal Issues and Cyberbullying **Breakout Discussion Groups:** Using presentation information and pre-reading **Reflection** and reporting on personal learning from the whole day: in Buddy Groups **Social Event:** Short Aussie film night.
Wednesday	**Presentation and Question Time:** Keynote speakers: Peter Smith and Donna Cross – Interventions and Cyberbullying **Breakout Discussion Groups:** Using presentation information and pre-reading. School visit (Melbourne Grammar, Wesley College, Berry Street NGO and Bendigo Telstra Project) and case studies of community responses to cyberbullying **Free evening**
Thursday	**Presentation and Question Time:** Keynote speakers: Barbara Spears, and Students from the Youth Affairs Council of Victoria – Engaging the Student Voice to reduce Cyberbullying **Breakout Discussion Groups:** Using presentation information and pre-reading **Presentation and Question Time:** Keynote speakers: Maritta Valimaki and Tolya Stoitsova – Cyberbullying Policy; Media Literacy **Breakout Discussion Groups:** Using presentation information and pre-reading **Reflection** and reporting on personal learning from the whole day: in Buddy Groups **Social Event:** Walking tour and Training School dinner
Friday	**Presentation and Question Time:** Keynote speakers: Maritta Valimaki, Ersilia Menesini and Donna Cross – Research Methods and Cyberbullying **Breakout Discussion Groups:** Using presentation information and pre-reading **Plenary (all Faculty) and Evaluation:** Revisiting the Challenges and Personal Learning **Closing address and evaluation:** Led by Georges Steffgen and Phillip Slee

Outcomes of the Training School

A systematic approach to project monitoring and evaluation was undertaken to ensure quality progress and outcomes of the Training School. First, trainees filled in a questionnaire on their expectations of the school, and preparations for it, before arrival. Second, trainees filled in questionnaires for each major thematic session, and at the end of the school. All in all, the findings of the evaluation showed that the school was very successful. The content and the teaching were perceived by most of the trainees as excellent. Moreover, the trainees indicated that they will collaborate in the future. It was concluded that the intended aims of the Training School were attained as well as the expected outcomes being achieved.

Asked for the professional benefit taken from the Australian Training School the trainees comments included:

- "a unique opportunity to interact with other researchers";
- "very well organized";
- "faculty had genuine interest in our learning";
- "exciting to learn from experienced academics; to debate and discuss, to inform future research";
- "expectations were far exceeded by the realities and opportunities provided".

One trainee noted:

> It has been almost a year now since we met in Melbourne for the COST Training School. For me this was certainly one of the absolute highlights in 2010 not only in terms of what I learnt, the networking with colleagues and heaps of inspirations for my projects, but also because I simply had a perfect time and very much enjoyed Australia.

The main benefits for the Faculty were:

- the collaboration opportunity;
- the collegiality and learning experience;
- meeting many young researchers;
- learning about the topic from colleagues.

Other outcomes

Professor Marilyn Campbell coordinated a special edition on Cyberbullying of the *Australian Journal of Guidance and Counselling* (Vol 20, no 2, December 2010) with seven refereed papers by trainees and faculty from the Training School. This was an excellent opportunity for early career researchers to get feedback on their work and see it published, often at an early stage in their publishing career.

Professor Slee was invited by Dr Julia Stamm, COST Science Officer for the ISCH Domain at the time, to attend the ninth meeting of the domain committee for Individuals, Society Cultures and Health review in Brussels in June 2010. A paper was presented on the significance of international cooperation and collaboration in research from an Australian perspective.

The four Australian researchers (Slee, Campbell, Cross, Spears) presented a paper to the Australian Academy of Science entitled: "Drivers of successful Australian engagement with COST actions in March 2011". Dr Gorlicki (COST CSO delegate for France) highlighted that these partnerships facilitate international cooperation between the EU and important scientific players all over the world. He outlined the shift from the old "Mare Nostrum" to Northern Atlantic Ocean during the early 20th century, and now to the Pacific Ocean as the emerging exchange arena. All participants agreed that Australia and New Zealand could play a major role in linking the region with the European Research Area.

The Finnish Training School

As a COST Action follow-up to the Training School in Melbourne, a two-day Training School was held in May 2011, at the University of Turku, Finland. The goal was to deepen students' knowledge level in advanced research methods related to adolescents and the use of social media and widen students' international networking. The topics were: (1) Systematizing knowledge base; (2) Innovative data collection methods; (3) Developing innovative interventions; (4) Implementing new interventions; and (5) Evaluation of the effectiveness of interventions.

International lecturers in the area of cyberbullying research presented overviews: Professor Peter Smith (UK), Professor Sonja Perren (Jacobs Center for Productive Youth, Switzerland), Professor Angela Costabile (University of Calabria, Italy), Professor Donna Cross (Edith Cowan University, Australia), Policy Coordinator Susan Flocken (ETUCE, Brussels), and Associate Professor Sheri Bauman (University of Arizona, USA). There was an open discussion session, chaired by Professor Ana Almeida (University of Minho, Portugal).

There were 26 young researchers (20 female, six male) from 12 different countries attending this Training School (from Finland, Greece, Sweden, Germany, Ireland, Italy, Poland, UK, Israel, Estonia, Latvia, Austria). Some participants came to Finland a few days before to help the organizing committee doing practical arrangements, such as venue arrangements and registrations. In addition, two early career researchers spent a week in Finland with an STSM from the COST Action.

The topic of the Training School was "Adolescents and Social Media Interventions: Methodological Issues, and Guidance and Coping Strategies for Cyberbullying". The second day of the Training School was combined with the 3rd Workshop of the COST Action (May 13, 2011). The Workshop was titled "Adolescents and Social Media: Guidelines and Coping Strategies for Cyberbullying". The aim of this workshop was to address the following questions: (a) What do we know from empirical findings about successful coping strategies against cyberbullying?; (b) What guidelines against cyberbullying exist in different countries and how should they be adapted?; and (c) How can positive use of new technologies enhance positive relationships in educational settings? The workshop was combined with poster presentations of interest for scientists, students, practitioners and other stakeholders interested in adolescents' use of social media and cyberbullying.

An international networking event, "Getting Together", was organized one evening at the Old Russian Army base, Upseerikerho. The aim was to support young researchers, senior researchers and students networking with each other. The event was run by Sami Saikkonen (a famous Finnish TV presenter). Students prepared an oral presentation (with PowerPoint) of their own country and culture. There were foods from each country, and slide shows. The goal of the event was to increase cultural sensitivity and create international cooperation in a multicultural environment.

Early Career Researchers were able to join the COST network meeting organized for 52 participants, on the last day, at *Rymättylä Herrankukkaro* (in English, *Mama's Pocket*). The place is an old fishing farm out in the Turku Archipelago. After the official meeting and program, participants were able to taste Finnish food (mainly fish, of course) as well as go to Finnish saunas and hot spas beside the sea.

Feedback was collected in anonymous written forms. The feedback was mainly positive. Practical arrangements, lecturers and the relaxed atmosphere received positive feedback. As an area to be developed, the students hoped that the course would have been longer so that there would have been more time for conversations between students and teachers.

A press conference was organized related to the event (Training School plus Workshop), and 12 persons from the Finnish media (from different Finnish newspapers) participated in the press meeting organized. All together 22 news items were published in Finland based on the press meeting.

Conclusions

The COST Action provided special opportunities for networking, and training opportunities. The Short-Term Scientific Missions were often quite short visits, but clearly highly appreciated by those involved, and productive in terms of outcomes. The two Training Schools provided valuable chances for early career researchers to interact with more senior faculty, as well as amongst themselves; and the more extended Australian Training School not only linked European and Australian researchers, but used a variety of innovative activities to ensure a useful and successful outcome.

References

Jäger, R.S., Fischer, U., and Riebel, J. (2007). *Mobbing bei Schülerinnen und Schülern in der Bundesrepublik Deutschland*. Landau: Zentrum für empirisch pädagogische Forschung.

Menesini, E., Nocentini, A., and Calussi, P. (2011). 'The measurement of cyberbullying: Dimensional structure and relative item severity and discrimination'. *Cyberpsychology, Behavior and Social Networking, 14*(5), 267–274.

Paul, S., Smith, P.K., and Blumberg, H.H. (2010). 'Addressing cyberbullying in school using the quality circle approach'. *Australian Journal of Guidance and Counselling*, [Special Issue: Cyberbullying] *20*, 157–168, doi: 10.1375/ajgc.20.2.157

——(2012a). 'Investigating legal aspects of cyberbullying'. *Psicothema*, [Special Section: Cyberbullying] *24*, 640–645, http://www.psicothema.com/pdf/4066. pdf

——(2012b). 'Comparing student perceptions of coping strategies and school interventions in managing bullying and cyberbullying incidents'. *Pastoral Care in Education*, [Special Issue: Violence and aggression in school] *30*, 127–146, doi: 10.1080/02643944.2012.679957

——(2012c). 'Revisiting cyberbullying in school using the quality circle approach'. *School Psychology International*, [Special Issue: Cyberbullying] *33*, 492–504, doi: 10.1177/0143034312445243

Perren, S., Dooley, J., Shaw, T., and Cross, D. (2010). 'Bullying in school and cyberspace: Associations with depressive symptoms in Swiss and Australian adolescents'. *Child and Adolescent Psychiatry and Mental Health, 4*, 1–10.

Plichta, P. (2010). 'Intellectually Disabled Students as Victims and Perpetrators of Peer-to-peer Aggression: the Educational Context'. In J. Pyżalski and E. Roland (eds.), *Bullying and Special Needs. A handbook*. The Pedagogy Academy in Lodz, Poland and Centre for Behavioural Research, University of Stavanger, Norway.

——(2012). 'Uczniowie z lekką niepełnosprawnością intelektualną jako ofiary agresji elektronicznej' [Students with Mild Intellectual Disability as Victims of Electronic Aggression]. *Studia Edukacyjne, 23*, 267–280. Wydawnictwo Naukowe UAM, Poznań.

Pyżalski, J. (2009). 'Lodz Electronic Aggression Questionnaire – a tool for measuring cyberbullying'. In B. Sapio, L. Haddon, E. Mante-Meijer, L. Fortunati, T. Turk, and E. Loos (eds.), *The Good The Bad and The Challenging. The user and the future of information and communication technologies*, (pp. 1018–1024). Copenhagen: COST.

Tarablus, T., Heiman, T., and Olenik-Shemesh, D. (2012). *Teen's violence in the internet vs. face to face violence*. The Open University of Israel.

Wachs, S., Wolf, K.D., and Pan, C.C. (2012). 'Cybergrooming – risk factors, coping strategies and associations with cyberbullying'. *Psicothema, 24*, 628–633.

Section 6

Commentaries

14 Cyberbullying research

Standing on the shoulders of international giants

Justin W. Patchin and Sameer Hinduja

Introduction

Cyberbullying is a problem affecting a meaningful proportion of youth as they embrace online communication and interaction. Increasingly, research is being conducted in a number of countries around the world. The problem, however, is that very little coordination exists among researchers involved in these investigations. COST IS0801 has taken great steps toward remedying this concern. Starting in October 2008 and continuing for four years, the COST Action entitled "Cyberbullying: Coping with negative and enhancing positive uses of new technologies, in relationships in educational settings", served to bring researchers together to share expertise, data, legal analyses, and relevant information about mass media and industry efforts to curtail cyberbullying. Moreover, the Action sought to increase awareness about the nature and extent of cyberbullying with a specific focus on improving the coordination of research activities. Our comments in this chapter serve to synchronize the activities of the COST Action with our own efforts in the United States.

Methodological differences

In the opening chapter of this volume, Smith, Steffgen, and Sittichai express concern that research into the problem of cyberbullying has been progressing with little to no coordination among chief investigators. We agree. Differences in the operationalization of key constructs and in fact even the conceptual and operational definition of "cyberbullying" hamper our ability to meta-synthesize the important work that has already been completed. In Chapter 2, Menesini and colleagues attempt to move our efforts forward by summarizing the main tenets of cyberbullying, emphasizing intentional, repeated acts of aggression using technology carried out against one who lacks power. This is consistent with our own definition that we developed over a decade ago and first published in 2006 (Patchin & Hinduja, 2006) and later updated (Hinduja & Patchin, 2009).

We also feel that it is important to identify the unique characteristics of the online version of bullying, but recognize that at its very root, bullying is bullying. Anonymity, publicity, virality, and the constancy of electronic communications can make cyberbullying experiences particularly problematic for some targets. However, the nature of technology itself can also be exploited to help identify the perpetrator and thereby end those problems. Even though there is a perception among many school-aged youth that one can be anonymous online and therefore do whatever one wants without fear of reprisal, the reality is that most of what is done online can be tracked back to the original creator allowing for appropriate accountability. In many ways this is more easily done in the online realm versus traditional contexts where investigations often results in a "he said, she said" situation with little else for an investigating educator (or other adult) to go on.

Chapter 3 builds on this further by examining various cyberbullying measurement instruments from published research from around the world. We echo Frisén and colleagues' concerns about the use of response sets that reflect bullying behaviors that occurred "at least once or twice". As repetition is a key construct in the definition of all forms of bullying that most scholars can agree upon, grouping those who have experienced an event "once" or "twice" is problematic. Similarly, investigators ask respondents to report of their experiences that variously occurred in the previous month, few months, six months, year, or lifetime. These differences across studies certainly make it difficult to compare results, and ambiguous timeframes make it especially hard to standardize experiences. Perhaps Olweus himself is partially to blame for these decisions as his widely adopted instrument asks students to report how often they have been bullied "in the past couple of months" and the response choices include "it has only happened once or twice". We believe it is necessary to move to a more consistent instrumentation protocol that utilizes a response set which distinguishes between singular events and repeated experiences within a timeframe window that is reasonably discrete.

In our own work, we have chosen to ask students about the bullying they have "ever" experienced along with noting the behaviors that have occurred within the previous 30 days. We believe that it is difficult for children (and adults) to remember exactly *when* something happened to them if it occurred too long ago. But they will remember if it ever happened to them, and we believe that if it happened to them within the previous 30 days, it is probably fairly accurate to say it was a recent experience. This way we can assess both long-term as well as short-term experiences.

The criminalization of cyberbullying

In Chapter 4, Campbell and Zavrsnik articulate some of the issues associated with a movement in many countries to more explicitly criminalize cyberbullying behaviors. We concur with their analysis that formal criminal sanctions are unlikely to deter most youth from participating in cyberbullying behaviors, and among those who would be deterred, most are unlikely to engage in the behaviors even without a law. Furthermore, the majority of teens do not know about these laws or the associated punishments. Even if they are vaguely aware of the illicit nature of their behaviors, they often find it hard to believe that they would ever be identified, caught, and sanctioned.

If not a deterrent, then what is the purpose of a cyberbullying law? In our view, it should help bring awareness to the problem and to empower local officials to take the necessary steps to respond. The vast majority of adolescent cyberbullying incidents can and should be dealt with informally by parents with the help and support of educators, other community leaders, and local law enforcement. Any cyberbullying incident that occurs, regardless of location, that results in a substantial disruption of the learning environment at school, or that makes it difficult for a student to learn, should be subject to reasonable school sanction (and of course parental punishment). Criminal prosecution should be reserved for the most serious forms of cyberbullying that result in significant harm to the target. The reality is that most countries already have various laws that can be applied in these circumstances (criminal harassment, hate speech, felonious assault, stalking, etc.). In addition, victims of cyberbullying are always allowed to pursue civil litigation against a bully (civil harassment, defamation of character, libel, intentional infliction of emotional distress, etc.). Thus, the possible cross-jurisdictional nature of cyberbullying behaviors can make it tricky and complicated when various local, state, federal, and even international authorities are implicated and become involved. From our perspective, this is even more reason to encourage local and informal remedies for cyberbullying when possible.

Industry and media involvement in reducing cyberbullying

In Chapter 5, Coyne and Gountsidou discuss the role of industry in preventing and responding to cyberbullying. Like them, we agree that it is naïve to assume that industry alone can eliminate cyberbullying, but corporations and businesses that profit from technology use certainly should be a part of a comprehensive solution. Industry leaders have an obligation to serve the consumer population by doing all that they can to ensure a safe online experience for their users. To be sure, Web site administrators and Internet Service Providers must respond quickly to investigate reports of harassment and remove any content that violates their Terms of Service. Moreover, security personnel within industry need to cooperate with law enforcement when online behaviors become criminal in nature. Beyond that, though, industry officials should develop platforms on which their users can educate themselves about these behaviors, and what to do if confronted. They can also sponsor educational initiatives in schools that equip the broader Internet audience with the necessary skills to be good digital citizens no matter where they venture. Most major companies are already involved in various activities, but they certainly could be expanded.

The media, too, has an obligation in this regard as well. As Vandebosch and others document in Chapter 6, the news media plays a vital role in shaping our views concerning cyberbullying behaviors. Understandably, the mass media often focus on the extreme or rare incident that is sensationalist in nature, but such an approach unfortunately depicts cyberbullying in a way that might not be completely accurate. For example, the emphasis on several teen suicides linked to experiences with cyberbullying result in a general population that comes to believe that "cyberbullying causes suicide". Also, the impact of news media reporting on suicidal behavior appears to be strongest among young people. Despite these tragedies, the vast majority of cyberbullying victims do not kill themselves, and those who do typically have experienced a constellation of stressors and other issues operating in their lives, making it difficult to isolate the influence of one specific personal or social problem as compared to others. As we have concluded elsewhere on this issue: "…it is unlikely that experience with cyberbullying by itself leads to youth suicide. Rather, it tends to exacerbate instability and hopelessness in the minds of adolescents already struggling with stressful life circumstances" (Hinduja & Patchin, 2010, p. 217). But this level of analysis is often missed in the headlines, as is the accompanying emotional tumult associated with teen suicide. The mass media has a responsibility to report unbiased information using validated sources of data, and should refrain from unnecessarily promoting the worst-case scenario in a way that marginalizes youth, blames parents or educators, or creates excessive and unhelpful fear and panic.

Preventing and responding to cyberbullying

Chapters 7 and 8 in this volume discuss issues related to preventing and responding to cyberbullying. McGuckin and colleagues address the response issue from the perspective of instilling effective coping skills in students who are targeted, but also in encouraging parents and educators to reduce risk by educating youth and to respond to *all* reports of cyberbullying in a way that stops the harassment and protects the target. This must be conveyed in a relatable and accessible way so that youth are inspired and motivated to maturely deal with peer conflict and to step up for their friends in meaningful ways.

The authors rightly acknowledge the close connection between the bullying that happens at school and the bullying being done online, and surmise that one way to prevent cyberbullying would be to prevent any and all forms of mistreatment that occur offline. Indeed, in our work we have observed that the vast majority of students who cyberbully also bully others at school. It remains to be seen, however, whether changes in behaviors at school will result in corresponding behavior changes online. It certainly does seem logical. In general, we agree that the same types of programs that would serve to reduce bullying at school might also result in decreases online – most notably those efforts that focus on the development of conflict resolution techniques, socioemotional skills, and empathy.

Finally, we concur with McGuckin and colleagues that the available empirical evidence regarding the effectiveness of various response strategies is seriously lacking. We likewise are not aware of any thorough evaluations or clinical trials that have examined the efficacy of intervention programming, or even any otherwise formal assessments of "what works" when responding to cyberbullying. Anecdotally, we hear about responses that seem effective, but still encounter some contradicting evidence. Indeed, research in the US has noted that telling an adult about cyberbullying is the most effective response (even though students report that doing so leads to improvements only about one-third of the time). We also know that most students are still reluctant to talk with adults about their experiences, and many adults still do not know how to respond (Davis & Nixon, 2010).

Some prevention and response efforts have now begun to empower students not directly involved in cyberbullying to become actively involved in its control. Research consistently finds that a large majority of students do not approve of bullying in their schools, and even though research also finds that most students have seen it happening, few do anything about it. In Chapter 8, O'Moore and colleagues review this research and conclude that encouraging bystanders to stand up in various ways against bullying is potentially productive.

We particularly feel that such an approach is promising in schools where a positive culture and climate is developed. Our work supports this model as much of our recent research has identified the capacity and utility of positive school climates in preventing cyberbullying and sexting (Hinduja & Patchin, 2012). Specifically, we argue (and have found evidence to support the idea) that there will be fewer problems at school *and online*, because students will not want to damage the positive relationships they have at school by doing anything that will disappoint or upset the adults or youth there to whom they are strongly bonded. Creating a culture of caring, it seems, is a potent prevention strategy for a host of problematic adolescent behaviors, regardless of whether they occur via technology or in the real world.

Cyberbullying among adults

In Chapter 9, Cowie and colleagues acknowledge that cyberbullying is not just a teen problem. As university professors ourselves, we have seen evidence of cyberbullying in our educational communities and regularly speak with university students in our institutions and elsewhere about these behaviors. There is little question that harassment occurs among adults (both among those who are enrolled in higher education and those who are not), and that efforts should made to curtail it in these populations as well. Surprisingly little formal research into the cyberbullying experiences of college students has been conducted, especially since they are often an easily accessible sample for researchers to corral. What data are available, suggest that cyberbullying does occur among older adolescents and probably for many of the same reasons as primary and secondary students. In some ways, it may be more difficult for university students to seek and obtain relief from cyberbullying since few universities have formal policies in place that address the misbehavior, and victims are often forced to utilize formal (civil or criminal) channels to respond – which may be inaccessible, inappropriate, or ineffective. This remains an area of study that is neglected and in need of attention and deeper inquiry; hopefully this coverage will pique the interest of others in further studying this particular set of victims in the hopes of better illuminating what can be done.

Most teens aren't cyberbullies

Chapters 10 and 11 of this book shift the focus away from blaming teens for everything that is bad online by recognizing the important benefits ICT offers adolescents, and by identifying the ways that teens themselves have been agents of understanding. Spears, Costabile, and associates begin by offering a counterpoint to the problematic behaviors which are the primary focus of this book by quite appropriately highlighting many positive developments that can be attributed to the motivation, brainpower, kindheartedness, and passion of adolescents in the Information Age. We need to clearly acknowledge that not all teen behavior online is bad. Moreover, the vast majority of teens do not cyberbully others. Over the last decade, we have surveyed over 14,000 students from different schools within the US. Among this group, approximately 15 per cent of respondents admitted that they had cyberbullied others. This number is consistent with the weight of the research that has been published by others (Patchin & Hinduja, 2012). Of course, this means that about 85 per cent of students have not cyberbullied others! Sometimes in our haste to deal with problem behaviors among youth, we forget to recognize that most are doing the right thing.

Spears, Costabile, and colleagues also point out that many of the features of ICT that make it ripe for cyberbullying also make it a positive venue for teens to work through the challenges that are common in adolescence. For example, the disinhibition and pseudonymity associated with online interactions allows young people to explore questions that they perhaps otherwise would avoid. In addition, they can experiment in social exchanges in ways that would otherwise be too risky if tried and failed locally among people they would see on a daily or weekly basis. Identity formation is an important part of adolescence, and teens are able to experiment by portraying and representing themselves in certain ways to receive affirmation and validation of who they are and who they want to be. Finally, the authors also note the various other skills that are developed and refined while interacting with technology, including fine motor movements such as pressing, clicking, swiping, etc., and the ability to work on several tasks simultaneously.

It may still be too early to assess the usefulness of these abilities, but there is little question that "millenials" are more adept at online interaction than those of earlier generations. Even so, adults who work with youth have a responsibility to model appropriate online behaviors and to encourage the safe and responsible use of technology. To that end, they should enlist the assistance of youth in their efforts to better understand how teens are using and misusing technology. As Spears and Kofoed advocate in Chapter 11, the youth voice is an important one that cannot and should not be ignored. Their involvement in helping to elucidate the nature of cyberbullying behaviors as well as to aid in a more complete understanding of what works in addressing it is crucial. And efforts to include their perspectives ought to move beyond collecting data via questionnaires from them. Focus groups, storytelling, and other in-depth conversations with youth about policy and programming can reveal a great deal about what is really going on, and will complement quantitative analyses that often can benefit from more personal perspectives. Relatedly, Cross and colleagues also acknowledge in Chapter 12 the importance of allowing youth to authenticate their cyberbullying experiences through active participation in research and analysis in several Australian initiatives. The focus here was also to integrate knowledge across projects in a way that aided in the development of prevention and response solutions.

Training, professional development, and the lasting legacy of the COST action

Chapter 13 of this book highlights the numerous opportunities made available through the COST Action for researchers (especially those who are early in their academic careers) to develop their research agendas through collaboration with investigators in other countries and by participating in a Training School in Australia or Finland. These networking opportunities led to interactions and partnerships among researchers who are interested in similar problems, but who may not have known about the comparable work being done elsewhere.

The problem of a lack of coordination is one that the COST Action has specifically sought to remedy, most notably by bringing together researchers from different academic traditions, methodological approaches, and geographic locations. Indeed, even within the United States where we conduct our research, there is little formal collaboration between scholars at different institutions – likely for the same reasons that the COST Action was created.

Indeed, a key feature of these kinds of efforts is to establish networks within which additional collaboration can take place. This volume is evidence of the effectiveness of the COST Action in that dozens of researchers from several countries within and outside of Europe have contributed. We are pleased to see that the topic of cyberbullying is on the forefront of research agendas across multiple countries, because it is through these inquiries that we collectively make progress in understanding the scope, prevalence, consequences, and contributing factors of the problem at hand. We must now continue to share knowledge created through these various empirical examinations, and then make a consistent effort to share the best practices that arise with all constituent audiences that can benefit from it while they work on the front lines. Finally, we must continue our relentless pursuit of understanding "what works" through more longitudinal and evaluation studies so that our scientific investigation of cyberbullying actually leads to a decrease in its relevance in the lives of the youth we aim to safeguard and serve.

References

Davis, S., and Nixon, C. (2010). 'Youth Voice Research Project: Victimization and Strategies'. Retrieved 20 March, 2013: http://www.youthvoiceproject.com/YVPMarch2010.pdf

Hinduja, S., and Patchin, J.W. (2009). *Bullying beyond the schoolyard: Preventing and responding to cyberbullying*. Thousand Oaks, CA: Sage Publications (Corwin Press).

——(2010). 'Bullying, cyberbullying, and suicide'. *Archives of Suicide Research, 14*(3), 206–221.

——(2012). *School climate 2.0: Reducing teen technology misuse by reshaping the environment*. Thousand Oaks, CA: Sage Publications (Corwin Press).

Patchin, J.W., and Hinduja, S. (2006). 'Bullies move beyond the schoolyard: A preliminary look at cyberbullying'. *Youth Violence and Juvenile Justice, 4*(2), 148–169.

——(2012). 'Cyberbullying: An update and synthesis of the research'. In J. Patchin and S. Hinduja (eds.), *Cyberbullying Prevention and Response: Expert Perspectives* (pp. 13–35). New York: Routledge.

15 Practitioner commentary from ETUCE

Anders Eklund and Susan Flocken

Introduction

It is with great interest and pleasure that ETUCE (European Trade Union Committee for Education) contributes to this book. This commentary does not intend to go deeply into the debate on the emergent themes, rather it will contribute with the findings of teacher unions in Europe on the topic at stake. In its work, ETUCE has used the terms "cyber-harassment" and "harassment". The reason for using "harassment" rather than "bullying" is on the one hand to clearly show the link to the European social partners' Framework Agreement and other EU legislation in this area; and on the other hand to demonstrate the fact that ETUCE focuses in its work on the protection of education workers' rights and therefore the prevention of harassment; whereas bullying in the school context is used to mostly refer to student-to-student relations.

This publication is the beginning of a closer liaison between researchers in the field of bullying, harassment and cyberbullying, cyber-harassment; it will hopefully, also, trigger a new relationship between research and those who daily promote the reduction of harassment and those who work with prevention in this area. These reviews are interesting for all who, in a more systematic way, try to come close to the essence of structures, emotions and values that provide the underlying core to all harassment. They are thought-provoking findings and deal with this issue in a scientific way which is promising for the future. New and good practices will arise out of quality research.

Violence, bullying and harassment, and in particular cyber-harassment, is a growing concern among ETUCE member organisations. The occupational health and safety of teachers and school staff have always been a key issue for ETUCE, as schools need to be a safe environment for teaching and learning so as to provide high quality education. Therefore, we believe that even in times of economic constraint, continuous public investment in education is needed at all levels.

ETUCE feels that there are many stakeholders in the discussion, when building the road towards improved management of addressing violence, bullying and harassment, and especially cyber-harassment. This contact could be the beginning of a movement from words to action. The articles in this book represent angles of cyberbullying and cyber-harassment that will be useful also in finding the road marks that we need to put along the road for better leadership in this area.

Before writing any more remarks on the texts in this book, some references to what ETUCE has achieved in this field should be presented.

ETUCE: European Trade Union Committee for Education

The ETUCE represents 135 Teacher Unions and 12.8 million teachers in all the countries of Europe (5.5 million teachers in the EU), from all levels of the education sector. ETUCE is a Social Partner in education at the EU level and a European Trade Union Federation within ETUC, the European Trade Union Confederation. ETUCE is the European Region of Education International, the global federation of teacher unions.

For several years ETUCE has carried out projects aimed at implementing the European framework agreement on violence and harassment related to work which is one of the major European framework agreements by the social partners in Europe. Among the different union confederations ETUCE is leading the way in acting upon these agreements. In two ways there has been a learning experience. First, ETUCE and its member organisations gained knowledge from different experts who contributed to seminars and conferences. Second, the multilateral exchange between teacher unions in Europe as regards sharing experiences, set backs and progress, has built an informal network. As a formal outcome this has resulted in the ETUCE Action Plan on Preventing and Tackling Violence at School, http://teachersosh.homestead.com/Publications/ETUCE_action_plan_HV_EN.pdf. In addition, ETUCE has compiled – together with the European Federation of Education Employers (EFEE) – an implementation guide on the prevention of the third party violence in the education sector, intended to be used in the social dialogue and collective agreements in the education sector at national, regional and local level.

Project on cyber-harassment

In 2010, ETUCE carried out the project 'Teacher Trade Unions concerned about violence at school II – Cyber-Harassment'; and conducted two surveys to gather information on whether and to what extent cyber-harassment is addressed in the countries of the ETUCE member unions. The second survey examined national teacher union strategies on cyber-harassment and collected good practices on how to continue developing and improving anti-cyber-harassment measures at national union level.

The survey report shows that an increasing number of national teacher unions have established or are developing strategies to prevent cyber-harassment against teachers and school staff. The survey contributions show a wide range of interesting approaches of how teacher unions can tackle cyber-harassment. The report also gives an overview of national union strategies on anti-cyber harassment measures in Europe so as to provide practical examples for inspiration and to facilitate a possible transfer of experiences and best practice models from one country to another. Focusing around five priority issues of awareness-raising, negotiations/co-operation with education employers and other stakeholders in education, whole-school approach, reporting incidents and teacher training, the report provided teacher unions with practical guidelines to address and tackle cyber-harassment.

The challenge for the future is to mainstream the importance of occupational health and safety for teachers and school staff and to continue to raise awareness on the issue in collaboration with other stakeholders in education. Also, it is essential that teacher unions carry on exchanging good practices on anti-cyber-harassment measures in schools and adjust them to the relevant national conditions.

Linking with the results of the cyber-harassment project, ETUCE carried out a joint project with EFEE that explored to what extent third-party violence and harassment are addressed in the education sector in EU and EFTA countries and outlined possible actions of teacher unions and education employers in preventing third-party violence and harassment. The main project outcome is the 'Implementation Guide for the Education Sector of the Multi-Sectoral Guidelines to Tackle Third-Party Violence and Harassment Related to Work', which was presented to the European Sectoral Social Dialogue Committee for Education in spring 2013. This project is based on a multi-sectoral initiative which clearly also addresses cyber-harassment as a form of third-party violence.

Thirteen chapters of knowledge

Turning now to the 13 main chapters in this book, it is noticeable that some of the summaries and conclusions suggest the need for further research. This is of course the responsibility of a researcher. Teachers in schools also need to take these issues further and would be grateful for more research. From a teacher union point of view, it seems to be clear that much previously acquired knowledge in traditional fields such as conflict management, harassment, violence and victimization applies to cyberbullying and cyber-harassment, too. Bullying and harassment, be it in the streets or in the school yard, has many of the same components as cyberbullying and cyber-harassment. In the chapter on definitions of cyberbullying these similarities are discussed. In the following chapters this point of view is also reflected upon from other angles. However, and this is important, the different chapters also point out the special features of cyberbullying. It is these aspects that widen the horizon of knowledge in this field.

The extensive chapters are mainly written addressing a reader with a scientific background. It is indeed important to bring all reasoning on the table for fellow scientists. From a practitioner's point of view, speaking from the teachers' and teacher unions' perspective, however, the results need to be presented to a larger audience in order to advance and gain even more understanding with the ultimate aim to further decrease the number of incidents and suffering from different forms of bullying and harassment. A main concern for many stakeholders in working environments, especially in education, is that research findings should lead and materialise into new practices. The road from findings to change of practice is often very long – if it is built at all. Often, when researchers have completed their quality work and successfully reported in their scientific clusters and journals, it remains the case that politicians, school leaders and teachers rely on what is known to them. Often that comes from their previous experience ("How did we do this last time?") or, for politicians, taking reference to their own time in school. Whether it is a researcher, a combination of practitioners, education authorities and researchers or the practitioners themselves who create this link from research into action is not the main issue. However, it is of vital importance that new findings reach schools relatively quickly.

With this collection of systematic understandable research, as represented in this book, one of the cornerstones for future discussion is laid. Steps have been taken to approach helpful solutions for promotion of quality standards and prevention of ill health because of cyberbullying and cyber-harassment.

There are some passages in the book that take a step even further than the rest of the text. Glimpses of pictures of the future are presented. Industry, technology, usability will be different when this book is read, than when the book was first conceived. What will come next after the iPhone or Twitter? The immediate response from a teenager is: "a lot". One only needs to go back a few years to understand how different the devices were that were common then. How can we anticipate in which direction bullying and harassment will develop with the rapid changes in technology?

Working in school as a teacher, one of the main sources of information about outside-school reality comes through pupils and students. Teachers and education staff are well prepared to run schools according to the curriculum and that is of course important, but looking into the future, teachers need support. Chapter 11, on youth as knowledge brokers, discusses using the knowledge the general school population already possesses. "Youth voices enable researchers to explore" as is stated in the conclusion. This is very important. To act ahead requires not only a profound historic knowledge; it also requires the knowledge of how to follow present developments and the imagination of what could be true tomorrow. Many of the findings in the chapters are enthralling, but it is good to acknowledge the fact that following the mind of the student is the most intriguing challenge for a teacher.

Remarks from the practitioners' side

Taking the work and findings presented in this book further, it is appropriate to highlight some observations that ETUCE has made concerning different aspects of violence, bullying and harassment in general and cyberbullying and cyber-harassment in particular. These observations concern the importance of working with fundamental values as a foundation for schoolwork: concentrating on school identity, strengthening the identity of students and pupils, and training. As one of the ETUCE projects showed, the nature of the daily mutual engagement of both students and teachers with this issue is essential to determining whether the incident rate goes up or down.

Training to tackle incidents

As is obvious from the research, teachers and education staff in general have to learn to handle cyber-harassment in action or after incidents, and to practice this situation over and over again. In this regard, this does not differ from any other harassing and/or violent incidents. Teachers are, in general, not trained to deal with such situations and tend to escalate incidents instead of defusing them. Education staff really need to train, evaluate and train again so as to build good practice of how to tackle and address bullying and harassment. Practitioners therefore indeed underline the necessity that cyberbullying and cyber-harassment, as opposed to other forms of violence, requires the knowledge and practice on how to handle specifically the "cyber" part. Education staff need networks to find the right access into groups of bullies that use digital devices.

Cyberbullying and cyber-harassment also differ from other forms of bullying, harassment and violence, because the victim very seldom can hide from what is happening. The victims who do succeed in hiding it and still have some integrity, often have accomplished this with strong support from their personal environment (friends) who care. It is important to be observant of victims, and offer support and shelter.

Possibility of assessment

The problem is where to start. Knowing this is hard, especially when in a school where you have not done anything on this issue before. This is not an uncommon situation. Initial opportunities to analyze the actual situation are necessary. There needs to be time and perhaps the possibility to pause for a while.

Often schools seek solutions from other schools that have already acted upon their own particular situation. Some schools might be lucky and the method could be transferred to their own situation, but in general this is not the case. Therefore school leaders and shop stewards, security representatives, sometimes the entire staff need to sit down and evaluate the situation. Key questions need to be dealt with: which support is needed, what could be done locally and which contacts could be of use? The more work put into this assessment at the beginning, the better and smoother the work will be later.

Room to handle fundamental values in school

Underlining the research done in the field of translating research into practice and the challenges faced therein, we believe that the very essence of successful work in dealing with cyberbullying and cyber-harassment, and any other forms of harassment and violence, is basic training in fundamental values of school and society. Respect for others, self-esteem and transparency. Without these prerequisites it will be hard to achieve any change in behaviours or attitudes. It is necessary to be able to trust students and pupils, and to get them to believe in what they can become, in order for schools to establish more confidentiality. The construction of a foundation of identity, values and rules that leads to a less aggressive environment is absolutely necessary in order to achieve any success in this area.

Time to work with identity of school and students

Experiences show that an effort to create a positive identity in a school results in lower incidence of harassment and bullying. Such a positive identity can be assisted, for example, by creating a school logo, school newspaper, and school activities to create a feeling of living and working together. Additionally, support to individuals in regular schoolwork results in less incidents. Supportive work with students outside school is also important. Through this work, staff are informed earlier about what is going on among the students.

Support to teachers

Teachers trust each other in their knowledge of teaching and education. In the matter of harassment and bullying, teachers cannot trust each other in the same way. Knowledge in this field is scarce and it does not help so much if only one or two members of staff have some experience with it. It is important to establish a support for teachers so they can trust each other before and after bullying or harassment occur. This support needs to level the knowledge of all teachers, and also produce individual and group support after incidents so that they can handle the situation in a better manner.

Conclusions

Working with identity, values and commonly decided rules will not show an immediate effect. It might even happen that the larger and broader recognition of the issue, it will provoke an increased incident rate at first, which will gradually decrease. To this, many of the practical suggestions mentioned in this book are relevant. Changing the school climate must be the prime objective.

One of the main questions to be asked is whether cyber tools are considered to be of value to society and school for their development and progress or whether they are seen as a threat to individuals' integrity. This is also brought up in Chapter 10. When this question is raised, it is important to be more reflective than only seeking a quick reply. Every new development is a challenge for any society and often first revealed in school. There is no valid evidence of youth being more hostile towards each other and others outside school than they were before. The big difference is transparency, which is widely discussed and written about. One concern when using cyber tools lies in the fact that the harassment is recorded and more widely spread. But on the other hand it can be more easily traced. With transparency a change of attitude has also developed. Behaviours of bullying and harassment that one generation back in some ways were accepted, are now no longer accepted. The competence that these chapters represent will provide further knowledge and transparency, and a more enlightened attitude on harassment and especially cyberbullying and cyber-harassment.

16 Addressing cyberbullying through more effectively bridging research and practice

Keith Sullivan

Introduction

Cyberbullying can be mean-minded, vicious, cumulative, and end in tragedy. In Ireland, over a three-month period in the second half of 2012, three young girls, Ciara Pugsley aged 15 of County Leitrim, Erin Gallagher aged 13 of County Donegal, and Lara Burns aged 12 of County Kildare all committed suicide. Cyberbullying was cited as a major reason or a contributing factor. Shannon Gallagher, the 15 year-old sister of Erin, also took her own life a few months after Erin's suicide and became a secondary victim of cyberbullying.

Similar scenarios have been repeated in various other locations around the world and have involved both boys and girls. The extreme situations that have caused children and young people to take their lives have also left permanent scars within families and school communities. They are stark and tragic and the bell they toll can't be ignored. They are also the tip of a deep and largely hidden iceberg. The most important outcome of our cyberbullying research is to reveal cyberbullying and dismantle it in order to put a stop to such extreme consequences.

Responding to cyberbullying

Cyberbullying through the new media: Findings from an international network is an excellent book and one of several publications that has emerged from the four-year EU-funded COST IS0801 process, entitled 'Cyberbullying: Coping with negative and enhancing positive uses of new technologies, in relationships in educational settings'. "The main aim of the Action was to share expertise on cyberbullying in educational settings, coping with negative and enhancing positive uses of new technologies in the relationships area, moving towards a common set of guidelines applicable in Europe" (https://sites.google.com/site/costis0801/). This aim was achieved and provides the basis for Chapter 8, 'Guidelines to prevent cyberbullying: a cross-national review'. In fact, much more has been achieved in this book and there were a substantial number of other significant accomplishments from the project as a whole, including the web of research connections made by participants not just from Europe but also from Australia, the US, Japan and Thailand.

The conceptual foundations upon which COST IS0801 was based are inspiring because rather than bringing a group of people together and funding a research process to produce a compilation of national reports from participant countries, it does something much more dynamic, exciting, productive and appropriate: it creates extensive connections and networking possibilities through conferences, research visits for early-career and established researchers, and the possibility of supervised or joint research work with colleagues who had similar interests but were in different locations. Two excellent research-training courses were provided in Australia and Finland, and the exchange of ideas and support in developing individual and joint research projects resulted in a number of publications and an extension of research knowledge and skills development. This high quality international book focusing on the important contemporary issues on cyberbullying echoes these creative international research synergies.

The theme of the project has provided a wide-ranging brief that has allowed us to get at the root of the problems cyberbullying creates and to identify and create ways to address them. In a strategic about-face, the positive use of ICT in educational contexts is addressed as a way of developing the skills, fluency and confidence for dealing with cyberbullying if and when it happens to individual students or their friends. It is an extensively referenced and complex exercise of exploration of the topic of cyberbullying by a group comprising psychologists and established or emerging experts in a particular specialisation within the topic of cyberbullying in educational settings. The formation of groups of experts to focus upon and write chapters in key areas has allowed a spotlighting of the research and scholarship of those working on a particular topic, which promotes the sharing of new knowledge in a critical and creative way.

This commentary asks the following question, "Is the research-generated knowledge in *Cyberbullying through the new media* transferable to and useful for those on the ground?" Primarily, it concerns those who have to deal with the prevention of cyberbullying and its effects. In school-related cyberbullying, the most important reason for addressing it is to get it to stop, to assist people who are being subjected to it to be relieved of the pain it has caused them, to deal with those who are causing it, and to address the bystanders and their role in supporting the cyberbullying, taking a stand on behalf of the targeted person or watching from the sidelines.

This topic is close to my heart. But it is much more than that. All the contributors to this book care about what they do, but it is in the process of joining together that we have the real ability, knowledge and power to challenge the status quo, to push out the boundaries, and to create new and useful knowledge that allows those in the firing line, the practitioners, to deal with the problem of cyberbullying in schools and other educational settings and within the contexts of the individual cultures of those institutions. The synergy that clearly occurred in COST IS0801 created a series of connections between researchers that went beyond their own countries and provided insights from different contexts that are mutually applicable.

This book offers an overview of our current knowledge: it provides helpful information, good advice, and a mixture of established, innovative and exploratory ideas. There is also some "putting of the cat amongst the pigeons" in order to go beyond description to analysis, and beyond analysis to reframing, innovation and restorative methodologies. Always the focus is on understanding the beast that is cyberbullying and taming it in order to restore safety.

Ko wai koe?

When working as a research fellow at Waikato University's Centre for Maori Studies and Research in New Zealand in the late 1970s and early 1980s, with my newly minted PhD and the only *Pakeha* (European) on a team examining *whaikoorero*, Maori oratory, I felt both excited and more than a little intimidated. The aim of the project was to preserve the rich traditional forms of the Maori language and to halt the process that seemed to be moving the language towards possible extinction and to firmly retain for and pass on this rich traditional linguistic body of knowledge to future generations. A Maori community's *marae* is the area for discourse and is located at the heart of their village usually in front of a carved wooden meetinghouse (*whare whakairo*). Here it is common for a senior male member of the community to ask "*Ko wai koe?*", meaning "who are you?" but implying, "As a *Pakeha*, what right do you have to examine and critique our treasure?"; "What are your qualifications and experience?"; "How am I connected to you?". This is not a question without context, as one of my colleagues, a *kaumatua* (elder) and Methodist minister, the late Te Uira Manihera informed me in semi-joking fashion that "The Pakeha stole our lands from under our feet while we were looking up at heaven" (see Mahuta *et al.*, 1981, Sullivan and Sullivan, 1984).

Although sometimes politely and quietly done, the question and its follow up could be very challenging. And these concerned individuals were right to challenge me as they were passionate about their culture and language and needed to know that I would be "a safe pair of hands". The reason I am relating this story is because I feel excited about this book as a culmination of and the container for excellent thinking and passionate writing about cyberbullying and its effects, and what we have learned about it, what we can do now and where we should go next.

So *Ko wai ahau*? Who am I? What right do I have to be writing this chapter, having visited the travelling COST roadshow late in the day and travelling only from Dublin to Paris to Vienna? What right do I have to be, in effect, critiquing this book and its contributions?

In many ways, I feel like "the odd one out" as my qualifications and inclinations are similar to but also different from those of my colleagues. I have a Master of Philosophy in Educational Psychology from Cambridge, and in the mid-1990s, I beat out competition from the legal profession for a fellowship in human rights at Oxford University to carry out research into bullying. My PhD, however, was a multidisciplinary study at the now gone Institute of Dialect and Folk Life Studies at Leeds University. My major focus was on the cultural and living role of folk music in the lives of the inhabitants of a traditional village community. So although I have training and experiences in educational settings with psychological and quantitative methodologies, my more substantive training was in qualitative approaches and this mix and my strengths have been reflected in my approach to educational, and specifically bullying, research. My research has focused on finding practical solutions for addressing both traditional and cyber bullying, with a particular concern for educating practitioners, students, parents and the wider educational community to pragmatically and effectively deal with bullying and cyberbullying.

Although I am currently the Statutory Professor of Education at the National University of Ireland, Galway, I have been a secondary school counsellor (with some teaching responsibility) in New Zealand, a secondary school teacher in Canada and England, a youth worker in England, the Head Counsellor of a community centre in Canada, and a management board member of an Irish primary school.

The role of the practitioner

Bridging research and practice is an important task and I would argue that this book does that up to a point. Although some of us manage to exist in the cultures of research and practice, there is sometimes a divide that is difficult to bridge and that often remains unassailable. The more we can build bridges or find other, perhaps more creative, ways to make the crossing, the more we may succeed in tackling cyberbullying effectively. I would argue that the following are the ideal qualities for the anti-cyberbullying practitioner (see also Bauman's 2011 excellent book).

1. A solid professional training, updated as appropriate: As a school counsellor, you would have trained specifically to deal with children and young people, to guide them through difficult issues and help them to deal assertively with problems in a way appropriate to the particular individual. Theoretically, you would be familiar with the boundaries of your role, the nature of bullying and cyberbullying, the nature and stages of human development and how these may come into play in the dynamic of cyberbullying.

2. Excellent counselling and personal skills and the ability to work creatively, sometimes in chaotic contexts: Over time you will have learned through your experiences and will have developed your skills and

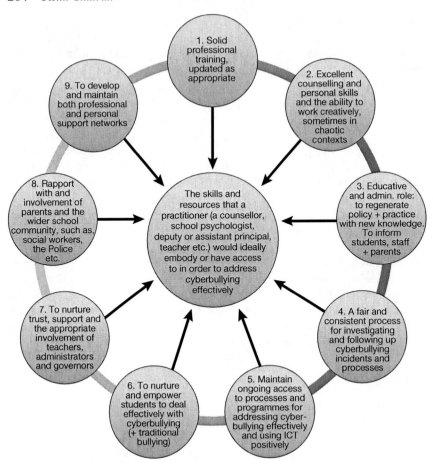

Figure 16.1 The resources and skills that a practitioner (a counsellor, school psychologist, deputy or assistant principal, teacher, etc.) would ideally embody or have access to in order to address cyberbullying effectively

insights, but also be cautious about generalising and getting to the "apparent" cause of the problem too quickly. Schools are busy places, although there will be ebbs and flows in the many demands of your job, which you will learn to respond to.

3. Educative and administrative roles: to regenerate policy and practice with new knowledge. To inform students, staff and parents.

A crucial and central role of the practitioner is to be the school's expert on cyberbullying. The school population, particularly other members of staff, governors and parents have a second-hand and popular understanding of the background issues to cyberbullying. The chapters discussing cyberbullying and the law, the ICT industry and the media clearly articulate the differences between popular impression and the actual reality. For instance, people often think that if you legislate against an issue like cyberbullying that it will stop it from happening and that it is appropriate to punish. In Chapter 4, Campbell and Zavrsnik argue that the response is at least to some degree a result of the chasm between the cyberliteracy of the parents and their children. Resorting to law is also an "ambulance at the bottom of the cliff" response and the role of the practitioner is to have processes in place so pupils are protected against jumping or being pushed over the cliff. Similarly, to address cyberbullying the ICT industry are largely happy to help and are involved in working to create a safe environment in the cyberworld, but there are loopholes such as their first obligation being towards the privacy of individuals, sometimes putting them in a position where they are unable to deal with the cyberabuse of a customer, for instance.

There is also the issue of websites flourishing (and generating extra income through the publicity) as a result of their refusal to cooperate in addressing cyberbullying that takes place on their site. The Latvian-based Ask.fm, for instance, was cited as allowing the anonymous postings of cyberabuse and refusing to take them down. In the case of two of the suicides by the Irish girls named at the beginning of this chapter, this website was identified as the place where inflammatory postings about them were placed. Despite requests and threats, the website owners have refused to take responsibility or change their policies. Chapter 6 on the media focuses on examining the quantity and quality of cyberbullying-related articles in popular and quality newspapers. Popular newspapers, tend to consider the newsworthiness of a particular item and frame it in a way that both conveys its content but also slants it so as to sell as many newspapers as possible (and generate profit), regardless of accuracy. The quality newspapers, on the other hand, tend to focus more on addressing the research and looking for positive steps to address cyberbullying. Overall, however, the context of cyberbullying as one of "the bad boys" of ICT attracts a lot of attention from a moral panic perspective.

From an anti-cyberbullying policy perspective, in Chapter 8 Mona O'Moore and colleagues have extracted "the best of the best" from the multi-country analysis of policy guidelines. It is an excellent source for schools for developing or updating their cyberbullying policies.

4. A fair and consistent process for investigating and following up cyberbullying incidents and processes: Students talk with each other and if you are seen as easily hoodwinked or inconsistent in your dealings, particularly in terms of fairness, students will avoid coming to you, particularly those that have had their confidence undermined. You need to carry out the process of examining and responding to cyberbullying fairly, consistently and with it being clear that you know what you are doing. Incidents are often one-off attacks, but a process is usually ongoing. Again, Chapter 8 is an excellent resource for how to carry out the investigative and decision-making processes relating to cyberbullying incidents and processes. See also Sullivan (2011) for guidelines for developing anti–cyberbullying policy and practice.

5. Maintain ongoing access to processes and programmes for addressing cyberbullying effectively and using ICT positively: Processes have been developed for understanding and teaching about the dynamics and intentions of cyberbullying. It is crucial to keep up to date with developments and to try out various options so that you can choose what you think will work for the particular situation. Get second opinions and constructive criticism, particularly from those whose culture it occurs in, that of the students (see Sullivan, 2011, specifically the chapters on social action drama and CPR; and AAC Action Against Cyberbullying in Sullivan, 2013; plus Chapters 7, 10 and 12 in this book).

6. To nurture and empower students to deal effectively with cyberbullying (and traditional bullying): To initiate this process, it is important to teach the students about the nature of cyberbullying and use this as a starting point for developing a sense of competence and trustworthiness amongst students so that you will be seen as someone they can come to. In terms of addressing the issue of cyberbullying and assisting students to deal with it, the quality of counselling is very important. From my experience, I agree with Fenaughty and Harré's insightful statement in relation to two studies they carried out concerning young people's successful resolution of distressing electronic harassment.

> The quality of intervention, rather than the type of intervention per se, seems to be critical in the successful resolution of harassment. Reflecting on both studies we suggest the need to increase young people's confidence in actively dealing with harassment as well as supporting adults and peers to provide effective support.
>
> (Fenaughty & Harré, 2013, p. 242; see also Chapter 11)

7. To nurture trust, support and the appropriate involvement of teachers, administrators and governors: While upholding your authority as a professional, it is also important to gain the trust and support of teaching staff, principals, deputy and assistant principals, deans and school governors. You may need their involvement and support, but the right of privacy for those involved and the issue of their trust in you is also crucial.

8. Rapport with and involvement of parents and the wider school community, such as social workers, the Police etc.: Problems that start within the school may spin out into the wider school community and the wider community outside the school. Taking care of problems before they get worse and contacting the appropriate people and calling on the expertise of those who may help are all useful.

9. To develop and maintain both professional and personal support networks: It is crucial to have a network of colleagues who can support you and with whom you can discuss things generally while at the same time maintaining confidentiality. It is also important to have a professional supervisor with whom you can confidentially discuss what you have been doing and from whom you can seek help in terms of things that didn't work (and to be acknowledged and think through what did work and why). Furthermore, having a circle of family, friends/a friend with whom you can escape from difficult and often stressful problems and with whom you can share enjoyable downtime is essential.

Cyberbullying through the new media as a toolbox for practitioners?

What became clear when I had read the book (twice) was the exceptional quality of what had been created. With no disrespect meant towards the editors, I decided to re-organize the chapters in order to make the most sense of them from a practitioner's point of view. I did this around five themes, as follows:

- **Theme 1** Foundational knowledge about cyberbullying: Chapters 1 and 2.
- **Theme 2** Prevention of and coping with cyberbullying: Chapters 7 and 8.
- **Theme 3** Combating cyberbullying through using ICT constructively: Chapters 10 and 12.
- **Theme 4** Important cyberbullying issues to consider: Chapters 4, 5, 6 and 9.
- **Theme 5** Research processes: strengthening versus breaking the mould: Chapters 3, 11 and 13.

All of these themes and the chapters within them will be of use to the practitioner.

The chapters in Theme 1, Foundational knowledge about cyberbullying, provide the reader with an overview both of the nature of the COST project that led to the formation of groups to examine the key areas identified, and gives an overview of the issues involved in creating a definition of cyberbullying, bearing in mind Olweus' definition. The characteristics of cyberbullying that we have identified to date are also discussed.

Theme 2, Prevention of and coping with cyberbullying generally provides the layers and diversity that shows us the range and variables of international cyberbullying, and its similarities with traditional bullying. It therefore increases our knowledge and a sense of a definition, while showing us its crazy, apparently out-of-control manifestations, and its dangerous flexibility and malevolence. It also shows us strategies that are as imaginative as the instances of cyberbullying are voracious and ever-spreading, as daring and as powerful. Theme 3 continues the account of the attack back, the wise moves based on accumulated knowledge and effective strategies whose aim is not only to ameliorate events of cyberbullying but also to stamp it out, to make it lack a viable social environment in which it can flourish.

Theme 4 is a more discursive collection that tackles the headline issues that flare up around cyberbullying: where it fits on the continuum of human cruelty and assault, where it could take off next, how it spreads like an epidemic for which there appears to be no viable remedy as it morphs and mutates. It looks at its impact in the wider world of which we are all part and how it can be reported, acknowledged, dissected and known, and thus be thwarted.

Theme 5 on research processes is extremely interesting. Chapters 3 and 11 are both useful overviews of the quantitative and qualitative approaches to research and application (with the authors of Chapter 11 arguing strongly for qualitative methodologies being seriously utilized within a methodological sharing of a mixed methods approach). Without being intended as such, a quantitative, qualitative and mixed methods conversation cum debate is crying out to be heard. In Chapter 3, the authors are very honest and constructive in arguing for the need to correct foundational issues of much of the quantitative research on cyberbullying. They argue that when placed under close scrutiny, results between studies using similar instruments were found to have different or no definitions of cyberbullying. They also compared other elements that seemed the same but also were not. They furthermore discovered a tendency to highlight positive significant results while ignoring less compelling ones. Therefore the arguments that emerged from such flawed comparative research process could only be flawed themselves. The authors correctly argue for tightening things up by, first and foremost, agreeing on a universally-accepted definition of cyberbullying and an agreement on what constitutes other variables to be measured and to carry out studies with instruments whose results could legitimately be compared so that valid and reliable results could be produced and appropriate comparisons made. They also call for the wider use of factor analysis.

In Chapter 11, Spears and Kofoed argue that the current mould needs to be recast so that it is more inclusive of school–centred qualitative research approaches. Through such process they are both seeking new knowledge but also to empower the student voice and support the agency of young people. Having been professionally raised on quantitative research methodologies themselves, they do not argue against quantitative methodologies but instead call for inclusion and a re-assessment in light of the needs of the current context. Of particular interest is having the site of the school as the main place of research and using a variety of qualitative approaches for understanding the nature of cyberbullying and the creation of strategic and efficacious interventions. They argue strongly and convincingly as they clearly intend to create substantive and meaningful inroads using qualitative methods (while perhaps also aspiring to change the statement in Chapter 1 that almost all bullying related publications in the area of cyberbullying are psychological and quantitative).

I would argue that although their foundations are very different and although there is a potentially rich argument about the value of qualitative versus quantitative research methodologies and vice versa, that although sometimes regarded as antithetical, both approaches are, in fact, aiming for the same target, which, as far as is humanly possible, is to erase cyberbullying in its various permutations in the lives of the children and young people in our schools and other educational institutions (See Johnson and Christensen, 2008, for more details).

A creative research process developed through COST IS0801 was that financial and intellectual support was provided to early career and established researchers to enable them to work and sometimes collaborate with international colleagues with similar research interests (see Chapter 13). These exciting opportunities inevitably led to stimulation, creativity and innovation for the participants. One instance is early career researcher Simone Paul's exploration of the Quality Circles approach (a tool normally associated within business rather than education or psychology) to creatively develop students' abilities to better understand and more effectively deal with complex and problematic issues. Simone, whose doctoral thesis I was an examiner for, put her newly-acquired skills into research practice in a low-SES, multicultural Inner London school. The school's administrators and teachers were innovative in their approach to education and, like Simone, were constantly seeking opportunities to turn demanding challenges into constructive change-processes. They were therefore sympathetic towards and supportive of her efforts. During the course of a school year and via a series of workshops utilising the Quality Circles approach, Simone taught the 30 students how to problem-solve effectively. They learnt to identify key (not necessarily immediately recognised) issues, to prioritise concerns and to analyse the problems that emerged. They were then taught to combine the knowledge acquired, generate solutions and to put them into effect. The students were able to take these newly acquired skills out into their school life, particularly in relation to gathering information about bullying and cyberbullying.

> The information gained from the QCs supported a transitory notion of bullying behaviour, whereby forms of bullying and cyberbullying continue to alter over time, thus prevention programmes must adapt to the changeable nature of this behavior to remain effective.
>
> (Paul, Smith, & Blumberg, 2012, p. 1)

Conclusions: How can researchers address cyberbullying more effectively in partnership with our schools?

This book is excellent in its own right and the individuals and groups of researchers both at the individual and group level have compiled a treasure trove of chapters that presents a "state of the art" view of a living, destructive creature, that is known as cyberbullying.

Cyberbullying through the new media: Findings from an international network provides us with ways of understanding cyberbullying and the potential also to creatively and constructively counter it. The book is both an intellectual and practical gift to fellow researchers, to contemporary thinkers reflecting on the impact of ICT in our individual countries, and to members of schools and higher education institutions who need to have avenues for understanding about and effectively dealing with cyberbullying.

It is also not the end of a journey but in many ways a beginning. There is also a blueprint already starting to emerge that doesn't say "Where to from here?" but rather "We have generated a great momentum together, shall we continue? Are you coming?" The direction, of course, is not yet decided but rather needs to be negotiated. On the one hand, there is a very strong argument for the direction and creative drive being towards a mixed methods approach and the releasing of the energy and potentially creative voice and agency of youth. On the other hand, we could continue to work in a complementary way whereby we choose to retain our individual research integrities but work for the greater good. Either way, *Cyberbullying through the new media: Volume 2: what's happening in the schools and what we can do about it?* seems a logical next port of call.

References

Bauman, S. (2011). *Cyberbullying: What counsellors need to know*. Alexandria, VA: American Counselling Association.

Fenaughty, J., and Harré, N. (2013). 'Factors associated with young people's successful resolution of distressing electronic harassment'. *Computers and Education, 61,* 242–250.

Johnson, B., and Christensen, L. (2008). *Educational research: Quantitative, qualitative, and mixed approaches*. Thousand Oaks, CA: Sage Publications.

Mahuta, R., Manihera, T., Simpson, M., and Sullivan, K. (1981). *Whaikoorero: Maori ceremonial farewells to the dead*. Wellington: Continuing Education Unit of Radio New Zealand.

Paul, S., Smith, P.K., and Blumberg, H.H. (2012). 'Revisiting cyberbullying in schools using the quality circle approach'. *School Psychology International, 33*(5), 492–504.

Sullivan, K. (2011, 2012 as an e-book). *The Anti-Bullying Handbook*. Second Edition. Los Angeles, London, New Delhi, Singapore, and Washington DC: Sage Publications.

——(2013). 'Action Against Cyberbullying (AAC): A programme for understanding and effectively addressing school-related cyberbullying'. In M. O'Moore and P. Stevens (eds.), *Bullying in Irish education: Perspectives in research and practice*. Cork: Cork University Press.

Sullivan, K. and Sullivan, G. (1984). 'Whaikoorero – Some social and political implications of Maori oratory', *Mentalities/Mentalités*, 12 (2), 1–6.

Index

Page references containing a 't' refer to tabulated information, for example, 'legal experts 13t' and *italicised* entries refer to titles of documents.